CHAUCER

VOLU

Troilus and Criseyde
& The Minor Poems

An Anthology edited by

RICHARD J. SCHOECK

and

JEROME TAYLOR

UNIVERSITY OF NOTRE DAME PRESS
NOTRE DAME   LONDON

First published 1961
Second printing August, 1962
Third printing September, 1963
Fourth printing February, 1965
Fifth printing May, 1968
Sixth printing May, 1970
Seventh printing July, 1971

Library of Congress Catalog Card Number: 60-10279
Manufactured in the United States of America by
NAPCO Graphic Arts, Inc., Milwaukee, Wisconsin

PREFACE

The works of Chaucer, more than the works of later English authors, require for their responsible interpretation a broad range of historical knowledge—cultural, intellectual, literary. No less than modern works, however, they require sound and sensitive critical method.

The seventeen essays in this volume have been selected in part because they supply historical knowledge important for an understanding of *Troilus and Criseyde*, *The Book of the Duchess*, *The House of Fame*, and *The Parlement of Foules;* in part because they build such knowledge into formally well-reasoned interpretations of the poems; and in part because, despite formally sound arguments, some (notably several dealing with the *Troilus*) disagree widely in their interpretations and evaluations of that poem. The disagreements appear to derive from too undeviating an attention to a single historical perspective, or, indeed, from allowing historical perspective as such to prejudice formal analysis. That some of the essays should invite consideration of dangers involved in the use of historical materials for critical purposes has seemed to the editors to add to their value.

The first essay, that by Dodd, succinctly outlines the conventions of courtly love and of the literature to which courtly love gave rise in the middle ages. In so doing it supplies the first of several historical bases which must underlie any adequate interpretation of the principal characters and situations in the *Troilus* and the minor poems. Chaucer does not simply adopt, he adapts courtly love conventions. He fuses them with elements of yet other traditions with a distinctive effect and point of view which, if one is to appreciate them, must be gauged against the courtly tradition in itself, as Dodd describes it.

Lewis's essay, the second in the anthology, is the first of twelve which deal with the *Troilus*. Examining Chaucer's alterations of Boccaccio's *Il Filostrato*, principal source of the *Troilus*, Lewis finds that they are of four types. Chaucer

added details from the medieval "matter of Rome"; he introduced medieval rhetorical techniques; he shaped the poem to
bring out "doctryne" and "sentence" as the middle ages conceived these; and, finally, he made of the story a more adequate representation of courtly love—indeed, "a great poem
in praise of love." Chaucer's fourfold "medievalizing" of
Boccaccio, Lewis argues, produces "an effect of greater
realism and nature and freedom" than does the Italian original, for "certain medieval things are more universal, in that
sense more classical . . . than certain things of the Renaissance"; indeed, courtly love itself "is at bottom more agreeable to those elements in human, or at least European, nature,
which last longest, than the cynical gallantries of Boccaccio."

Lewis's characterization of the *Troilus* as "a great poem in
praise of love" and his somewhat idealizing view of courtly
love are not shared by the authors of the next several essays.
Turning from literary and social history, from rhetorical and
courtly conventions, to intellectual history, Curry, in the third
essay, analyzes the workings of Providence and destinal
forces as set forth in Boethius's *Consolation of Philosophy*, a
work which Chaucer translated. Curry argues that Chaucer's
selective use of Boethian ideas in the *Troilus* is such as to
make of the poem a "deterministic tragedy," in which "an
absolutely inescapable destiny governs the progress of the
story." As a consequence, he argues, the *Troilus* "transcends
the conventional mediaeval ideas of what a tragedy ought to
be"—simply the story of a highly placed man's fall from
prosperity into misery. Its superiority lies in its dramatizing
the "tragic conflict between Troilus and the mysterious destinal powers overshadowing him," a dramatization which
lifts the poem to "a sort of middle ground artistically between
the ancient Greek tragedy [in which "we sense a mysterious
and unalterable Fate or Necessity back of human action"]
and the modern tragedy of Shakespeare" [in which "emphasis
is laid upon the fact that a man is the architect of his own
fortunes"]. Troilus's long soliloquy on predestination, rather
than free will, as the universal cause of events Curry judges
to be not the ill-digested pedantry which other critics have
alleged it to be but a dramatically appropriate recognition by
the protagonist of the "settled determinism" ruling his life.
In the so-called epilogue of the poem, on the other hand,
Curry finds a "nest of contradictions": the Christian con-

demnation of a love which Troilus was not free to avoid is unjust; the dedication to "moral Gower" and "philosophical Strode," who would have eschewed the poem's determinism, is illogical and in bad taste; and the ascent of Troilus's soul "to an apparently Christian bliss" is dramatically the most inappropriate ending that can be imagined.

The essays immediately following Curry's—those by Patch, Robertson, Stroud, Shanley, and Denomy—in effect provide rebuttal or qualification for various of Curry's conclusions. Patch's essay, expressly a rebuttal to Curry, scrutinizes the meaning of "determinism," considers what the necessary emotional and moral response to a strictly deterministic plot would be, argues that none of the alleged determinism in the *Troilus* eliminates the operation of free choice on the part of the characters, and explains as consistent the features of the epilogue with which Curry had found fault. Like Patch, Robertson argues that the entire poem, including the epilogue, manifests "an intellectual coherence that is firmly rooted in Christian doctrine and Boethian philosophy." The basis of his argument, however, is a definition of the "typical Chaucerian tragedy" which he takes from Chaucer's Monk's Tale and various Christian sources, including Boethius's *Consolation of Philosophy*. Observing, as Curry did not, that it is Fortune which, in medieval tragedy, is responsible for a protagonist's fall and that susceptibility to the caprices of Fortune is the effect of concupiscence, or earthly love, usurping the place of charity, or love of God, Robertson would interpret Troilus, Criseyde, and Pandarus as alike guilty of this sin and would read the poem as a perfect instance of Chaucerian—and medieval—tragedy.

Stroud, concerned like Lewis with Chaucer's modifications of Boccaccio and like Curry and Robertson with Chaucer's use of Boethius, contends that Chaucer revised the *Filostrato* "in a fashion which would supplement the conclusions of Boethius in an area of human activity [namely, courtly love] which Boethius had neglected" in the *Consolation of Philosophy*. The *Troilus,* while on one level it is a romance, is, on another level, "an allegory concerning man's quest for the moral laws of the universe." Shanley, citing passages from the poem to prove that the epilogue's criticism of earthly love is in fact worked into the entire texture of the story, sees the *Troilus* as demonstrably unified. Moreover, unlike Roberton, he finds that the text establishes Criseyde as "gentle and lovely," and unlike Stroud, he finds no deficiency of mind or will, no effeminacy, in Troilus. Denomy, applying his well-known theory about the relation of courtly love to the double-truth heresy, sees the poem as embodying not a single attitude toward love, certainly not a Christian one, but two mutually exclusive codes of morality, one heretical, one orthodox. The heretical code—courtly love—governs the action of the story proper. Chaucer, who "states again and again that he is not writing on love from personal knowledge gained from experience or from his own feelings on the subject," comes at length, in the epilogue, to condemn the love of Troilus and Criseyde, perhaps from "fear of incurring blame and displeasure . . . for what he knew to be not only immoral but also heretical," perhaps "to salve a conscience thoroughly Christian, a conscience revolted at the utter incompatibility of Courtly Love with the tenets of Christian morality and faith." For Denomy, then, the poem is hardly, as for Lewis, "a great poem in praise of love"; instead, as for Curry, the epilogue and the poem stand opposed, though for quite different reasons from those Curry adduced.

The next five essays focus upon selected aspects of the poem's technique rather than upon the meaning or value of the poem as a whole, though not without bearing upon that larger problem. Owen, drawing upon Root's earlier textual studies of Chaucer's composition of the *Troilus,* finds in Chaucer's revisions both formal and thematic significance: "Not only did they strengthen the contrasting parallels and the symmetry of the poem's structure, but they made more explicit the thematic oppositions which the poem holds in tension, the opposition between fate and free will, the opposition between love and 'charity.'" Kaske, examining the tradition of the *aube* in European literature, finds evidence that Chaucer has redistributed the conventional *aube* elements in such way as to reverse the roles of lover and lady. Sams contrasts the "actual, basic time-scheme of three years," which underlies the action of the poem, with the "artistic scheme of one year, or the coming and departure of one summer," found in the imagery. Boughner, concentrating upon elements of the "high style" in the poem, argues that these are traceable to medieval *artes poeticae* and that their presence, inspired by the poetic principles and practice of Dante and Boccaccio, helps "exalt the *Troilus* to the level of those supreme poems" of which the Italian masters most approved. Bloomfield observes that the *Troilus* narrator "plays his role with a striking difference" from what one finds in the minor works and in *The Canterbury Tales,* in which the narrator is cast "as one of the dramatis personae, and participates in the action." In *Troilus,* he writes, Chaucer assumes the mask of a faithful and sympathetic historian who "meticulously maintains a distance between himself and the events in the story," a distance "conveyed to us in . . . temporal, spatial, aesthetic, and religious ways" and which accounts both for the pre-destinarian handling of events in the story proper and the Christian "escape" from the tragic pressure of events at the end.

Miss Bethurum's essay forms a bridge to the remaining essays, which treat the minor poems. Examining the narrative points of view of Chaucer's love poems in chronological order, she finds in them a "clear development up to the complex and subtle presentation in *Troilus.*" Sketching the influence upon Chaucer of Neoplatonic notions of love current in the middle ages, she argues that certain modern critics (notably Robertson and Denomy) slight the *Troilus*-narrator's high regard for earthly love. The "heart of Chaucer's position as narrator" is not invidious contrast between earthly and heavenly love but contrast "between the stable world of learning and the fragile world of love" without detriment to either. "From his appreciation of *both* worlds comes his incomparable poise."

Lawlor argues that Chaucer, in offering the widowed John of Gaunt "the consolations of the religion of love" in *The Book of the Duchess,* "is making no forced transition from the world of married lovers to a region appropriate only to adulterous passion." Rather, the Knight, in rehearsing his loss to the Dreamer, "is brought to celebrate again the heaven of requited love." In so doing he receives not only the consolation of the Dreamer's understanding but the consolation of recalling "that Fortune is not to be railed against, since the heaven of requited love is not granted for the lover's deserving but of the Lady's grace; and that the loss of this heaven by death is not so great as its loss by infidelity." Ruggiers, addressing himself to "the often repeated charge against the *House of Fame* that it lacks a clear plan," finds the key to the poem's unity in "the progressively universalizing impulse which determines its form." Thus, its first book "presents us with a love story in which Fame, much like Fortune, plays an important role in the lives of two lovers"; the second, "while maintaining both the motive power of a love-vision and the force of a quest, gives us a view of an orderly universe of which Fame is a part"; the third, "satisfying the demands of the quest and the love-vision, reveals the actual distribution or withholding of renown in such a universe." McDonald reads the *Parlement of Foules* as a poem "in which Nature plays the role of a tolerant mediator between apparently contradictory points of view [toward love], and in which the usual roles of the naive and sophisticated are delightfully reversed." In this poem, he concludes, "a genuine love of nature and natural conduct is balanced against the artificialities adopted by those who consider love a fit subject for rules and regulations according to an arbitrary, 'sophisticated' pattern of courtly conventions." Chaucer thus renders his judgment against the conventions outlined by Dodd in the first essay in the anthology.

Of the essays presented in this volume, one (Kaske's on the *aube*) has not been printed before; several have been revised by their authors for this reprinting. Limitations of space have made it necessary for the editors to eliminate some of the original documentation, but notes identifying the source of quotations or essential to the argument have been retained. To aid the general reader, the editors have supplied translations of Latin, Old French and Italian passages, placing these in the footnotes or substituting them for the original in the text as seemed best in particular cases. References to articles which present notably contrary or qualifying points of view have also been added.

R. J. S.
J. T.

July 31, 1961

CONTENTS

1

The System of Courtly Love

WILLIAM GEORGE DODD

It is in the south of France and at a very early period that we must look for the origin of the system of Courtly Love. Gathered about several small courts, there existed, as early as the eleventh century, a brilliant society, in which woman held the supreme place, and in which under her influence, vast importance was attached to social etiquette and decorum. Definite rules governed the sexes in all their relations, and especially in matters of love. It was to this society that the troubadours belonged, and it was love, chiefly, that was the inspiration of their songs. In the troubadours, therefore, we find the earliest expression of the ideas of courtly love.

In time, these ideas were introduced into northern France, largely through the influence of Eleanor of Aquitaine [c. 1122-

Reprinted, by permission of Harvard University Press, from *Courtly Love in Chaucer and Gower,* Harvard Studies in English, Vol. I (Boston: Ginn & Co., 1913), pp. 1-20. To supplement Dodd, see C. S. Lewis, *The Allegory of Love* (Galaxy paperback, GB 17; New York: Oxford University Press, 1958), pp. 1-43; Sidney Painter, *French Chivalry* (Baltimore: Johns Hopkins University Press, 1940), pp. 95-148; and for philosophical-theological backgrounds, A. J. Denomy, C.S.B., *The Heresy of Courtly Love* (New York: Declan X. McMullen Co., 1947). Valuable for full quotations from original texts (translations in appendix) and secondary sources is Thomas A. Kirby, *Chaucer's Troilus: A Study in Courtly Love* (Gloucester, Mass.: Peter Smith, 1958; reprint), pp. 1-87; special section on courtly love in Boccaccio, *Il Filostrato,* source of Chaucer's *Troilus,* pp. 91-118.

1204]. This amorous duchess took a lively interest in the doctrines, as well as the practices, of courtly love. Before leaving her southern home to become queen of France, she received, and, it seems, encouraged, advances of a very familiar nature from the troubadour Bernart de Ventadorn. At the northern court, also, she lent her authority to the new doctrines. In this she was followed by her daughter, Marie of Champagne, and other noble ladies, who amused themselves and the fashionable society about them by rendering decisions on difficult questions which were argued before the mock Courts of Love. Naturally, such decisions soon came to be regarded as definite rules and regulations of the courtly system. Thus, in northern France, the new ideas of love received from the first the sanction and support of women of high rank, through whose influence they found their way into contemporary literature. Marie of Champagne, for instance, impressed them upon Chrétien de Troies [her *trouvère,* or court poet], and he, in turn, introduced them into the romances of the Round Table. Under his hands, the Arthurian romances became the representatives *par excellence* of the chivalrous and courtly ideal of twelfth-century society. His *Conte de la charrette* [Tale of the Cart], which reflects in an especial manner the conceptions of the courtly love, owes its existence, as he himself tells us, to Marie of Champagne.

The ideas of love in the romances of Chrétien are the ideas found in the lyrics of the troubadours; but in many instances the genius of the French poet has transformed them into something peculiarly his own. The fancies and conceits of the earlier poetry he elaborates highly; mere hints he develops into formal doctrines. He subjects the emotions of the human heart to delicate and subtle analysis, and philosophizes upon them with astonishing minuteness. The result of this process of refinement was the formulation of certain doctrines, the observance of which became equally obligatory upon courtly lovers and upon later writers who dealt with the subject.

As the system was left by Chrétien, so it was to remain. It would be wrong, however, to suppose that the crystallizing of the courtly sentiments was due to him alone. The process had begun in the poetry of the troubadours. Even for them love was an art to be practised rather than a passion to be felt. It was largely a matter of behavior. To regulate his conduct in strict accord with the rules and restrictions with which the art

was hedged about, became the lover's chief concern. Naturally, the literature which drew its inspiration from such love
was devoid of spontaneity and real feeling. In the poetry of
Bernart de Ventadorn, it is true, there is to be found what
seems to be earnest passion; but the writings of the troubadours after Bernart are to a great extent characterized by
artificiality and monotony of sentiment. Through each poet's
imitation of his predecessor, the very emotional experiences
of lovers became stereotyped. The exaggerations employed
to give a semblance of intensity to an artificial passion became
poetical conventions. It was with such material that Chrétien
worked. His contribution to the courtly system was the fixing
of ideas already present in twelfth-century literature, the development of others, and the introduction of them all into
the romances of the Round Table.

The interest in courtly love is nowhere more clearly manifested than in certain works roughly contemporary with
Chrétien, which treat of love as an art, setting forth in a
scientific manner the principles of the system and codifying
the laws upon which it was based. This method of treatment
had its origin in the erotic writings of Ovid, the favorite poet
of the mediaeval schools. His *Ars amatoria* was several times
translated into French, curiously altered to suit the manners
and customs of mediaeval society, the sensualism of the
original being newly interpreted in accord with the chivalrous
spirit. Of the works of this period which, following the plan
of Ovid, treat of love as an art, the most important is the *De
arte honeste amandi* [The Art of Loving Decently] by Andreas
Capellanus.[1] Here we have fully worked out the jurisprudence
of that courtly system which is exemplified in the romances of
the Round Table. Andreas treats with scholastic precision the
following questions: What is love? What are its effects? Between whom can it exist? How is it acquired, retained, augmented, diminished, terminated? What is the duty of one
lover when the other proves unfaithful? He is chiefly concerned, however, with showing whom the lover should choose
for his *amie*, how he may win her, and how her favor may be
retained. This threefold division was common with the mediaeval imitators of Ovid, and is manifestly copied from the
plan of the *Ars amatoria*. The second of his three questions
Andreas answers by means of eight imaginary conversations
between model lovers of various ranks. He also deals with the

love of clerks, monks, courtesans, and rustics; he condemns love which is acquired by means of money, as well as that obtained with too little difficulty. Chapter seven of the second book contains twenty-one decisions rendered by noble ladies, on disputed points of love. Chapter eight gives the thirty-one statutes which bear the stamp of authority of the god of Love himself. Besides the thirty-one rules, there is also in the work a short code of twelve which purport to have been revealed to a knight in a vision of the Palace of Love. These two codes sum up the whole doctrine of Andreas. His third and last book is entitled *De reprobatione amoris,* and is modeled on Ovid's *Remedia.* Throughout the work there are references to Eleanor of Aquitaine, Ermengarde of Narbonne, and the Countess Marie of Champagne, oftenest to the last named. Obviously it was her theories which, to a large degree, inspired Andreas to write his treatise.

The book of Andreas furnishes us a ready means of understanding the abstract principles and the laws underlying the courtly system. These principles, which are few in number, are:

1. *Courtly love is sensual.* Andreas makes this clear at the outset by defining love as a passion arising from the contemplation of beauty in the opposite sex, and culminating in the gratification of the physical desires thus awakened.[2] On this definition the whole system rests. The insistence with which the sensual element is dwelt upon throughout the book, contrasts strangely with the high ideals of conduct and character presented at the same time. For this incongruity, however, Andreas is not responsible. The love which was practised by the courtly society of southern France, and which spread to the North, though essentially impure, was yet exalted as uplifting and ennobling and productive of every virtue.

2. *Courtly love is illicit and, for the most part, adulterous.* Indeed, in the courtly system marriage has no place. The Countess Marie is reported by Andreas to have decided, in a disputed case, that "love cannot exist between two people joined together in the conjugal relation."[3] The idea is again expressed, on the authority of the same Countess, in the excuse which a certain lover offers for seeking love out of wedlock, although he has a beautiful wife whom he professes to love "totius mentis affectione maritali" [with the marital affection of his whole mind]. In accord with these opinions, and

probably based upon them, is the first law of the longer code, which frankly states that a woman cannot plead marriage as a sufficient excuse for denying a lover's petition.[4]

3. *A love, sensual and illicit, must needs be secret.* The shorter code lays this down as a law;[5] and the longer adds, as the reason, that a love which is divulged, rarely lasts. No article of the code is so important as this, and none is insisted upon so much. "Qui non celat, amare non potest" [He who is not secretive cannot love]. He who reveals the secrets he should keep, is branded as a traitor to the god of Love. Nothing is so despicable as to blab after having received favors. But not only must love be secret; it must also be furtive. It was the element of furtiveness, largely, that made the courtly love incompatible with the legal relations between husband and wife. The necessity of secrecy gives rise in the literature to a constant fear of spies: a fear exaggerated, no doubt, but not without foundation, if we may accept the romances as reflecting contemporary life. In these stories, it is often the role of the false steward to spy upon lovers and to report their actions to the lady's father or husband.

There were grounds of a very practical nature for the insistence upon secrecy. Chaucer, describing the violation of Lucretia, tells us:

> Thise Romain wyves loveden so hir name
> At thilke tyme, and dredden so the shame,
> That, what for fere of slaundre and drede of deeth,
> She loste bothe at ones wit and breeth,
> And in a swough she lay. (*LGW*, 133-7)

Fear of slander has disturbed the mind of many a woman far less chaste than Lucretia. As the Wife of Bath aptly puts it,

> "For, be we never so vicious withinne,
> We wol been holden wyse and clene of sinne." (*WBT*, 943-4)

Despite the moral laxness of the society out of which the courtly love grew, there were some, perhaps many, to whom its ideas were abhorrent. However this may be, the women of that society felt it necessary to protect their good name. Chastity might be dispensed with without scruple, but a sullied reputation was unbearable. Once the lady had satisfied herself that the aspiring lover would be true to her, her greatest fear was that their *liaison* should become known, and that she might be subjected to the aspersions of talebearers.

Another reason for secrecy may be found in the peculiar relations between husband and wife among the higher classes of medieval society. Marriage was rarely a matter in which the heart was concerned. Business affairs and political considerations often brought about unions in which no affection could exist. Yet the integrity of the tie and the exclusive rights pertaining to the married state seem to have been insisted upon by husbands. By the theory of courtly love, jealousy could not exist between a man and his wife, and since jealousy was a requisite of love, no love could exist between them. As a matter of fact, jealous husbands are execrated in love poetry from the early carols of the peasant girls of Poitou and Limousin to Chaucer. Criseyde says:

> "Shal noon housbonde seyn to me 'chek mat!'
> For either they ben ful of jalousie,
> Or maisterful, or loven novelrie." (*TC*, II, 754-6)

What action the husband of an unfaithful wife was expected to take, in case her infidelity was discovered, we may infer from the summary and severe punishment dealt out to such offenders, as it is pictured in romances, ballads, and chronicles. Due precaution for the maintenance of strict secrecy would therefore be dictated by wisdom and common sense.

4. *Love, to meet the requirements of the courtly system, must not be too easily obtained.*[6] This idea receives great stress because of the lofty position which woman held in the courtly society. The concrete working of the rule is seen in the coldness and capriciousness of the lady, which are the cause of all the lover's woes as they are pictured in the poetry of the troubadours.

We have already observed that courtly love was exalted under the system as a virtue which ennobled those who practised the art. In theory, love is the fount and origin of every good. It is constantly associated in the literature with courtesy and "largess." Andreas declares that love is "ever banished from the domicile of avarice." In another passage, he states specifically that love makes the rude and uncouth excel in every grace; that it enriches those of low birth with real nobility of character; and that it makes the true lover show a becoming complaisance to all. And then he breaks out rapturously: "O, how wonderful is love, which causes a man to be effulgent in virtue, and teaches every one to abound in good manners!" It was to achieve these virtues that the courtly lover sought his lady's favor. Strangely enough, the "good" was all on one side. If this love was like mercy, which "blesseth him that gives and him that takes," it is not so stated in the manual of Andreas. This again is due to the high position held by woman in the society of the time, and the reverence with which she was regarded. From her lofty place, as the perfect being, she dispensed favors which were at the same time the reward of noble deeds and the incentive to further effort.

It must be noted that the ideals of the courtly system, if we disregard the element of sensualism, were high. This was true, not only in matters of decorum, but of honor as well. Constancy was of the utmost importance.[7] No more grievous fault could be committed, no breach of the canons could be more serious, than for a lover, man or woman, to be unfaithful. This idea is insistently dwelt upon by Andreas, and it appears conspicuously in the other erotic literature of the period and of the following centuries. "Supplanting" also was strictly forbidden.[8] To choose for his mistress one whom he would be ashamed to marry, was thought unworthy of a lover. Though sensual love lay at the bottom of the system, voluptuousness was regarded as fatal to real love. Indeed, though according to the courtly ideas love is in essence sensual, and should be secret and furtive, yet it incited the lover to worthy deeds; it demanded of him nobility of character and moderation in all his conduct. It is a love evil at the heart of it, yet it is a love which "loses half its evil, by losing all its grossness."

Such was the theory of the courtly system. For its practical side, we turn to the poetry of the troubadours. Inspired, professedly, by real and actual love affairs, their lyrics present the concrete workings of the sentiment which afterward became the basis of the erotic philosophy not only of Chrétien de Troies but of Andreas himself. In the poems of the troubadours, therefore, we find portrayed the birth and progress of their love, their emotional experiences, their relation and attitude toward the ladies whose favor they sought, and their behavior as affected by their passion.

The lady is regularly represented as perfect in all her attributes. The basis of this idea is, of course, the high social

position of woman. Her good qualities were doubtless exaggerated, however, because of her rank; for the poet was often
politically her subject, as well as her humble lover. Her perfection is pictured in her physical beauty, her character, and
her influence upon others. Her physical beauty, when portrayed, accords with the mediaeval ideal. Her hair is blond
or golden; her eyes beautiful; her complexion fresh and clear;
her mouth rosy and smiling; her flesh white, soft, and smooth;
her body slender, well formed, and without blemish. In
character, she is distinguished for her courtesy, kindness, refinement, and good sense. In short, all that makes the perfect woman, in soul or in manners, the poet's love possesses.
Her influence on others is always ennobling. Her goodness
affects all who come near her, making them better. One poet
fondly sings: "There is not in the whole world a vile person
so ill-bred that he will not become courteous, if he speaks a
word with her." Another declares: "The most ignorant man
in the company, when he sees and gazes at her, ought at parting to be wise and of fine bearing."

As a perfect being, the lady occupies a position of exalted
superiority in respect to the lover. He becomes her vassal and
protests absolute submission and devotion to her. "Good
lady," begs Bernart de Ventadorn in his humility, "I demand
nothing more of you than that you take me for a servant, for
I will serve you as one serves a good master, whatever be my
reward." Even power of life and death is in the lady's hands.
The same poet says: "In her pleasure may it be, for I am at
her mercy: if it please her to kill me, I do not complain of it
at all." His love for her surpasses all other things in value;
the slightest token from her makes him rich. "She, whose
liegeman I am without recall, kills me so sweetly with desire,
that she would make me rich with a thread of her glove, or
with one of the hairs that falls on her mantle." The service
which he professes is often carried to the extreme of worship,
and he adores her as a divinity, giving and commending himself to her with hands joined and head bowed.

The lady rarely appears as a personality in the poetry of the
troubadours, but remains indistinct in the background. From
the poet's portrayal of his own feelings, however, her attitude
toward him is clear enough. We have seen that she possesses
every good quality; her kindness, however, the lover seldom
experiences. To him she is cold, disdainful, capricious, and

domineering. In vain does he implore pity; in vain does he complain of her cruelty and beg for mercy; her rigor is unabated. This coldness of the lady is the keynote of by far the larger part of the poetry which we are now considering. Originating in the instinctive hesitancy of the woman to yield too easily, it is here exaggerated beyond all naturalness. In later erotic literature it becomes a convention and is the motive of almost all the love-poetry of France for the next four centuries.

Nobility of rank was not a requisite in the troubadour-lovers of Provence. Poetry seems to have been a common meeting-ground for knight and burgher, for prince and peasant. The first troubadour whose work is extant is William IX, Count of Poitiers. Piere Vidal, one of the most prolific writers, was the son of a furrier. Alphonso II of Aragon, one of the great rulers of his age, like Richard the Lion-Hearted, was not only the friend and patron of the troubadours, but a maker of verses himself. Bernart de Ventadorn, who loved and was loved by Eleanor of Aquitaine, was "of low degree, son, to wit, of a serving man, who gathered brushwood for the heating of the oven wherein was baked the castle bread." All who sang of love, however, agreed as to the ennobling effect of love on the character of the lover. Specifically, because of his love, he becomes courteous, gentle, humble, generous, and courageous. As one lover proudly says, "Happy is he whom love keeps joyous, for love is the climax of all blessings, and through love, one is gay and courteous, frank and gentle, humble and proud."

I have spoken of the absolute devotion of the lover to the lady, of his service, and his submission to her will. In their efforts to emphasize these features of their love and the power which that love exerted over them, the troubadours made use of as extravagant fancies as their imaginations could invent. The effects of love, which Professor Neilson aptly speaks of as "symptoms," are described as suffering, or a severe sickness; sleeplessness; confusion and loss of speech in the lady's presence; trembling and pallor when near the loved one; fear to make an avowal to the lady; and dread of detection by others.[9]

Certain other ideas and conceits, though frequent in the poetry of the troubadours, are important rather because of the elaborate treatment of them by Chrétien de Troies. Three especially are to be mentioned: the idea that love is caused by the beauty of the opposite sex; the conceit that through the eyes, beauty enters the heart, inflicting a wound which only the lady can heal; and the fancy that, though absent from the loved one, the lover leaves his heart with her. Because of Chrétien's subtlety in dealing with these ideas, they may be regarded as his particular contribution to the conventional stock.

The idea that love is caused by beauty is illustrated in the *Cligès,* where Alexander is represented as thinking of the charms of Soredamors. "Love pictures to him her beauty, on account of which he feels himself *fort grevé* [greatly distressed]. It has robbed him of his heart, nor does it allow him to rest in his bed: so much is he delighted to remember the beauty and the countenance of [Soredamors]."

More subtlety is displayed in the poet's use of the second idea, in the passage from the same poem where Alexander undergoes a rigid self-examination on the manner in which love has attacked him. He says: "It has wounded me so severely, that even to the heart his (Love's) dart has penetrated. . . . How then does it penetrate the body when the wound does not appear on the outside? . . . Through what has it penetrated? Through the eye. Through the eye? And yet it has not put out the eye? In the eye it has not hurt me at all, but in the heart it hurts me grievously. Tell me then: how has the dart passed through the eye so that it is neither wounded nor destroyed? If the dart enters through the eye, why does the heart suffer, and not the eye which received the first blow? — And so he continues to analyze this all-important question until he hits upon the explanation that, as the sunlight penetrates glass without breaking it, so the light of beauty pierces the eye without harming it, and reaches the heart.

Chrétien's treatment of the third idea is quite as subtle. When Ivain found it necessary to leave Laudine and to accompany Sir Gawain and the king to Britain, the poet tells us, the lover departed from his lady very unwillingly, although his heart did not depart from her at all. "The king can take away the body, but the heart not a bit; for it is so joined and holds so fast to the heart of her who remains behind, that he has not the power to take it. While the body is without the heart, it can in no wise live; and if the body does live without the heart, such a wonder no man has ever seen. This wonder has come to pass; for the body [of Ivain] has kept its life without the heart which used to be there, and which does not wish to follow it more."

The quotations given illustrate the minuteness of Chrétien's philosophizing on questions of love, and his process of refinement, which later poets regarded with delight, and which, as far as they were able, they imitated in their own work.

In general, then, we have seen that the ideas of the troubadours, derived in the main from Ovid, but developed and exaggerated in the south of France, became in the north the principles and requirements of a fixed code. Chrétien made certain conceits into formal doctrines, which were accepted as such by later writers. Still other fancies became rules of conduct in matters of love. The coldness of the lady is reflected in Andreas's law: "The easy attainment of love renders it contemptible; difficult attainment makes it to be held dear." The idea of fear in the lady's presence became a philosophical principle: "Amorosus semper est timorosus."[10] The same is true of the trembling: "In repentina coamantis visione cor contremescit amantis."[11] Sleeplessness, at first a result of love, became a requirement imposed upon lovers: "Minus dormit et edit, quem amoris cogitatio vexat."[12] In short, the ideas of the troubadour lyrics are the basis of the whole courtly system; and Andreas's book is but a quasi-scientific attempt to reduce to laws the practices of the troubadours and other courtly lovers of the time.

Besides the elements thus far treated, which belong to the essential theory of courtly love, certain incidental features of the courtly literature must be briefly mentioned. A number of conventional devices were of such frequent occurrence in mediaeval love-poetry that they became characteristic of the tradition with which this study is concerned. Many erotic poems, for example, were cast in the form of dreams or visions, doubtless in imitation of the apocalyptic writings of the Church. Thus the love-vision came to constitute a distinct literary type, and for a long time was perhaps the prevailing mode of expression of courtly sentiment. Poems of this class commonly tell the story of the experience of a hero in the service of love. The events are usually assigned to the springtime, in keeping with an old and lasting association between love and that season of the year. The hero is often

conducted by a guide to the god of love, whose habitation is
more or less fully described. Allegorical figures abound, ex-
hibiting various phases of love or the virtues and faults of
lovers; and the person of the divinity himself is conceived in
accordance with certain definite traditions.[13]

The personification of love as a god is an inheritance from
classical times, and a good example may be found in the first
elegy of Ovid's *Amores.* . . . This personification of love as a
god, with the appurtenances of quiver and arrows, is in constant use in the mediaeval love literature. The hero of the
Pamphilus de Amore, which is in the spirit of Ovid throughout, suffers from a wound inflicted by the god's arrows. It
is a shot from his bow that brings Chrétien's hero, Alexander,
low. Yvain, too, is a victim of the deadly dart. Without the
accompaniment of his weapons, Love is frequently depicted
as an all-powerful deity, to express the idea that to all suitable
young persons love is not only a duty, but a fate which they
cannot escape. In the early poetry of the troubadours, Love
is a goddess whose power is irresistible, whose command is
law to the lover, who at times is cruel, at others, neglectful of
her servants. Bernart de Ventadorn sings: "I have no power
at all that can defend me against Love; . . . when I think to
free myself, I cannot, for Love holds me." He says of himself,
"I alas! whom Love forgets," and addresses the cruel goddess
thus: "Whatever you command me to do, I shall do, for so it
is fitting, but you do not well always to make me suffer."
Chrétien also personifies love to express the same idea of a
resistless god. Soredamors is helpless in his hands; against
Love she thinks to defend herself, but it is useless. He brings
her to grief and avenges himself upon her for her great pride
and indifference.

The classical conception of the god of Love is still familiar
in literature. In mediaeval writings, however, the deity often
took on special characteristics borrowed from the religious
conditions of the time. Thus in the *Concile de Remiremont,*[14]
a Latin poem of the twelfth century, a council is assembled by
one who acts under the commands of the god of Love. Its
members are all enlisted in his service, and they regulate their
lives in accordance with his precepts and wishes. The meeting
is opened with a ceremony of worship; but the form of procedure is clearly borrowed from the service of the Church, and
is inconsistent with the worship paid to a heathen divinity. The

Concile is representative of a large class of erotic literature in which a systematic religion of love is set forth, modelled on that of the Church. The New Jerusalem of the Apocalypse became the Paradise in which dwelt the god of Love, and in which were reserved places for his disciples. There was also a Purgatory where those who refused to bow to his commands were punished. In the book of Andreas, both these places are elaborately described. The new religious system had its gospel, its commandments, its apostles and teachers; examples of the two former we have seen in the codes of Andreas's book. In short, adaptations of all the important features of the mediaeval Christian worship may be found in the erotic literature of the time.

Alongside the conception of the god of Love just noticed, there appears another in which the characteristics of the deity reflected rather social than religious conditions. To him were given the attributes of a feudal lord, to whom, as to their chief, lovers swear loyalty and obedience. In return for faithful service, the god, who now often becomes a king, acts as their protector and has at heart the welfare of his vassals. Disputes are carried to him for arbitration; and in his court, surrounded by his barons, he administers justice. This conception of the god of Love was well known to Chrétien. Alexander remarks: "A servant ought to tremble with fear when his lord calls him or sends for him. And whoever commends himself to Love, makes him his lord and master, and it is right that such a one hold him in reverence and fear him and honor him much, if he indeed wishes to be of his court." The same ideas appear in varying degrees in many documents of the period. In the Old French *Florance and Blancheflor,* in particular, the feudal character of the god is made prominent. He here becomes a king, with a court of bird-barons, to whom a case is referred for settlement. The "inconsistency in the use of 'king or god'," as Professor Neilson has remarked with reference to this poem, ". . . is suggestive of the process by which the classical divine court took on a feudal character. The birds are just about to be brought in, not merely as attendants on the god of Love, but as barons with deliberating power, and almost unconsciously, it might seem, the poet begins to speak of a king instead of a god."[15] An interesting example of the same process is also furnished by two other French pieces, *Li Fablel dou Dieu d'Amours* and *Venus la*

Deese d'Amour, which are in reality only different versions of a single story. In the former, there is no suggestion of the judicial character of the god; he is simply the classical divinity who comes to the aid of one of his worshippers in trouble. In *Venus la Deesse*, his role as judge is brought out with distinctness and in detail. He holds his court, before which the case of the lover is argued, and renders the decision which restores to the hero his lady.

In the consideration of the love deity in the literature which it is the purpose of this study to examine, the three conceptions pointed out in the preceding paragraphs will be distinguished by the terms "classical," "ecclesiastical," and "feudal." It is clear, however, that, since the classical deity took on the peculiar attributes consistent with the ecclesiastical and feudal conceptions, there may appear a blending of the classical with the ecclesiastical, or of the classical with the feudal. . . . instead of a god, or along with him, a goddess often appears, to whom is attributed the same power and authority. Venus as the goddess of Love is frequently found with Cupid the god of Love, as was seen in *Venus la Deesse*. Often she appears alone, either as the goddess or as the queen of Love. In general, poets do not consistently discriminate between Venus and Cupid as the love deity.

Notes

1 Ed. E. Trojel (Copenhagen, 1892). [English translation by John J. Parry, *The Art of Courtly Love of Andreas Capellanus*, Columbia University Records of Civilization: Sources and Studies, No. 33 (New York: Columbia University Press, 1941)].

2 "Amor est passio quaedam innata procedens ex visione et immoderata cogitatione formae alterius sexus, ob quam aliquis super omnia cupit alterius potiri amplexibus et omnia de utriusque voluntate in ipsius amplexu amoris praecepta compleri." Trojel, p. 3. ["Love is a certain passion, born within one and proceeding from sight of, and from immoderate reflection upon, the physical appearance of a person of the opposite sex; because of it one desires above all things to become possessed of the other's embraces and to fulfill all the promptings of love, by common consent, in the other's arms."—Ed.]

3 "Dicimus enim et stabilito tenore firmamus, amorem non posse suas inter duos iugales extendere vires." Trojel, p. 153. ["We declare and affirm with fixed intention that love cannot manifest its power between two married persons."—Ed.]

4 "Causa coniugii ab amore non est excusatio recta." Trojel, p. 310. ["The allegation of marriage is no proper excuse for not loving."—Ed.]

5 "Amoris tui secretarios noli plures habere." Trojel, p. 106. ["Do not have several confidants whom you tell of your love."—Ed.]

6 "Facilis perceptio contemptibilem reddit amorem, difficilis eum carum facit haberi." Trojel, p. 310. ["Easy attainment makes love cheap; difficult attainment causes it to be held dear."—Ed.]

7 "Nemo duplici potest amore ligari." Trojel, p. 310. ["No one may be bound in two love affairs."—Ed.]

8 "Alterius idonee copulatam amori scienter subvertere non coneris." Trojel, p. 106. ["You shall not knowingly attempt to seduce a woman suitably joined to another in love."—Ed.]

9 The place of secrecy in the courtly system has been noticed in considering the work of Andreas. It may be added that secrecy was a quality which the troubadour-lovers prized very highly in themselves; they seldom omit it from the list of their virtues, when recommending themselves to their ladies' favor. Yet, the maintenance of secrecy was a difficult matter. Slanderers and talebearers are constantly execrated. Apparently the talebearer did not confine himself to mere tattling. Misrepresentation of the lover's actions to the lady herself furnished to unscrupulous persons an easy means of "supplanting," and the lover sometimes had to warn his lady not to believe such reports. Thus Rambaut de Vanqueiras says: "Beautiful worthy lady, courteous and well bred, do not believe calumniators nor evil-speakers about me, for I am constant to you." See Mahn, *Die Werke der Troubadours* (Berlin, 1846), I, 374.

10 Trojel, p. 311. ["A man full of love is also full of fear."—Ed.]

11 *Ibid.* ["At the unexpected sight of his beloved, the heart of the lover trembles."—Ed.]

12 *Ibid.* ["A man obsessed by love sleeps and eats less."—Ed.]

13 The love-vision as a literary type is well described and illustrated by W. O. Sypherd in his *Studies in the "Hous of Fame,"* Chaucer Society, 1907.

14 Printed by G. Waitz in *Zeitschrift für deutsches Alterthum,* VII, 160ff.

15 William A. Neilson, *The Origins and Sources of the Court of Love,* Harvard Studies and Notes in Philology and Literature, Vol. VI (Boston, 1899), p. 38.

2

What Chaucer Really Did to *Il Filostrato*

C. S. LEWIS

A great deal of attention has deservedly been given to the relation between the *Book of Troilus* and its original, *Il Filostrato,* and Rossetti's collation[1] placed a knowledge of the subject within the reach even of undergraduate inquirers. It is, of course, entirely right and proper that the greater part of this attention has been devoted to such points as specially illustrate the individual genius of Chaucer as a dramatist and a psychologist. But such studies, without any disgrace to

Reprinted, by permission of author and editor, from *Essays and Studies by Members of the English Association*, XVII (1932), 56-75. Further discussion of the *Troilus* by Lewis in *The Allegory of Love* (Galaxy paperback, GB 17; New York: Oxford University Press, 1958), pp. 157-97. Against Lewis's view that the *Troilus* is "a great poem in praise of love," Roger Sharrock, "Second Thoughts: C. S. Lewis on Chaucer's *Troilus*," *Essays in Criticism*, VIII (1958), 123-37, argues that it is "a great poem about human frailty and exposedness, tender in its recognition of the limited human goodness of passionate love . . . ." Text of Boccaccio's *Il Filostrato* with facing English translation and valuable introduction on the affair with Maria d'Aquino which inspired his poem, on the sources, on the poem as courtly love document, and on differences between the *Filostrato* and Chaucer's *Troilus* in Nathaniel E. Griffin and Arthur B. Myrick, *The Filostrato of Giovanni Boccaccio* (Philadelphia: University of Pennsylvania Press, 1929). English translation of the story as told in Bendît de Sainte-Maure, *Roman de Troie* (c. 1160), and Boccaccio (1336), Chaucer's text, and Robert Henryson's 15th-century sequel, *The Testament of Cressid*, in R. K. Gordon, *The Story of Troilus* (London: J. M. Dent and Sons, Ltd., 1934).

themselves, often leave singularly undefined the historical position and affinities of a book; and if pursued intemperately they may leave us with a preposterous picture of the author as that abstraction, a *pure* individual, bound to no time nor place, or even obeying in the fourteenth century the aesthetics of the twentieth. It is possible that a good deal of misunderstanding still exists, even among instructed people, as to the real significance of the liberties that Chaucer took with his source. . . . I shall endeavour to show that the process which *Il Filostrato* underwent at Chaucer's hands was first and foremost a process of *medievalization*. One aspect of this process [courtly love] has received some attention from scholars, but its importance appears to me to be still insufficiently stressed. In what follows I shall, therefore, restate this aspect in my own terms while endeavouring to replace it in its context.

Chaucer had never heard of a renaissance; and I think it would be difficult to translate either into the English or the Latin of his day our distinction between sentimental or conventional art on the one hand, and art which paints 'Life'—whatever this means—on the other. When first a manuscript beginning with the words *Alcun di giove sogliono il favore* ["Some are wont the favor of Jove"—opening line of the *Filostrato*] came into his hands, he was, no doubt, aware of a difference between its contents and those of certain English and French manuscripts which he had read before. That some of the differences did not please him is apparent from his treatment. We may be sure, however, that he noticed and approved the new use of stanzas, instead of octosyllabic couplets, for narrative. He certainly thought the story a good story; he may even have thought it a story better told than any that he had yet read. But there was also, for Chaucer, a special reason why he should choose this story for his own retelling; and that reason largely determined the alterations that he made.

He was not yet the Chaucer of the *Canterbury Tales*: he was the *grant translateur* of the *Roman de la Rose,* the author of the *Book of the Duchesse,* and probably of 'many a song and many a lecherous lay'.[2] In other words he was the great living interpreter in English of *l'amour courtois.* Even in 1390, when Gower produced the first version of his *Confessio Amantis,* such faithful interpretation of the love tradition was still regarded as the typical and essential function of Chaucer:

he is Venus' 'disciple' and 'poete', with whose 'ditees and songes glade . . . the lond fulfild is overal'. And Gower still has hopes that Chaucer's existing treatments of *Frauendienst* [courtly service to a Lady] are only the preludes to some great 'testament' which will 'sette an ende of alle his werk'.[3] These expectations were, of course, disappointed; and it is possibly to that disappointment, rather than to a hypothetical quarrel (for which only the most ridiculous grounds have been assigned), that we should attribute Gower's removal of this passage from the second text of the *Confessio Amantis*. It had become apparent that Chaucer was following a different line of development, and the reference made to him by Venus had ceased to be appropriate.

It was, then, as a poet of courtly love that Chaucer approached *Il Filostrato*. There is no sign as yet that he wished to desert the courtly tradition; on the contrary, there is ample evidence that he still regarded himself as its exponent. But the narrative bent of his genius was already urging him, not to desert this tradition, but to pass from its doctrinal treatment (as in the *Romance of the Rose*) to its narrative treatment. Having preached it, and sung it, he would now exemplify it: he would show the code put into action in the course of a story—without prejudice (as we shall see) to a good deal of doctrine and pointing of the amorous moral by the way. The thing represents a curious return upon itself of literary history. If Chaucer had lived earlier he would, we may be sure, have found just the model that he desired in Chrestien de Troyes. But by Chaucer's time certain elements, which Chrestien had held together in unity, had come apart and taken an independent life. Chrestien had combined, magnificently, the interest of the story, and the interest of erotic doctrine and psychology. His successors had been unable or unwilling to achieve this union. Perhaps, indeed, the two things had to separate in order that each might grow to maturity; and in many of Chrestien's psychological passages one sees the embryonic allegory struggling to be born. Whatever the reason may be, such a separation took place. The story sets up on its own in the prose romances—the 'French book' of Malory: the doctrine and psychology set up on their own in the *Romance of the Rose*. In this situation if a poet arose who accepted the doctrines and also had a narrative genius, then *a priori* such a poet might be expected to combine again the two elements—now fully grown—which, in their rudimentary form, had lain together in Chrestien. But this is exactly the sort of poet that Chaucer was; and this (as we shall see) is what Chaucer did. The *Book of Troilus* shows, in fact, the very peculiar literary phenomenon of Chaucer groping back, unknowingly, through the very slightly medieval work of Boccaccio, to the genuinely medieval formula of Chrestien. We may be thankful that Chaucer did not live in the high noon of Chrestien's celebrity; for, if he had, we should probably have lost much of the originality of Troilus. He would have had less motive for altering Chrestien than for altering Boccaccio, and probably would have altered him less.

Approaching *Il Filostrato* from this angle, Chaucer, we may be sure, while feeling the charm of its narrative power, would have found himself, at many passages, uttering the Middle English equivalent of 'This will never do!' In such places he did not hesitate, as he might have said, to *amenden* and to *reducen* what was *amis* in his author. The majority of his modifications are corrections of errors which Boccaccio had committed against the code of courtly love; and modifications of this kind have not been entirely neglected by criticism. It has not, however, been sufficiently observed that these are only part and parcel of a general process of medievalization. They are, indeed, the most instructive part of that process, and even in the present discussion must claim the chief place; but in order to restore them to their proper setting it will be convenient to make a division of the different capacities in which Chaucer approached his original. These will, of course, be found to overlap in the concrete; but that is no reason for not plucking them ideally apart in the interests of clarity.

I. Chaucer approached his work as an 'Historial' poet contributing to the story of Troy. I do not mean that he necessarily believed his tale to be wholly or partly a record of fact, but his attitude towards it in this respect is different from Boccaccio's. Boccaccio, we may surmise, wrote for an audience who were beginning to look at poetry in our own way. For them *Il Filostrato* was mainly, though not entirely, 'a new poem by Boccaccio'. Chaucer wrote for an audience who still looked at poetry in the medieval fashion—a fashion for which the real literary units were 'matters', 'stories', and the like, rather than individual authors. For them the *Book of Troilus* was partly, though of course only partly, 'a new bit of the Troy story', or even 'a new bit of the matter of Rome'. Hence Chaucer expects them to be interested not only in the personal drama between his little group of characters but in that whole world of story which makes this drama's context: like children looking at a landscape picture and wanting to know what happens to the road after it disappears into the frame. For the same reason they will want to know his authorities. Passages in which Chaucer has departed from his original to meet this demand will easily occur to the memory. Thus, in I, 141 et seq., he excuses himself for not telling us more about the military history of the Trojan war, and adds what is almost a footnote to tell his audience where they can find that missing part of the story—'in Omer, or in Dares, or in Dyte'. Boccaccio had merely sketched in, in the preceding stanza, a general picture of war sufficient to provide the background for his own story—much as a dramatist might put *Alarums within* in a stage direction: he has in view an audience fully conscious that all this is mere necessary 'setting' or hypothesis. Thus again, in IV, 120 et seq., Chaucer inserts into the speech of *Calkas* an account of the quarrel between *Phebus* and *Neptunus* and *Lameadoun*. This is not dramatically necessary. All that was needed for *Calkas's* argument has already been given in lines 111 and 112 (cf. *Filostrato*, IV, xi). The Greek leaders did not need to be told about Laomedon; but Chaucer is not thinking of the Greek leaders; he is thinking of his audience who will gladly learn, or be reminded, of that part of the cycle. At lines 204 et seq. he inserts a note on the later history of *Antenor* for the same reason. In the fifth book he inserts unnecessarily lines 1464-1510 from the story of Thebes. The spirit in which this is done is aptly expressed in his own words:

> And so descendeth down from gestes olde
> To Diomede.   (v, 1511-12)

The whole 'matter of Rome' is still a unity, with a structure and life of its own. That part of it which the poem in hand is treating, which is, so to speak, in focus, must be seen fading gradually away into its 'historial' surroundings. The method is the antithesis of that which produces the 'framed' story of a modern writer: it is a method which romance largely took over from the epic.

II. Chaucer approached his work as a pupil of the rhetoricians and a firm believer in the good, old, and now neglected maxim of Dante: *omnis qui versificatur suos versus exornare debet in quantum potest* [Every versifier should embellish his verses as much as he can]. This side of Chaucer's poetry has been illustrated by Mr. Manly[4] so well that most readers will not now be in danger of neglecting it. A detailed application of this new study to the *Book of Troilus* would here detain us too long, but a cursory glance shows that Chaucer found his original too short and proceeded in many places to 'amplify' it. He began by abandoning the device—that of invoking his lady instead of the Muses—whereby Boccaccio had given a lyrical instead of a rhetorical turn to the invocation, and substituted an address to *Thesiphone (Filostrato,* I, i-v, cf. *Troilus,* I, 1-14). He added at the beginning of his second book an invocation of *Cleo* and an apology of the usual medieval type, for the defects of his work (II, 15-21). Almost immediately afterwards he inserted a *descriptio* of the month of a May (an innovation which concerned him as poet of courtly love no less than as rhetorician) which is extremely beautiful and appropriate, but which follows, none the less, conventional lines. The season is fixed by astronomical references, and *Proigne* and *Tereus* appear just where we should expect them (II, 50-6, 64-70). In the third book the scene of the morning parting between the two lovers affords a complicated example of Chaucer's medievalization. In his original (III, xlii) Chaucer read

> Ma poich' e galli presso al giorno udiro
> Cantar per l'aurora che surgea
> [But when near day they heard the cocks
> Crow for the rising dawn].

He proceeded to amplify this, first by the device of *Circuitio* or *Circumlocutio; galli,* with the aid of Alanus de Insulis, became 'the cok, comune astrologer'. Not content with this, he then repeated the sense of that whole phrase by the device *Expolitio,* of which the formula is *Mutiplice forma Dissimuletur idem: varius sis et tamen idem* [Disguise the same matter under multiple form: be various while yet the same], and the theme 'Dawn came' is varied with *Lucifer* and *Fortuna*

Minor, till it fills a whole stanza (III, 1415-21). In the next
stanza of Boccaccio he found a short speech by *Griseida,* expressing her sorrow at the parting which dawn necessitated:
but this was not enough for him. As poet of love he wanted
his *alba* [song as lovers part at dawn]; as rhetorician he wanted his *apostropha.* He therefore inserted sixteen lines of address to Night (1427-42), during which he secured the additional advantage, from the medieval point of view, of 'som
doctryne' (1429-32). In lines 1452-70 he inserted antiphon-
ally Troilus's *alba,* for which the only basis in Boccaccio was
the line *Il giorno che venia maledicendo* [cursing the approaching day] (III, xliv). The passage is an object lesson for
those who tend to identify the traditional with the dull. Its
matter goes back to the ancient sources of medieval love
poetry, notably to Ovid *Amores* i. 13, and it has been handled
often before, and better handled, by the Provençals. Yet it is
responsible for one of the most vivid and beautiful expressions that Chaucer ever used.

> Accursed be thi coming into Troye,
> For every bore hath oon of thi bright eyen.   (III, 1452-3)

A detailed study of the *Book of Troilus* would reveal this
'rhetoricization', if I may coin an ugly word, as the common
quality of many of Chaucer's additions. As examples of
Apostropha alone I may mention, before leaving this part
of the subject, III, 301 et seq. (*O tonge*), 617 et seq. (*But o
Fortune*), 715 et seq. (*O Venus*), and 813 et seq., where
Chaucer is following Boethius.

III. Chaucer approached his work as a poet of *doctryne*
and *sentence.* This is a side of his literary character which
twentieth-century fashions encourage us to overlook, but, of
course, no honest historian can deny it. His contemporaries
and immediate successors did not. His own creatures, the
pilgrims, regarded *mirthe* and *doctryne,*[5] or, as it is elsewhere
expressed, *sentence* and *solas,*[6] as the two alternative, and
equally welcome, excellences of a story. In the same spirit
Hoccleve praises Chaucer as the *mirour of fructuous entende-
ment* and the universal *fadir in science*—a passage, by the
by, to be recommended to those who are astonished that the
fifteenth century should imitate those elements of Chaucer's
genius which it enjoyed instead of those which we enjoy. In
respect of *doctryne,* then, Chaucer found his original deficient,

Storymithia story

and *amended* it. The example which will leap to every one's mind is the Boethian discussion on free will (IV, 946-1078). To Boccaccio, I suspect, this would have seemed as much an excrescence as it does to the modern reader; to the unjaded appetites of Chaucer's audience mere thickness in a wad of manuscript was a merit. If the author was so 'courteous beyond covenant' as to give you an extra bit of *doctryne* (or of story), who would be so churlish as to refuse it on the pedantic ground of irrelevance? But this passage is only one of many in which Chaucer departs from his original for the sake of giving his readers interesting general knowledge or philosophical doctrine. In III, 1387 et seq., finding Boccaccio's attack upon *gli avari* a little bare and unsupported, he throws out, as a species of buttress, the *exempla* of *Myda* and *Crassus*. In the same book he has to deal with the second assignation of Troilus and Cressida. Boccaccio gave him three stanzas of dialogue (*Filostrato*, III, lxvi-lxviii), but Chaucer rejected them and preferred—in curious anticipation of Falstaff's thesis about pitch—to assure his readers, on the authority of *thise clerkes wyse* (III, 1691) that *felicitee* is felicitous, though *Troilus* and *Criseyde* enjoyed something better than *felicitee*. In the same stanza he also intends, I think, an allusion to the *sententia* that occurs elsewhere in the Franklin's Tale.[7] In IV, 197-203, immediately before his *historial* insertion about Antenor, he introduces a *sentence* from Juvenal, partly for its own sake, partly in order that the story of Antenor may thus acquire an exemplary, as well as a *historial* value. In IV, 323-8 he inserts a passage on the great *locus communis* of Fortune and her wheel.

In the light of this sententious bias, Chaucer's treatment of Pandarus should be reconsidered, and it is here that a somewhat subtle exercise of the historical imagination becomes necessary. On the one hand, he would be a dull reader, and the victim rather than the pupil of history, who would take all the doctrinal passages in Chaucer seriously: that the speeches of Chauntecleer and Pertelote and of the Wyf of Bath not only *are* funny by reason of their sententiousness and learning, but are intended to be funny, and funny by that reason, is indisputable. On the other hand, to assume that sententiousness became funny for Chaucer's readers as easily as it becomes funny for us, is to misunderstand the fourteenth century: such an assumption will lead us to the preposterous view that *Melibee* (or even the Parson's Tale) is a comic work— a view not much mended by Mr. Mackail's suggestion that there are some jokes *too* funny to excite laughter and that *Melibee* is one of these. A clear recognition that our own age is quite abnormally sensitive to the funny side of sententiousness, to possible hypocrisy, and to dulness, is absolutely necessary for any one who wishes to understand the past. We must face the fact that Chaucer's audience could listen with gravity and interest to edifying matter which would set a modern audience sleeping or sniggering. The application of this to Pandarus is a delicate business. Every reader must interpret Pandarus for himself, and I can only put forward my own interpretation very tentatively. I believe that Pandarus is meant to be a comic character, but not, by many degrees, so broadly comic as he appears to some modern readers. There is, for me, no doubt that Chaucer intended us to smile when he made Troilus exclaim

> What knowe I of the queene Niobe?
> Lat be thyne olde ensaumples, I thee preye.   (I, 759)

But I question if he intended just that sort of smile which we actually give him. For me the fun lies in the fact that poor Troilus says what I have been wishing to say for some time. For Chaucer's hearers the point was a little different. The suddenness of the gap thus revealed between Troilus's state of mind and Pandarus's words cast a faintly ludicrous air on what had gone before: it made the theorizing and the *exempla* a little funny in retrospect. But it is quite probable that they had not been funny till then: the discourse on contraries (I, 631-44), the *exemplum* of Paris and Oenone, leading up to the theme 'Physician heal thyself' (652-72), the doctrine of the Mean applied to secrecy in love (687-93), the *sentences* from Solomon (695) and elsewhere (708), are all of them the sort of thing that can be found in admittedly serious passages, and it may well be that Chaucer 'had it both ways'. His readers were to be, first of all, edified by the doctrine for its own sake, and then (slightly) amused by the contrast between this edification and Troilus's obstinate attitude of the plain man. If this view be accepted it will have the consequence that Chaucer intended an effect of more subtility than that which we ordinarily receive. We get the broadly comic effect—a loquacious and unscrupulous old uncle talks solemn platitude at interminable length. For Chaucer, a *textuel* man talked excellent doctrine which we enjoy and by which we are edified: but at the same time we see that this 'has its funny side'. Ours is the crude joke of laughing at admitted rubbish: Chaucer's the much more lasting joke of laughing at 'the funny side' of that which, even while we laugh, we admire. To the present writer this reading of Pandarus does not appear doubtful; but it depends to some extent, on a mere 'impression' about the quality of the Middle Ages, an impression hard to correct, if it is an error, and hard to teach, if it is a truth. For this reason I do not insist on my interpretation. If, however, it is accepted, many of the speeches of Pandarus which are commonly regarded as having a purely dramatic significance will have to be classed among the examples of Chaucer's doctrinal or sententious insertions.

IV. Finally, Chaucer approached his work as the poet of courtly love. He not only modified his story so as to make it a more accurate representation in action of the orthodox erotic code, but he also went out of his way to emphasize its didactic element. Andreas Capellanus had given instructions to lovers; Guillaume de Lorris had given instructions veiled and decorated by allegory; Chaucer carries the process a stage further and gives instruction by example in the course of a concrete story. But he does not forget the instructional side of his work. In the following paragraphs I shall sometimes quote parallels to Chaucer's innovations from the earlier love literature, but it must not be thought that I suppose my quotations to represent Chaucer's immediate source.

1. Boccaccio in his induction, after invoking his mistress instead of the Muses, inserts (I, vi) a short request for lovers in general that they will pray for him. The prayer itself is disposed of in a single line

> Per me vi prego ch'amore preghiate.
> [For me I pray you that you pray to Love.]

This is little more than a conceit, abandoned as soon as it is used: a modern poet could almost do the like. Chaucer devotes four stanzas .(I, 22-49) to this prayer. If we make an abstract of both passages, Boccaccio will run 'Pray for me to Love', while Chaucer will run 'Remember, all lovers, your old unhappiness, and pray, for the unsuccessful, that they may come to solace; for me, that I may be enabled to tell this story; for those in despair, that they may die; for the fortunate, that they may persevere, and please their ladies in such manner as may advance the glory of Love'. The important point here is not so much that Chaucer expands his original, as that he renders it more liturgical: his prayer, with its careful discriminations in intercession for the various recognized stages of the amorous life, and its final reference *ad Amoris majorem gloriam* [to the greater glory of Love], is a collect. Chaucer is emphasizing that parody, or imitation, or rivalry—I know not which to call it—of the Christian religion which was inherent in traditional *Frauendienst*. The thing can be traced back to Ovid's purely ironical worship of Venus and Amor in the *De Arte Amatoria*. The idea of a love religion is taken up and worked out, though still with equal flippancy, in terms of medieval Christianity, by the twelfth-century poet of the *Concilium Romaricimontis* [The Council of Remiremont][8] where Love is given Cardinals (female), the power of visitation, and the power of cursing. Andreas Capellanus carried the process a stage further and gave Love the power of distributing reward and punishment after death. But while his hell of cruel beauties (*Siccitas*), his purgatory of beauties promiscuously kind (*Humiditas*), and his heaven of true lovers (*Amoenitas*) can hardly be other than playful, Andreas deals with the love religion much more seriously than the author of the *Concilium*. The lover's qualification is *morum probitas* [moral uprightness]: he must be truthful and modest, a good Catholic, clean in his speech, hospitable, and ready to return good for evil. There is nothing *in saeculo bonum* which is not derived from love: it may even be said in virtue of its severe standard of constancy, to be 'a kind of chastity'— *reddit hominem castitatis quasi virtute decoratum* [it adorns a man, in a way, with the virtue of chastity].[9]

In all this we are far removed from the tittering nuns and *clerici* of the *Concilium*. In Chrestien, the scene in which Lancelot kneels and adores the bed of Guinevere (as if before a *corseynt* [holy relic]) is, I think, certainly intended to be read seriously: what mental reservations the poet himself had on the whole business is another question. In Dante the love religion has become wholly and unequivocally serious by fusing with the real religion. . . . It is this quasi-religious element in the content, and this liturgical element in the diction, which Chaucer found lacking in his original at the very opening of the book, and which he supplied. The line

> That Love hem bringe in hevene to solas (I, 31)

is particularly instructive.

2. In the Temple scene (Chaucer, I, 155-315; *Filostrato*, I, xix-xxxii) Chaucer found a stanza which it was very necessary to *reducen*. It was Boccaccio's twenty-third, in which Troilus, after indulging in his 'cooling card for lovers', mentions that he has himself been singed with that fire, and even hints that he has had his successes; but the pleasures were not worth the pains. The whole passage is a typical example of that Latin spirit which in all ages (except perhaps our own) has made Englishmen a little uncomfortable; the hero must be a lady-killer from the very beginning, or the audience will think him a milksop and a booby. To have abashed, however temporarily, these strutting Latinisms, is not least among the virtues of medieval *Frauendienst*: and for Chaucer as its poet, this stanza was emphatically one of those that 'would never do'. He drops it quietly out of its place, and thus brings the course of his story nearer to that of the *Romance of the Rose*. The parallelism is so far intact. Troilus, an unattached young member of the courtly world, wandering idly about the Temple, is smitten with Love. In the same way the Dreamer having been admitted by Ydelnesse into the garden goes 'Pleying along ful merily'[10] until he looks in the fatal well. If he had already met Love outside the garden the whole allegory would have to be reconstructed.

3. A few lines lower Chaucer found in his original the words

> il quale amor trifisse
> Piu ch'alcun altro, pria del tempio uscisse.   (I, xxv)
> [whom Love transfixed
> More than any other before he left the temple.]

Amor trafisse in Boccaccio is hardly more than a literary variant for 'he fell in love': the allegory has shrunk into a metaphor and even that metaphor is almost unconscious and fossilized. Over such a passage one can imagine Chaucer exclaiming, *tantamne rem tam negligenter* [so great a thing so quickly tossed off]? He at once goes back through the metaphor to the allegory that begot it, and gives us his own

thirtieth stanza (I, 204-10) on the god of Love in anger bend-
ing his bow. The image is very ancient and goes back at least
as far as Apollonius Rhodius. Ovid was probably the intermediary who conveyed it to the Middle Ages. Chrestien uses
it, with particular emphasis on Love as the avenger of contempt. But Chaucer need not have gone further to find it
than to the *Romance of the Rose*,[11] with which, here again,
he brings his story into line.

4. But even this was not enough. Boccaccio's *Amor trafisse*
had occurred in a stanza where the author apostrophizes the
Cecità delle mondane menti [blindness of worldly minds],
and reflects on the familiar contrast between human expectations and the actual course of events. But this general contrast seemed weak to the poet of courtly love: what he wanted
was the explicit erotic *moral,* based on the special contrast
between the $\H{v}\beta\rho\iota\varsigma$ [pride in the face of the gods] of the
young scoffer and the complete surrender which the offended
deity soon afterwards extracted from him. This conception,
again, owes much to Ovid; but between Ovid and the Middle
Ages comes the later practice of the ancient Epithalamium
during the decline of antiquity and the Dark Ages: to which,
as I hope to show elsewhere, the system of courtly love as
a whole is heavily indebted. Thus in the fifth century Sidonius
Apollinarus in an Epithalamium, makes the bridegroom just
such another as Troilus: a proud scoffer humbled by Love.
. . . . In a much stranger poem, by the Bishop Ennodius, it is
not the $\H{v}\beta\rho\iota\varsigma$ of a single youth, but of the world, that has
stung the deities of love into retributive action. . . . In Chrestien the role of tamed rebel is transferred to the woman. In
Cligès Soredamors confesses that Love has humbled her
pride by force, and doubts whether such extorted service will
find favour. In strict obedience to this tradition Chaucer inserts
his lines 214-31, emphasizing the dangers of $\H{v}\beta\rho\iota\varsigma$ against
Love and the certainty of its ultimate failure; and we may be
thankful that he did, since it gives us the lively and touching
simile of *proude Bayard.* Then, mindful of his instructional
purpose, he adds four stanzas more (239-66), in which he
directly exhorts his readers to avoid the error of Troilus, and
that for two reasons: firstly, because Love *cannot* be resisted
(this is the policeman's argument—we may as well 'come
quiet'); and secondly because Love is a thing 'so vertuous in
kinde'. The second argument, of course, follows traditional

lines, and recalls Andreas's theory of Love as the source of all secular virtue.

5. In lines 330-50 Chaucer again returns to Troilus's scoffing—a scoffing this time assumed as a disguise. I do not wish to press the possibility that Chaucer in this passage is attempting, in virtue of his instructional purpose, to stress the lover's virtue of secrecy more than he found it stressed in his original; for Boccaccio, probably for different reasons, does not leave that side of the subject untouched. But it is interesting to note a difference in the content between this scoffing and that of Boccaccio (*Filostrato* I, xxi; xxii). Boccaccio's is based on contempt for women, fickle as wind, and heartless. Chaucer's is based on the hardships of love's *lay* [law] or religion: hardships arising from the uncertainty of the most orthodox *observances*, which may lead to various kinds of harm and may be taken amiss by the lady. Boccaccio dethrones the deity: Chaucer complains of the severity of the cult. It is the difference between an atheist and a man who humorously insists that he 'is not of religioun'.

6. In the first dialogue between Troilus and Pandarus the difference between Chaucer and his original can best be shown by an abstract. Boccaccio (II, vi-xxviii) would run roughly as follows:

> *T.* Well, if you must know, I am in love. But don't ask me with whom (vi-viii).
>
> *P.* Why did you not tell me long ago? I could have helped you (ix).
>
> *T.* What use would *you* be? Your own suit never succeeded (ix).
>
> *P.* A man can often guide others better than himself (x).
>
> *T.* I can't tell you, because it is a relation of yours (xv).
>
> *P.* A fig for relations! Who is it? (xvi).
>
> *T.* (after a pause) Griseida.
>
> *P.* Splendid! Love has fixed your heart in a good place. She is an admirable person. The only trouble is that she is rather *pious* (*onesta*): but I'll soon see to that (xxiii). Every woman is amorous at heart: they are only anxious to save their reputations (xxvii). I'll do all I can for you (xxviii).

Chaucer (I, 603-1008) would be more like this:

> *T.* Well, if you must know, I am in love. But don't ask me with whom (603-16).

P. Why did you not tell me long ago? I could have helped
you (617-20).

T. What use would *you* be? Your own suit never succeeded
(621-3).

P. A man can often guide others better than himself, as we
see from the analogy of the whetstone. Remember
the doctrine of contraries, and what Oenone said. As
regards secrecy, remember that all virtue is a mean
between two extremes (624-700).

T. Do leave me alone (760).

P. If you die, how will she interpret it? Many lovers have
served for twenty years without a single kiss. But
should they despair? No, they should think it a guerdon even to serve (761-819).

T. (much moved by this argument, 820-6) What shall I
do? Fortune is my foe (827-40).

P. Her wheel is always turning. Tell me who your mistress
is. If it were my sister, you should have her (841-61).

T. (after a pause)—My sweet foe is Criseyde (870-5).

P. Splendid: Love has fixed your heart in a good place.
This ought to gladden you, firstly, because to love
such a lady is nothing but good: secondly, because
if she has all these virtues, she must have Pity too.
You are very fortunate that Love has treated you so
well, considering your previous scorn of him. You
must repent at once (874-935).

T. (kneeling) Mea Culpa! (936-8).

P. Good. All will now come right. Govern yourself properly: you know that a divided heart can have no grace.
I have reasons for being hopeful. No man or woman
was ever born who was not apt for love, either natural
or celestial: and celestial love is not fitted to Criseyde's years. I will do all I can for you. Love converted
you of his goodness. Now that you are converted,
you will be as conspicuous among his saints as you
formerly were among the sinners against him (939-
1008).

In this passage it is safe to say that every single alteration
by Chaucer is an alteration in the direction of medievalism.
The Whetstone, Oenone, Fortune, and the like we have already discussed: the significance of the remaining innovations
may now be briefly indicated. In Boccaccio the reason for

Troilus's hesitation in giving the name is Criseida's relationship to Pandaro: and like a flash comes back Pandaro's startling answer. In Chaucer his hesitation is due to the courtly
lover's certainty that 'she nil to noon suich wrecche as I be
wonne' (778) and that 'full harde it wer to helpen in this
cas' (836). Pandaro's original

> Se quella ch'ami fosse mia sorella
> A mio potere avrai tuo piacer d'ella   (xvi)
> [If she whom you love were my sister,
> I would do my best to give you your pleasure of her.]

is reproduced in the English, but by removing the words that
provoked it in the Italian (È tua parenta [is your relative],
xv) Chaucer makes it merely a general protestation of boundless friendship in love, instead of a cynical defiance of scruples
already raised (Chaucer, 861). Boccaccio had delighted to
bring the purities of family life and the profligacy of his
young man about town into collision, and to show the
triumph of the latter. Chaucer keeps all the time within the
charmed circle of *Frauendienst* and allows no conflict but
that of the lover's hopes and fears. Again, Boccaccio's Pandaro has no argument to use against Troilo's silence, but the
argument 'I may help you'. Chaucer's Pandarus, on finding
that this argument fails, proceeds to expound the code. The
fear of dishonour in the lady's eyes, the duty of humble but
not despairing service in the face of all discouragement, and
the acceptance of this service as its own reward, form the substance of six stanzas in the English text (lines 768-819): at
least, if we accept four lines very characteristically devoted
to 'Ticius' and what 'bokes telle' of him. Even more remarkable is the difference between the behaviour of the two Pan-
dars after the lady's name has been disclosed. Boccaccio's,
cynical as ever, encourages Troilo by the reflection that female
virtue is not really a serious obstacle: Chaucer's makes the
virtue of the lady itself the ground for hope—arguing scholas-
tically that the *genus* of virtue implies that *species* thereof
which is *Pitee* (897-900). In what follows, Pandarus, while
continuing to advise, becomes an adviser of a slightly different
sort. He instructs Troilus not so much on his relationship to
the Lady as on his relationship to Love. He endeavours to
awaken in Troilus a devout sense of his previous sins against
that deity (904-30) and is not satisfied without confession

(931-8), briefly enumerates the commandments (953-9), and
warns his penitent of the dangers of a divided heart.

In establishing such a case as mine, the author who transfers relentlessly to his article all the passages listed in his
private notes can expect nothing but weariness from the
reader. If I am criticized, I am prepared to produce for my
contention many more evidential passages of the same kind.
I am prepared to show how many of the beauties introduced
by Chaucer, such as the song of Antigone or the riding past
of Troilus, are introduced to explain and mitigate and delay
the surrender of the heroine, who showed in Boccaccio a
facility condemned by the courtly code. I am prepared to
show how Chaucer never forgets his erotically didactic purpose; and how, anticipating criticism as a teacher of love,
he guards himself by reminding us that

> for to winne love in sondry ages,
> In sondry londes, sondry ben usages.   (II, 27-8)

But the reader whose stomach is limited would be tired, and
he who is interested may safely be left to follow the clue for
himself. Only one point, and that a point of principle, remains
to be treated in full. Do I, or do I not, lie open to the criticism of Professor Abercrombie's 'Liberty of Interpreting'?

The Professor *quem honoris causa nomino* [whom I name
to honor him] urges us not to turn from the known effect
which an ancient poem has upon us to speculation about the
effect which the poet intended it to have. The application of
this criticism which may be directed against me would run
as follows: 'If Chaucer's *Troilus* actually produces on us an
effect of greater realism and nature and freedom than its
original, why should we assume that this effect was accidental-
ly produced in the attempt to conform to an outworn convention?' If the charge is grounded, it is, to my mind, a very
grave one. My reply is that such a charge begs the very
question which I have most at heart in this paper, and but for
which I should regard my analysis as the aimless burrowings
of a thesis-monger. I would retort upon my imagined critic
with another question. This poem is more lively and of deeper
human appeal than its original. I grant it. This poem conforms
more closely than its original to the system of courtly love.
I claim to prove it. What then is the natural conclusion to
draw? Surely, that courtly love itself, in spite of all its shabby

origins and pedantic rules, is at bottom more agreeable to those elements in human, or at least in European, nature, which last longest, than the cynical Latin gallantries of Boccaccio? The world of Chrestien, of Guillaume de Lorris, and of Chaucer, is nearer to the world universal, is less of a closed system, than the world of Ovid, of Congreve, of Anatole France.

This is doctrine little palatable to the age in which we live: and it carries with it another doctrine that may seem no less paradoxical—namely, that certain medieval things are more universal, in that sense more classical, can claim more confidently a *securus judicat* [freely, "a guarantee of sound judgment"], than certain things of the Renaissance. To make Herod your villain is more human than to make Tamburlaine your hero. The politics of Machiavelli are provincial and temporary beside the doctrine of the *jus gentium*. The love-lore of Andreas, though a narrow stream, is a stream tending to the universal sea. Its waters move. For real stagnancy and isolation we must turn to the decorative lakes dug out far inland at such a mighty cost by Mr. George Moore; to the more popular corporation swimming-baths of Dr. Marie Stopes; or to the teeming marshlands of the late D. H. Lawrence, whose depth the wisest knows not and on whose bank the hart gives up his life rather than plunge in.

Notes

1 [William Michael Rossetti, *Chaucer's Troylus and Cryseyde Compared with Boccaccio's Filostrato*, Chaucer Society, First Series, Vols. XLIV and LXV (London, 1875-83).]

2 *CT*, X (I), 1086.

3 John Gower, *Confessio Amantis*, VIII, 2941-58.

4 John Matthews Manly, "Chaucer and the Rhetoricians," *The Proceedings of the British Academy*, XII (1926), 95-113. [Reprinted in R. J. Schoeck and J. Taylor, eds. *Chaucer Criticism: The Canterbury Tales* (Notre Dame, Indiana: University of Notre Dame Press, 1960), pp. 268-90.]

5 *CT*, VII (B²), 2125.

6 *CT*, I (A), 798.

7 *CT*, V (F), 762.

8 See above, Dodd, "The System of Courtly Love," n. 14.

9 Andreas Capellanus, *De arte honeste amandi*, ed. E. Trojel (Copenhagen, 1892), p. 10.

10 *Romaunt of the Rose*, 1. 1329.

11 *Ibid.*, 11. 1330 ff.; 1715 ff.

3

Destiny in *Troilus and Criseyde*

WALTER CLYDE CURRY

Chaucer's *Troilus and Criseyde* is a tragedy, strongly deterministic in tone, the action of which is presided over by a complex and inescapable destiny. Professor Kittredge has already given an excellent exposition of the fate which hangs over the chief characters and over the doomed city of Troy, and has analyzed the sources of the feeling that we are "looking on at a tragedy that we are powerless to check or to avert."[1] And Professor Root, remarking upon the high seriousness and the moral import of Chaucer's poem, says:

> He has called *Troilus* a tragedy; and it is a tragedy in the medieval sense of the term—the story of a man cast down by adverse fortune from great prosperity and high estate into misery and wretchedness. The five books into which he has disposed his story suggest the five acts of the tragic drama. There is, moreover, a quite tragic insistence on the idea of destiny.[2]

It seems to me probable, however, that the destiny in this poem is perhaps more hugely spread than has been hitherto conceived and that the tragedy of it is far in advance of the

Reprinted, by permission of author and publisher, from *Chaucer and the Mediaeval Sciences* (2nd ed.; New York: Barnes and Noble, Inc., 1960), pp. 241-98.

usual mediaeval idea. It is the aim of this study, therefore, to attempt an exposition of one mediaeval conception of fate or destiny—the sources and nature of its power, its various manifestations, its relations to providence, fortune, chance, and human free-will—and to indicate its vital and complex functioning in Chaucer's *Troilus*.

Undoubtedly Chaucer's idea of destiny is derived primarily from the *Consolation of Philosophy*, though he may draw occasionally upon the conceptions of other writers. That part of Boethius's philosophical system pertinent to the *Troilus* is comparatively simple, schematized, mechanical, and rigid. In general it deals with God's simplicity or one-ness in relation to the heterogeneity and multifariousness of His creations; in particular it treats of questions concerning the nature of Providence, the orders of destiny, the processes of fortune, the significance of so-called chance or accident, and the relation of all these to human free-will. How does God, infinitely removed, intervene in the affairs of men dwelling upon this mundane sphere? This God, stable, indivisible, and benevolent, transmits the power of His will through successive stages of action, each one of which, as it is discovered to be further and further away from the unchangeable source, shows more and more diversity, change, and alteration than the one before. First, standing outside and aloof upon the tower of His one-ness, God plans in His divine reason a universe as a complete and final whole, an entirely unified conception so infinite that it embraces every possible part—the creation of all things, the progressions of changing nature, all forms, causes, movements that have been or can be. This ordinance, assembled and unified in the divine thought, is called Providence. Secondly, in order that this conception may be realized in all its diverse particulars, God in His Providence delegates executive powers to a blind force called Destiny, which administers in detail whatever has been planned. But because Destiny is somewhat removed from the absolutely stable center of divine intelligence, it necessarily becomes split up and divided into many manifestations; Providence is One, but He administers through Destiny in many manners and at various times that which as a whole He has ordained. Destiny is, therefore, the disposition and ordinance inherent in movable things by which Providence knits all things together in their respective orders. Thus

whether Destiny be exercised by divine spirits (servants of
Providence), or by some soul (*anima mundi*), or by all
Nature serving God, or by the celestial movings of stars, or
by virtue of angels, or by the machinations of devils, by
any of these or by all of them together, the destinal ordinance is woven and accomplished.

Thirdly, this Destiny so divided and distributed sends
its influences outward and still further away from the stable
center until they move upon still another blind and capricious force called Fortune, whose function it is (being
personified as a sort of goddess) to rule over the checkered
careers of human beings in this world. And because this
plane of activity is the farthest possible removed from the
one-ness characteristic of God, the chief qualities of Fortune are mutability, change, instability, and irrationality. In
other words, whatever comes to a man in this precarious
existence—for example, birth, riches, power, happiness, grief,
sorrow, reverses, friendship, love, death, anything and everything—is the immediate gift of Fortune. This unsympathetic,
erratic force which continually whirls human beings from
good to bad, from poverty to riches, or from eminence to
destruction, cares no more for one man than for another; its
activities *seem* in their infinite capriciousness and diversity to
be entirely illogical and chaotic.

But they only *seem* so to those who are ignorant or themselves blinded by success or adversity. For Fortune has two
aspects: namely, (a) that "common" Fortune, which represents all common experiences of humanity, and (b) that
more personal fortune, according to which an individual may
be born at a given time and place, grow up in this or that
environment, love one person in particular, and die in youth
or middle age by war or flood or poison. Thus any individual
experience is likely to be the complex result of the combined
influence of two or more destinal forces. Fortune as "common" comes from the moving of Nature-as-destiny. Or in
more poetic terms, God binds together the diverse elements
of His creation and maintains their proper status by the universal bond of Love; planets move in prescribed courses without faltering, seasons follow in regular order, neither day nor
night encroaches upon the other, the sea remains within its
bounds, men's lives progress in general from birth and youth
to age and death, and men and women are joined in the

sacrament of marriage—all this because God has bound them
with the chain of Love. But Fortune in its more personal
bearings may be the result also of other destinal forces such
as, for example, that of the erratic stars. It is Fortune in this
latter aspect that is sometimes spoken of a chance or "hap"
or "aventure of fortune" or accident. But if accident be taken
to mean that which comes to pass without cause or design,
there is really no such thing. What through ignorance is called
chance is nothing more than an occurrence whose causes are
not understood. When, say, a man finds a pot of gold in a
field, no one should say that this chances without a cause.
The causes for this and for everything else, though perhaps
not perceived by finite men, stretch back in an unbroken
order through Destiny to the divine plan in God's mind. For
all things are inescapably bound together and unified in the
ordinance of Providence. It is only because men are shortsighted that they rail at the mutability of Fortune or the
cruelty of Destiny or even at Providence itself. But the philosopher whose thought is stayed upon the stability of God may
rise in some measure above the vicissitudes of Fortune. The
relation between human free-will and the Destiny prepared
in the Providence of God we shall discuss anon.[3]

Now of all the destinal forces manifesting themselves in
the affairs of men—"whether exercised by divine spirits
(servants of Providence), or by some soul, or by Nature
serving God, or by the celestial movings of stars, or by virtue
of Angels or by the machinations of devils, by any of these
or by all of them together"—that which seems usually to
appeal most strongly to Chaucer as artist is the celestial moving of the erratic stars. The personal fortunes of Palamon and
Arcite in the *Knight's Tale* are presided over by the planets
Saturn and Mars. Again, in the *Merchant's Tale* the narrator
is in light mood undecided what combination of destinal
forces brings May to bestow her love upon Damian: "Whether it was by destiny or chance, by the influence (of spirits),
or by nature, or by the power of a constellation thus-
or-so placed in the heavens that it was a favorable time for
presenting a love-letter to a woman to get her love, I cannot
say; let that great God above, who knows that no act is
causeless, judge the matter."[4] The destiny governing the Wife
of Bath resides in a conjunction of Mars and Venus in
Taurus; it is evident that the destinal forces hanging over

Hypermnestra in the *Legend of Good Women* are associated with the movements of Venus, Jupiter, and Saturn, and that Constance's fortunes in the *Man of Law's Tale* are in large measure subject to the power of Mars and Luna cadent from an angle in Scorpio and the eighth house. These more or less capricious and uniquely personal fortunes are caused by the destinal forces emanating from the erratic stars or planets as they move through the heavens.

The "common" fortunes of men—birth, growth, love, reproduction, death, and so on—are, as we have said, under the control of Nature, which serves God in the capacity of Destiny. We must now observe that, according to some mediaeval thinkers, this Nature is the product of the regular movements of the fixed stars. Aristotle says:

> The motion of the heavens, to which all change on earth is due, is two-fold, and has a twofold effect upon sublunary matter. The perfect diurnal motion of the fixed stars from east to west constitutes the principle of permanence and growth; whereas the motion of the planets, running their annual courses at irregular paces from west to east athwart the diurnal motion of the fixed stars, constitutes the principle of earthly change.[5]

But it is the Arabian, Albumasar, who develops the theory more fully:

> All that is born and dies on earth depends upon the motions of the constellations and of the stars. . . Now the seven wandering planets march along the zodiac more swiftly than do the constellations, often changing from direct to retrograde. They are, therefore, better adapted than the upper spheres to produce the effects and the motions of the things of this world. To the sphere of the constellations is assigned a general rule; whereas to the wandering stars belongs the care over the details of earthly life. . . The more rapidly a planet moves, and the stranger the course it follows, the more powerful will be its influence on things below. The motion of the moon is swifter than that of any other planet; it has, accordingly, more to do than any other in regulating mundane affairs. The fixed stars govern what is stable in the world, or what suffers gradual change. The celestial sphere of the fixed stars encircles the earth with a perpetual motion; the stars never alter their pace, and maintain invariably their relative distance from the earth. The seven planets, on the contrary, move more rapidly and with diverse motions, each running its own variable course. . . As the motions of these wandering stars are never interrupted, so the generations and alterations of earthly things never have an end. Only by observing the great diversity of planetary motions can one comprehend the unnumbered varieties of change in this world.[6]

Thus, we may safely conclude, the regular progressions of Nature—the successions of the seasons, birth, growth, death—and consequently the common fortunes of men are ultimately attributable to the motion of the fixed stars.

That Boethius shows familiarity with some such theory as this seems evident. . . . In Book iv meter 6, Boethius seems to imply that the destinal power of the Chain of Love is inherent first and primarily in the movement of the sphere of the constellations and that its influence is projected thence outward and farther away from God, the stable center, into certain movements of the Sun and Moon and into the natural order of things upon the earth:

> If thou, being wise, wilt judge in thy thought the laws of the high Thunderer, behold the heights of the sovereign heaven. There the stars, by the rightful alliance of things, keep their old peace. . . . Thus Love creates concord in the everlasting courses, and thus is conflict put out of the country of the stars. This concord controls in a uniform manner the elements, so that the moist things striving with the dry things yield place at times; and the cold things join themselves by faith to the hot things. . . By the same causes the flowery year yields sweet savours in the first summer-season warming; the hot summer dries up the corn; the autumn comes again, heavy with apples; and the heavy rain washes the winter. This concord brings forth and nourishes everything that has life in the world; and this same concord, destroying, hides, snatches away, and overwhelms under the last death all things that are born.

Thus the power of Love, communicated by God first to the constellations of the eighth sphere, is transmitted through the more regular movements of the planets (especially the Sun and Moon) and through the elements so that it becomes finally in this mundane sphere Destiny-as-nature, which produces the common fortunes of men.

With this exposition of the destinal forces in mind, let us return to a study of Chaucer's *Troilus and Criseyde*. It must be observed at once that in this tragedy the poet has not been able, or perhaps has been unwilling, to define the limits of the destiny back of the story's action with such precision and accuracy as he has employed elsewhere. He insists time and again, as we shall see, that the common fortunes of Troilus and Criseyde are caused by Nature-as-destiny and hence by God, who is the author of Nature; he suggests as often that the special, individual fortunes of the protagonists are directed by the destinal power inherent in the

movements of the erratic stars. But he nowhere postulates a
more definite system of destinal forces. Still one is made to
feel—by means of reference to this or that planet, by striking
suggestions of destructive influences hanging over the doomed
city of Troy, and by mysterious intimations of tragedy announced by dreams, oracles, and divinations that the days of
Troy are numbered and that the cloud of fate hovering over
Troilus and Criseyde will presently overwhelm them in the
general disaster.

For example, in the beginning of Book I, Chaucer states,
with his usual swift artistry, that the story deals primarily
with the double sorrow of Troilus, who loved Criseyde and
who was in the end forsaken by her. But, like a true tragedian,
he conceives the brilliant idea of throwing the lamentable
history of the two lovers against the dark background of the
Trojan war, which has already progressed nearly ten bloody
years and which is on the point of ending with the fall of
the great city. Apollo's unappeasable enmity is about to
strike; and in some sense the movements of the stars are
bound up with the city's imminent destruction. For Calchas,
celebrated astrologer, magician, and augurer, receives an-
nouncements from a variety of sources all agreeing that
mysterious powers are about to meet in one line for the doom
of Troy. Apollo speaks to him through an oracle, saying that
the Greeks will shortly be victorious; "by calculynge," i.e.,
by astrological observation, he finds the same message written
among the stars; and "by sort," i.e., by the casting of lots, or
by the chance opening of sacred books, or perhaps by augury
from the flights of birds, his conclusions are further confirmed. Then since his native city must fall, Calchas departs
from it, and seeks sanctuary among the enemy Greeks (I,
64-83). But in the meantime fighting continues for a season,
bringing successes now to one side, now to the other; Fortune
turns her wheel, and each in succession is whirled aloft to
victory and afterwards under to defeat (I, 134 ff.). Since it is
not apposite, however, to tell the whole process of the city's
destruction, the author directs the reader to Homer, Dares,
and Dictys (I, 141 ff.). Thus, at the very beginning of the
story, Chaucer has suggested the lively pageantry of a romantic war and has sketched back of this narrative of chivalry
and love the destinal forces which produce the city's downfall. And when the protagonists appear upon the scene, one

senses that a doom is already prepared for them. This method of precipitating tragic characters into a situation already overshadowed by a gloomy fatality is characteristic of Shakespeare in his greatest tragedies.

Troilus is introduced scoffing at love and deriding lovers, but Nature-as-destiny is preparing his inevitable subjugation to her laws. When he sees a knight or squire feasting his eyes upon a lady and sighing, he smiles contemptuously upon such folly. But the angry god of love prepares to pluck the fine feathers of this peacock. At this juncture, Chaucer introduces a long, independent passage in which he philosophizes upon the power of Love (Nature-as-destiny) that is presently to subdue the proud heart of Troilus. It is the nature of man and, therefore, his destiny to love. Since love binds all things together and no man may escape the law of Nature, let no man refuse to be bound by Love (I, 214-66). So Chaucer initiates the love-story with the announcement of one source of the destinal power which is to direct the life and actions of Troilus; the Boethian principle of Love, which binds together all parts of God's creation, is invoked to explain why the proud Trojan is made to love at all [Cf. Boethius ii. m. 8].

Having fallen in love with Criseyde, Troilus himself seems to recognize that Nature-as-destiny is in large measure responsible for his experience, which is in a sense common to all men. But since his code enjoins absolute secrecy and since she can know nothing of his passion as yet, he is constrained to lament the fate which has decreed that his particular fortune should be to love Criseyde, and not perhaps some other woman. This is the fool who laughed at love's pains; now he, too, is caught in the snare and gnaws his own chain (I, 507,09). If this were known (he thinks) no doubt his friends would jeer and say:

> O thou woeful Troilus, since thou must of necessity love through thy destiny, would to God that thou hadst centered thy affections upon one who might know of thy woe, even though she should lack pity. But thy lady is as cold toward thee as frost under the winter moon, and thou art fordone as is snow in fire (I, 519-25).

He does not understand the destinal origin of this individual fortune which has come upon him; consequently when Pandarus comes and offers to medicine his complaint, he rails at Fortune and refuses aid (I, 835-40). And now to comfort him Pandarus, following Boethius, postulates that Fortune is not to be greatly blamed, because she is in some measure common to all men. If she should stop turning her wheel for a single moment, she would cease to be Fortune. Troilus should take this comfort to his soul: if the joys given by Fortune must pass away, so also must the sorrows—for her wheel cannot stop turning. Who knows but that, out of her very mutability, she may be preparing happiness for the woeful lover? (I, 840-54) [Cf. Boethius ii. m.l; ii. pr. 2]. At any rate, Troilus should not be ashamed to love Criseyde; nothing but good comes of loving well and in worthy place. He ought not to call this hap or chance but rather grace, i.e., a special mercy of whatever destinal or divine forces there are (I, 895 ff.). Pandarus himself will entreat Criseyde for his friend with hope of success, for wise men say that there was never yet man or woman who was unapt to suffer heat of love, either celestial or natural; it would become her much more to love and cherish a worthy knight like Troilus (I, 975-86). Here Chaucer is showing that the mysterious movings of Nature in the capacity of destiny have conquered the proud heart of Troilus and may influence the decision of Criseyde. But as to why either lover, as an individual, should choose the other and not somebody else, he has nothing to say as yet.

In Book II, however, one is made to feel that the wandering or erratic stars, especially Venus and Luna, exert a powerful influence upon the personal fortunes of Troilus and Criseyde. For example, before Pandarus sets out to woo his niece for Troilus, he deems it necessary to set up a figure of the heavens in order to learn whether the Moon is favorable to such a journey; and having determined that the election is favorable, he proceeds with confidence (II, 74 ff.). We are not told in precisely what position he finds Luna, nor how she is aspected by other planets, but he shows himself wise in astrological lore in assuming that Luna especially must be consulted when one starts upon a journey of any sort and particularly upon a journey for the purpose of acquiring love or friendship. Albohazen Haly says:

> For an election to determine the best time for beginning a journey Luna should be crescent in light, free from the influence of the infortunes, and not in the second, or eighth, or sixth, or the twelfth house of the figure; she should be in good aspect with the fortunes;

Mercury should not be combust and should be free from the infortunes; the lord of the ascendant should not be combust or unfortunately placed, but in good position; and a fortune should be
found in the ascendant or in any one of the angles. Such an election
signifies health of the body, promptness, and joy in the journey. . . .
When Luna is separated by a degree from conjunctions with Sol and
is in trine or sextile aspect with Saturn, and afterwards comes into
aspect with any fortune, it signifies that whatever is undertaken at
that time will be completed, be durable, and will bring joy. And
if your going forth is to a woman, apply Luna to Venus situated in
a masculine sign.[7]

Pandarus, no doubt, applies Luna to Venus, since he is going
forth to Criseyde. . . . At any rate, assured of the benevolent
aspect of the heavens, Pandarus sallies forth jauntily.

Criseyde's knowledge of God, Providence, and Destiny is
apparently slight, but she is acquainted in some measure
with the eccentricities of Fortune. Consequently, when Pandarus comes to her with an appeal on behalf of Troilus, his
message is couched in terms which she can readily understand.
He arouses her curiosity at first by referring mysteriously to
a "fair adventure" (II, 224) which has befallen her, and
urges her to seize upon it. She has lightly found good fortune,
and she must accept it lest it should abate (II, 281-91).
Troilus loves her and, if fortune wills it so, must hasten to
die unless she will requite his love (II, 335 ff.). "Alas! for
woe," says she playing slyly, "I should have thought that, if
it had been my misfortune to love him or Achilles or Hector
or any other man, you would have had no mercy on me"
(II, 415-19). But Pandarus assuages her assumed perturbation
by recounting Troilus's eloquence in bewailing his woe to
Love. Here, strangely enough, the god of love is made to have
the power and momentarily to take the place of the Boethian
God, who in his Providence directs through Destiny the
fortunes of every man. "O god," says Troilus, "who at thy
disposition leadest the end of every man, by just Providence,
accept my confession and send me such penance as seems
good" (II, 526-30). In the meantime, while Pandarus and
Criseyde talk, Troilus comes riding by on his return from
battle, and she sees him as he is, a romantic and attractive
figure. Why should he have come at this precisely psychological moment? It is destiny, fate, necessity, says Chaucer,

For which, men say, may nought disturbed be
That shal bityden of necessitee (II, 621).

We are not yet informed what the source of this necessity is. But it is suggested that Nature-as-destiny is responsible for Criseyde's beginning to pity the woe of Troilus (II, 1373-75); and after that, her first inclination toward love is deepened into real passion partly by contemplating his manhood and pain, and through his good service to her.

But here Chaucer emphasizes that, in the development of Criseyde's budding love for Troilus, the destinal influence of the planet Venus is, if not the most potent of the destinal forces, at least powerfully contributory. It is suggested, in the first place, that Venus was not entirely unfavorable ("nas nat al a fo") to Troilus in his nativity (II, 684). If this may be interpreted to mean that this planet was the ruling influence at his birth, we can account in some measure for his character in general and for his personal attractiveness to women in particular. As I have shown elsewhere, it is the province of Venus to bestow upon her children beautiful and elegantly formed bodies, together with characters inclined to luxuriousness and passionate love but withal honorable and upright. Though voluptuous and temperamental by nature, the children of Venus possess a fine sense of duty, a ready faith, great refinement, good breeding, delicacy of feeling, and kindliness of heart. They easily become leaders and perform whatever they undertake with facility. They are given to games, to laughter, to joyous living, rejoicing in the companionship of friends and relying upon others to the point of being often deceived. So Troilus is described. He is said to be so well grown in stature and to be of such complete proportion that Nature might not amend it; he is young, fresh, strong, hardy as a lion, and in every situation true as steel. He is so endowed with good qualities that there are few like him in the world (V, 826-33). And Criseyde loves him finally, in part, for his innate honesty and trustworthiness, for his wisdom in making love, for his secrecy, and for his honor in affairs of the heart. His every act indicates that he is a child of Venus.

Moreover, at the precise moment when Troilus seeks the full love of Criseyde, Venus is said to be so well situated in the heavens that she aids materially in furthering the amatory cause. This naturally benefic planet is favorably located in the seventh house of the heavens, having other planets disposed in such good aspect to her that she helps poor Troilus to escape his woe (II, 680 ff.). Since we are not told specifically how the other planets stand in relation to Venus, it is impossible to interpret fully the astrological situation. But Chaucer is correct when he suggests that, in elections to determine a favorable time for securing the love of a woman, Venus should be located in the seventh house of the heavens. To this house are referred all questions concerning love, marriage, the quarrels of lovers, pleasure, passion, and desire. As Professor Root well says:

> For any question concerning love, the astrologer inquires what planets are at the moment in the seventh house, which "gives judgment of marriage and all manner of love-questions." A malefic planet—Saturn or Mars—in the seventh house causes ill fortune in love. But Venus is a benefic planet, and especially concerned with affairs of love. Venus in the seventh house marks a very propitious hour.[8]

In this instance Chaucer is careful to indicate that, at the critical moment when Criseyde (urged at first by Nature-as-destiny) is on the point of making up her mind to love the individual, Troilus, the wandering planets in favorable combinations exert their destinal power and aid in producing the special fortunes of the characters.

It is in Book III, however, where Troilus finally secures and enjoys the love of Criseyde, that Chaucer shows most effectively the combined and intricately working forces of destiny. He has apparently confused the influence of the planets, sometimes with that of the pagan gods and goddesses of the same names and sometimes with the power of the Boethian bond of Love. But here is in reality no confusion; the mythological dress is a poetical device, and with a clear mind the poet has demonstrated how the destinal urge emanating from the erratic stars combines and intermingles with that having its source in Nature-as-destiny. In order to make this idea immediately emphatic he removes Troilo's song (based on Boethius ii. m.8) from its natural position in Boccaccio's *Filostrato* to the beginning of Book III and raises it to the dignity of a Proem (III, 1-38).

Here Venus in several aspects is praised as the source of all love and unity in the world. As Professor Root has it:

> In this passage, Venus is addressed sometimes as the pagan goddess, sometimes as the planet with astrological influence. She is the

power of Love, both in its earthly aspect as sexual attraction, and
in its platonic aspect as the unifying principle of the universe.[9]

It is the favorable light of the planet Venus, the Sun's friend,
which adorns the third heaven and which, always ready to
repair into gentle hearts, is in part the cause of that whole-
some joy accompanying the advent of love. It is Venus, the
symbol of unifying Love, whose might is felt in earth and
sea, in heaven and in hell; all created things feel at times her
eternal and all-pervasive influence. God loves and will refuse
nothing to love; and in this world no creature has worth or
may endure without it. The planet Venus appeases the wrath
of the infortune, Mars; Venus, the symbol of unity, over-
comes the tendency of created things to fly asunder and to
destroy themselves in conflict. Venus—in both her philosophical and astrological aspects—holds realm and house together; she is the true cause of friendship; she knows all the
hidden qualities of things—i.e., "the disposition and ordinance
inherent in movable things," which, according to Boethius,
is destiny—at which people wonder so, when they cannot
understand why this woman loves that man, or why another
loves elsewhere, or why this fish and not that comes into the
weir. She has established an inescapable law in the universe
(III, 1-36). Consequently, we may conclude that Venus in
both her aspects is largely responsible for the consummation
of Troilus's love.

But the other planets are also in general accord with her.
When Criseyde visits Pandarus on the fatal night and is on the
point of returning home without having seen Troilus, her
Fortune ruled over by a combination of planets compels her
to remain. "But, O Fortune, executrix of fates," says Chaucer
of this critical moment, "O influence of these high heavens,
it is truth that, under God, you are our shepherds, though to
us beasts the causes are hidden. Criseyde started home, but by
the god's will it was executed other than she desired. For the
bent Moon joined with Saturn and Jupiter in Cancer brought
such a deluge of rain that she was compelled to remain" (III,
617-25).[10] Moreover, just before Criseyde is made to come to
Troilus, the apprehensive lover appeals for assistance to every
planet except Saturn. It must be recalled that Venus exerted
a favorable influence in his nativity. Consequently, he prays
that, if Venus the happy planet had bad aspects of Mars or
Saturn or if she were combust at his birth, she may ask her

father Jupiter, a powerfully benefic planet, to turn aside these evil influences (III, 715-21). In this situation he is particularly wise in asking to be relieved of the possible bad aspects of Mars and Saturn, for as Albubather says:

> When Venus and Mars, without the good influence of Jupiter, are *in medio coeli* or in the East, the native will be a fornicator and of evil reputation. . . . When Venus is located in Pisces and Mars aspects her from his exaltation, the native will be given to much fornication and from it shall procure his death. . . . When Venus and Saturn are unfortuately joined in the tenth house and peregrene, the native will be impotent.[11]

And Ptolemaeus points out the dangers in even more sweeping terms:

> If Venus is combust and in any one of the angles, and without beneficent aspect of Jupiter, the native will commit many secret acts contrary to nature, and especially so if Venus is found in any of the incontinent signs.[12]

Well may the gentle-minded Troilus, going in honor to enjoy his love for the first time, pray to be delivered from the dishonorable and unnatural acts which Venus, if she were under the evil influence of Saturn or Mars or if she were combust at his birth, might impose upon him.

Moreover, lest any loop-hole should be neglected through which malefic influences may be streamed upon him in this situation, Troilus is careful to supplicate all the planets with the single exception of Saturn. Astrologically speaking, Saturn is the cold and dry planet, the malignant infortune, sending violent death by inundation and storms of pestilential winds, fomenting conflicts of all kinds, dealing destruction by poison, in prison, and by means of disease. He is never favorable under any circumstances, and that is why Troilus asks to be delivered from his bad aspects (III, 716) and why his help is not solicited. . . . Finally, Troilus appeals again to whatever destinal forces there may be, using this time the symbol of the pagan Fates:

> O fatal sustren, which, er any cloth
> Me shapen was, my destine me sponne,
> So helpeth to this werk that is bygonne! (III, 733-35).

Apparently the lover's intelligent prayers are answered in some detail. At any rate, when Troilus finds that success has

crowned his efforts and Criseyde lies in his arms, he renders
thanks to precisely those destinal forces upon which he called
for aid. He expresses fervent gratitude to "the blisful goddes
sevene" (III, 1202), that is to say, gratitude to the benefic
planets no doubt for their active and favorable interference
in his behalf and to the malignant infortunes for their apathy
or indifference. He acknowledges especially that Venus, "the
wel-willy planete" (III, 1257), has had an important part in
bringing the lovely lady to his arms. . . . Chaucer is very careful to state that this relation between Troilus and Criseyde is
no madness or folly; here is no wicked love which might lead
to base actions (III, 1373-94). The love of Troilus and
Criseyde, watched over and guided by the kindly planets, has
taken no taint from the possible bad aspects of the infortunes.
The practice of it only "souneth in-to gentlenes" (III, 1414).

But Troilus does not forget in the first flush of his happiness to praise also Nature-as-destiny. When he holds Criseyde
in his arms for the first time, he acclaims that benign Love,
the holy bond of all things, through whose grace he, the
former rebel against love's laws has been raised to a place of
boundless contentment (III, 1261-74). And after he has enjoyed the companionship of Criseyde for a season, he is
accustomed to descant to Pandarus upon the perfections of
his love, and to sing a joyous hymn in praise of that mysterious power which holds them together.

> It is Love that establishes laws in the high heavens, in the earth,
> and in the hearts of men and women, so that all things obey their
> respective natures. Without Love all Nature would be in chaos and
> human life useless. May God, who is the author of Nature, bind
> with the power of Love all human hearts so that no man may
> escape (III, 1740-71).

So Troilus pays his final respects to the great power which
has been instrumental in giving him the consummation of his
desires.

We must observe in passing, however, that the hymn to
Love sung by Troilus at this juncture is not found in manuscripts supposed to represent the first draft of the poem. Professor Root says:

> At this point in *Filostrato*, Troilo sings to Love a hymn (III,
> 74-9) which is based in part on this Metre of Boethius [ii. m.8].
> These stanzas of *Filostrato* Chaucer has used as a Proem (lines

1-38) to his third book. Having so used them, it was necessary to find new material for the song of Troilus; and Chaucer turned back to the passage in Boethius from which Boccaccio had received his inspiration. . . . It would seem that the poet did not in the first draft provide a song for Troilus to sing.[13]

In that case, why should Chaucer feel it expedient to return to his original manuscript and add this particular song for Troilus? Our analysis of the destinal forces back of the third book supplies the answer to this question: he wanted to give climactic emphasis to the conception of Nature-as-destiny, with which the book begins and which underlies the progress and consummation of the love affair. Fearing that his readers might possibly miss the technical significance of the Proem and of Troilus's earlier song (III, 1254-74) he returned and inserted, near the end of the book and at the point where the lovers are most supremely happy, this full-throated song which reiterates and confirms the inescapable power of Love. In this way he has to some degree palliated what may have seemed to his age a rather immoral situation; and he has bestowed dignity upon ephemeral human relationships by linking them up with the processes of cosmic forces. Having so established his purpose, he does not refer again to Nature-as-destiny.

Then comes the turning point of the story's action. It is in Book IV that we have the reversal of personal Fortune out of which grows the tragedy of Troilus and Criseyde. Up to this time the lovers have been for the most part increasingly happy and successful; Nature-as-destiny had decreed their passion and destinal forces residing in the erratic stars have determined in large measure the conditions, times, and places which figure in their joyous coming together. But, well-away the while, says Chaucer remembering Boethius, for all too short a season endures such joy, thanks to Fortune! She seems most favorable when she is just on the point of beguiling. From Troilus she turns aside and hides her bright face, and takes no heed of him; she casts him completely out of his lady's grace, and sets Diomede on her wheel. The poet himself feels compelled now to write with quaking pen the story of how Criseyde forsook Troilus, or at least how she was unkind; may the Furies and cruel Mars help him (IV, 1-28).

And at this inauspicious moment, when Fortune seems to withdraw her favor from the protagonist, Chaucer the artist emphasizes again the imminent doom of Troy. Through the first three books we are likely to forget the ominous warnings concerning the city's coming destruction, seeing that Troilus and Criseyde are apparently the darlings of Fortune and feeling that destiny itself subscribes to them; the tragic qualm which we experienced at the beginning of the story has been allayed to some extent by the growing sense that cosmic forces are arrayed on the lover's side. But now the old gray Calchas, who fled from Troy long ago because he knew it must fall, begins his croakings again. He demands of the Greeks that this daughter, Criseyde, be exchanged among other prisoners of war in order that she may escape the general holocaust. He tells the Greeks:

> On peril of my life, I do not lie, Apollo has taught it to me faithfully; I have also known it to be true by astrological observation, by the casting of lots, and also by augury; and I prophesy that the time is close at hand when Troy shall be reduced to dead ashes! For certainly Apollo and Neptune, who built the walls of Troy, are so angry with the city that they shall bring it to confusion out of spite for King Laomedon. He would not pay their wages; therefore, the town of Troy shall be set on fire (IV, 113-126).

The ancient enmity of the incensed gods still hangs over the city, and we hear closer and more pronounced rumblings, as it were, of the Fate which is soon to be unloosed upon it. How shall Troilus survive when he is caught in the maelstrom of such colossal forces?

When he learns that Criseyde must depart from Troy, Troilus is at first thrown into a panic. In his progressive happiness he has been able to discern, back of his common and individual fortune, the destinal powers moving under the direction of God. But now he is so blinded by grief and so unphilosophical that he can understand nothing beyond the waywardness of Fortune. Conceiving of her as a pagan goddess, he laments pathetically:

> O Fortune, why hast thou taken away Criseyde without a reason? I have honored thee above all the gods; I am too insignificant to have incurred thy enmity. If Criseyde had been left, I would have scorned thy gifts. It is thy nature to bereave a creature of his dearest possession, and in that way to prove thy changeable violence. All is lost! (IV, 260-86).

He does not understand why the lord of Love, who knows his heart and the travail he has undergone for Criseyde, can permit this separation, since it was Love in the first place who brought him and Criseyde into his grace and sealed their hearts (IV, 288-94). Whatever else he may do while suffering this life of torment and cruel pain, he will always complain this "infortune or this disaventure" which has come upon him (IV, 295-98). And he prays that, after his soul has fled from his heart, these lovers who are now set high upon the wheel of Fortune in good "aventure" may find their loves as true as steel (IV, 323-29).

The sympathetic Pandarus also weeps out his observations upon the fickleness of Fortune. "Who would have thought," says he, "that in so short a time Fortune would have so overthrown our joy! For in this world there is no creature who ever saw stranger ruin than this, through 'cas or aventure.' But such is the way of this world. Therefore, I thus conclude: no one may consider what Fortune sends to be his own peculiar possession; her gifts are in common to all men" (IV, 384-92). He holds out to Troilus the consolation, however, that Fortune supports the hardy man in his undertakings and abandons wretches who exhibit cowardice (IV, 600-2). But Troilus is a fatalist and can derive no comfort from such an idea; a dire necessity has been imposed upon him from without, and nothing he can do will have the least effect in altering it. And when upon his last painful visit to Criseyde she falls into a swoon so deep that he thinks her dead, he rails at both God and Fortune:

> O cruel Jove and you, adverse Fortune, you have falsely slain Criseyde; and since you can do no worse to me, fie upon your power and upon your contradictory works! You shall never win over me in this cowardly manner; no death shall separate me from my lady. For since you have slain her thus, I shall also die (IV, 1192-1200).

Though Criseyde also senses a kind of fatality back of her parting from Troilus, still she is self-reliant and is willing to oppose her woman's cleverness and wit against whatever may be the decrees of Fortune. She once attributes her present misfortunes to the fact that she must have been born under a cursed constellation (IV, 745). But she is philosophically shortsighted and is apparently ignorant of the relations of Destiny to God and Fortune; or her conception of Fate (if she has one) is so dim and limited that she does not realize the futility of human struggles against what God ultimately has planned. Or perhaps she is so superficial in her thinking and so conventional that she actually places no faith in her father's prognostications regarding the doom of Troy; or maybe her feminine childishness is responsible for the supposition that, in hoodwinking her father into believing his own prophecies false, she may be averting the city's destruction altogether. At any rate, she is undoubtedly the clever woman planning an immediate return to her lover, provided she may be able to secure her father's permission. Desire of gold will so blind his soul that she will be able to do anything she pleases with him; for neither Apollo, nor his clerk's laws, nor his astrological prognostications shall avail him three haws! And if Calchas attempts to prove by divination that she lies, she will pluck him by the sleeve and assure him that he has not well understood the gods; for the gods speak in ambiguities and, of a truth, they tell twenty lies. She will insist to him that dread first created the gods and that his coward heart made him interpret amiss the gods' text, that time when he fled for fear out of Delphi after having received the oracle concerning Troy's fall (IV, 1395-1411). She attempts to comfort Troilus further with the idea that the man who pays no attention to Fortune is lord of her; for she subdues nobody but the wretch (IV, 1586-89). Troilus may expect her return within ten days. But Chaucer makes us feel already the irony of the situation: a weak woman ignorantly contemning Fortune and either disregarding the decrees of Destiny that have gone forth concerning herself and Troilus or opposing to them her puny strength. As Professor George Lyman Kittredge wisely remarks: "She soon discovers that she has matched her woman's wit, not against her dotard father merely, but against the doom of Troy."

After this manner Chaucer must have represented, in the original draft of the poem, the destinal forces working back of the fourth book. But when he came finally to revise his text, he apparently found that the general effect produced was not precisely, or at least not completely, what he had intended. Consequently, at the intense moment when reversal of fortune strikes the protagonist, he chose to introduce Troilus's now celebrated soliloquy on the relation of God's foreknowledge to man's free-will (IV, 955-1085). And that the insertion of the passage satisfied permanently whatever purpose he may have had seems to be attested by the fact that he never withdrew it.

Perhaps no passage in Chaucer's works has received quite such universal condemnation as has Troilus's monolog on predestination. Professor Lounsbury, for example, says:

> It is the grossest instance of the failure on the part of Chaucer to comply with the requirements of his art. . . . The passage is a versification of the argument on the subject of God's foreknowledge and man's free-will that is contained in the fifth book of the treatise of Boethius. It utterly interferes with the movement of the story. It is tacked to it by the flimsiest of fastenings. . . . The bad taste exhibited by the poet in such passages will be conceded by all. His most fervent admirers would be readiest to admit the justice of this censure.[14]

Ward thinks the matter is "pedantically put, perhaps, and as it were dragged in violently by means of a truncated quotation from Boethius."[15] T. R. Price says: "The passage is the chief artistic blemish."[16] Professor Manly is of the opinion that the poet "did not restrain within proper limits the ideas brought up by association (note the famous passage on predestination in the *Troilus*)."[17] Professor Root defends the passage to a certain extent: "Prolonged beyond its due proportion it may be; but it is no more a digression than are the soliloquies of Hamlet. It is thoroughly in accord with the character of Troilus as Chaucer conceived him."[18] And Professor Kittredge concludes: "Doubtless the passage is inartistic and maladjusted; but it is certainly not, as some have called it, a digression. On the contrary, it is, in substance, as pertinent as any of Hamlet's soliloquies."[19]

As to Chaucer's probable purpose in writing and introducing the passage, scholars are still in disagreement. For instance, some will have it that the soliloquy "has a special interest in showing us the settled determinism of Chaucer's philosophical conception of human life";[20] others are of the opinion that he uses Boethius "for a moral tone to emphasize the stages of the action." Ten Brink says: "It is his tragic intensiveness that leads the poet into such depths, and makes him express ideas in sonorous verses, which agitated deeply the most eminent minds of his age, ideas which touch strongly on the doctrine of predestination."[21] Professor Patch states tentatively: "Interested in a certain conception of philosophy, he may have seized an occasion to preach. After the story itself had grown cold for him, he picked up his manuscript and saw in one of the most intense scenes of the tragedy a

splendid opportunity to point a moral."[22] But he later seems
to come to the conclusion that the passage is neither too long
nor inappropriate since it reveals the character of Troilus as
Chaucer conceived him and illustrates the subtle humor for
which the poet is celebrated. . . .

Misconceptions concerning the function of this passage
originate, it seems to me, in a misunderstanding of Chaucer's
artistic methods. The supposition that the argument on predestination is too long or that it interrupts the action of the
story may imply that in this case a pedantic poet has dumped
an unassimilated knowledge of Boethius into the smooth flow
of a simple narrative of human affairs. We must observe, however, that Chaucer is not writing a simple story; he is evidently giving a very complex account of the intricate relations
between the happy or miserable human being and the destinal
forces which rule the universe. Again, the idea that he is
here pointing a moral or giving expression to his own personal beliefs suggests that he is at times primarily a philosopher. If this be true, the passage is an almost perfect expression of a philosophical point of view, but it has no place
whatever in the story. It seems more reasonable to assume
that Chaucer is primarily the literary artist, particularly in an
objective and dramatic work like the *Troilus,* using philosophical material wherever necessary to secure an artistic
effect presumably aimed at. And finally, the more or less
light tone of the first three books has influenced some critics
in concluding that he lacks high seriousness in his repre-
sentations of human life and that his "all-pervasive humor"
may imply a want of artistic earnestness. But such assumptions are apparently without adequate foundations. Let us put
out of our minds for a moment the idea that, in Troilus's
argument about predestination, Chaucer is trying to express
his own settled determinism or that he is being facetious or
that he is carried away by dramatic intensity or that he is
betrayed into a digression for whatever purpose. And let us
assume for once that he is primarily the objective artist,
deliberately putting back of the story's action *for purely
dramatic effect* the conception of Destiny which actually finds
expression there. In that case, we shall doubtless find the
passage in question dramatically appropriate and of such
tremendous importance that it emerges as the pivotal point
upon which turns the destinal action of the story.

Emphasis cannot be too strong when placed upon the fact that in *Troilus and Criseyde* an absolutely inescapable necessity governs the progress of the story. The Boethian God may be discerned back of every incident working out the plans of Providence through His ministers, Destiny and Fortune. All Nature-as-destiny (serving God) makes it inevitable, as we have seen, that Troilus should love; and the destinal powers of the erratic stars, in conjunction possibly with other forces, impose upon him the doom of loving Criseyde. Both Chaucer and the protagonist insist time and again that the lovers' coming together precisely as they do is unavoidable. And so long as God in his Providence gives Troilus what of his own free will he would choose, the happy lover is vastly contented with the plan upon which the universe is run; he even praises the inevitability which places upon him the necessity of loving and being loved. But just so soon as it becomes apparent to him that reversals of fortune are also included in the divine plan, he revolts, ironically and humanly enough, against precisely those forces which before he praised so fervently. Criseyde is to be taken from him, and his first reaction to adversity is naturally a grief-stricken cry against the immediate cause of it, Fortune!

But it is not the nature of Troilus to rest content with childish railings at Fortune. That he should be blinded for a moment by sorrow is dramatically appropriate, but that he should remain insensible of the higher destinal forces which have shaped his life from the begining is inconceivable. Consequently, when Chaucer came to revise his poem, he must have recognized the inconsistency in his representation of Troilus's character at this point and must have realized that this most critical reversal of fortune was not properly motivated by reference to the fatality which informs the remainder of the tragedy. In the revised text, therefore, Troilus's naturally philosophical mind is represented as reasserting itself and as urging him to push to their logical conclusions the Boethian principles which he has espoused all along. In the depths of despair he retires into a temple where he prays to the pitying gods for the privilege of dying and communes with himself upon the relations between God's fore-knowledge and man's free-will. But he is perfectly honest with himself and uniformly consistent in his attitudes toward Destiny or Fate. Just as before his love for Criseyde was considered inevitable, so now in adversity he recognizes that "all that comes to a man, comes by necessity"; and just as his happiness was the inescapable product of destinal forces, so now he acknowledges that to be lost is also his destiny (IV, 958-59). For he seems to be sure that the foresight of divine Providence saw from the beginning of the world that he must forego Criseyde, since God without doubt sees all things and disposes them, through His ordinance and according to their merits, as they shall come by predestination (IV, 960-66). But, after all, the Boethian conception of God's relation to his universe is grim and forbidding when Providence is seen to involve human suffering as well as happiness. And Troilus now experiences a quite human revulsion of feeling against the whole scheme of things when it appears to include his loss of Criseyde; there must be something wrong either with his philosophy or with God's plan. At least, his whole argument represents a powerfully dramatic struggle in his mind to find some way out of the web of fate which seems to have been woven for him. His emotional upheaval urges him to review all the arguments at his command with the idea of determining whether there may not be some logical escape from his long-engrafted conviction that Destiny rules the world and the fortunes of men; there are some great clerks who postulate an inescapable Destiny, but there are others who hold that there is no such thing because man has been given the power of free-choice and is capable, therefore, of directing his own life (IV, 967-73). If he can only convince himself that the latter point of view is true, then the energies of his apathetic body and mind may be released for effective action.

His arguments, however, lead him to one inevitable conclusion. Since as some clerks say, God foresees everything and since He may not be deceived, then everything must transpire precisely as He has foreseen it; if from all eternity He has known our thought and our deed, then we have no free choice (IV, 974-80). For if God's foresight is perfect, then we can have only such thoughts and deeds as he has foreseen; and if the contrary were possible, then we should have to ascribe to God imperfect knowledge, which is heresy (IV, 981-94). There are other clerks, however, who assert that God's prescience does not cause the happening of events but that He foresees them because they are to happen. In that case, we have merely changed the order of causes without

having altered the quality of necessity imposed upon everything that occurs; for it seems to Troilus that, whether God's
foreknowledge is the cause or not, whatever He foresees, be
it fair or foul, must come to pass by necessity (IV, 995-1023).
For example, if a man sits in a chair, he sits by necessity; if
we see him sitting, then the truth of our seeing is also determined by necessity (IV, 1023-43). In like manner, God's
foreknowledge of coming events is governed by necessity; and
that which He foresees must transpire of necessity (IV, 1045-
56). Troilus is not greatly concerned with the necessity which
compels God to foresee; he is interested mainly in the inevitability of events which happen to men and in the im-
possibility of free-choice. Consequently, he states his original
conclusion finally and for the fourth time: God necessarily
foresees all things that come to pass; and whatever He foresees may not be escaped in any manner (IV, 1075-78). In
other words, Troilus in his happiness is a fatalist; and in his
grief, even after he has gone over thoroughly the grounds
upon which he bases his philosophy, he is still consistently
the fatalist. He does not here raise the question of God's
justice in thus imposing a dire necessity upon the lives of both
good and bad men, who have not a chance of escape; nor
does he emphasize his own merits or demerits. Still, in spite
of his firm conviction that events transpire precisely as ordained, he is tragically human enough to pray to Almighty
Jove that He may have pity upon his sorrow and slay him or
return Criseyde and deliver him from this distress (IV, 1079-
82). But we are made to feel that Jove is not moved by the
prayers of men; governed Himself by necessity, He has planned in his Providence a universe, his destinal decrees have
gone forth and cannot be recalled; and the Fortune of Troilus,
conceived from the foundation of the world, must be executed
with inevitable precision.

That Chaucer fused such a fatalistic philosophy into the
structure of his tragedy and that he did it with calculating
deliberation cannot, it seems to me, be doubted. It is now
well known that, in the passage under discussion, he put into
the mouth of his dramatic character, Troilus, a paraphrase of
precisely those deterministic arguments which Boethius represents himself as addressing to Lady Philosophy in the
Consolation of Philosophy [v. pr.3]. The poet undoubtedly
knew the later reply of Philosophy to Boethius, in which man's

free-will is reconciled with the necessity residing in God's foreknowledge.

> She resolves the conflict by declaring that necessity is of two sorts: simple necessity, which cannot be avoided, and conditional necessity. The necessity which derives from God's foreknowledge is of the second sort. *If* God foreknows that a man will do a certain thing, he will necessarily do it; but the man's action is free, and is not constrained by God's foreknowledge of the choice that he will freely make.[23]

Moreover, Chaucer was evidently acquainted with the solutions of the problem offered by Augustine, Bradwardine, and other thinkers of the time. . . . We must observe, however, that Chaucer was apparently not writing philosophy; he was not in the *Troilus* interested personally in the problem of predestination and, therefore, offered no solutions such as he might have evolved had he been writing philosophy. He was probably orthodox in his own beliefs; but in the drama proper I can find no indication of his personal views. But he was, for his time, undoubtedly an extremely intrepid artist who conceived that the action of a great tragedy should be under the direction of a stern necessity and that the doom of a struggling protagonist should be inevitable. Admirers of Sophocles and Shakespeare would scarcely criticize this principle of tragic composition. The speech of Troilus on predestination is the most powerful element of the poem in the confirming of that fatality which governs the tragic action; it makes clear that the ultimate power behind the destinal forces inherent in movable things is the arbitrary will of God, whose plans for the universe do not include human free-choice. Representing merely a fragment of the Boethian discussion, it serves to warn the intelligent reader emphatically that solutions of the protagonist's tragic problems have been deliberately ignored for dramatic purposes. The whole speech is in character and is dramatically appropriate; and since its philosophical import is in conformity with the settled determinism which the enlightened artist has fused into his tragedy throughout, its length seems to be nicely proportionate to the great sweep of the poem's action.

Accordingly, Book v represents the final consummation of the fate prepared for Troy and its inhabitants. At the beginning of the book we are warned that the fatal destiny, which Jove has at His disposal and which He turns over for execution to the three angry sisters, the Parcas, approaches swiftly; Criseyde must of necessity leave the city, therefore, and Troilus must remain in pain until Lachesis no longer spins his thread of life (v, 1-7). Fortune intends to glaze the hood of the lover more thoroughly still (v, 467) and to trick him in the end (v, 1134).

After Criseyde has departed for the Greek camp, Troilus is inconsolable. In his frenzy he now curses Jove, whose Providence he has praised before, and Venus—together with her servants, Cupid, Ceres, and Bacchus—whose power has been instrumental in bringing the lovers together; he curses his birth, himself, his fate, all Nature—indeed, every creature save only his lady (v, 205-10). When he slumbers, his dreaming mind is disturbed by the most dreadful things that could be imagined. Sometimes it seems to him asleep that he is alone in some horrible place; sometimes he is fighting with his enemies and falls into their hands; and again he seems to be pitching from some high place into the depths below. Starting out of his slumber, he feels a quaking dread about his heart, and his body trembles with fear (v, 250-60). Pandarus attempts to comfort him with the opinion that dreams have no significance, or at least that no man knows how to interpret them aright (v, 360-77); indeed, as I have indicated elsewhere,[24] this sort of dream does not bear the marks of even a respectable *somnium animale,* however much the mind of Troilus may have been disturbed over the going of Criseyde. In this case he is merely oppressed by the fumes arising from too much melancholy in the blood; he is experiencing a *phantasma,* or having a nightmare, or being shaken to fear by an incubus. Still, he himself is convinced that these dreams and the shrieking of that fatal bellman, the owl, undoubtedly foretell his approaching death (v, 316-20). And Troilus's qualm in the presence of these supposed harbingers of coming events communicates itself to the sympathetic reader, who is also made to feel that the protagonist has not long to live.

This feeling is deepened and confirmed when it transpires that a subsequent dream is an authentic *somnium coeleste,* sent by that divine Intelligence which has control over his destiny. After Criseyde does not return upon the appointed tenth day, Troilus complains his fate and desires death. And one day he dreams that, while walking through a forest, he

beholds a boar with great tusks asleep in the sun, and by his
side lies the bright Criseyde, folding him in her arms and
kissing him again and again (v, 1238-41). Now Troilus's
faith in his lady is shaken at last; he believes that the blissful
gods, through their great might, have shown him in his dreams
that Criseyde has satisfied her heart elsewhere (v, 1247-52).
In spite of Pandarus's comforting interpretation (v, 1275 ff.),
he is still convinced that Jove in his Providence has shown
him, through the figure of a boar seen in his dream, the significance of Criseyde's untruth and his own misfortune (v,
1445-49). But in order to be absolutely sure of it, he calls
upon the sibyl, Cassandra, for an interpretation.

Cassandra's elaborate exposition of the vision, introduced
independently by Chaucer, proves conclusively that Troilus's
surmise about the divine origin of this warning is correct.
The prophetess begins with a smile to recount how Fortune
overcame many lords in ancient times. She tells him how,
once upon a time, Diana was angry with the Greeks because
they would do no sacrifice upon her altars and how she sent
a great boar to destroy their corn and vines; how a beautiful
maiden came to look upon the destroyer, and Meleager, lord
of that country, became so enamoured of her that he man-
fully slew the boar and sent its head to her for a present;
how from Meleager descended Tydeus, who made war upon
the strong city of Thebes and perfomed many wonderful
deeds of valor; and finally, how from Tydeus descended
Diomede. And concluding her narrative—which is based
largely upon the *Thebais* of Statius—Cassandra gives her
interpretation to Troilus: "This boar which you have seen in
a dream betokens Diomede, the son of Tydeus, descended
from Meleager who made the boar to bleed; and wheresoever
your lady may be, Diomede has her heart and she has his.
Weep, therefore; for without doubt this Diomede is in, and
you are out" (v, 1457-1519). Though Troilus at first refuses
to believe the accursed Cassandra (v, 1520 ff.), he is presently confronted with indisputable evidence of his lady's
perfidy (v, 1660-95). And being convinced, he is again
forced to the inevitable conclusion that in sundry forms the
gods foreshow in dreams the coming of both joy and sorrow;
at least this dream, sent by the gods and interpreted rightly
by Cassandra, has come true to the letter (v, 1710-15). In
this manner Chaucer strengthens our impression that the

destiny prepared for Troilus is inescapable.

Moreover, the linking of Troilus's doom with the destruction of Troy is finally further emphasized with splendid
effect. Diomede wins the love of Criseyde in part through
the argument that Troy must inevitably fall.

> The folk of Troy are in prison, and not one of them shall escape.
> Such revenge shall be taken upon them for the ravishing of Helen
> that men shall always fear to do the like again. Calchas exchanged
> Antenor for Criseyde because he knew that the city should be
> destroyed. She must let Troy and Trojans pass from her heart
> (v, 869-917).

It must be remembered, moreover, that Cassandra's account
of the battles waged about the city of Thebes and her report
of the fatalities which overtook eminent lords of ancient times,
serve as a fitting background against which to cast the waning fortunes of Troy. She tells Troilus how Archimoris was
buried, how Amphiorax was swallowed up in the earth, and
how Tydeus was slain; how Ypomedon was drowned, and
Campanëus was blasted by a stroke of lightning; how Eteocles
and Polynices slew one another before the walls of Thebes,
and how Thebes was itself finally destroyed by fire (v, 1485-
1510). So Fortune overthrew the lords of old (v, 1460). And
now this same Fortune, who has immediate rule over the
transmutation of things in this world as it is committed to
her through the Providence and disposition of high Jove, who
regulates the passing of realms from the hands of one people
into those of another or determines the destruction of nations
—this same Fortune now begins to pull away the bright
feathers of Troy from day to day until its inhabitants are
bare of weal (v, 1540-47). Among other dire misfortunes,
now approaches the end of that period of life assigned to the
great hero, Hector: Fate purposes the unbodying of his soul
and shapes the means by which it is to be driven forth.
Against this Fate his struggles are in vain; he goes into battle
and is slain (v, 1548-54). There remains only the final catastrophe; read Dares for an account of the last battles (v,
1771).

Into this maelstrom of battle between two mighty peoples
Troilus rushes seeking death. Since Criseyde has given her
heart to Diomede, there is nothing further for him to do in
this world except to take vengeance upon his enemies. The
gods have warned him in dreams that his end is already

decreed, but he goes out struggling admirably. He slays his thousands, raging cruelly through the Greek hosts. But most he seeks for Diomede, with whom he fights many bloody battles. Fortune has determined, however, that neither of these enemies shall die by the other's hand (v, 1763-4). For in the last great battle Troilus is slain by the fierce Achilles. And this eventuality, the poet is careful to state, is brought about by the will of the gods (v, 1805-6). Such is the inescapable doom of a protagonist whose common and individual fortunes have been, in the Providence of God, directed in part by Nature-as-destiny and partly by that destiny inherent in the movements of erratic stars.

We must observe in passing, however, that there is a third destinal force, postulated by Boethius, which Chaucer has not forgotten in presenting the spectacle of Troilus caught in a web of fate. Among the other agencies to which God turns over the executive of His plan, Boethius mentions *anima mundi*, which Chaucer understands to mean "some soul" [Boethius iv. pr.6; cf. Chaucer's trans.]. That is to say, there is in this mundane sphere a destinal power exerted through the influence of one soul upon another in ordinary human relationships. In a certain mediate sense, moreover, the character of an individual himself constitutes one of the "movable things" to which cleave the disposition and ordinance of destiny. For a character, with the stamp of Nature and of the stars upon it at birth, is itself responsible in large measure for whatever fortune it suffers. But Boethius maintains that it is possible for a man to dominate his fortunes and to transcend the necessity of his destiny in proportion as he cleaves to the steadfastness of the thought of God [iv. pr.6). And Thomas Aquinas is of the opinion that, since a man's will and intellect are not corporeal, they do not directly come under the compelling influence of the stars, but that, since will and intellect are connected with the body, they may indirectly be influenced through the passions, which are subject to the stars. Says he:

> The majority of men, in fact, are governed by their passions, which are dependent upon bodily appetites; in these the influence of the stars is clearly felt. Few indeed are the wise who are capable of resisting their animal instincts. Astrologers, consequently, are able to foretell the truth in the majority of cases, especially when they undertake general predictions. In particular predictions, they do not attain certainty, for nothing prevents a man from resisting

the dictates of his lower faculties. Wherefore the astrologers themselves are wont to say that "the wise man rules the stars," forasmuch, namely, as he rules his own passions.[25]

Therefore, the man who does not exercise his free-will in the control and direction of his emotions, finds himself presently without free-choice in the guidance of his actions when the power of the stars descends upon him or when he comes in contact with the destinal force inherent in other people's influence.

His creator has been at considerable pains to make Troilus such a man. Though Troilus possesses a philosophical attitude of mind, his thinking is limited and incomplete where his emotions are concerned; indeed, he never entertains the conception that a man may transcend destiny by virtue of controlling his passions. Consequently, near the beginning of the story he is so harassed and perplexed by the driving power of his overwhelming love that he likens himself to a man caught upon the sea in a rudderless boat and tossed to and fro by conflicting winds (I, 415 ff.). So he is throughout the drama. He is a great warrior and a pure-minded lover, but his emotional and sentimental nature leaves him the sport of every human influence brought to bear upon him. The consummation of his love is brought about largely through the influence and machinations of Pandarus; he comes to his tragic end partly through the persuasions and treachery of Criseyde. The whole action of the story *seems* to evolve so logically from the interplay of character upon character that Professor Price is moved to conclude:

> Only by force of human will, by ardor of human passion, by cleverness of human contrivance and persuasion, is any character to be led, or to be driven, under the influence of some other character, to its own inevitable action.[26]

But Professor Price is betrayed by appearance into such an overstatement of the truth. As we have seen, Chaucer has linked his drama of human passions with the destinal power of the stars and of Nature, and has created his tragedy of human experiences against a mysterious background of divine foreordination.

Thus Chaucer's conception of tragedy as exemplified in the *Troilus* transcends the conventional mediaeval idea of what a tragedy ought to be. Dante writes: "Tragedy in its beginning is admirable and quiet, in its ending or catas-

trophe foul and horrible." Chaucer himself glosses his translation of Boethius: "Tragedie is to seyn, a ditee of a prosperitee for a tyme, that endeth in wrechednesse" [ii. pr.2,
Chaucer's trans.]. And the Monk prefaces his series of
'tragedies' with the remark:

> Tragedie is to seyn a certeyn storie,
> As old bokes maken us memorie,
> Of him that stood in greet prosperitee
> And is y-fallen out of heigh degree
> Into miserie, and endeth wrecchedly
>
> (*C.T.*, VII (B^2), 3163 ff.).

Now, because Chaucer has defined tragedy in the mediaeval
sense and has exemplified it in the *Monk's Tale,* most critics
seem to reason after this fashion: Chaucer evidently understands the mediaeval conception of tragedy; he has called
Troilus a tragedy (v, 1786); therefore, *Troilus* must be a
tragedy in the mediaeval sense. Such a conclusion is a *non
sequitur.* Though *Troilus* (and almost any other great tragedy,
for that matter) may in a measure be brought within the
limits of the mediaeval definition, still it ultimately shatters
the old form and, in the hands of a genius, flowers into an
original and independent creation which embodies a sublimity comparable to that of ancient Greek tragedy and a
dissection of the human heart which presages modern drama.

For one thing, the *Troilus* is artistically far in advance of
other mediaeval "tragedies" because it is essentially dramatic.
As Professor Price well says:

> Chaucer, in this poem, is dramatic, not because he allows action
> to dominate or run riot in his work, but because he deduces action,
> with a profound psychological skill, from the working of emotion.
> . . . He is dramatic, because with intense realism of effect, he has
> made each spoken word of each character, and each action of each
> character . . . spring as inevitable necessity . . . from the soul of
> the character that he has imagined. And, in the highest sense of all,
> Chaucer in this poem is dramatic, because, in tracing the emotional
> life of his chief characters, he has led that play of passion to its
> final expression in definite action. . . . And so, in this great poem,
> we have, as nowhere else in our literature, the evolution of literary
> form from narrative to drama.[27]

Moreover, the five books, into which the fifty scenes of the
story are cast, suggest the five acts of the modern drama. In
addition to being dramatic in quality, the poem represents
a powerful conflict between the protagonist, Troilus, and

such forces of character, circumstances, and destiny as are arrayed against him; and conflict has come to be recognized as the main essential of all tragedy. No one can help seeing that, externally, the dramatic action of this story is concerned with Troilus's earlier struggle to consummate his happiness in love and with his later efforts to recapture and maintain it. The turning point of this struggle comes in the dramatic scene where Chaucer represents the grief of the lovers at the prospect of separation (IV, 1128-1701). Internally, however, the main tragic conflict is between Troilus and the mysterious destinal powers overshadowing him. He may be classed among those other essentially noble protagonists whose "blindness of heart" brings them to destruction; his tragic fault lies in the fact that his passions leave him unable to exercise his free-will in transcending the destinal decrees promulgated by Nature and the stars. He fights at first against the destinal powers that would give him Criseyde for a season; he struggles against the forces which would finally take her away from him. And the climax of this conflict comes in the soliloquy on predestination and free-will (IV, 960-1085), at the point where Troilus signally fails to rationalize his true relationship to the necessity of destiny. Here the passion-blinded protagonist, as we have already seen, makes his last stand against the powers which have decreed his destruction. Having made up his mind to a settled determinism, he rushes forth pitifully enough to the doom prepared by destiny. The tragedy of Chaucer's *Troilus* may be defined, therefore, as the representation in a dramatic story of an essentially noble protagonist of heroic proportions who is brought into conflict with circumstances and with the destinal powers—character, Nature, and the stars—and who, because his passions over-shadow and becloud his reason and judgment, is brought into subjection to adverse destiny and finally to his destruction.

This dramatic narrative, founded ultimately upon a medi-aeval philosophy, occupies a sort of middle ground artistically between the ancient Greek tragedy and the modern tragedy of Shakespeare. It is wholly like neither, yet it participates spiritually in the characteristics of both. In Greek tragedy, on the one hand, we sense a mysterious and unalterable Fate or Necessity back of human action, imposing its judgments arbitrarily from without upon men and women whose criminal actions, intentional or otherwise, have brought them into conflict with these destinal powers. In Shakespearean tragedy, on the other hand, while one may dimly glimpse a shadowy fatality connected with a mysterious moral order, the principal destiny which rules the fortunes of men is the fatality of character. In other words, in Greek tragedy the emphasis is put upon the mystery of those powers which force men to destruction; in Shakespeare the emphasis is laid upon the fact that a man is the architect of his own fortunes.[28] Now Chaucer, in the *Troilus,* has placed approximately equal stress upon the external and internal sources of human happiness and misery. No one can help perceiving that Troilus's fortunes are in large measure the result of the action and inter-action of character upon character—which, it must always be remembered, is itself one aspect of destiny. But it is one of the glories of Chaucer's tragic art that he should have dignified his drama of human experiences by linking them up with those more mysterious and awe-inspiring forces of destiny which govern both men and the universe. No purely psychological work can ever have such a powerful tragic effect as does the tragedy in which human actions are made to have cause-and-effect relationships with whatever external forces there are in the world. . . . [Chaucer] has gained such an effect in the *Troilus* by creating back of his tragedy the mystery which shrouds the activities of Nature, and the stars.[29] And this deterministic tragedy is entirely complete when Troilus is brought to his death by an inescapable destiny (v, 1806).

What follows in the Epilog to the completed drama (v, 1807-69) is dramatically a sorry performance. From one point of view one may lament the fact that an enlightened artist, who has held himself with admirable courage to the composition of a stirring tragedy, should have in the end deemed it expedient to drop into the role of an extraordinary moralist, pointing out to his contemporaries that earthly joy is but false felicity. Here in the Epilog the poet, without having given the slightest hint of warning, suddenly denies and contradicts everything that has gone before in the poem. The love-affair of Troilus and Criseyde, which he has presented with gusto and which we have watched with sympathy develop into a tragedy, is now condemned as worldly vanity: such is the end of Troilus's false love and desire, and such is the end of all this world's frailty (v, 1828-34). He expresses the pious wish that all young people may repair home from such vanities and cast their countenances up to that true God in whose image they are made, for this world is but a fair which, like a flower, soon passes away. May they set their love upon that Christ who died for our souls upon the cross, arose, and sits in heaven above; He will play false to no man whose heart is fixed wholly upon Him. Since love to Christ is best, what need is there to seek a false love? (v, 1835-41). Moreover, having taken great pains to throw about his story a pagan cloak and, as it were, to tinge it with a pagan coloring, Chaucer now condemns the ancient pagan rites attendant upon the worship of such unavailing gods as Jove, Mars, and Apollo; behold Troilus, whose end is the finish of those who put faith in such "rascaille" (v, 1849-55). And all this is in denial of those figures in the story who, as gods, have not a vestige of power over the fortunes of the protagonist; the names of the pagan gods, as we have seen, are employed merely as a literary device to symbolize the real destinal forces back of the drama. In the next place, the dedication of the poem is illogical and in bad taste, or at least inappropriate. Having written deliberately what must have seemed to his age an immoral poem, Chaucer proceeds to dedicate it to the "moral Gower," who would have disapproved heartily of the whole action; having fused into his drama an entirely deterministic philosophy, he has the temerity to dedicate it in part to the "philosophical Strode," whose adherence to the "school of the middle" would have made him abhor Troilus's attitude toward predestination (v, 1856-59).[30] And finally, the poet closes his worldly poem with a fervent prayer to the Trinity for protection against invisible foes and for divine mercy. As Professor Tatlock well says:

> We must not regard this ending as merely throwing back an ironical light over what precedes, so that we should read the story a second time with quickened understanding. The feeling in the Epilog is in no way foreshadowed at the beginning or elsewhere; it does not illuminate or modify; it contradicts. The heart-felt worldly tale is interpreted in an unworldly sense. He tells the story in one mood and ends in another.[31]

But Chaucer is not yet content with that nest of contradictions, the Epilog; having finished his sermon, he must needs return to his manuscript and insert the three stanzas (v, 1807-27) which represent the flight of Troilus's spirit through the heavens to the realm of true felicity. This Troilus, who—according to the Epilog—has served false gods to his destruction and has concerned himself with the gratification of this wretched world's appetites, now sails serenely to an apparently Christian bliss.[32] This Troilus, who—as implied in the Epilog—did not set his heart's love upon Christ but upon the vanity of this world, is rewarded with perfect felicity in heaven. And this Troilus, looking down from his coign of vantage above, laughs at those who weep for his death and condemns all human experiences motivated by blind desire, which is evanescent, realizing at last that every man should set his heart upon heaven and not upon worldly things. I cannot imagine a more dramatically inappropriate end for a great tragic protagonist than this or a more illogical solution of the philosophical problem involving the relationship between the false felicity of this world and the perfect felicity hereafter. Fortunately, however, this Troilus is in no sense to be indentified with that Troilus of the tragedy proper who suffers for love, struggles against an inescapable destiny, and dies like a hero.

One may deplore, therefore, the tendency of certain critics to interpret the action of the whole story in the light of this entirely contradictory Epilog, with the result that the tragic quality of the poem is blurred and the supreme artistry of it vitiated. Professor Root, for example, commenting upon the moral that earthly joy is but false felicity, says: "The modern reader who dissents from this moral may disregard it, if he will, and find the story but little injured for his taste by its concluding stanzas. Yet it is no mere tacked-on moral. It is implicit in the whole poem." And basing his criticism apparently upon the assumption that the passage representing Troilus's flight to heaven constitutes an integral part of the unified work, Professor Root concludes: "And yet the story does not make on us a really tragic effect. It is rather a tragic story handled in the spirit of high comedy. Chaucer has not treated his theme with *tragic* intensity. Great tragedy leaves us with the sense of irreparable loss, of a hurt for which there is no healing. Hamlet dies with the unforgettably tragic words: 'The rest is silence.' The last we hear from Troilus is a peal of celestial laughter."[33] It should be observed, however, that no modern reader is justified in either approving or rejecting the Epilog to *Troilus* because the moral of it happens to flatter or disagree with his taste in morals. The main point is that the passing of Troilus's more or less pagan spirit through the heavens toward a Christian realm of perfect felicity destroys the tragedy of this drama with as much effectiveness as would have been the case in *Hamlet* had Shakespeare, following the pious suggestion of a conventional Horatio, actually represented Hamlet's spirit's being sung to its rest by flights of angels. Fortunately, however, the Epilog is not a part of the whole and is detachable at will, and one need not of necessity consider it at all in an interpretation of the drama.

In fact, the line of cleavage between the two productions is so abruptly and sharply drawn that it may fairly be said to represent the complete separation of the pure artist from the religious man. Considered by itself, the Epilog is a poem of great beauty, lyrical in quality, the spirit of which is exalted by the undoubted sincerity and religious fervor of its author. And the drama proper, considered in its own right, is the most effective tragedy written in mediaeval times. It is to Chaucer's everlasting glory that in the composition of this work of art he should have suppressed his private beliefs (as indicated in the Epilog) and that, in an age when man and artist were not readily separable, he should have been courageous enough to exercise his artistic faculties alone in the creation of *Troilus*.

Notes

1 G. L. Kittredge, *Chaucer and His Poetry* (Cambridge, Mass.: Harvard University Press, 1915), pp. 112-17.

2 R. K. Root, *The Book of Troilus and Criseyde by Geoffrey Chaucer* (Princeton: Princeton University Press, 1945), p. xlix.

3 [Cf. B. L. Jefferson, *Chaucer and the Consolation of Philosophy of Boethius* (Princeton: Princeton University Press, 1917), pp. 47 ff. and H. R. Patch, *The Goddess Fortuna in Mediaeval Literature* (Cambridge, Mass.: Harvard University Press, 1927).]

4 *CT*, IV (E), 1967-76.

5 *Meteorologica* i. 2. Quoted from T. O. Wedel, *The Mediaeval Attitude Toward Astrology* (New Haven: Yale University Press, 1920), p. 3.

6 *Introductorium in astronomiam* iii. 1. Quoted from Wedel, p. 57.

7 *Liber in judiciis astrorum* (Venice, 1485), pp. 120-21. Cf. Lynn Thorndike, *A History of Magic and Experimental Science* (New York: Macmillan, 1923), I, 680-82.

8 Root, p. 446.

9 Root, p. 463.

10 Chaucer is astrologically correct in attributing this deluge of rain

to the "great conjunction" of Luna, Saturn, and Jupiter in the "watery sign," Cancer. One early anonymous writer says that such a conjunction produces "submersiones et diluvia" [floods and inundations]. . . .

11 *Liber nativitatum de Arabico in Latinum translatus* (Venice, 1501), B_4v; C_2v.

12 Quoted in Abraham ibn Ezra *De nativitatibus* (Venice, 1484), sig. b_7.

13 Root, pp. lxxi, 494.

14 T. R. Lounsbury, *Studies in Chaucer* (New York, 1892), III, 372.

15 A. W. Ward, *Chaucer*, Vol. IX, English Men of Letters Series (New York: Macmillan, 1909), p. 92.

16 T. R. Price, *"Troilus and Criseyde*, a Study in Chaucer's Method of Narrative Construction," *PMLA*, XI (1896), 311.

17 J. M. Manly, "What is Chaucer's *House of Fame?*" *Anniversary Papers of G. L. Kittredge* (Boston: Ginn and Co., 1913), p. 77.

18 R. K. Root, *The Poetry of Chaucer* (Boston: Houghton Mifflin Co., 1922), p. 117.

19 G. L. Kittredge, *Chaucer and His Poetry* (Cambridge, Mass.: Harvard University Press, 1915), p. 115.

20 Price, p. 311.

21 B. Ten Brink, *History of Early English Poetry* (trans. W. C. Robinson; New York, 1893), II, 92.

22 H. R. Patch, "Troilus on Predestination," *JEGP*, XVII (1918), 3.

23 Root, *Book of Troilus*, p. 517; cf. Boethius v. pr. 4-6.

24 *Chaucer and the Mediaeval Sciences*, chap. 8, "Mediaeval Dream Lore"; see esp. p. 209.

25 *Summa theologica* i. 1. 115. 4. Quoted from Wedel, p. 68.

26 Price, p. 314.

27 Price, p. 310.

28 W. C. Curry; *Shakespeare's Philosophical Patterns* (Baton Rouge, 1937; reprinted, 1959), chap. 4, esp. pp. 131-37.

29 I conclude, therefore, that, since Chaucer has created a tragedy which is artistically so far in advance of mediaeval theory and practice, he must be conscious of that fact and is probably satirizing not only the Monk but also the mediaeval conception of tragedy when he defines it in the prologue to the *Monk's Tale* and illustrates it with those monstrosities of rhetorical dullness called 'tragedies.' Or, if he could conceive no better *theory* than that of his contemporaries, at least his genius has enabled him to create a tragedy which successfully transcends the theory.

30 Root, *Book of Troilus*, p. 564.

31 J. S. P. Tatlock, "The Epilog of Chaucer's *Troilus*," *MP*, XVIII (1920-21), 636.

32 Chaucer gets the materials for the stanzas on Troilus's flight to heaven from the *Teseide* of Boccaccio, who in turn is dependent for the idea upon Cicero's *Somnium Scipionis*. It should be observed, however, that Clement and Origen elaborated the same conception. See Origen, *De principiis*, II, cap. iii, tr. *The Ante-Nicene Fathers*, IV, 274.

33 Root, *Book of Troilus*, Introduction, p. 1.

4

Troilus on Determinism

HOWARD R. PATCH

Words are often flung about in critical usage, until a few
of them stick to a subject and grow there like barnacles, as
if their attachment were foreordained and their appropriateness inevitable. Thus in regard to Chaucer's interest in fatalism
the word 'determinism' has more and more crept into use with
reference to his thought, and even Price remarks of the
famous soliloquy of Troilus that it has a 'special interest in
showing us the settled determinism of Chaucer's philosophical
conception of human life'. When so significant an expression
is used so often it must be scrutinized afresh, first for its own
meaning in the modern vernacular, and secondly for its accuracy in describing the poet's philosophical ideas.

The need for such a word arises when we try to indicate
the stages in the theoretical relation between the opposite poles
of human freedom and external compulsion or necessity.
What appears to be its readiest implication is that of the
extreme of absolute compulsion—'determinism,' when you
look at it, after all a hard word,—and, in fact, that is the usual
meaning attached to it to-day. If it is used to connote only a
degree of compulsion, then it loses in definiteness; for nearly
everybody, the orthodox Christian, the pagan, the modern
scientist, everyone but an out and out libertarian (as the

Reprinted, by permission of author and editor, from *Speculum,* VI
(1929), 225-43.

Pelagians do vainly talk), would be a determinist. There are other terms to cover the fact of *some* external influence in human life, and we need one which excludes the theory of *any* trace of free will. In this paper, then, I shall confine the use of 'determinism' and allied expressions to such a meaning. I shall consider whether in this sense it has any applicability to the views expressed in Chaucer's *Troilus*, and what conclusions may be drawn regarding the poet's own ideas on the subject. First it will clarify the situation to look briefly into the discussion of the subject during the Middle Ages as a background to the poet's theory.

I

The importance of the question in literary history is not only intellectual but aesthetic. In literature artistic appeal varies as one sees depicted, on the one hand, a character moved entirely by what amount to external forces (whether heritage, humors, or motives over which the individual has no control), and, on the other, a character morally responsible because, in part at least, free to choose his course. Without raising the issue of art for art's sake, we may note that the values of a work of art may include moral patterns as well as others, and that the emotional response may be changed by the fact that the onlooker cannot put aside the situation as in any way isolated, or as unrelated to his own action in the future. Reflection may be added to pity and terror if one has the conviction that one can affect one's own destiny in part, and that the future is something more than a question of mere luck. In comparison, an entirely fatalistic tragedy seems less rich in variety, and to many will appear even warped as a picture of life. With such an art as that of fatalism there is nothing to do but weep. But whether the experience of moral tragedy is salutary or not, we may observe that it is different in important ways from the spectacle of the action of irresponsible puppets.

The aesthetic importance of the distinction was clearly perceived by Aristotle, who, in discussing tragedy, at first points out that for hero an entirely virtuous man will not do, for his adversity will merely shock us. On the other hand, in what is really an inductive fashion, inferring his principles from the drama of his day, and trying to formulate them in relation to his philosophy, Aristotle traces the development of a tragedy to an essential weakness in the hero. This, it is true, need not be a moral weakness, but there can be little doubt that Aristotle deliberately chose the inclusive expression ἁμαρτία ["hamartia," mistake] because he was giving special attention to his favorite tragedy, the *Oedipus Tyrannus*. For elsewhere in his works the necessity of moral responsibility and of moral value is never ignored, and he shows definitely his belief in an element of human free will. The gravity of the question, however, is reflected in the discussion among critics as to the precise meaning of ἁμαρτία and as to the real cause of the tragedy in the story of Oedipus. For the latter one critic has maintained, with apparent justice, that even there a moral weakness furnishes the spring to the action: 'Yet Sophocles plainly shows even in his case that [Oedipus's] own traits of character brought on and augmented the catastrophe."[1] . . . And of the characteristics of the Greeks the same writer remarks: 'Freedom of thought, freedom of action, love of the beautiful, joy in living, incessant activity . . . all these are diametrically opposed to any fatalistic doctrine, to anything bordering on patient and unquestioning submission to the fixed and unalterable decrees of fate.' While the Greeks had a sense of destiny, they were able to sustain the paradox of fate and free will, so well recognized and discussed in the Middle Ages. The critic's enthusiasm shows the instinctive revolt almost anyone feels at any kind of moral slavery.

The fact that Aristotle puts the cause of real tragedy in a flaw, moral or otherwise, in the leading character, rather than in the crushing power of more purely external circumstance, suggests that his own preference was typically humanistic—that he held that character, rather than forces outside the individual, is destiny.[2] By this we cannot mean that character is only another variety of destiny (inasmuch as character is partly a gift of nature); for it is an impressive fact that Aristotle does not put the prime cause in outer nature or in the plan of the gods. The whole point of the ἁμαρτία is not that it is the necessary hypothesis for destruction, but that it brings the one touch of human nature in which we may resemble the hero and apply his case to ours and ours to his. We may have tragedies where the whole action is concerned with the helpless destruction of a group of beings, where every cause is external, where no gesture or action springs from a vital spark of freedom, and thus where all the lines of artistic appeal form a beautiful harmony in their direction downward like a sentimental shower. The cross currents introduced by the interplay of free motivation will be lacking. But such tragedies will represent the sort of art left to us when the pseudo-scientist and certain psychological faddists have done their worst with human nature, and they will really embody determinism. Such, however, is not the tragedy of the Greeks, where irony springs from the reality of the human will striving in conflict with fate. Even if one holds that the human will always succumbs in any conflict with fate, and thus produces a sentimental philosophy of pessimism, the result will be other than deterministic. On the other hand, to maintain that on certain occasions the will is of no avail, and that occasionally the innocent suffer, is a still different conception. Such, I believe, is the view of Sophocles.

The real difficulty in dealing with the problem of fatalism in art comes from the fact that the mind is likely to reject the paradox of fate and free will as a contradiction. When the element of fate in a plot is successfully demonstrated, one may rush to the conclusion that free will is excluded. But the Greeks retained some belief in both; and the Middle Ages, from St. Augustine and Boethius on, kept the same tradition in their analysis of predestination or grace and their recurrent insistence on human freedom and moral responsibility.[3] But the difficulty in keeping a balance between the ideas appears in the medieval debate and modern accounts of it. Thus St. Thomas Aquinas follows the Aristotelian tradition of making the will subject, in a sense, to the intellect; so much so that Windelband, writing of the Occamist and Thomist controversy, speaks of St. Thomas's view as that of 'intellectualistic determinism.' Now I suppose that to-day no one would seriously maintain that in the ordinary sense of the word Thomas Aquinas was really a determinist. The great Doctor certainly held that, where knowledge is clear, choice will move immediately to what is best. But in actual fact knowledge is seldom so clear, and rarely is full freedom of that kind made our own (until the Truth makes us free). For the present argument it is sufficient to bear in mind that St. Thomas allows choice between differing values; and one may further consult his argument that man does not choose of necessity,[4] and read again his sections on the goodness of the will, on merit and demerit.

The solution of the problem lies partly in the fact that man may suffer worldly tragedy and yet, like Job, win spiritual victory. This to some will be as unsatisfactory as the spiritual reward seems unreal; and for a valid free will they may insist that the human will should have power to control material destiny, although that is quite another matter. Boethius resolves the difficulty by putting the whole question where it belongs—in eternity, where Divine foresight is unlimited, and parallel lines are at last to meet. It is thither, we recall, that after his debate on fate and free will the soul of Troilus takes its flight.

II

From the present discussion of the paradox it is obvious that in considering Chaucer's ideas of determinism, heaping up instances of his apparent fatalism is a futile task. The gods rule the story of Palamon and Arcite as they rule life in general; astronomical forces touch the life of Constance; and we know from the discussion of God's prescience in Boethius that any man's death is 'shapen' ere his 'sherte.' But we lose enormously in appreciating Chaucer if we assume that because 'it is one of the glories of Chaucer's tragic art that he should have dignified his drama of human experiences by linking them up with those more mysterious and awe-inspiring forces of destiny which govern both men and the universe,'[5] he has therefore eliminated the meaning and artistic value of human free will. In the *Knight's Tale*, Chaucer has taken pains to draw on Boethius for his references to chance, and, as I have shown elsewhere, has gone out of his way *for some reason or other* to reproduce the Christian portrait of Fortune in Dante in his own account of Destiny—Destiny who carries out the 'purveiaunce' of God, which, as any reader of Boethius knows, cannot and does not affect the power of human free will. Furthermore, when Arcite suffers, we remember that it was in defiance of his oath of brotherhood that he turned rival to Palamon, who after all (and it is another of Chaucer's alterations) was the first to see the lady. The gods themselves are indeed for a time doubtful about the issue. Whatever the degree of sentimentalism in the story told by Boccaccio,

Chaucer has gone to the trouble of restoring 'poetic justice,' and, though a sense of proportion would keep one from pressing too hard the element of moral responsibility in a story of this kind, if this is a case of determinism then it is the most flexible and gentle determinism known to man.

It is a ponderous business to analyze these tales for moral implications; but it is only by so doing that we can get a hint of the author's point of view. The same difficulty rises in discussing the *Troilus,* which is a poem of youth written with incomparable lightness and charm. In dealing with it, however, we are bound to observe that, whatever the poet's joy in the telling, he has not taken the composition lightly; and a point of cardinal importance for penetrating to his own ideas is the necessity of comparing the poem with its source for evidence of the nature of the changes introduced. One might have supposed that this was somewhat axiomatic in the field of scholarship to-day. The important elements in these changes (in comparison with the *Filostrato*), often noted before, are chiefly directed toward a deep intensification of the values which Chaucer found in his original. This is true, whether it is a question of the subtlety of Criseyde and her candor with herself, or the physical details of the love-affair. Pandarus is set more in contrast to Troilus because he is older, and achieves a special individuality thereby; but his function thus becomes the clearer, and in more perfect harmony with his vicarious satisfaction in the success of Troilus, and with his futility when Criseyde is faithless. Diomede as well is more Diomede than ever, when (as in Benoit) he makes love to Criseyde at once on her return instead of later. And finally the element of fate is dignified by additions from Boethius on the philosophical side, and deepened by astrological material. These additions might lead one to regard the poem as a study of a particular case of the slings and arrows of outrageous Fortune.

But one must not overdo the matter. While character, love, and the 'influences of these hevenes hye,' and fate itself in various ways, affect the actions of the characters in the poem, we can hardly have a right to put all these elements together, as merely separate aspects of destiny, to show the total effect of destiny on the reader or hearer. Some theorizers, it is true, did analyze fate or fortune into such separate manifestations; but we cannot assume that the average reader could be relied upon to perform the reverse process, to achieve the synthesis of all these various things, and thus to read into the poem an overwhelming power of fate which would make unreal a single stirring of merely human impulse. Few readers, I think, would see in Troilus's impulse to love the same force as that which ruled the doom of Troy. Moreover, the great majority of Chaucer's references to Fortune or Fate are based on similar passages in the *Filostrato*, and there the same fatal scheme is in process. But even if Chaucer wanted to pile Ossa upon Pelion in his attempt to increase the brooding sense of fate, yet, as we have seen, mediaevally he may not have had the slightest intention of excluding human free will. Most of his additions on the subject are taken from the argument of Boethius, and yet the conclusion of that argument in what is almost his 'favorite book' is a defense of free will. What more could fate do against Boethius, and yet what else do we learn in the *Consolatio* but the power of man in spite of odds? There is no more in the *Troilus* on the subject of destiny, astrology, or the grace of God than in the *Divine Comedy*, and yet Dante's poem is chiefly occupied with the expectations of moral responsibility.

But we do not have to concede so much as all that. At least three times [III, 617-23; V, 1541-7; V, 1835-48] Chaucer has taken pains to show his own point of view by departing from his source in passages carefully made to reveal what he thought. These resemble in some respects the corresponding passages in the *Knight's Tale* and his full discussion in the *Balade* on Fortune. If ever a writer expressed clearly and emphatically what he thought in such a case, Chaucer most certainly did. In the famous soliloquy of Troilus in Book IV, 653-1078, the hero gives, it is true, considerable expression to what, for the sake of the argument, we may call determinism —although I think he is rather complaining against predestination and trying to exonerate himself without impiety. In any case, there is no reason to suppose that this monologue is spoken for other than dramatic effect. It shows the youth in a typical mood, giving way to his feelings rather than to his intellect, with all the solemnity of his despair in a situation on which the poem as a whole sheds ironic light. In the three passages referred to, however, Chaucer deliberately modifies the philosophy of the story he found in Boccaccio, giving definite expression to a Christian point of view—in two [III,

617-23; v, 1541-7], adopting from Boethius and Dante the
description of a Christian Fortuna, which removes the element
of caprice from destiny, and restores the control to a rational
rather than an arbitrary God; and in the third, the Epilogue
[v, 1835-48], expressly interpreting the whole plot on Christian terms. It was unnecessary to call on Boethius and Dante
for the ideas of Fortune as subservient to God, if the story
was simply one of disaster and fatalism; the two passages are
in harmony with the third, which they precede and interpret.
Moreover the two passages occur at the crises of the plot,
and with the third at the end bind the philosophical construction of the plot together. Thus, for anyone who reads the
story as Chaucer wrote it, there is no break between the early
part where Troilus gives himself up a willing victim to the
Court of Love, and the end where he sees that in his tragedy
were the elements of folly and learns that he has suffered
from the consequences of his own choice. Of the Epilogue
Root has finely said: 'Yet it is no mere tacked-on moral. It
is implicit in the whole poem. . . . Chaucer is not so much
pointing a moral; as giving us at the end his own verdict as to
the permanent values of those aspects of our human life
which are for the moment of such passionate importance.'[6]

Here is the main-spring of the tragedy, and here is the
answer to Troilus's own soliloquy and modern assumptions of
determinism in the poem. To take the words of Mr. Curry:
'. . . . the man who does not exercise his free-will in the
control and direction of his emotions, finds himself presently
without free-choice in the guidance of his actions when the
power of the stars descends upon him or when he comes in
contact with the destinal force inherent in other people's influence' [see above, p. 63]. That is well put, except that we
must note that the point of choice for the man comes when he
'does not exercise his free will.' One would suppose, however,
that the three important additions to the poem were sufficiently clear indications of Chaucer's own ideas, written with the
greatest care, darting here for a word and there for a phrase,
and finally putting the whole matter as forcibly and beautifully as ever the conclusion of a poem could. If we leave out
passages like these because they conflict with our theories,
we may read the *Consolation of Philosophy* as a fine study
of settled determinism, and the *Divine Comedy* as a superb
pagan tragedy.

III

Let us waive all previous argument, however, and try to imagine that the *Troilus* was meant to embody determinism. What then would be its meaning? In the first place, much of the criticism of the poem written so far must be discarded as worthless. Thus when Kittredge observes of Criseyde, 'She soon discovers that she has matched her woman's wit, not against her dotard father merely, but against the doom of Troy,'[7] we realize that she has done nothing of the kind. Nature-as-Destiny has given her the woman's wit, and the stars have given her the impulse to match it against the Doom of Troy. Hers is a case of Fate against Fate, nothing less and nothing more. When Mr. Curry remarks of Troilus, 'He fights at first against the destinal power that would give him Criseyde for a season; he struggles against the forces which would finally take her away from him,' [see above, p. 65] (an acute piece of criticism which reveals something that I shall speak of later—the element of symmetry in the poem), we object, Not so! Nature-as-Destiny has given him the character which under the influence of the stars here conflicts with other destinal powers. I shall not go on listing instances where critical insight is based on the assumption that Chaucer's characters have free will, but the evidence is sufficiently abundant, and on any other terms, of course, the characters represent nothing more than fate fighting with itself.

Must we give up the full meaning of Criseyde's character, that of a clear-headed young woman who looks the facts calmly in the face until she learns the necessity of self-deceit? Shall we say that her paradox is only that produced by destiny, and that her candor is only an entirely meaningless reverie in which a human being is under the illusion that she is deciding her future course of action (whereas she is passive and impotent, while forces work and stimuli produce their quota of reaction)? No blame attaches to anybody in this scheme, not even to Calchas, time-server that he is, but fortunate indeed on this plan; for all are moved by the wind, the weather, and the rain. And if modern criticism has generally proceeded on a false basis, allowing some degree of responsibility to the characters, Geoffrey Chaucer has been just as guilty, and at least part of the time has been under the same illusion; for in the *Legende of Good Women* [Prologue, F-text, 332-4; G-text, 264-72] he refers with apparent sincerity to the sin of Criseyde, and even in the *Troilus* [v, 1096, 1775] acknowledges her 'gilt' when it would have been a matter of the greatest simplicity, in the very passage in which he writes her defense, to say that she was really the victim of circumstance. He would, he says, excuse her for very pity. Why then, at this point, does he fail even so much as to mention fate and the stars? But it is clear that we have no right to trust Chaucer's honesty, if he is really a determinist; for in the Epilogue he speaks of the pagans' cursed ancient ways and lauds Christian ethic (although we know from the passion in the earlier lines that he secretly prefers the warm sensuality of the story which contradicts it.) The Epilogue, in fact, he added only as a sop to the pious, and then (as we are fairly certain that he inserted the soliloquy of Troilus still later) he went back to deepen the pagan element (which, according to some critics, was really opposed to his own philosophy.)[8] Surely this is a new Chaucer, and one that we have never met hitherto.

Is this really the upshot of the story? If so, why not leave the matter at the meager summary given in the opening lines of the poem? The author's purpose is merely to tell of Troilus

> In loving how his aventures fellen
> Fro wo to wele, and after out of joye.'   [I, 3-4]

Do we conceive of Chaucer writing the long and admittedly beautiful Epilogue to keep the orthodox undisturbed, and then returning to the poem to intensify elements out of harmony with it? Is most of the criticism up to date based on illusions in the critics no less than on those in the characters, especially when that criticism finds a richer meaning in the poem from the very fact of its implications of free will? All this is no exaggeration of our problem. If anyone uses determinism to imply merely an emphasis on the occasional futility (and not the unreality) of human will power in gaining material ends, then let us have that clearly stated; but such a view is in accordance with orthodox medieval philosophy (as the whole tradition of Fortune and Fate shows),[9] and even that interpretation is not wholly fair to the action of the piece. Chaucer, and for some centuries his readers as well, have been concerned with the degree of blame to attach to Criseyde, who is often cited as guilty of the cardinal sin of faithlessness.

It is absurd to compare the poem with tragedies like *Macbeth* and *Othello* and *Lear*, but in all these cases the touch of human frailty explains what follows, and greater consequences follow the 'dram of eale' than the characters can foresee.

But the *Troilus* is not to be taken on such a scale. It is a poem of youth. Its high seriousness is in part that of youth, and its suffering really ends with Troilus's grief over losing Criseyde. The death of the hero, as Chaucer makes quite clear, is not an immediate part of the tragic sequence. It is caused in an affair entirely outside of his connection with the story of Criseyde (v, 1763-1764, and 1806. Cf. *Filos.* VIII, st. 26-27.) His death must come sometime and it comes in this way to release his spirit for the flight that permits him to scan his own career and see its meaning. His flight to a Christian heaven is no stranger than the original flight of Scipio Africanus or the later one of Pompey the Great to what is substantially the same heaven. Dante shows us the Trojan Ripheus in Paradise, and we understand the point. Again Chaucer took great pains in composing the passage; and in this celestial region we as critics, like Troilus, may learn a sense of proportion. Among other things we may learn to understand that the sin of Troilus was not grave or mortal, nor his tragedy of stupendous and lasting significance (we do not observe that as a sop to the pious Troilus was plunged into hell), and that the apparatus of the Court of Love is mere tinkling symbolism as the strife of the critics is often sounding brass. The Epilogue no more contradicts the mood of the poem than various tendencies of human nature in one person contradict one another; on any other terms every Christian would have to be a complete ascetic and every Catholic a puritan. It is an aspect of Chaucer's greatness and his breadth that he can enter as heartily into the love affair as into the vision of the limitation of earthly things and the supreme value of lasting idealism.

IV

Surely it is a safe principle in criticising a great work of art to assume that the interpretation in harmony with all parts of the poem is the one nearest to the intention of the author. We should suppose that critics would hesitate before finding a passage like the Epilogue, in one of the most serious works of one of our greatest authors, a 'sorry performance,' or a 'nest

of contradicitions.' Another good principle to assume is that
a great artist knows what he is about, and that he has a right
to be understood on his own terms. In all fairness in the interpretation of the *Troilus,* how can we reject the Epilogue
and deny any Christian meaning in the passages on Fortune?
Can we throw overboard all criticism up to now because of
a recrudescent psychological fad? Shall we hold that Chaucer
intended one meaning for the Christians of his day and another, assuming that they were a different group, for those
who liked a kind of pagan tragedy, the very existence of which
is doubtful in that period? And, finally, can we assume that,
for the sake of the thrill, the poet used an alien philosophy to
get his effects?

This last point is one that deserves a moment's special attention. Has Chaucer used determinism for artistic purposes
in the body of the poem (assuming, for the moment,—as we
cannot—that the poem will bear such a reading), and then
added the Epilogue as a later *confessio fidei* to set the public
at rest about himself? This is a wholly different matter from
Milton's using the Ptolemaic system of astronomy for *Paradise Lost,* or from Wordsworth's calling on Platonism for the
poetic truth of the *Ode* on *Intimations of Immortality.* Determinism implies a special attitude toward life as a whole. It
is, I believe, an unworthy conception of the nature of art to
hold that a writer may adopt for the nonce whatever philosophy has artistic value and play it for its effect as if it meant
nothing in particular. Before we commit ourselves to such a
theory we must see important examples of the trick furnished
by great writers, examples generally accepted as such by com-
petent critics. To play with philosophy for the sake of a sen-
sation is hardly characteristic of any poet who sees art as a
source of something more than ordinary pleasure.

If we accept Chaucer's terms the poem is in harmony with
his philosophy. Troilus on earth may expound determinism
with all the determination of his desperate nature; but from
the heights of heaven, looking back with more humor, he
abandons the idea and admits his folly. There are thus two
layers of meaning in the poem symmetrically adjusted to each
other: Troilus was guilty of sinning against the Court of Love,
and was punished by Criseyde's infidelity; from the Christian
point of view, he was guilty of yielding to blind pleasure, and
he suffered. Doubly therefore he was responsible for what

occurred. The dedication to Gower and Strode, which causes difficulty for those who take another view, is thus explained as delightfully appropriate. The poet, not too gravely and not without impudence, agrees with these gentlemen for at least once. It has been remarked earlier in this study that the poem may seem almost like the presentation of a particular case of the workings of chance with the *Consolation of Philosophy* as a background. The caprice of Fortune exalts and lowers the unhappy Troilus; the question of free will is raised, and the process is roughly similar to that of the *Consolatio* up to the solution. Here again we may observe that the solution in the poem is precisely that furnished by Boethius, who also bids mankind to lift its eyes to the contemplation of eternal values; Troilus in fact proceeds to eternity where all these difficulties are made plain. The conclusion of Boethius, although suggesting no verbal influence, represents in sum the moral of the Epilogue:

> "And god, biholder and for-witer of alle thinges, dwelleth above; and the present eternitee of his sighte renneth alwey with the dyverse qualitee of oure dedes, despnsinge and ordeyninge medes to goode men, and torments to wikked men. Ne in ydel ne in veyn ne ben ther nat put in God hope and preyeres, that ne mowen nat ben unspeedful ne with-oute effect, whan they ben rightful.
>
> "Withstond thanne and eschue thou vyces; worshipe and love thou virtues; areys thy corage to rightful hopes; yilde thou humble preyeres a-heigh. Gret necessitee of prowesse and vertu is encharged and commaunded to yow, yif ye nil nat dissimulen; sin that ye worken and doon . . . biforn the eyen of the Iuge that seeth *and demeth* alle thinges." *To whom be glorye and worshipe by infinit tymes.* Amen.   [*De cons.* v. pr. 6, 299 ff.]

Even to the prayer the spirit of the *Consolatio* is in the *Troilus*, its hymns are taken over in various parts of the poem, its philosophy quoted here and there, and the final moral is the same. To urge that in the *Troilus* the feeling of sections regarding love and passion is really pagan, and therefore totally opposed to the mood of the Epilogue, is like objecting to the sympathetic presentation of the grief of Boethius in the *Consolatio* when the moral enlightenment bestowed by Philosophy is later to follow. In the Epilogue the influence of Boethius on Chaucer's own conception of life in its more important aspects is finally complete.

Elsewhere Chaucer again studies the problem of fate. Chauntecleer in the *Nun's Priest's Tale* is fearful of what

destiny has in store for him, his wife causes him much trouble,
and his tragedy is linked with that of Troy and Rome as well
(B. 4546 ff.). One might take the following lines as indicative
of Chaucer's settled determinism:

> 'O destinee, that mayst nat been eschewed!
> Allas, that Chauntecleer fleigh fro the bemes!
> Allas, his wyf ne roghte nat of dremes!
> And on a Friday fil al this meschaunce.'   (B. 4528 ff.)

But the fates seem to be in conflict once more, Fortune steps
in to help the hero, and apparently if a man keeps his eyes
open he can take advantage of celestial indecision.

> 'For he that wynketh, whan he sholde see,
> Al wilfully, God lat him nevere thee!'   (B. 4621-4622).

Haec fabula docet [this fable is instructive]. Chaucer's head
was where it should be, and he did not cultivate a sentimental
art at the expense of common sense.

Notes

1 Abby Leach, 'Fate and Free Will in Greek Literature,' in *The
Greek Genius and its Influence*, etc., ed. Lane Cooper (New Haven,
1917), p. 148. Cf. T.D. Goodell, *Athenian Tragedy*, etc. (New Haven,
1920), pp. 137-138; Evelyn Abbott, *Hellenica* (N.Y., 1898), pp. 31 ff.
and on p. 59 citing cases of free will; and J. R. Wheeler, "Tragedy,' in
Greek Literature, a Series of Lectures, etc. (N. Y., 1912), p. 114:
'With Aeschylus it is a stern law that suffering is the reward of sin.
. . . Sophocles, on the other hand, clearly holds that the innocent do
suffer. . . .'

2 See S. H. Butcher, *Aristotle's Theory of Poetry and Fine Art* (London, 1911), pp. 354 f. and in particular Abbott, *Hellenica*, p. 57: "If
destiny, as something apart from and superior to the will of the gods,
plays such an important part in Greek tragedy, it is remarkable that
Aristotle should have no allusion to it in his *Poetics*. . . ."

3 See Boethius *De cons*. v. pr. 3. In another paper I have said that
"The Church Fathers held to a faith in divine predestination of human
affairs, but they reconciled it with human free-will none the less. Those
who held independent views on these points would be considered
heretical and, like the Lollards, would be marked extraordinary. If
Chaucer introduced such alien doctrines [as determinism] into the
moral of his poem, he must have been deliberate in the fact and he
must have been conscious that he was thereby making his work conspicuously revolutionary." *JEGP*, XVII (1918), 409-10.

4 *Summa theol.* IaIIae, Q. 13, Art. 6. Cf. Etienne Gilson, *Saint
Thomas D'Aquin* (Paris, 1925), pp. 85ff., and M. deWulf, *Philosophy
and Civilization in the Middle Ages* (Princeton, 1922), pp. 184ff.

[5]W. C. Curry, "Destiny in *Troilus and Criseyde," Chaucer and the Mediaeval Sciences* (New York: Barnes and Noble, 1960; rev. ed.), p. 293 [reproduced above, pp. 34-70; see p. 66].

[6]R. K. Root, ed. *The Book of Troilus and Criseyde* (Princeton: Princeton University Press, 1945), Introduction, p. 1.

[7]G. L. Kittredge, *Chaucer and His Poetry* (Cambridge, Mass.: Harvard University Press, 1915), p. 120.

[8]Thus Mr. Curry: "It is to Chaucer's everlasting glory that in the composition of this work of art he should have suppressed his private beliefs (as indicated in the Epilog). . . ." [see above, p. 69].

[9]See H. R. Patch, *The Goddess Fortuna in Mediaeval Literature* (Cambridge, Mass.: Harvard University Press, 1927), pp. 23 f. (n. 4) and 83 f. That man forms his own destiny is preached by Gower, *Conf. Amantis,* pro. 520 ff., and *Vox Clam.,* ii, 201 ff.; also by Lydgate, cf. Brie, *Engl. Stud.,* LXIV (1929), 261 ff. The mediaeval attitude toward Fortune is really shown in lines, which, although spoken by Pandarus, I think we are justified in taking at their face value:

> "For to every wight som goodly aventure
> Som tyme is shape, if he it kan receyven;
> But if that he wol take of it no cure,
> Whan that it cometh, but wilfully it weyven,
> Lo, neyther cas ne fortune hym deceyven,
> But ryght his verray slouthe and wrecchednesse:
> And swich a wight is for to blame I gesse."

(ii, 281-287.)

5

Chaucerian Tragedy

D. W. ROBERTSON, JR.

Chaucer's observations concerning tragedy are well known and have been frequently discussed. But the implications of what he says are sometimes neglected, both in studies of the *Troilus* and in comments on what is called the *de casibus* theme as it appears in later drama. This essay seeks to examine certain of these neglected implications, especially those that concern the philosophical background afforded by the *De consolatione* of Boethius and by other works of a more obviously theological character. It is assumed here that Chaucer, like most of his medieval predecessors, thought of the *De consolatione* as a Christian document and that he considered its philosophical message to be of profound importance. For illustrative purposes, I wish to show that the *Troilus* may be thought of as a typical Chaucerian tragedy, at present confining the implications for later dramatic tragedy to a few incidental allusions.

In the first place, Chaucer found the definition of tragedy which he followed in the Monk's Tale imbedded in a discussion of Fortune in the *De consolatione*. He translated it as follows:

> What other thyng bywaylen the cryinges of tragedyes but oonly the dedes of Fortune, that with unwar strook overturneth the realmes of great nobleye? (*Glose. Tragedye is to seyn a dite of a prosperite for a tyme, that endeth in wrecchidnesse.*)
>
> (ii. pr. 2)

Reprinted, by permission of author and editor, from *ELH*, XIX (1952), 1-37.

It should be observed that the gloss explains only that the word *tragedy* indicates a special kind of "dite"; it does not elaborate the concept of "dedes of Fortune," which is explained in the treatise itself. In the prologue to his tale, the Monk gives a superficial literary definition of tragedy, elaborating the idea in the gloss just quoted but avoiding the idea of Fortune (*CT*, VII [B²], 1973-81). Fortune is introduced, however, in the little preface within the tale proper:

> I wol biwaille, in manere of tragedie,
> The harm of hem that stoode in heigh degree,
> And fillen so that ther nas no remedie
> To brynge hem out of hir adversitee.
> For certein, whan that Fortune list to flee,
> Ther may no man the cours of hire withholde.
>
> (*CT*, VII [B²], 1991-6)

Fortune is referred to several times in the course of the individual tragedies, to appear finally in the summation at the close of the last story:

> Tragedies noon oother maner thyng
> Ne kan in syngyng crie ne biwaille
> But that Fortune alwey wole assaille
> With unwar strook the regnes that been proude;
> For whan men trusteth hire, thanne wol she faille,
> And covere hire brighte face with a clowde.
>
> (*CT*, VII [B²], 2761-6)

It is fairly obvious that Chaucer's conception of tragedy is dependent on his conception of Fortune, and that we cannot understand what he meant by *tragedy* unless we understand also what he meant by *Fortune,* and what happens "whan men trusteth hire."

Fortune was regarded in the Middle Ages as a useful designation for an idea which fitted nicely into the scheme of Christian theology. One did not "believe in" Fortune any more than one believed in the goddess Venus; but Fortune, like Venus, was used to express a kind of behavior to which almost everyone is subject. The concept, as a matter of fact, appears once in the Bible, where we are shown some of the implications of "trusting" Fortune (Isa. 65: 11-14):

And you, that have forsaken the Lord, and have forgotten my holy mount, that set a table for Fortune, and offer libations upon

it, I will number you in the sword, and you shall fall by slaughter:
because I called and you did not answer: I spoke and you did not
hear: and you did evil in my eyes, and you have chosen the things
that displease me. Therefore thus saith the Lord God: Behold my
servants shall eat, and you shall be hungry: behold my servants
shall drink, and you shall be thirsty. Behold my servants shall
rejoice, and you shall be confounded: behold my servants shall praise
for joyfulness of heart, and you shall cry for sorrow of heart, and
shall howl for grief of spirit.[1]

The *Glossa ordinaria* explains that such persons are those who
submit to false doctrines, thinking that everything is governed
by changing fortune or the course of the stars.[2] The speaker
at the beginning of the *De consolatione* is one among them.
He is exiled from his own country in a spiritual sense; he has
forsaken God and forgotten the Celestial City, or the holy
mount. As Philosophy explains to him (i. pr. 5):

For yif thow remembre of what cuntre thow are born, it nys nat
governed by emperoures, ne by governement of multitude, as weren
the cuntrees of hem of Atthenes; but o lord and o kyng, and that is
God, is lord of thi cuntre, which that rejoisseth hym of the duellynge
of his citizeens, and nat for to putten hem in exil; of the whiche lord
it is a sovereyn fredom to ben governed by the brydel of hym [sc.
"reason"] and obeye to his justice.

He has forgotten his true nature and submitted to false
doctrine (i. pr. 5). It is important to observe that Philosophy
considers the plight of the speaker to be his own responsibility. He could very well have avoided his distress, since,
as she explains, no one is exiled from the Celestial City except through his own volition.

The exile of the speaker is thus not due to chance. One of
the false doctrines to which he was subject was a belief in
"happes aventurous." Philosophy seeks to show him the
"wey" to his "contre" by explaining (v. pr. 1) that "hap nis,
ne duelleth but a voys (*as who seith, but an idel word*), with-
outen any significacioun of thing summitted to that voys."
What appears to be chance is "an unwar betydinge of causes
assembled in thingis that ben doon for som oothir thing."
That is, those things which appear to happen by chance are
actually part of a larger design. Nor does Fortune represent
any kind of absolute destiny. Destiny is the operation of
providence in particular instances, but there are some things
which "surmounten the ordenaunce of destyne" (iv. pr. 6),
notably the free will of man. We cannot say, then, that the

victim or "hero" of a Chaucerian tragedy is either the victim of chance or the victim of an inevitable destiny. Like the speaker in the *De consolatione,* he is the victim of his own failure. This failure may come about in various ways, some of which are described at length in the *De consolatione.* If he sets his heart on wealth, dignity, power, fame, physical pleasure, or on any other wordly goods of this kind, he loses his freedom and becomes a slave to Fortune. True freedom is a thing of the spirit which cannot be affected by externals. It is maintained by the reason and lost when reason is abandoned. "Wherefore," Philosophy says (v. pr. 2), "in alle thingis that resoun is, in hem also is liberte of willynge and nillynge." Thus to be subject to Fortune is to be subject to vices, to wander from the way to the true good in search of false and unreasonable worldly satisfactions. If, on the other hand, a man remains confident in providence, in the essential, though obscure, reasonableness of creation, he can neither be affected by adversity ("evil" fortune) nor by prosperity ("good" fortune). "Whoso it be," Boethius explains (i. met. 4), "that is cleer of vertu, sad and wel ordynat of lyvinge, that hath put under fote the proude weerdes and loketh, upright, upon either fortune, he may holden his chere undisconfited." Fortune can neither elevate nor cast down the virtuous man, since its gifts are by nature transitory and trivial. Philosophy explains (ii. pr. 1) "thou shalt wel knowe that, as in hir [i. e., Fortune], thow nevere ne haddest ne hast ylost any fair thyng." The evils of adversity are merely apparent, arising from the uncertainty of the reason (ii. pr. 4), "and forthi nothyng is wrecchid but whan thou wenest it." All Fortune, whether "good" or "evil" on the surface, is essentially good (iv. pr. 7), "so as al fortune, whethir so it be joyeful fortune or aspre fortune, is yeven eyther bycause of gerdonynge or elles of exercisynge of goode folk, or elles bycause to punysshen or elles chastisen shrewes; thanne is alle fortune good, the whiche fortune is certeyn that it be either ryghtful or elles profitable." Specifically, Fortune represents the variation between worldly prosperity and worldly adversity. Reason is able to discern that however superficially disappointing this variation may be, it is due neither to chance nor to destiny, but is a manifestation of the divine will, a function of the chain of love which holds creation together. To love the uncertain and transitory rewards of the world is to subject oneself to their fluctuations. To love God is to acquire freedom and peace of mind.

These formulations are entirely consistent with conventional medieval theology. In the first place, the false goods of the world as described in the *De consolatione* are all objects of cupidity, and the subjection to Fortune in vice described there is sufficiently commonplace to appear, in slightly different terms, in the Parson's Tale:

> Ne a fouler thral may no man ne womman maken of his body than for to yeven his body to synne. Al were it the fouleste cherl or the fouleste womman that lyveth, and leest of value, yet is he thanne moore foul and moore in servitute. Evere fro the hyer degree that man falleth, the moore is he thral, and moore to God and to the world vile and abhomynable.
>
> *(CT,* X [I], 145-7)

The idea that sin is a departure from reason is also common. The Parson puts this in terms of order. The reason should be subject to God; and "sensuality," or the desire for worldly satisfactions, should be subject to the reason. When the "sensuality" triumphs so that the reason loses sight of what Boethius calls the "verray good," the proper order of things is disturbed so that sin results:

> And ye shul understonde that in mannes synne is very manere of ordre or ordinaunce turned up-so-doun. For it is sooth that God, and resoun, and sensualitee, and the body of man been so ordeyned that everich of thise foure thynges sholde have lordshipe over that oother; as thus: God sholde have lordshipe over resoun, and resoun over sensualitee, and sensualitee over the body of man. But soothly, whan man synneth, al this ordre or ordinaunce is turned up-so-doun. And therfore, thanne, for as muche as the resoun of man ne wol nat be subget ne obeisant to God, that is his lord by right, therfore leseth it the lordshipe that it sholde heve over sensualitee, and eek over the body of man. And why? For sensualitee rebelleth thanne agayns resoun, and by that wey leseth resoun the lordshipe over sensualitee and over the body. For right as resoun is rebel to God, right so is bothe sensualitee rebel to resoun and the body also.
>
> *(CT,* X [1], 259-66)

Sin, the disturbance of reason through the desire of temporal satisfaction, makes man subject to both "good" and "evil" fortune, that is, to prosperity and to adversity:

> Certes, synful mannes soule is bitraysed of the devel by coveitise of temporeel prosperitee, and scorned by deceite whan he cheseth

flesshly delices; and yet is it tormented by impacience of adversitee, and bispet by servage and subjeccioun of synne; and atte laste it is slayn fynally. (*CT*, X [I], 275)

The Parson is no less certain than Boethius that complaints against "evil" fortune are foolish:

Agayn God it is, whan a man gruccheth agayn the peyne of helle, or agayns poverte, or los of catel, or agayn reyn or tempest; or elles gruccheth that shrewes han prosperitee, or elles for that goode men han adversitee. And alle thise thynges sholde man suffre paciently, for they comen by the rightful juggement and ordinaunce of God. (*CT*, X [I], 499-500)

Finally, if the false goods which Boethius describes are typical objects of cupidity, the root from which all evils may be said to spring, the "verray good" which he describes is the object of charity, God Himself; and it is from charity that all virtues arise. Thus the *De consolatione* develops in a systematic way, but in the guise of a philosophical dialogue, the contrast between the two loves, charity and cupidity, which is the cornerstone of medieval theology.

To return now to our definitions of tragedy, it is clear that the subject of a Chaucerian tragedy is not only a man of high degree but also a man who has allowed himself to be elevated spiritually by "good" fortune. Having achieved this eminence, he is beset by "evil" fortune or adversity, before which he falls. Tragedy describes the downfall of "regnes" that are proud, that is of "orders," both internal and external, that are elevated by the vices as symbolized by the chief vice, pride. The tragic "hero" turns from the way and seeks false worldly satisfactions, abandons reason and becomes subject to Fortune. In short, through some sort of cupidity the protagonist loses his free will so that when adversity or "evil" fortune strikes, his doom has a certain inevitability. It may be objected that the tragic protagonist cannot be a sinner, since he is sometimes treated with sympathy, as he is in the *Troilus*. But in the Middle Ages it was widely recognized that we are all sinners. Moreover, the attitude toward sinners was not necessarily one of unreserved condemnation. The Parson's evident contempt was sometimes modified by a more philosophical attitude. In the *De consolatione,* Philosophy explains that (iv. pr. 4):

no wyght nil haten gode men, but yif he were overmochel a fool, and
for to haten shrewes it nis no resoun. For ryght so as langwissynge
is maladye of body, ryght so ben vices and synne maladye of corage;
and so as we ne deme nat that they that ben sike of hir body ben
worthy to ben hated, but rather worthy of pite; wel more worthy
nat to ben hated, but for to ben had in pite, ben thei of whiche the
thoughtes ben constreyned by felonous wikkidnesse, that is more
cruwel than any langwyssynge of body.

The pity here advocated is not a sentimental pity, not a desire
to eliminate the symptoms of the malady without alleviating
the malady itself, but a desire to cure it. Theologically, the
departure from reason involved in a sin is a corruption of the
Image of God. Hence a sinner loses his potentiality as a man
and becomes a beast. Philosophy says of sinners that (iv. pr.
3) "when thei ben perverted and turned into malice, certes,
thanne have thei forlorn the nature of mankynde." An avaricious man is like a wolf, a felonious man like a dog, and so
on. The loss of potential involved in the destruction of what
was thought of as man's essential humanity, his reason, or
the divine image, is a pitiable thing. But one does not cure
an avaricious man by giving him gold, nor a gluttonous man
by giving him food. "What brydles myghte withholden to
any certeyn ende," exclaims Boethius (ii. met. 2), "the dis-
ordene covetise of men, whan evere the rather that it fletith
in large yiftes, the more aye brenneth in hem the thurst of
havynge?" In Biblical terms, the effort to destroy appetite
by feeding it is figuratively expressed in the water of the
Samaritan woman. He who drinks of it shall thirst again.
Those who burn with cupidity, whether in prosperity or
adversity, are thus pitiable; but the kind of pity desired is
exactly the kind exhibited by Philosophy for the speaker in
the *De consolatione*. She did not restore his lost dignities,
his wealth, or his physical freedom. Instead she gave him
spiritual freedom, restoring his essential humanity. She
taught him to "laugh at gilded butterflies."

The general pattern of the tragic fall as it was seen in
the Middle Ages is vividly described in the opening chapter of
the *Policraticus* by John of Salisbury, where the temptations
of "good" fortune are discussed. This account includes all
of the salient features of the scheme we have described: the
worldly temptation, the abandonment of God for the sake
of vices, the loss of reason, and the destruction of the
divine image. John suggests one additional element, neglect

of duty. The tragic protagonist was a man of high degree, a prince or other dignitary. In the Middle Ages, an elevated degree carried with it certain moral obligations. A prince was theoretically a wiser man than any of his subjects, formed of a more refined metal better able to bear the divine image. His fall thus involved an especially disturbing loss of potential and, at the same time, through his neglect of duty, a significant disruption of the earthly hierarchy. John of Salisbury was discussing an actual pattern of behavior, not a "dite." But this pattern, as an examination of the *De consolatione* reveals, is implicit in the statement that tragedy bewails the "dedes of Fortune." The external structure of the "dite" implied for Boethius, and for Chaucer, a very real and significant content. It is to this content and to the artistry and forcefulness with which it is expressed that we should attach primary importance. The overthrow of "regnes that been proude" is a characteristic theme of earlier English literature, from Hrothgar's speech over the sword hilt left by the giants in the earth to Sidney's statement that a tragedy makes "kings fear to be tyrants." And it is a theme firmly rooted in the philosophy of medieval Christianity.

Certain further implications of Chaucer's conception of tragedy may be seen in the Monk's Tale itself, although the little tragedies presented there are not sufficiently elaborated to serve as a very full basis for discussion. The series begins with the fall of Lucifer. This is not a true tragedy, since "Fortune may noon angel dere," but it is a necessary preliminary to the tragedies which follow. Without the influence of Satan, no man would abandon reason and subject himself to Fortune. Satan, in medieval terms, offers to each man the opportunity to exercise his free will, to acquire virtue through resistance or to succumb and move toward a deserved punishment. Satan's actions, incidentally, are all "good" in exactly the same way that the actions of Fortune are, and his temptations are traditionally expressed in terms of prosperity and adversity. Satan cannot avoid the order of providence. The first man to abandon reason and turn away from God under Satan's influence was Adam, whose story appears as the first of the true tragedies. Adam, through "mysgovernaunce," turned away from God and became, as it were, the first fool of Fortune. It is noteworthy that Adam was neither destined to fall nor the victim of an unlucky chance. Traditionally, he had perfect freedom of choice, and his downfall came as a result of his own decision to submit to Eve. The implications of the fall of Adam are very significant, since all tragic protagonists in the Chaucerian sense follow Adam's footsteps. Some of the implications would have been evident to many in Chaucer's audience without any elaboration on his part. For example, the story of Adam and Eve may be taken tropologically as well as literally, so that it not only affords a model for external events in other tragedies but also is a model for events in the mind of the tragic protagonist. These inner implications of the story were well known in the Middle Ages. They are explained at length in St. Augustine's *De Trinitate* (Lib. XII, Cap. 12), in the *Sententiae* of Peter Lombard (Lib. II, Dist. XXIV, Cap. VI ff.), and in many subsequent works.[3] Briefly, Adam, Eve, and the serpent correspond to the higher reason, the lower reason, and the motion of the senses in an individual. The function of the higher reason is wisdom, or *sapientia,* and that of the lower reason is worldly wisdom, or *scientia.* The higher reason, which perceives the laws of God, should dominate the lower reason, which perceives the laws of nature, just as the husband should rule the wife. There is thus an inner marriage within man. Just as the serpent tempted Eve and Eve tempted Adam, so the motion of the senses tempts the lower reason, and this womanly faculty in turn tempts the higher reason. Parenthetically, an individual dominated by the senses or the lower reason is frequently characterized as "effeminate." If the lower reason resists the tempting motion of the senses, the resulting sin is venial. If the lower reason indulges in pleasurable thought ("delectatio cogitationis") when the senses tempt it but the fruit is rejected by the higher reason, the sin is still venial. But the sin is mortal and the individual falls just as Adam fell if the higher reason consents to the temptation or if the lower reason persists too long unchecked in pleasurable thought. In Boethian terms, Fortune is recognized by the higher reason to be an illusion which conceals providence, but the lower reason sees Fortune as blind chance or fate. When the higher reason bows to the lower reason, when the pleasurable thought of Eve triumphs, the individual becomes a slave to Fortune, to Satan, or, figuratively, to the God of

Love, whom Isidore calls the "demon of fornication." The result is a corrupt inner marriage, an "up-so-doun" condition of the soul which is frequently described in terms of fornication or adultery. The tragic protagonist who through a misdirected worldly love becomes an "unseemly woman in a seeming man" presents a local illustration of the fall of the first and noblest of men.

Finally, two further characteristics of tragedy may be formulated on the basis of the Monk's stories. The definitions of tragedy do not stipulate that the protagonist may not be saved by an ultimate repentance after his fall. The tragedies of "Nabugodonosor" and his son illustrate the two possible alternatives here. The first hero was a "proude kyng" who became through his iniquity "lyk a beest." But after his downfall, he "thanked God" and acknowledged His "myght and grace." His son was also "rebel to God," but he died unrepentant at the height of his good fortune. The problem of sympathy for the tragic protagonist is also illustrated. Little pity is wasted on Nero, who seems completely "fulfild of vice," so that when he killed himself in desperation, "Fortune lough, and hadde a game." Cenobia, on the other hand, displays admirable physical competence, virtue, wisdom, generosity, and learning. But her costly array, her dignity, and her power are gifts of Fortune to which she devoted herself, and like all gifts of Fortune, they are unstable. Her loss is obviously the loss of a considerable potential for good, in spite of her devotion to *scientia* for worldly reasons. When the tragic protagonist is treated with some sympathy, the audience can participate in his experiences, sharing, for the moment, his hopes and fears. This kind of participation is desirable at times, for the lesson of a tragedy is the lesson of the fall of man. The more readily we sympathise with the victim, the more easily we may recognize the fact that the fall establishes a tempting precedent for almost anyone to follow. The serpent lurks about us in unexpected places, in a fair face, a sudden honor, or an unforseen misfortune. The tragedian points him out for us; and his work is more effective when he can show him in the guise of commonplace events and superficially attractive individuals.

The following account of the *Troilus* is not intended to be in any sense a complete discussion of the poem, it is, rather,

an attempt to show that the poem is a tragedy, whatever
else it may be also.[4] The topics discussed, moreover, are
treated only in a preliminary way. Chaucer makes it perfectly clear at the beginning that his hero is to be treated
sympathetically; that is, Troilus is, as it were, Adam as
Everyman rather than Adam as the evil sinner. Adopting the
attitude recommended by Boethius, the poet says,

> For so hope I my sowle best avaunce,
> To preye for hem that Loves servauntz be,
> And write hire wo, and lyve in charite,
>
> And for to have of hem compassioun,
> As though I were hire owne brother dere.
>
> (I, 47-51)

The servants of love, already mentioned in line 15, are
servants of Cupid, or Satan. Chaucer proposes to describe
their "wo" and live in "charite." That is, he will take pity
on the followers of the wrong love and seek to maintain the
right love in himself. He will "advance" his own soul best
in this way, for, as Boethius explained, one should "have
pite on shrewes." Love's servants are suitable tragic material, since those subject to cupidity are those subject to
Fortune, with whose "dedes" a tragedy is concerned. The
literary task of maintaining both a sympathetic attitude and
at the same time an attitude which will make clear the protagonist's deviations for the "wey" is a difficult one. If the
foolishness of the hero is too apparent, the audience may
find his plight irrelevant to themselves. On the other hand,
if the departure from reason is not apparent enough, the
result will appear to display blind chance or fate rather than
providence. Chaucer solves the difficulty by maintaining
with fair consistency a sympathetic attitude on the surface,
referring at times to his sources or pretended sources for
confirmation, or calling attention to the antiquity of his
subject. But this sympathy is tempered by a consistent irony.[5]
Since critical discussions of the poem sometimes carry the
sympathetic attitude to an almost sentimental extreme, the
present essay emphasizes the irony, not, however, with the
implication that the sympathy does not exist.

Speaking generally, Troilus subjects himself to Fortune in
Book I, rises to the false heaven of Fortune's favor in Books
II and III, and finally descends to a tropological Hell in Books

IV and V. By the close of Book III, he has been distracted by "good" fortune to the extent that he has no freedom left with which to avoid the ensuing adversities. He reaches a point at which there is "no remedie." His doom thus becomes a matter of destiny, or providence, since he loses the power to transcend Fortune. Indeed, it is the function of the "digression" on free will in Book IV to make this point clear and emphatic. The three stages of tragic development—subjection to Fortune, enjoyment of Fortune's favor, and denial of providence—correspond to the three stages in the tropological fall of Adam: the temptation of the senses, the corruption of the lower reason in pleasurable thought, and the final corruption of the higher reason. This correspondence is pointed by the emphasis on Criseyde's external attractions in Book I, by the worldly wisdom developed under the guidance of Pandarus in Book II, and by the substitution of Criseyde for divine grace in Book III. Books IV and V show the practical result of this process: confusion, despair, and death. Troilus becomes one of those who *cry for sorrow of heart* and who *howl for grief of spirit*.

When we first meet Troilus, he is very much aware of the foolishness of lovers: of the labor of winning, of the doubts of retaining, and of the woe of losing (I, 197-203). If his observations had been made on the basis of wisdom rather than as a manifestation of pride, they might have proved useful. But they are made at a religious festival in honor of Pallas, goddess of wisdom,[6] to whom Troilus pays no attention whatsoever. Instead, he and his youthful companions are engaged in looking over the pretty girls who are present, deliberately inviting the temptation of the senses. Troilus is thus guilty of sloth, or neglect of duty, as well as pride, and sloth is traditionally the "porter to the gate" of earthly delights.[7] It should be noticed that he knows very little of Criseyde before he sees her. Whether she is virtuous, wise, agreeable, or in any way reasonable are matters of no importance; what is important is her appearance:

> And upon cas bifel that thorugh a route
> His eye percede, and so depe it wente,
> Til on Criseyde it smot, and ther it stente.
>
> And sodeynly he was therwith astoned,
> And gan hir bet biholde in thrifty wise.

"O mercy, God!" thoughte he, "wher hastow woned,
That art so feyr and goodly to devise?"

(I, 271-7)

The concluding question was probably about as serious in
tone in the fourteenth century as it is now. As Troilus continues to stare, the initial reaction is confirmed, passing from
the eye to the heart (I, 295-298), where the effect is so
profound that "hym thoughte he felte deyen . . . the spirit
of his herte." A famous clerk, describing this process in a
pastoral discussion of sin, remarked, "Beauty is introduced
through the sight into the soul, where it remains fixed, willy
nilly, nor may a man escape from it afterward." The death
of the spirit implied in Chaucer's lines was observed by a
still older clerk (Ecclus. 9: 7-9): *Look not round about thee
in the ways of the city, nor wander up and down in the
streets thereof. Turn thy face away from a woman dressed
up, and gaze not about upon another's beauty. For many
have perished by the beauty of a woman, and hereby lust is
enkindled as fire.* The fire alluded to here is remarked several times in the poem (e.g., ll. 436, 445, 449, 490). What
Troilus experiences is the motion of the senses stimulated
through the eye. The serpent, in this instance, is concealed
in the "aungelik beaute" of Criseyde. This is the temptation, the invitation to pleasurable thought and subjection to
Fortune.

Troilus reacts to his predicament in exactly the wrong way.
In his chamber alone, he makes a "mirour of his mynde,"
indulging in what Andreas Capellanus calls "immoderate
thought upon the beauty of the opposite sex," or in what
Peter Lombard speaks of as "pleasurable thought." What he
sees in this mirror of Narcissus is Criseyde's "figure." The
song he sings is a foreshadowing of the course of his love,
typical of those who abandon reason for Fortune. He has
tasted the water of the wrong spring, the water of the Samaritan woman, so that the more he drinks the more he thirsts
(I, 406). He is "al steereles within a boot." Petrarch is
merely an intermediary for this figure, whose source is Prov.
23: 33-34: *Thy eyes shall behold strange women, and thy
heart shall utter perverse things. And thou shalt be as one
sleeping in the midst of the sea, and as a pilot fast asleep,
when the stern* [i.e., "rudder"] *is lost.* The perverse doctrines
are evident in the last two stanzas of the Cantus. Troilus gives

himself up to the god of love, regards his lady as a goddess," and resigns his "estat roial" into her hand. This is the neglect of which John of Salisbury warned, and specifically a violation of the wisdom of Ecclus. 9:2: *Give not the power of thy soul to a woman, lest she enter upon thy strength and thou be confounded.* Troilus has no desire to love Criseyde for her virtue, her potential virtue, or her reason—no desire to take her as a wife. Instead, he wishes to submit to her, to turn the order of things "up-so-doun." The external submission to Criseyde recalls not only Adam's submission to Eve, but also the submission of the reason to the "sensualitee," the wit to the will. The song, however, is an expression of a process that is not actually completed until Book III. But Troilus has already gone so far that no other fear except that of losing Criseyde assails him (I, 463-464). This is the wrong fear that accompanies the wrong love,[8] a fear which takes away Troilus' sense of duty and leads to confusion and despair. In spite of a display of false virtue to capture Criseyde's attention,[9] Troilus soon wishes for death.

The character of Pandarus is a masterpiece of medieval irony. On the surface, he is an attractive little man, wise, witty, and generous. But his wisdom is clearly not of the kind Lady Philosophy would approve, and his generosity is of the type which supplies gold to the avaricious and dainties to the glutton. In short, he is a sentimentalist and a cynic by turns, for sentimentality and cynicism are but two sides of the same coin. His prototype is Jonadab, a *very wise man,* and the device he uses to bring the lovers together is strikingly like that used by his Biblical predecessor (2 Kings 13). Beneath his superficially attractive surface, his real function is that of intermediary between a victim of *fol amor* and the object of his love. As an intermediary of this kind, he acquires some of the characteristics of a priest. Indeed, there is more than a suggestion in the poem that Pandarus is a blind leader of the blind (I, 625-630), a priest of Satan. It is true that he is not a Mephistophelian figure, in part because the Devil had not yet been romanticised when Pandarus was created. He is externally pleasant, somewhat commonplace, and a little unctuous. But this deceptiveness is part of Chaucer's artistry. His "devel," as Troilus once calls him (I, 623), is convincingly decked out in sheep's clothing. Pandarus' first remarks reveal a witty contempt for "remors

of conscience," "devocioun," and "holynesse" (i, 551-560).
And when Troilus, with the blind unreasonableness of a
typical tragic protagonist, complains against Fortune (i, 837),
Pandarus can reply only that everyone is subject to Fortune
and that she is by nature fickle (i, 844-854). Neither here
nor elsewhere does he ever suggest that it is possible to rise
above Fortune. His almost complete lack of scruple is
revealed in his offer to get Troilus anyone, even his sister
(i, 860-861).

When Pandarus discovers that Criseyde is the object of
Troilus' desire, he gives him a little sermon, emphasizing
Criseyde's "pitee," a characteristic which she shares with
May in the Merchant's Tale. He closes with an admonition
to Troilus to repent his earlier remarks about the foolishness
of lovers. Like a good priest, he leads his sinner in prayer:

> "Now bet thi brest, and sey to God of love:
> 'Thy grace, lord; for now I me repente,
> If I mysspak, for now myself I love;'
> Thus sey with al thyn herte in good entente."
> Quod Troilus: "A, lord! I me consente,
> And preye to the my japes thow forvive,
> And I shal nevere more whyle I live."
>
> (i, 932-8)

He further admonishes perseverance and devotion, asserting
that of the two loves Criseyde is much more inclined toward
what is actually the wrong one. In Pandarus' estimation, she
would be vicious to engage in celestial love (i, 981-987). In
other words, Troilus thus acquires not true humility, but
humility before a gift of Fortune, for both loves humiliate
just as both loves inflame. He confirms and fortifies his
tendency toward pleasurable thought, promising to maintain
it. Finally, he obtains assurance of Criseyde's "grace." She
will "cure" his appetite by satisfying it. A little appalled by
the point to which Pandarus has led him, however, he protests that he desires nothing but "that that myghte sounen
into goode." Pandarus' reaction is cynical enough:

> Tho lough this Pandare, and anon answerede:
> "And I thi borugh? fy! no wight doth but so."
>
> (i, 1037-8)

That is what they all say. Pandarus is perfectly aware of what
Troilus wants, or thinks he wants, and is determined to get

it for him. As for Troilus, he falls on his knees, embraces
Pandarus, and submits to him completely. "My lif, my deth,
hool in thyn honde I ley," he says. His senses have been
moved to such an extent that he is willing to place his trust
completely in worldly wisdom, in the *scientia* advocated by
Pandarus.[10]

Book II is a study in false "curtesie," the Curtesie who
leads the lover to the old dance in *The Romaunt of the
Rose,* the Curteysie who accompanies Aray and Lust in *The
Parlement of Foules.* It consists of nothing more than the
corrupted lower reason operating in a sophisticated society.
Figuratively, the corruption of the lower reason is the corruption of Eve, and in this book, significantly, Chaucer
concentrates attention on the corruption of Criseyde. In doing so, he gives us a vivid picture of "manners" in fourteenth
century England. His scenes in the parlor, in the garden, and
in the bedchamber combine to form what may be called the
first comedy of manners in English. Since what happens in
this little comedy reveals a great deal about Criseyde's character, it will repay us to examine it in some detail. It is important to determine whether Criseyde's love, for which
Troilus is to suffer the extremity of sorrow, is a "fair thing,"
or whether it shares the usual deceptive character of Fortune's
gifts. At the same time, the book also reveals much about
Pandarus, the "friend" in whom Troilus has placed his trust.
The book opens on May 3, an unlucky day for Pandarus and
for all other followers of Venus, goddess of lechery. For it
was on May 3 that Chaucer and his contemporaries celebrated
the deeds of St. Helena, who cast down the idol of Venus
and set up the Cross in Jerusalem. Pandarus is especially
"green" on that day; it was the Cross which finally separated
his master, the God of Love, from his first sweetheart, Eve.
Pandarus can never enjoy any kind of love himself, but he
can suffer the pangs of desire, and he can lead others down
the road to what Andreas Capellanus calls "Amoenitas."
With many a clever flourish, he proceeds to guide Criseyde.
Since Troilus is no Diomede, he must rely on his friend for
this service; but once the proper lies have been told to the
proper people, once the lady has made her bow to Fortune,
he is very willing to cooperate.

The meeting between Pandarus and Criseyde is characterized by a meticulous attention to the social graces. Pandarus

finds her with two other ladies, listening to the tale of Thebes, from which she does not seem to learn a great deal. She rises, takes him "by the hond hye," and seats him on a bench, meanwhile beginning some appropriate small talk which gives Pandarus the opportunity to introduce the subject of "love." He is careful to begin his work at some distance from its object, and first asks Criseyde to dance in an effort to undermine the restraint of her widowhood. But she is perfectly aware of the moral obligations of her status:

> "It sate me wel bet ay in a cave
> To bidde and rede on holy seyntes lyves;
> Lat maydens gon to daunce, and yonge wyves."
>   (II, 117-18)

Widowhood in the Middle Ages bore an analogy to the contemplative life, called the "status viduarum," and a widow was supposed to look upon her bereavement as an opportunity to renounce the flesh and devote herself to God. At the same time, in pastoral theology, a widow was thought to be not altogether responsible, having, presumably, lost the wise guidance of a husband. Pandarus seeks to take advantage of Criseyde's vulnerable position, and, simultaneously, to remove the inhibitions of her status. He has one advantage. Criseyde is afraid, at this point afraid of "Grekes." As Mr. C. S. Lewis has pointed out, she is almost always fearful, but he does not go on to say that this fear, which is never fully justified, is always the wrong fear which accompanies the wrong love and leads to transgression. In this respect, her fear is like that developed earlier by Troilus, except that it is not centered on a single object, and, in fact, never becomes fully centered in that way. Playing on the present fear of "Grekes," Pandarus finds an opportunity to praise Troilus at some length, preparing the way for his message (II, 157 ff.). Finally, he offers to leave without telling her what he has come for, at the same time repeating his invitation to dance: "let us daunce, and cast youre widwes habit to mischaunce" (II, 221-222). Like that of Curtesie in the *Romaunt,* his invitation has more than one meaning.

Criseyde, overcome by curiosity, will not let him leave. He plans very carefully his next move (II, 267-273), opening this time with some remarks about good fortune. He who does not make the most of it when it comes is foolish, he says,

seeking to tempt her with rumors of prosperity. She remains
fearful (II, 134), so that he can safely reveal his message.
When he does so, he asserts that Troilus will die if he does
not get her. Indeed, he will himself die also, cutting his own
throat. "With that the teris burste out of his eyen." All this
is obviously a carefully prepared bit of acting. It is followed
by a long sentimental lament, which has the desired effect of
increasing Criseyde's fear. He is, he asserts, not a "baude";
all he wants is "love of frendshipe," a "lyne" which Diomede
also uses with great success later on (V, 185). Criseyde is
very much aware of what Troilus and Pandarus actually
want: "I shal felen what ye mene, ywis" (II, 387). But after
Pandarus has driven his point home with a little false philosophy derived from Wisdom, 2, she pretends shock and astonish-
ment. At this, Pandarus offers to go again, apparently hurt by
her suspicions. But she catches his garment and agrees to
"save" Troilus provided that she can also save her "honor."
Criseyde has a great deal to say on this subject in the remainder of the poem, but the "honor" she seeks to preserve
is not any kind of real honor; it is the honor of appearances,
a middle class virtue not altogether harmonious with the
"aristocratic" qualities some critics have wished to see in her
behavior.

To reassure Criseyde, Pandarus offers a little picture of
Troilus as he expresses his love. In a "gardyn, by a welle," a
typical setting for first steps in idolatry.[11] Troilus confesses
his "sins" to the god of love:

> "Lord have routhe upon my peyne,
> Al have I ben rebell in myn entente;
> Now, *mea culpa*, lord, I me repente! . . ."
>
> (II, 523-5)

Again, Troilus is depicted lamenting sorrowfully in bed. So
enthusiastic does Pandarus wax in his description that he slips
a little, revealing the underside of his "process," although the
"slip" may be intentional:

> "Whan ye ben his al hool, as he is youre:
> Ther myghty God yit graunte us see that houre!"
>
> (II, 587-8)

Criseyde's response to this is worth looking at again. She
sees what Pandarus has in mind and pretends shock, but he is
able to gloss over the situation with very little effort:

> "Nay, thereof spak I nought, ha ha!" quod she;
> "As helpe me God, ye shenden every deel!"
> "O! mercy, dere nece," anon quod he,
> "What so I spak, I mente nat but wel,
> By Mars, the god that helmed is of steel!
> Now beth naught wroth, my blood, my nece dere."
> "Now wel," quod she, "foryeven be it here."
>   (II, 589-95)

What Pandarus means by "meaning well" has already been
sufficiently revealed. And the oath he swears by Mars has its
humor too, for Mars was caught in a trap not unlike that
being prepared for Troilus. Criseyde's forgiveness is also
interesting in view of the fact that she has never seen Troilus
to know him. When she does see him shortly thereafter, the
serpent lifts its head again, this time in a somewhat more
calculating way. The lady's eyes betray her:

> Criseÿda gan al his chere aspien,
> And leet it so softe in hire herte synke,
> That to hire self she seyde: "Who yaf me drynke?"
>   (II, 649-51)

When Troilus saw Criseyde, he thought only of her "figure."
In addition to his shape, however, she considers his prowess,
estate, reputation, wit, and "gentilesse." These things all contribute to a vast self-satisfaction:

> But moost hire favour was, for his distresse
> Was al for hire. . . .   (II, 663-4)

Ultimately, her love is self-love of the wrong kind, the kind
which seeks the favor of Fortune.[12] The stars have something
to do with it (II, 680-686). Criseyde will always be true to
herself; she will always seek to escape from the fear of misfortune, no matter what effects her actions may have on others.
If Troilus wished to turn the order of things "up-so-doun" by
submitting to Criseyde, she is equally determined that no
husband will rule her (II, 750-756). Like the Wife of Bath,
that fourteenth century cousin of the Samaritan woman, she
wants the "maistrie." The mastery of a man like Troilus, a
man of prowess and renown, a prince, and a handsome prince
at that, would be quite an achievement. The temptation of
Criseyde is not unlike the temptation of Eve. Just as Eve was
tempted to relinquish her obedience to God and to Adam by
prospects of good fortune and dominion, Criseyde is tempted

to forsake the obligations of her status for dominion over Troilus.

In the remainder of Book II, we are given some lessons in "Messagerie," who accompanies "Foolhardinesse," "Flaterye," "Desyr," and "Meede" in the Temple of Venus (*PF*, 227-228). Pandarus instructs Troilus carefully in the art of writing an effective love-letter in which one says not necessarily what one actually thinks or feels, but what will have the desired effect on the recipient. A tear or two shed in the right places may help. Criseyde, having reluctantly permitted Pandarus to thrust Troilus' literary efforts in her bosom, knows well enough how to write an artfully ambiguous reply. With a quaint little ruse, Pandarus gets her to the window where she may see Troilus again, and again she reacts to externals:

> To telle in short, hire liked al in-fere
> His person, his aray, his look, his chere.
>
> (II, 1266-7)

Meanwhile, initial success makes the "fir" of Troilus' desire hotter than ever. And Pandarus arranges his little plot to bring the young couple together. The plot involves lying to Deiphebus, to Hector, to Helen, and to Paris, not to mention lying a little also to Criseyde. But Troilus is quite willing to cooperate, to feign sickness like his illustrious predecessor Amnon, so that he and Criseyde may come together, like Adam and Eve still earlier, under cover of lies.[13] When the company is assembled and Troilus' illness is being discussed, Criseyde once more reveals the pride and self-love upon which her "love" for Troilus is based:

> For which with sobre cheere hire herte lough.
> For who is that ne wolde hire glorifie,
> To mowen swiche a knyght don lyve or dye?
>
> (II, 1592-4)

This is the love for which Troilus meets his death, the lady for whom he sacrifices his wisdom, his honor, and his obligations to his country. Criseyde is attractive enough externally, witty, graceful, amiable, and above all, good to look at. But underneath her sentimental appeal, she is self-seeking and vain, an easy victim to the temptations which misled her great mother Eve. At the end of Book II, it is clear that Troilus has allowed his lower reason to be perverted to the ends of his sensual desire. Full of pleasurable thought, he has submitted to the god of love and allowed that god's priest to lead him into the deceit, the lies, and the hypocrisy of perverse worldly wisdom. In Books I and II the first two steps of the Fall, the first great tragedy, find both an internal and an external echo. The serpent has spoken and Eve has lent a willing ear.

In Book III there is a great deal of religious imagery. Literary historians are apt to say that it is "conventional," that it reflects the traditions of "courtly love." One has gone so far as to say that in the fourteenth century love had nothing to do with marriage, that it had a religion of its own which people like Chaucer found acceptable. There is no historical evidence for this sort of thing, however, and there is good reason to doubt that the term "courtly love" as it is usually understood has any validity at all. One distinguished historian has found it necessary to warn his readers that the average knight was "untroubled by the thought that to be truly chivalrous, he must be chronically amorous." In any event, Chaucer certainly does not "accept" the behavior of Troilus. In fact, the religious imagery is intended to suggest the values from which the hero departs, and, at the same time, to furnish opportunity for ironic humor. Much criticism of medieval literature is vitiated by a certain pedantic seriousness on the part of the critics. Specifically, the religious imagery of Book III is used to show the corruption of Troilus' higher reason as he substitutes the "grace" of Criseyde for providence. Once this substitution is made, the fall is complete. In the opening scene, both the "religion" and the humor are displayed. Troilus is busily concocting proper speeches to use when Criseyde approaches. But he is not very learned in the seductive arts, a man cut out perhaps for higher things. All he can do when she comes in is to mumble twice "mercy, mercy, swete herte!" But finally he explains that he is all hers, and suggests that now that he has spoken to her, he can do no more. There is nothing left but death. But Pandarus, shedding some well timed tears, digs Criseyde persistently in the ribs:

> And Pandare wep as he to water wolde,
> And poked evere his nece new and newe,
> And seyde: "Wo bygon ben hertes trewe!
> For love of God, make of this thing an ende,
> Or sle us bothe at ones, er ye wende."

(III, 115-19)

Criseyde prettily feigns not to understand. But after some preliminaries in which Troilus promises to put himself under her "yerde," and Criseyde stipulates that she will keep her "honour sauf" and at the same time retain the "sovereignete," she assures Troilus that he will for every woe "recovere a blisse." She then takes him in her arms and kisses him. This is a triumph for Pandarus, an event of truly liturgical significance for our little priest, the *elevatio* of his mass:

> Fil Pandarus on knees, and up his eyen
> To hevene threw, and held his hondes highe;
> "Immortal god," quod he, "that mayst nought dyen,
> Cupid, I mene, of this mayst glorifie;
> And Venus, thow mayst maken melodie!
> Withouten hond, me semeth that in towne,
> For this merveille, ich here ech belle sowne."
>
> (III, 183-9)

God, or at least Cupid, is rapidly drawing matters to what the Wif of Bath would call a "fruitful" eventuality. This is the "miracle" Pandarus had hoped for; soon perhaps he can prepare the way for his communion, a "revel" accompanied by the "melodie" of Venus like that enjoyed by Nicholas and Alisoun:

> "But I conjure the, Criseyde, and oon,
> And two, thow Troilus, whan thow mayst goon,
> That at myn hous ye ben at my warnynge,
> For I ful wel shall shape youre comynge."
>
> (III, 193-6)

Criseyde's "honour sauf," the two young people will, of course, engage in a little light conversation:

> "And eseth there youre hertes right ynough;
> And let se which of yow shall bere the belle,
> To speke of love aright!" — therwith he lough. . . .
>
> (III, 197-9)

Troilus can walk any time now, and he is very anxious to talk —"how longe shal I dwelle, or this be don?" Evidently the few words spoken earlier were not really enough. There may be some other things to say before he dies, after all. Eleyne and Deiphebus approach, so that Troilus, to keep his "honour sauf," falls to groaning, "his brother and his suster for to blende." This is the son of a king whose country is in danger of destruction by a foreign enemy, a young man, physically strong, well bred, valiant in battle. But he has a fiddle to play too.

When Pandarus and Troilus are alone again, Pandarus decides to confess openly what he has been doing all along. Troilus will not now object. He has become, he says, "bitwixen game and ernest" a "meene" between a man and a woman. This sentimental statement has won for Pandarus many adherents in addition to the one being addressed. But the "game," as Book II abundantly illustrates, was always simply a pleasant and clever device to ameliorate his real intention, to put a "witty" and hence "harmless" face on the matter. The technique is still employed. Now he is serious, however. He admonishes Troilus solemnly and at length to keep his counsel, to treasure Criseyde's reputation. Troilus returns a solemn promise. The surfaces must be kept clean. As for Pandarus' pandaring, why it was only "gentilesse," "compassioun," "felawship," and 'trist." To show that he too has these noble virtues, Troilus says that he will be glad to do the same for Pandarus. His sisters, for example, or Helen, might please that gentleman:

> "I have my faire suster Polixene,
> Cassandre, Eleyne, or any of the frape,
> Be she nevere so faire or well yshape,
> Tel me which thow wilt of everychone,
> To han for thyn, and lat me thanne allone."
>
> (III, 409-13)

Whether any of the "frape" are suitable or not, Troilus is anxious to have Pandarus finish his business. He is thirstier than ever: "Parforme it out; for now is most nede." Morally, Troilus has descended to the level of Pandarus, who, at the outset, offered to get his own sister for Troilus.

After this first exchange of courtesies at Deiphebus' house, Pandarus keeps at his task "evere ylike prest and diligent" to "quike alwey the fir." He is no man to put the fire out as a true priest or a true friend should. In his "messagerie" he shoves "ay on," arranging the proposed conversation at his house. Troilus devises an excuse to explain any absences from his usual haunts. He will be at the temple of Apollo, a god whom medieval mythographers interpreted morally to suggest "truth."[14] But Troilus has long since abandoned any kind of truth. Pandarus invites Criseyde to supper, swearing that Troilus is not at his house (III, 570). Troilus, serving Apollo with diligence, is comfortably ensconced in an attic there, where he can see Criseyde approaching. After supper, when the time comes for her to go home, Fortune intervenes by making it rain. And Criseyde's fear again helps Pandarus; she is afraid of the storm. This storm may well be a literary reminiscence of another storm which sent Aeneas and Dido into a conveniently honorable cave; but storm or no storm, Criseyde knows why Pandarus wishes her to remain. She "koude as muche good as half a world."

Pandarus gets her safely bedded in an inner chamber and goes for Troilus. Still unmindful of Pallas and not very deeply concerned about Apollo, Troilus says a little prayer to "seint Venus." Now that he is ready to go into "hevene blisse," he will need her energies. But another ruse is neces- sary, another lie to get Troilus honorably into Criseyde's chamber. Never at a loss in such matters, Pandarus devises a little story of jealousy by means of which he succeeds in arousing Criseyde's "pitee" so that she agrees to let Troilus enter. When he kneels by the bed, she somehow fails to ask him to rise; she wants him within reach, sitting beside her (III, 967-973). But unfortunately the two lovers find it necessary to engage in considerable talk, to "speke of love," as Pandarus promised. They are impeded further by Troilus' confusion, which is brought on by his own lies. He is so troubled that he falls "a-swowne." Pandarus, ever ready with the sentimental remedy, tosses him in bed with Criseyde and disrobes him "al to his bare sherte," admonishing Criseyde to "pullen out the thorn." But even after Troilus recovers, more talk ensues before "sodeynly avysed," Troilus embraces Criseyde. Pandarus, at last satisfied that he is no longer needed, offers one bit of parting counsel: "swouneth nat now." When Criseyde perceives Troilus' "trouthe and clene entente," she makes him a joyful "feste." In the resulting "hevene," at a feast which is not exactly the Feast of the Lamb, Troilus appropriately sings a hymn. The hymn is a paraphrase of Dante on the Blessed Virgin Mary, in the original an aspect of the New Song of Jerusalem, but in Troilus' version a song to Cupid, who is ironically called "Charite." It is the grace of Cupid which Troilus praises, a grace which passes "oure desertes," a grace to which, at this time, he can offer only "laude and reverence." His higher reason has now lost sight of providence, of divine grace, and he has turned instead to the "grace" of the world, the "grace" of Fortune. Troilus is no longer a free agent, no longer a man. He is a pawn to Fortune, a star-crossed lover, Fortune's fool. The priest of Satan has led him to his highest sacrament.

But the "hevene" in which Troilus finds himself is not without its qualms, the "doutances" which he foresaw. The blessed are afraid in the midst of their bliss; they find

> That ech from other wende ben biraft,
> Or elles, lo, this was hir mooste feere,
> Lest al this thyng but nyce dremes were. . .
>
> (III, 1340-2)

Indeed, things of this kind are dreams, the fleeting appearances which are rounded with a sleep. The lovers are disturbed by the parting of night, a necessary adjunct to the deed of darkness (III, 1422-1442), and they curse the light of day.[15] Parting is torture for them, especially for the fearful Troilus (III, 1472-1491). Although he treasures Criseyde's affection more than "thise worldes tweyne," after he has left her, he is far from satisfied. If he was tormented by desire before, he is tormented more than ever now (III, 1536-1547; 1650-1652). As one old moralist put it, "And just as fire does not diminish so long as fuel is applied, but rather becomes hotter and more fervent when more fuel is cast upon it, so also the sin of lechery burns more fiercely the more it is exercised."[16] Pandarus brings the lovers together again occasionally,

> And thus Fortune a tyme ledde in joie
> Criseyde, and ek this kynges sone of Troie.
>
> (III, 1714-15)

This is the uncertain bliss, the fearful joy for which Troilus has sacrificed his "estat roial." To protect himself, he makes of his own feeling a cosmic force, this time paraphrasing Boethius on divine love, for which he substitutes a generalization of his idolatrous lust (III, 1744-1771). Troilus has made the pleasure he finds in Criseyde's bed the center of the universe, a center that actually rests within himself.

"But al to litel," as Chaucer says at the opening of Book IV, "lasteth swich joie, ythonked be Fortune." Fortune can "to fooles so hire song entune" that they are utterly misled. Troilus is one of these fools. If he called for night and cursed the day, he will now reap the consequences, for Night's daughters "that endeles compleynen evere in pyne" control him. Specifically, the "unwar strook" which unsettles his proud realm appears when he learns that Criseyde is to go to the Greek camp in exchange for Antenor. Thinking of her "honour," Troilus can do nothing to arrest the transaction. In despair he is like a bare tree (IV, 225-231), for the false leaves of vanity have blown away.[17] As he mourns alone in his chamber, he is like a "wylde bole," a beast rather than a man, since he has neglected his reason. He complains bitterly against Fortune, asking "is ther no grace?" He has honored Fortune above all other gods always (IV, 260-268); his subjection to it is complete and self-confessed. He also blames the "verrey lord of love," Cupid, whose "grace" but a short time ago was all-pervasive. Actually, the difficulty is of his own making. "Nothyng is wrecchid but whan thou wenest it." Nothing destined him to subject himself to Fortune or to Cupid, but now his reason has lost "the lordshipe that it sholde have over sensualitee." Pandarus offers no real comfort. No person, he says, can "fynden in Fortune ay proprietee." He knows that Fortune is fickle and recommends expediency: he can find Troilus "an other." Moreover, absence, he affirms, "shal drive her out of herte." But Troilus is no mere sinner in the flesh. He is too far gone in idolatry, too much a loyal servant to Cupid to seek solace elsewhere. We may commend him as a "faithful" lover, and indeed his persistence shows a potentiality for devotion; but his is the inverted faith of idolatry which leads him lower than any casual anthologist like Diomede could descend.[18] The only feasible solution seems to him to be suicide, the final act of despair and the consummation of the irremissible sin against the Holy Spirit, against the true love for which he has substituted a false one. Criseyde's condition is almost as bad. With a touch of the comedy of manners developed in Book II, Chaucer shows her beset by her familiar companions, a group of chattering women full of the gossip of her departure. She thinks of herself "born in cursed constellacioun," for like the Wife of Bath, she is subject to the stars. She will do herself to death. Pandarus finds her with her "sonnysh heeris" falling untended about her ears, a condition which may be regarded in a person of her vanity as a "verray signal of martire."

In the process of arranging another meeting between the two lovers, Pandarus discovers Troilus in a temple, full of despair. The frustrated prince laments that "al that comth, comth by necessitee" and that to be lost is his "destinee." This conclusion is followed by a long supporting discussion based on the false reasoning of the speaker in the *De consolatione* and omitting Philosophy's answer. Chaucer's elaborate paraphrase suggests that answer and makes it clear that at this point Troilus has lost his free will almost completely. He can no longer offer any resistance to Fortune, for he has been led by *his* friendly Mephistopheles to fall into the error of wishing, in connection with his heaven of physical bliss: "Verweile doch! du bist so schön." From now on, he has no real choice. He is a slave to his desire, a victim of his sin. Like old Januarie in the Merchant's Tale, or like Adam himself, Troilus has made a woman's love the controlling feature in his universe. When this love fails, "chaos is come again," a chaos resulting from the universalisation of a selfish passion. Again, Pandarus is of little help. His "wise" philosophy is mere shallow stoicism:

> "Lat be, and thynk right thus in thi disese:
> That in the dees right as ther fallen chaunces,
> Right so in love ther come and gon plesaunces."
>
> (IV, 1097-9)

The old doctrine of "happes aventurous" can afford no real help to Troilus, just as it cannot help the speaker in the *De consolatione*.

The lovers meet once more. Criseyde is so overcome by emotion that she swoons. Thinking her dead, Troilus offers to kill himself in Promethean defiance (IV, 1192 ff.). He will conquer Fortune by committing suicide, a device attempted by Nero in the Monk's Tale, "Of which Fortune lough, and hadde a game." Since neither Jove nor Fortune is responsible for Troilus' plight, his defiance is a little hollow. It is especially empty when we consider the character of the lady whom Troilus finds more important than either his country or life itself. When she awakes, she finds a characteristic solution to their mutual problem. If reason fails, something else might help:

> "But hoo, for we han right ynough of this,
> And lat us rise, and streight to bedde go,
> And there lat us speken of oure wo."
>
> (IV, 1242-4)

Once in bed, Criseyde promises to return in ten days, in spite of Calkas, the Pandarus between the Greeks and the city. Troilus is doubtful, but she engages in a long and verbose promise of fidelity connected with that ancient symbol of fickle Fortune, the moon. Her doctrine is, on the surface, a little better than that offered by Pandarus:

> "And forthi sle with resoun al this hete!
> Men seyn: 'the suffrant overcomith,' parde;
> Ek, 'whoso wol han lief, he lief moot lete.'
> Thus maketh vertu of necessite
> By pacience, and thynk that lord is he
> Of Fortune ay, that naught wol of hire recche;
> And she ne daunteth no wight but a wrecche."
>
> (IV, 1583-9)

Criseyde can quote Scripture and paraphrase Boethius, but it is too late. There is no stopping the "hete" of the fire lighted at the festival of Pallas now. Neither Troilus nor Criseyde has any notion of how to become "lord of Fortune." She knows that "love is thyng ay ful of bisy drede," but this fact is adduced as a reason why Troilus should remain faithful to her, not as something to discourage him from being a "wrecche." The book closes with one final touch of irony. Criseyde explains her love for Troilus:

> "For trusteth wel, that youre estat roial,
> Ne veyn delit, nor only worthinesse
> Of yow in werre or torney marcial,
> Ne pomp, array, nobleye, or ek richesse
> Ne made me to rewe on youre distresse;
> But moral vertu, grounded upon trouthe,
> That was the cause I first hadde on yow routhe!
>
> "Eke gentil herte and manhood that ye hadde,
> And that ye hadde, as me thoughte, in despit
> Every thyng that souned into badde,
> As rudenesse and poeplissh appetit,
> And that youre resoun bridlede youre delit:
> This made, aboven every creature,
> That I was youre, and shal whil I may dure."
>
> (IV, 1667-80)

"Who yaf me drynke?" This is indeed a beautiful little picture of what might have been if Troilus had loved Criseyde for a little more than her "figure" and competence in bed, if he had maintained the integrity of his lower reason and his "moral vertu," and if he had not debased his higher reason.

It shows what might have been if Criseyde had actually been interested in "vertu," rather than in "his persone, his aray, his look, his chere." But as it stands, this little picture could not be more false, more distant from the events as Chaucer describes them. Troilus' courtship was hardly "grounded upon treuthe." Both lovers have insisted on an "up-so-doun" relationship directly contrary to reason. And Troilus very carefully renounced his denunciations of "poeplissh appetit." Criseyde can always think of some high-sounding doctrine to rationalize her situation, but she perverts it into so much idle talk. And idle talk cannot now save Troilus from pains "that passen every torment down in helle."

Book v is a picture of the Hell on earth which results from trying to make earth a heaven in its own right. In medieval terms, when the human heart is turned toward God and the reason adjusted to perceive God's Providence beneath the apparently fortuitous events of daily life, the result is the City of Jerusalem, radiant and harmonious within the spirit. But when the will desires one of God's creatures for its own sake, placing that creature above God, the reason can perceive only the deceptive mutability of Fortune, and the result, as one cloud-capp'd tower after another fades away, is the confusion and chaos of Babylon. Troilus has defied the gods and placed Criseyde above them. When adversity strikes, he becomes the "aimlessly drifting megalopolitan man" of the modern philosophers, the frustrated, neurotic, and maladjusted hero of modern fiction. The destiny he brought upon himself by preparing a table for Fortune, by substituting the feast of the flesh for the feast of the spirit, descends upon him. He is hypersensitive, sentimental, a romantic hopelessly involved in a lost cause. In this book Chaucer's ironic humor becomes bitter and the pathos of the tragedy profound.

It is Troilus who leads Criseyde out of Troy to meet the Greek convoy. All he can say at parting is "Now hold youre day, and do me nat to deye." Diomede recognizes the general feature of the situation at once, being an old hand at pulling finches. He takes Criseyde by the "reyne," and for a time the little filly is his, but she has no bridle that will hold her "to any certeyn ende." Like Polonius or Iago, Diomede is a man true to himself: "He is a fool that wol foryete hym selve." Since he has nothing to lose but words, he begins the old game played by Pandarus in Book II, but without cir-

cuitous preliminaries. Just as Pandarus requested at first love
"of frendshipe," Diomede asks to be treated as a "brother"
and to have his "frendshipe" accepted. He will be hers "aboven
every creature," a thing which he has said to no other woman
before. This is the first time. This is different. And sure enough,
by the time they reach the Greek camp, Criseyde grants
him her "frendshipe." She has nothing to lose either and can
be thoroughly depended upon to be to her own self true. In
the Greek camp, Diomede does not neglect his opportunity:
"To fisshen hire, he leyde out hook and lyne." On her "day,"
when she was supposed to return to Troilus, she welcomes
Diomede as a "friend," and is soon lying to save appearances
again:

> "I hadde a lord, to whom I wedded was,
> The whos myn herte al was, til that he deyde;
> And other love, as help me now Pallas,
> Ther in myn herte nys, ne nevere was."
>
> (v, 975-8)

Although she is enticingly ambiguous at the close of their
conversation, she gives Diomede her glove (v, 1013). Her
fear helps Diomede, just as it helped Pandarus; moreover,
Diomede is a man of "grete estat," a conquest to please her
vanity. That night she goes to bed

> Retornyng in hire soule ay up and down
> The wordes of this sodeyn Diomede,
> His grete estat, the perel of the town,
> And that she was allone and hadde nede
> Of frendes help; and thus bygan to brede
> The cause whi, the sothe for to telle,
> That she took fully purpos for to dwelle.
>
> (v, 1023-9)

"Wo hym that is allone." These are the same causes which led
her to succumb to Troilus, for she was also fearful and "alone"
in Troy, and Troilus was a man of "estat roial." Criseyde has
not changed at all. She is beautiful and socially graceful, but
fearful, susceptible to sentimental "pite," and "slydynge of
corage." When the die is cast and Diomede has what he wants,
she says "To Diomede algate I wol be trewe." She meant to
be true to Troilus too, but she is actually faithful only to her
own selfish desires of the moment. As one of the most distinguished of her critics has said, Criseyde "takes the easiest
path." She drifts in the world's winds, a "gilded butterfly."

Her beauty is sensuous beauty of the world and her fickleness is the fickleness of Fortune. Neither Criseyde nor Diomede is capable of the idolatry of which Troilus is guilty, of the depths to which Troilus descends.

Left in Troy, Troilus curses all the gods together, including Cupid and Venus. But he is still a slave to his cupidity, a "great natural" with no place to hide his bauble. In bed he wallows and turns like "Ixion, in helle," for he has nothing but a pillow "tenbrace." His "lode sterre," substituted for a providence which affords *a way even in the sea, and a most sure path among the waves* (Wisdom 14:3), has gone. In sleep, he is beset by nightmares, particularly by one in which he seems to fall "depe from heighe olofte," a symbolic revelation of his actual situation. Pandarus gets him off "to Sarpedoun," where singing and dancing are provided. But there is no "melodie" left for Troilus. The Old Song which he once sang in "heaven" has a bitter ring. He spends his time, like a jilted schoolboy, moping over his beloved's old letters. Hastening back to Troy, he hopes to find her there, but in vain. The places where he has seen or enjoyed Criseyde have a perverse fascination for him, and he must visit them again. First, having found an excuse to go into town, he visits her house. When he sees it, he exclaims:

> "O paleys desolat,
> O hous of houses whilom best ihight,
> O paleys empty and disconsolat,
> O thow lanterne of which queynt is the light,
> O paleys, whilom day, that now art nyght. . ."
>
> (v, 540-4)

The ironic pun in line 543 is a bitter comment on what it is that Troilus actually misses, and the change from day to night is, ironically again, the fulfillment of his own wish in Book III. The house is a shrine "of which the seynt is oute," the "up-so-doun" church of Troilus' love. Everywhere he goes, he finds memories of Criseyde. He becomes intensely self-conscious, aware of the eye of every passing stranger on the street, Everyone sees his woe:

> Another tyme ymagien he wolde,
> That every wight that wente by the weye
> Hadde of him routhe, and that they seyn sholde,
> "I am right sory Troilus wol deye."
>
> (v, 624-7)

His spirit is the painful focus of creation, protected neither by the "harde grace" of Cupid with which he surrounded it in Book III, nor by his false hopes that Criseyde may return. Each new rationalization leads only to more bitter frustration. On the walls of the city, the very wind itself is a wind that blows from Criseyde straight to him. It blows nowhere else, only where he stands, and as it blows it sighs, "allas, why twynned be we tweyne?" She lurks in the form of every distant traveller, even in a "fare-cart." At last, jealousy adds to his discomfort, and with it comes another nightmare. He tries an exchange of letters, but the letters only make matters worse, for the artfulness of Criseyde's epistolary style is now painfully apparent. One day he sees the brooch he gave her at parting on Diomede's armor. Now his worst fears and Cassandra's prophesy are confirmed: "Of Diomede have ye al this feeste?" (v, 1677). He no longer furnishes the "revel and the melodie" for Criseyde; his goddess has withdrawn her grace, and there is nothing left now but death. In the depths of despair, Troilus goes out to seek death on the battlefield. His is no heroic defense of the city, no fulfillment of his political obligations, but a quest for revenge and for death to end his woes. This is the ultimate loneliness, a loneliness he has brought upon himself. In so far as the revenge is concerned, Troilus fails, fortunately for Criseyde, but "Ful pitously him slough the fierse Achille."

If Fortune "lough" at the self-destruction of Nero, Troilus can in spirit share that laughter as he rises above Fortune's realm. When the flesh with its cumbersome desires has been left behind, he see the foolishness of his earthly plight. There the "jugement is more clear, the wil nat icorrumped."

> And in hymself he lough right at the wo
> Of hem that wepten for his deth so faste;
> And dampned al oure werk that folweth so
> The blynde lust, the which that may nat laste,
> And sholden al oure herte on heven caste.
>
> (v, 1821-5)

The laughter is the ironic laughter with which Chaucer depicts Troilus' "wo" from the beginning, a laughter which he, and Troilus from his celestial vantage point, would bestow on all those who take a sentimental attitude toward such love as that between Troilus and Criseyde. Chaucer adds an admonition to his audience to love Christ, for He "wyl falsen no wight." The wrong love, no matter what form it may take, leads to subjection to Fortune and to the old tragedy of Adam. If a man loves Christ, "lord he is of Fortune ay," a fact of which Troilus and Criseyde, both "payens," were unaware. But neither was willing to use the wisdom by means of which even a pagan like Job might triumph over the world's mutability.

To summarize, Chaucer's *Troilus* follows in its general outlines the pattern of Chaucerian tragic theory. Troilus subjects himself to Fortune by allowing himself to be overcome by the physical attractions of Criseyde. His fall is an echo of the fall of Adam. When his senses are moved, he proceeds to indulge in "pleasurable thought," allowing his lower reason to be corrupted as he cooperates with Pandarus in deceits and lies. Once his object is attained, he substitutes the grace of Cupid as manifested in Criseyde for providence, thus corrupting his higher reason and turning away completely from "love celestial." Not only is his relationship with Criseyde "up-so-doun," but the "regne" of his mind is inverted too. His "capability and godlike reason" are neglected, so that he becomes, like "Nabugodonosor," a "beast, no more." And as a beast, he is completely at Fortune's mercy. There is thus a remarkable logic in the events of Chaucer's tragedy, an intellectual coherence that is rooted firmly in Christian doctrine and Boethian philosophy. The tragedy of Troilus is, in an extreme form, the tragedy of every mortal sinner. The law of the "payens" arises again with each new generation, and it is only with a struggle that any individual can learn to follow the New Law. The "queynte world" continues to have its charms; so great are they, in fact, that

> Evermoore we moote stonde in drede
> Of hap and fortune in oure chapmanhede.

The old words of the prophet are painful in the memory. For the inevitability of providence, which is the inevitability of Chaucerian tragedy, is not especially pleasing to think of when the butterflies seem fair: *And you, that have forsaken the Lord, and have forgotten my holy mount, that set a table for Fortune, and offer libations upon it. . . .* It is not impossible that later tragic heroes may owe their fates, at least in part, to a like inspiration, and that the *de casibus* theme

may imply more than the somewhat mechanical fall of men
of high estate.

Notes

1 The Bible is quoted here and elsewhere in the paper in the Douay
version, which is much closer to the medieval Vulgate than the King
James Bible. The latter does not mention Fortune in this passage.

2 *Patrologia Latina*, CXIII, 1310. Cf. St. Jerome, *Comm. in Isa.*,
ibid., XXIV, 663-4. See also D. W. Robertson, Jr., and B. F. Huppé,
Piers Plowman and Scriptural Tradition (Princeton, 1951), p. 130.

3 See O. Lottin, "La Doctrine morale des mouvements premiers de
l'appetit sensitif aux XIIe et XIIIe siècles," *Archives d'histoire doctrin-
ale et littéraire du moyen âge*, VI (1931), 49-173. For the common
view, see esp. pp. 51-3. The three steps of sin correspond to a wide-
spread formula; e.g., see Bede, *In Matt.*, *Patrologia Latina*, XCII, 28:
"and thus one arrives at sin by three steps: by suggestion, by delight,
and by consent." Since the idea of "courtly love" has been introduced
in discussions of the *Troilus*, it is not irrelevant to observe at this point
that the above pattern is reflected at the beginning of the *De amore*
by Andreas Capellanus. When Andreas says that love, by which he
means sexual love centered on a single object, proceeds from vision and
immoderate thought, he refers to the first two steps: the motion of the
senses and the corruption of the lower reason through inordinate
pleasurable contemplation. The result[ing] "love" represents the corruption of the higher reason as the object of desire is substituted for
God. In general, Andreas's familiarity with the theology of his day
has been unnecessarily slighted.

4 The interpretation advanced here incorporates elements from the
very brief but excellent account of the poem by Professor Patch in
The Tradition of Boethius (New York, 1935), pp. 71-72. It also resembles in some respects the interpretation suggested by J. L. Shanley,
"The *Troilus and Christian Love*," *ELH*, VI (1939), 271-281 [repro-
duced below, pp. 136-46]. In 1931 Professor Patch published a spirited
defense of Chaucer's unity of purpose in the poem, *Speculum*, VI,
225-243 [reproduced above, pp. 71-85]. This is an effective answer to
those who would consider Troilus' speech on free will and the conclusion of the poem superfluous. Recently, the concept of "courtly
love" has introduced a new kind of "dualism" in accounts of the poem,
however. See especially A. J. Denomy, "The Two Moralities of Chaucer's *Troilus and Criseyde*," *Trans. Roy. Soc. of Canada*, XLIV (1950),
Ser. III, 2, pp. 35-46 [reproduced below, pp. 147-59]. Professor Denomy
assumes that Andreas intended to be serious, rather than ironic and
humorous, in the first parts of the *De amore*, and that the resulting
artificial system was important enough in the fourteenth century for
Chaucer to attack it at length. The assumption is reinforced by certain
hypotheses about Provencal poetry which have by no means been
demonstrated. However, the importance of Boethius to an understanding of the *Troilus* has been emphasized again by T. A. Stroud, "Boethius' Influence on Chaucer's *Troilus*," *MP*, XLIX (1951), 1-9 [see next
essay—Ed.].

5 In the article referred to above, Professor Stroud calls attention

to the medieval theory of poetry in accordance with which a poem is said to have a surface meaning and an inner meaning, or a *cortex* and a *nucleus*. Cf. D. W. Robertson, Jr., "Some Medieval Literary Terminology," *SP*, XLVIII (1951), 669-692. In this instance, I believe that the irony is used to develop the *nucleus* of the poem.

6 Pallas was associated with theoretical arts or wisdom. See Hugh of St. Victor, *Didascalicon*, II, 18 [trans. Jerome Taylor, *The Didascalicon of Hugh of St. Victor: A Medieval Guide to the Arts* (New York: Columbia University Press, 1961), p. 73 and p. 204, n.63]. There are many examples of *allegoria*, the device of saying one thing to mean another, in the poem. They all point toward the inner meaning or *nucleus*. For this purpose Chaucer uses both figures from classical sources, like Cupid or Pallas, and Scriptural signs, like "night," discussed below. Only a few of these, however, are indicated in the present essay. In connection with the general background of the poem, it is pertinent to recall that Troy was sometime thought to represent the human body and the Trojan horse lechery. See Bernard Silvestris, *Comm. super sex libros Eneidos Virgilii*, ed. G. Riedel (Gryphiswaldae, 1924), pp. 15-16, 102-103. Chaucer's Troilus is thus, in a sense, a personification of Troy as it was understood by medieval interpreters. The destruction of a man is the destruction of a city when we consider that every man builds either Babylon or Jerusalem within himself and that Babylon is doomed to fall. For a description of the destruction of Jerusalem through lechery, or its transformation into Babylon, see *De David li prophecie*, ed. Fuhrkens (Halle, 1895), ll. 437 ff.

7 See D. W. Robertson, Jr., "The Doctrine of Charity in Medieval Literary Gardens: A Topical Approach through Symbolism and Allegory," *Speculum*, XXVI (1951), p. 41.

8 *Ibid.*, p. 28.

9 Troilus is at pains to acquire military glory and popular acclaim. His valor and generosity, as well as Criseyde's "honor," should be considered in the light of a principle expressed by Alanus de Insulis in his treatise on the virtues, the vices, and the gifts of the Holy Spirit, ed. O. Lottin, *Mediaeval Studies*, XII (1950), 20-56. It is explained there (p. 27) on the basis of a distinction from Boethius, *De cons.*, that a virtue must have both its proper "office" and its proper "end." As its end, a virtue must be directed toward God, and the actions in which the virtue is manifest must be performed in charity. The virtues of Troilus are directed toward Criseyde and performed in cupidity, and Criseyde's honor is completely a matter of self-love. It was not uncommon in the Middle Ages to distinguish "true" virtues from "false" virtues. See Huppé and Robertson, *Piers Plowman and Scriptural Tradition*, pp. 226-227. The "virtues" of the lover as described ironically by Andreas Capellanus are of the worldly variety. They are illustrated vividly and humorously, for example, in Aucassin's valorous behavior in the upside-down land of Torelore.

10 Troilus' behavior in Book I is typical of those who are moved by some false goal, whether in feminine guise or not, to depart from what Boethius calls the "wey" and thus subject themselves to Fortune. The fact that this particular temptation involves the beauty of a woman should not be taken as too much of a limitation. Feminine beauty was thought to typify the attractions of the world generally, and sexual

passion was a figure for all the vices. Thus Scotus Erigena, *De div. nat., Patrologia latina*, CXXII, 975-976, wrote: *"Whosoever shall look on a woman to lust after her, hath already committed adultery with her in his heart* (Matt. 5:28), obviously referring to the beauty of all sensible creatures as a woman. . . . All vices, in fact, which are contrary to the virtues, and which seek to corrupt nature, are described generally as lechery." Sexual love might be used to describe any form of cupidity, especially when it was carried to the point of idolatry. The temptation of Troilus may thus readily be universalised to include any of the false goals against which Boethius warns.

11 See Robertson, "The Doctrine of Charity," p. 44.

12 Self-love based on a knowledge of immortality leads ultimately to charity, but self-love based on worldly satisfaction may be thought of as the source of all the vices. Cf. Robertson and Huppé, *Piers Plowman and Scriptural Tradition*, pp. 27-8.

13 See Robertson, "The Doctrine of Charity," pp. 25-6.

14 See the tables of values for various deities in H. Liebeschütz, *Fulgentius metaforalis* (Leipzig, 1926), pp. 56-7.

15 Night was traditionally associated with spiritual ignorance or blindness and with adversity. E.g., see Gregory, *Moralia, Patrologia latina* LXXV, 510 and 563; Alanus, *Distinctiones, Patrologia latina*, CCX, 876; Bernard Silvestris, *op. cit.*, p. 101. Conversely, the day was associated with spiritual understanding or reason. In Bk. III Troilus and Criseyde wish to hide from the light of reason and in doing so invite the night of adversity which descends upon them in Bk. IV. Anagogically, day and night suggest the opposition between Christ, who said "I am the day," and Satan. Both spiritual ignorance and adversity are works of Satan, so that the two "nights" are basically aspects of the same thing. For an early literary use of this convention, see Prudentius, "Hymnus matutinus."

16 Gérard of Liège, ed. Wilmart, *Analecta reginensia* (Vatican, 1933), p. 201.

17 See Robertson, "The Doctrine of Charity," p. 26.

18 On the lover's malady as an aspect of idolatry, see Liebeschütz, *Fulgentius metaforalis*, p. 71.

6

Boethius' Influence on Chaucer's *Troilus*

THEODORE A. STROUD

Boethius' contribution to the terminology and the atmosphere of Chaucer's *Troilus* has long been recognized. Many readers agree that the poem is, in essence, "a practical study in real life of the working out of the Boethian teaching."[1] Illustrative of that position is Farnham's contention that Chaucer employed Boethian materials in altering *Il Filostrato* to achieve the perfect *De casibus* tragedy, to show how the Wheel of Fortune condemns all human endeavor.[2] But other and highly diverse interpretations of the poem continue to appear, with no sign of a reconciliation.

In the hope of reducing the disagreement, I have chosen to re-emphasize the influence of *De consolatione philosophiae,* especially some features of it which scholars of eminence have overlooked or casually mentioned. I say "casually," for that is how Patch treated his observation that the poem falls into stages roughly comparable to those discernible in the *Consolation.*[3] Exploring this comment, together with several interrelated aspects of the work, has led me to propose (1) that the poem not merely illustrates but extends the principle of the "turning wheel" and (2) that the poem, viewed in relation to the *Consolation,* has a significantly allegorical cast.

For half a century Chaucerians have been vitally concerned

Reprinted, by permission of author and publisher, from *Modern Philology*, XLIX (1951-2), 1-9. Copyright, 1951, by the University of Chicago.

with the alleged defects in *Troilus,* such as Pandarus' gar-
rulousness, Troilus' soliloquies, and Criseyde's infidelity. Their
reactions have been as varied and as irreconcilable as the
critical principles they have brought to the work. I—for one
—once hoped that these issues could be resolved by the
techniques of formal analysis. If it could be shown that
Chaucer selected a limited number of character traits and
other sources of plot complexity and arranged the events in a
plausible order which left the causes exhausted, in that no
expectations were aroused without being satisfied, then the
defects would be superficial and the poet's reputation en-
hanced. But at least one issue seems to defy resolution, that
is, the emotional confusion we experience at reading the
palinode. Nothing adequately prepares us for Chaucer's con-
demning every vestige of the morality not merely by which
his characters have acted but in terms of which the narrator
comments on those actions. The most rewarding alternative,
in my opinion, is to trace the conception of the work as it
evolved, testing our conjectures by their illumination of the
poem.

Anyone who accepts Root's conclusion that Chaucer added
three long passages to *Troilus,*[4] two taken directly from the
Consolation and one (as I shall argue later) indirectly, will
probably agree that Chaucer was concerned with its intellectual cast. In addition, of course, there are frequent phrasal
echoes, beginning perhaps with the Boethian conceit "drery
vers of wretchidness weten my face with varry teres" [*De
cons.*i. m. 1], which becomes "Thise woful vers, that wepen
as I write" [*TC*, I, 7]. At the time *Il Filostrato* was transformed into *Troilus,* Boethius was a basic stimulant to Chaucer's creative imagination. Many readers must have considered
the possibility that he sought to exemplify the philosophical
stages of the *Consolation,* somewhat as Dante did for Aquinas'
hierarchy of sins. Although Boethius had already cast his
work in narrative form, Chaucer might consider a further
attempt to meet the human demand for philosophy "concealed with the poetic veil."[5] He had learned his techniques
from the allegorical *Roman de la rose* and employed them,
though somewhat lightly, in various short poems. Note that
he explicitly compares *Troilus* with poems the meanings of
which, according to Boccaccio, are deliberately concealed by
the poets to remove them from the gaze of the irreverent.[6]

Let us suppose that he viewed Troilus *also* as a "Boethius"
who is driven by the alternations of Fortune rather than led
by Philosophy up the levels of metaphysical comprehension
traversed in the *Consolation*. This interpretation is not confirmed by any personified abstractions or supernatural details, nor is there a unit-by-unit correspondence between
Troilus' "double sorrow" and "Boethius' " quest. Yet we may
still ask whether the poem approaches the character of an
allegory, requiring some Gower or Strode to apprehend "the
doctrines that cloak beneath the strangeness of the verses."[7]
Does the hero ask the questions and learn their answers as
"Boethius" might appropriately have done if he had lacked
the assistance of Philosophy?

We may formulate the stages of the poem as they correspond to the sequence of arguments in the *Consolation* as
follows: Troilus is a "Boethius" well-nigh demented by his
sudden loss of freedom [cf. *De cons.* i. pr. 4; *TC*, I, 731].
Pandarus and then Criseyde administer "somdel lyghtere
medicynes" [*De cons.* 1. pr. 5] which Philosophy first applied
to "Boethius." Then, during his successful love affair, Troilus
is "Behooldyng ferst the false goodes" [*De cons.* iii. m.l],
though not with Philosophy's gloss. His loss of Criseyde is
equivalent to the "more egre medicynes" in the *Consolation*
[i. pr. 5; iii, pr. 1], consisting of the arguments that adversity
is peculiarly beneficial. For Troilus the gain is in his perspective: his ensuing soliloquy on predestination actually lifts
a long passage from "Boethius' " climactic challenge to the
position which Philosophy had advanced. That Troilus was
reduced ironically to asking the same question of dumb idols
is significant. His interminable period of frustration prepares
the reader emotionally for his reward of viewing the world
sub specie aeternitatis, which involves actualizing what Philosophy promised her pupil:

> I schall ficchen fetheris in thi thought, by which it mai arise in
> heighte. . . . Whanne the swifte thoughte hath clothid itself in the
> fetheris, it despiseth the hateful erthes, and surmounteth the rownd-
> ness of the gret ayr; and it seth the clowdes byhynde his bak, and
> passeth the heighte of the regioun of the fir . . .til that he areyseth
> him into the houses that beren the sterres . . . he shal forleten the
> last hevene and he schal pressen and wenden on the bak of the
> swifte firmament. . . . But yif the liketh thanne to looken on the
> derkenesse of the erthe . . . thanne shaltow seen . . . tirantz . . .
> exiled. . . . [*De cons.* iv. pr. 1, m.l]

If, as I noted before, Chaucer added two long Boethian passages and one which resembles this passage, it seems plausible that the *Consolation* inspired all three. Of course, a passage from the *Teseida* was the direct source. But here are the elements Troilus surmounted and the spheres on which he rested to survey earthly wickedness. Above all, here is the only feasible answer to Troilus' soliloquy—in context.

Perhaps these limited, sometimes even fanciful, correspondences between the two works might be dismissed, if they were not germane to an illuminating view of the epilogue of *Troilus*. This diffuse and multiple section, interrupted by the completion of the narrative, is far from characteristic of Chaucer's endings. Tatlock has observed that the ending contains seven distinct units, including the prudential caution against rakes.[8] Of these units, any two or three would have served adequately; upon examination they fall into two opposed, but self-contained, conclusions, separated by the narrative (Troilus' death and ascent). The first conclusion finds Troilus, the pitiful dupe of faithless love, unable either to avenge himself on his supplanter or to find surcease in death. Having stated that Troilus' further activities are irrelevant and having protested against charges of slander, Chaucer turns with his usual sympathetic irony to educe his moral— a caution against trusting false lovers. With his genial apostrophe to "litel myn tragedy" to characterize his poem as an unpretentious effort, he has completed the story of two young lovers, each unequal to the demands of romantic love, but in neatly contrary respects.

But the poem does not end there. With a prayer that the poem be preserved—and understood!—Chaucer reverts to the narrative, a move artistically justified by the craving for relief already evoked in his readers. Troilus is granted release from his agony and an answer to his questions. Afterward that answer is expanded in Chaucer's apostrophe on Troilus' "fyn," and the moral is redressed: youth should avoid the Wheel of Fortune by loving only the Savior, whose power and perfection are antithetical to such pagan gods as Love. At this stage Chaucer is no longer submissive to pagan poets but only to moral or religious authorities and ultimately to God himself.

With the confirmation of this double ending, I maintain that this love story, which satisfies both a medieval definition of a tragedy and the modern conception of a novel, is also a philosophical "quest" in certain respects parallel to the *Consolation*. . . . The interpretations which seriously distort the nature of the poem are those which ignore or minimize its philosophical level, for instance, by dismissing the predestination soliloquy as an excrescence.[9] Even the diction of Troilus, fluctuating between simple, idiomatic passages and those of "high style,"[10] employing all the rhetorical techniques of the epic, suggests the two levels. But no terms are available to describe the relationship. The system of interpretation so familiar to Boccaccio and other Italian poets whom Chaucer took as his masters during this stage of his career was not reserved for obvious instances.[11] Today, however, when two of their nonliteral meanings (tropological and anagogical) are forgotten and allegory is a pejorative word, used either to label clumsy examples of symbolism or to serve as the opposite of symbolism, the tendency is to ignore nonliteral meanings or to view the story as illustrating some doctrine (an exemplum). Thus Farnham concludes that *Troilus* is a leisurely *De casibus* tragedy, illustrating the Boethian concepts of Fortune. But the relationship is really more complex: not only is Troilus unlike Boccaccio's illustrious men (and Chaucer's Monk's) in that he actually gropes for the *De contemptu mundi* lesson, but he alone seems so concerned with it that he does not struggle in any way to achieve Fortune's favors or to preserve them against the turning of the wheel. Chaucer's concern with a nonliteral level of meaning in the poem, at whatever point in his composition it began to influence his treatment of the story, needs to be borne in mind as we consider why he chose the *Filostrato* and what he added from the *Consolation*.

After the Provençal poets had disseminated the doctrines of *l'amour courtois*, many medieval readers were probably conscious of a glaring oversight in Boethius' treatment of "false goods." In Philosophy's eyes, these are power, dignities, and fame [iii. pr. 2 ff.]. Having shown how each is a source of vice and misery, she dismisses "delyces of body" as bestial, hardly worth considering [iii. pr. 7]. As the power of love became a conspicuous myth in the medieval culture, however, the possession of the loved one became a treasure hardly to be mentioned in the same breath with a worldly honor or power. It was a *bonum in saeculo* [a worldly good], a source of virtue and ultimately of happiness compared to which the Boethian goods were indeed trivial.

Perhaps Chaucer first glimpsed the need for Boethian arguments against such possessions as he studied the chapters in which Jean de Meung insists that lovers invite the caprice of Fortune no less than do ambitious men. Yet, during the entire argument between Reason and the Lover, Jean does not mention a single lover who suffered the outrage of Fortune—only dignitaries.[12] Later Chaucer came upon the early poems of Boccaccio, in which he sang affectingly of both the felicity and the torment of love, and then upon his *De casibus virorum illustrium* [*On the Falls of Illustrious Men*], which curiously failed even to mention love as a pinnacle from which men could fall. Meanwhile, within Chaucer's immediate circle, the relation between courtly and divine love was being imaginatively analyzed and illustrated, notably by John Gower, the prose-poet Thomas Usk, and perhaps Sir Thomas Clanvowe. We can only conjecture about any accompanying conversations.

Out of these circumstances, I believe, came Chaucer's decision to revise *Il Filostrato* in a fashion which would supplement the conclusions of Boethius in an area of human activity which he had neglected. An expansion of this view will show that it minimizes many of the cruces in the design of *Troilus*, or at least permits an accurate estimate, for example, of assertions about Chaucer's "lack of real grip on a human Troilus"[13] or about the intractability of his materials for executing his conception. It has not been sufficiently recognized that the problem concerns not merely what he added or changed in his source but what he retained. For Boccaccio's poem has an explicit rhetorical function: his appeals to a "bella donna" and his identification with Troilo give appropriateness to many passages which his narrative could not otherwise sustain. Thus, only if the hyperbolic descriptions and protestations acquire a new function, can Chaucer be justified in retaining, much less expanding, them. Surely, it is inadequate to assume that they were the conventional accouterments of courtly love literature; if genius means anything, it is that its manifestations exhibit a more organic rationale than poetic conventions alone can provide. In the affair of Troilo, Chaucer saw an exemplum of the lesson which the *Consolation* promulgated; in his version the token of fortune which Troilus acquired was altered to offer a greater illusion of sublimity than any other "good" of this terrestrial world. To heighten the receptivity of his audience, he eliminated such potentially offensive doctrines as the added relish that secrecy imparts to love [cf. *Filostrato*, II, 74]. To narrator and reader his "service of love" becomes a temporal bliss rivaling any religious ecstasy. If at last it also collapses miserably, the Boethian lesson is a fortiori confirmed.

Chaucer, it would seem, has constructed a romance, intensely pathetic, faintly satirical, to which he added a level commingling the functions of an illustration for a thesis and of an allegory concerning man's quest for the moral laws of the universe. Whether this view obviates the critical defects of the poem is, of course, a matter for the reader to decide after we have surveyed its implications for the various events and characters in the poem, with the evolving personality of Troilus as our center.

In his supreme innocence,[14] Troilus begins by mocking the religion of love. Once converted, he reveals a passivity, a craving for failure, hardly typical of the courtly lover, much less of romance in general.[15] Specifically, his reaction exceeds that of Troilo, whose function is to symbolize the paralyzing effect of love on the narrator himself. Troilus' desire for secrecy, which again the convention is inadequate to explain, leads him to resist all but the most vehement of Pandarus' attempts to tender aid. Instead, Troilus immediately focuses on the implications of his new religion; with "Boethius" his initial reaction is that "Fortune is my fo." His wholesale questioning in the *Canticus Troili* and the slavish homage to his lord reflect an introspective tendency which makes him, however heroic on the battlefield, incapable of actions relevant to his emotional drives.[16] The result is a pathetic story, many incidents of which appear humorous to both Pandarus and the reader. Yet when Troilus is forced or passively led along the stages of love to its consummation, the very sensitiveness and speculativeness which hamper him also enable him to analyze the states of personality evoked by love in a more comprehending fashion than other lovers could. If for this species of love, "Men must axe at seyntes if it is/Aught fair" [II, 894-95], Troilus is our saint. Every detail of his longing to possess Criseyde physically has overtones of a religious devotee agonizingly praying for a mystical union.

For those who can laugh, with Pandarus, at his fainting by
Criseyde's bedside, Chaucer has achieved a *reductio ad ab-
surdum* of the potentialities of courtly love.[17]

To these stages of Troilus' affair Pandarus contributes both
motivation for the episodes and elements of Boethian doctrines. Thus Pandarus is the philosophical antithesis of Troilus
as he defends Fortune against Troilus' strictures: since it is the
nature of the goddess to alternate her favors, man has no right
to blame her; in fact, he should take courage in adversity that
her wheel does revolve. From this position, derived from the
first stage of the *Consolation,* Pandarus never varies. When
he seeks to introduce a note of caution to a Troilus reveling
in his ecstasy [III, 1618-37], a few months later, the fact that
the wheel is still turning strikes Troilus as highly irrelevant;
he has not united misfortune in the manner of the *De casibus*
heroes, who achieve prominence by unlimited exertion; he is
passive and far from "rakle." If humility will save him, he has
learned it perfectly—along with all the other virtues—as is
witnessed by the narrator's paean to his nobility. What guilt
could undermine his felicity? He does lack moderation, but
it is an excess antithetical to the excess of rulers, who thereby
nourish their vices, for Troilus is immoderate in an attachment
which nourishes his virtues. At this point, anyone could agree
that this is a poem "in praise of love."

Chaucer's reconstitution of the philosophy in the *Consolation* is also implicit in Troilus' song glorifying the universal
bond of love. It is taken directly from that work, "and differs
from it only in that some of the parts are changed about."[18]
But the difference consists precisely in that Boethius stresses
the Empedoclean principle of attraction in the universe and
mentions matrimony only incidentally toward the end, whereas in *Troilus* "holsom alliaunce / Halt peples joined" appears
in the opening lines of his song. This reversal is meaningful in
itself but should be viewed as a climax in a series of songs.
In his first song [I, 400-20], Troilus is dismayed at the inexplicable power operating in his heart, though as yet unconscious of its universality. Then, having been accepted as
a suitor, he is living testimony to the regeneration which
Antigone's song promises lovers: love is a source of felicity
accompanied by an increase in physical prowess and moral
virtue [II, 827-75]. Next, if the proem to Book III is a reflection of Troilus' expanding conception, he now recognizes

love as a *sine qua non* of life itself. With the consummation of his affair, he discerns the universal and infinite grace of this force apotheosizing lovers. During his sojourn in grace, he views love as synonymous with God's power in the universe—a concept Troilus in his saintliness symbolizes so persuasively that the reader is somehow shocked by his final recantation. It seems misleading, therefore, to describe him as "sunk in all the blind error of unphilosophical attachment to the temporal world."[19] How could he be more philosophical —in Troy?

During the events of the first three books, Criseyde is presented as charming and intelligent, utterly feminine in her curiosity and sympathy. Her fears and desire for social approval hardly seem abnormal, particularly in view of her precarious status in Troy. It is obvious that Pandarus required more influence and ingenuity to gain her for Troilus than did his prototype. The skill with which he manipulates her emotions and the wit she matches against his increase the richness of the love story. It is generally agreed that she makes a more fundamental moral sacrifice in acquiescing to this clandestine affair and therefore can sustain its felicity more intensely and comprehensively than Boccaccio's heroine. But she is so appealingly human in her rationalizations to avoid responsibility that, however she may be temporarily inspired by Troilus' worship, she is at no time a potential saint of Love.

The *verbal* contribution she makes to the early stages of his education consists primarily of a speech on false felicity [III, 813-40, 1016-22]. She reflects a deeply rooted pessimism as she inquires how man can ever be truly happy, since his happiness must result either from ignorance of Fortune's laws or from temporary forgetfulness. Under the pressure of human attraction, she does commit herself to turn Troilus' bitter "al into swetnesse" [III, 179]. But her major contribution to his quest results from her infidelity, an action which readers invariably have trouble reconciling with her previous behavior. The numerous studies arguing for highly divergent conclusions concerning her traits, one even denying her guilt,[20] are signs that, whatever his intention, Chaucer did not make her betrayal aesthetically acceptable to his audience. In my opinion, the solution hinges on Farnham's view of her as the worldly possession of which Troilus must be deprived. To satisfy Chaucer's purpose, she must be the finest gem that earth affords, yet flawed to her very core. As a heroine of a love story, she deserves Pandarus' curse [v, 1731-43]; as a token of Fortune, the narrator's pity and regret [v, 1093-99]; and as an exemplum of "blind lust," Troilus' contempt (which she shares, however, with all mankind). This ambivalence in treating her character may explain the apparent discrepancy in the time required for Diomede to triumph. Whether he obtained her love on the eleventh day or whether months were required to overcome her fidelity is quite obscure [cf. v, 1030-6 and 1086-92]. Allegorically, Troilus should be stripped of his bauble instantaneously; yet, as a principal of a pathetic love story, Criseyde's "goodness" will not permit such haste. Again, Chaucer chose to stress Diomede's boorish nature, exemplifying the principle that Fortune indifferently distributes her goods, although this trait alone would almost have insured his rejection by the earlier Criseyde. No wonder we are unwilling to credit her infidelity!

Given these discrepant functions, we are hardly surprised to find an article devoted to the evidence that *Troilus* has "two concentric and contradictory time-schemes," for which no explanation is offered.[21] For this view of the poem, the feature seems significantly appropriate: one scheme, which connects the major events with the seasons successively from spring to winter, symbolizes Fortune's wheel and focuses on the universality of the sequence of events; the other scheme extends the story over several years to heighten the pathos and concomitant emotions of the individualized story. Yet Chaucer was ordinarily able to reconcile these disparate ends: for example, the three years of Troilus' blessedness lack events to give them a sense of immediacy, and need none. After the one night of love, which is supremely individualized, all we learn is that Troilus became a quasi-saint, matchless in devotions and virtuous activities.

Until the announcement in "parlement," he was convinced that his homage to Fortune and his moral perfection were adequate to propitiate that force, to free him from the wheel. His first reaction of disillusionment was to rail against her while he considered alternate courses of action, eliminating any which would involve energetic opposition to his lot. Then he glimpses the connection between Fortune and Destiny, a power subsuming all the apparent capriciousness of events.

At first this is personal, but the threat of separation from his source of felicity is sufficient to conjure up in his imagination an eternity of desolation, and to thrust his mind into metaphysical speculation. And the various ironies of the situation (for instance, that a traitor is depriving him of his love in exchange for a potential traitor, Antenor) help the reader to follow his lead. He yearns to die, not to have Criseyde urge her abduction [IV, 638-40, 950-5]. Within a few hours he has formulated the issue in its most general terms, as though any success he might achieve by setting "the world on six and seven" would be futile unless in some way it obviated the predicament facing all men. Thus Pandarus finds him proving the foreordination of all men's actions and eliminating the alternative in any unsystematic but thorough fashion (a lengthy paraphrase from the *Consolation*). Though no longer blinded by his false felicity, he lacks a substitute for the religion it evoked. It has been his role from the outset to raise the questions which "Boethius" did, with no equivalent of Philosophy to answer them. Having now risen to a point where he understands the nature of the human dilemma a little less imperfectly than his associates, he can turn only to graven images. Certainly, Pandarus, who merely rephrases his conception of Fortune, is no longer a source of support, though he sympathizes intensely with Troilus' plight.

Many of the chronological inconsistencies discernible in Book V, especially the confusion in the number and sequence of the letters from Criseyde, are perhaps devised—or left unrevised—to reflect Troilus' psychological state. The interminable agony of his living death, as he fluctuates among despair at her loss, hope of her reurn, desire for revenge, and craving for death, serves Chaucer's dual ends. In speculation, Troilus can go no further, unless he is granted perspective by some divine means. To be permanently deprived of his goddess is hardly enough to evince his transcendent merit; he must experience her symbolic destruction (as she makes unfounded accusations against him and dedicates herself to a "boar"), without himself becoming a heretic to love. His situation, with neither revenge nor suicide to give surcease, is drained of every pleasure that pathos affords (compare Chaucer's treatment of the Griselda story). Also, by this suffering, Troilus is finally made to deserve a momentary glimpse of truth, so that his "quest" ends successfully, before Mercury assigns him to his dwelling.

The fate of Troilus, as has often been observed, is set against the symbolic background of the fall of Troy. For the poem constituted as a love story, this background tends to minimize our lack of sympathy for Troilus' passivity and Criseyde's weakness, increasing the pathos, yet blurring its implications for our existence. But for the poem as a philosophical quest, the background imparts an intense degree of fatalism to the events: Chaucer felt, at least in the conception of this story, that mankind faces ruin through the very nature of its activities. He does not even seem to share Boethius' belief that man can grasp the principle reconciling foreordination and free will. All men are dwelling in a beseiged Troy. To show the quest against a backdrop of any other pattern would be to falsify the picture of human existence, to make it atypical indeed.

What was said earlier about the parallelism between the *Consolation* and *Troilus,* particularly the duality of the epilogue, should be confirmed by this survey of the events. Here are no allegorical trappings to be facilely stripped away, but an allegory none the less, ordering the philosophical implications of the story. The most tenable conclusion seems to be not that Chaucer was unconcerned or unaware of the need for a unified effect but that the fusion his conception required was not entirely feasible. Certainly, I prefer not to conclude that Book v, where most of the difficulties occur, is "perhaps a mass of undigested materials."[22] To some degree my hypothesis serves to explain both what Chaucer added to *Filostrato* and how he could retain and even add hyperbole to the protestations and the soul-searchings which were functional in Boccaccio's poem as persuasion. Of course, some of the episodes in *Troilus* defy interpretation on the different levels. But commentators are also unable to distinguish the levels of meaning signified by numerous sections of the *Divine Comedy*, even though Dante himself described it as systematically polysemous.[23] Considering the frequency of allegorical interpretation in the Middle Ages, I feel justified in disregarding the modern disdain for allegory, the feeling that any sententiousness is an artistic defect, if this attitude has helped to clarify the complex interplay of events and intellectual issues which readers generally discover in *Troilus*.

Notes

1 B. L. Jefferson, *Chaucer and the "Consolation of Philosophy" of Boethius* (Princeton, 1917), p. 120.

2 W. Farnham, *The Medieval Heritage of Elizabethan Tragedy* (Berkeley, Calif., 1936), pp. 137 ff.

3 H. R. Patch, "Troilus on Determinism," *Speculum*, VI (1929), 242. [reproduced above, pp. 71-85; see p. 83].

4 R. K. Root, *The Textual Tradition of Chaucer's "Troilus"* (London, 1916), pp. 155-57, 216-20, 245-47.

5 *Genealogia deorum gentilium*, trans. C. G. Osgood, in his *Boccaccio on Poetry* (Princeton, 1930), p. 68.

6 *Ibid.*, pp. 59-60.

7 A paraphrase of Dante's *Inferno*, IX, 62-63.

8 J. S. P. Tatlock, "Epilogue of Chaucer's *Troilus*," *MP*, XVIII (1921), 625 ff.

9 C. S. Lewis, "What Chaucer Really Did to *Il Filostrato*," *Essays and Studies by Members of the English Association*, XVII (1932), 16 [reproduced above, pp. 16-33; see p. 23].

10 D. C. Boughner, "Elements of Epic Grandeur in the *Troilus*," *ELH*, VI (1939), 200-210 [reproduced below, pp. 186-95]. As R. A. Pratt ("Chaucer's Use of the *Teseida*," *PMLA*, LXII [1947], 608-13) points out, many of these elevated passages are derived from the *Teseida*, but Chaucer's motive for adding them remains obscure.

11 After insisting that Petrarch's pastorals were written for their nonliteral significance, Boccaccio writes: "I would also cite my own eclogues, of whose meaning I am, of course, fully aware . . ." (Osgood, p. 54). In any serious writing of this school we may assume the writer's awareness of at least one nonliteral level of meaning: tropological (or moral), allegorical, or anagogical. For some idea of the meaning and application of these terms in fourteenth-century England see G. R. Owst, *Literature and Pulpit in Medieval England* (Cambridge, 1933), pp. 56-109.

12 *Le Roman de la rose*, ed. E. Langlois (Paris, 1920), ll. 4229-6978. This section contains several passages which certainly caught Chaucer's attention; e.g., Virginius (PhT), Nero and Croesus (MkT).

13 J. S. P. Tatlock, "People in Chaucer's *Troilus*," *PMLA*, LVI (1941), 92.

14 In contrast, Troilo could boast at least one successful excursion into the cult of love (I, 24-25).

15 Ordinarily the obstacles are largely external. But according to D. de Rougement, *Love in the Western World*, trans. M. Belgion (New York, 1940), pp. 29 ff., the essence of the Tristan myth was a lover craving and creating obstacles to union with his lady, thereby symbolizing love of death. His position is suggestive for *Troilus*, however dubious one may be about its applicability to courtly love romances in general.

16 W. G. Dodd (*Courtly Love in Chaucer and Gower* [Milford, 1913], p. 145) fails to make this distinction as he denies that Troilus is weak and inactive. Also when Tatlock ("People," p. 91) argues that Troilus is fundamentally practical, the evidence that he is often consulted by his associates seems rather weak: the first (II, 510-11) is

Pandarus' imaginary explanation of how he discovered Troilus' passion; the other (II, 1627, 1692-1701) concerns a pretext to eliminate Helen and Deiphebus from the scene (another example of Pandarus' ingenuity).

17 In contrast, Troilo fainted in the midst of "parlement" upon learning that he would *lose* his mistress.

18 Jefferson, p. 67.

19 Farnham, p. 146.

20 J. S. Graydon, "Defense of Criseyde," *PMLA*, XLIV (1929), 141-77.

21 H. W. Sams, "Dual Time-Scheme in Chaucer's *Troilus*," *MLN*, LVI (1941), 94-100 [reproduced below, pp. 180-85].

22 J. M. Manly and E. Rickert, *The Text of the Canterbury Tales* (1940), II, 36. Miss Rickert also initiated a Master's thesis maintaining that Book V is at many points composed of inconsistent and unassimilated paraphrases of Chaucer's various sources [Grace A. Olson, *The Peculiar Features in the Fifth Book of Chaucer's* Troilus and Criseyde, University of Chicago, 1940—Ed.].

23 C. S. Singleton, "Dante's Allegory," *Speculum*, XXIV (1950), 81 ff.

7

The *Troilus* and Christian Love

JAMES LYNDON SHANLEY

> O yonge, fresshe folkes, he or she,
> In which that love up groweth with youre age,
> Repeyreth hom fro worldly vanyte,
> And of youre herte up casteth the visage
> To thilke God that after his ymage
> Yow made, and thynketh al nys but a faire
> This world, that passeth soone as floures faire.
> And loveth hym, the which that right for love
> Upon a crois, oure soules for to beye,
> First starf, and roos, and sit in hevene above;
> For he nyl falsen no wight, dar I seye,
> That wol his herte al holly on him leye.
> And syn he best to love is, and most meke,
> What nedeth feynede loves for to seke?
>
> [*TC*, v, 1835-48]

Critics have seen these lines of the *Troilus* as no part of the whole and perfect deterministic tragedy;[1] as a completely unexpected return from the Renaissance to the Middle Ages;[2] or as the repudiation of an immoral code which Chaucer had pretended to uphold.[3] This paper will attempt to show that these views are wrong and that the correct one is: that the epilogue is no mere tacked-on moral but is implicit in the whole poem.[4] It will seek to show that there is a more fundamental connection between the story and the epilogue than Professor Robinson suggests in his introduction:

Reprinted, by permission of author and editor, from *ELH*, VI (1939), 271-81.

It [the epilogue] expresses . . . exactly the feeling by which Chaucer might have been possessed at the moment when he was deeply moved by his tale of "double sorwe." . . . The artistic propriety of the epilogue may always be a matter of dispute, and its acceptability to the reader will depend in some measure upon his attitude toward explicit moralization. But it is not necessary to find any deep conflict between the epilogue and the story.[5]

We should not consider the *Troilus* as simply a romance of courtly love, a psychological novel, or a drama, even though it has characteristics in common with all these types. Most simply stated, what Chaucer did was to recast a narrative poem; and he caused a fundamental difference between the *Troilus* and *Il Filostrato* when he retold the story in the light of an entirely new set of values, determined not only by this world and man's life in it but by the eternal as well. He did not merely retell the story of an engaging young man who, because he trusted in a woman, was made unhappy when she proved faithless. The ultimate reason for Troilus's woe was not that he trusted in a woman but that of his own free will he placed his hope for perfect happiness in that which by its nature was temporary, imperfect, and inevitably insufficient.

We shall not be surprised at the suggestion that Chaucer meant his thoughtful readers to understand this fact long before Troilus did if we remember that at the heart of mediaeval philosophy and religion was the conviction of the inherent insufficiency of things earthly, no matter how noble and good, and, on the other hand, of the reality and completeness of heavenly bliss and the individual's responsibility in attaining it. But the statement of these ideas, in the light of which I think the moral Gower and the philosophical Strode would have read the *Troilus,* points only to a possibility. An examination of the poem will perhaps make it appear a probability.

Accustomed to the conventions of courtly love, Chaucer's readers would have found nothing unfamiliar in the early stages of the love affair. They would have accepted Troilus's great misery and sorrow as natural in one who had not yet gained the love of his mistress; further, Chaucer had assured them that Troilus's worthiness would be rewarded. But the readers also knew that Criseyde would forsake Troilus before she died. Therefore, when Troilus, on his return from the temple where he first saw Criseyde, willingly and completely gave himself over to Love, the pity and the irony of the situation marked the tale as no ordinary courtly romance.

Yet all proceeds favorably for the lovers, and there seems to be no reason why they should not possess happiness when, after Criseyde decides to remain at Pandar's, the consummation of their love is made certain. The reader knows, however, that it is to be only temporary, that the lovely and gracious Criseyde will forsake Troilus. And the reader is not only reminded of this but is also shown the lovers' fundamental error just as they are apparently to have their utmost desires fulfilled. For, when she is told of Troilus's supposed jealousy, Criseyde cries that worldly happiness, called false felicity by the learned, is mixed with bitterness because it is unstable, and her conclusion is:

> trewely, for aught I kan espie,
> Ther is no verray weele in this world heere.
>
> [III, 835-6]

The word of Troilus's jealousy seems to bring home to her for a moment the quality of earthly joy and shows to the reader the reason for Troilus's pathetic situation: It is not that he thinks Criseyde and love good, but that he has made them the things upon which all his happiness depends.

As soon as she has allayed the stings of jealousy and all is well, Criseyde herself quite naturally forgets the warning she gave. But the reader does not and what follows only heightens the irony. For, after the fashion of courtly lovers, Troilus and Criseyde describe their joy and give thanks to Love in the religious terms constantly used in speaking of God, the everlasting good:

> Benigne Love [says Troilus]
> . . . .
> Yet were al lost, that dar I wel seyn certes,
> But if thi grace passed oure desertes.
>
> [III, 1261-7]

And Criseyde, as deeply in love as Troilus, replies to his protestations of entire love:

> Welcome, my knyght, my pees, my suffisaunce.
>
> [III, 1309]

Nothing remained to be said after this; both gave themselves completely to love. Following Criseyde's surrender, Pandar attempted to make Troilus see that worldly joy "halt nought

but by a wir" [III, 1636], but in vain; for Troilus and Criseyde
had such joy that "felicitee" could not describe their state,
wherein "ech of hem gan otheres lust obeye" [III, 1690-4].
But before the mediaeval mind seriously and religiously concerned with life and happiness were divine peace and felicity,
perfect and eternal, to be achieved not when individual wills
were drawn to one another, but when they were drawn to
God's, for it was His will that was peace.

> Brother, the quality of love stilleth our will, and maketh us long
> only for what we have, and giveth us no other thirst.
> . . . .
> Nay, 'tis the essence of this blessed being to hold ourselves with-
> in the divine will, whereby our wills are themselves made one.
> So that our being thus, from threshold unto threshold through-
> out the realm, is a joy to all the realm as to the king, who draweth
> our minds to what he willeth;
> and His will is our peace; it is that sea to which all moves that
> it createth and that nature maketh.[6]

Nothing could break the peace of which Dante was told
and of which the reader is reminded by Criseyde's words. But
the peace of Troilus and Criseyde, the reader knows, is to be
broken. Criseyde once more recalls this fact to his mind when
she exclaims, on learning of the parliament's decree:

> Endeth thanne love in wo? Ye, or men lieth!
> And alle worldly blisse, as thynketh me.
>
> [IV, 834-5]

But again she forgets, and later in the Grecian camp, bemoan-
ing the delay of her return to Troy, she resolves to take no
heed of gossip and censure but to return to the city, for, she
says:

> Felicite clepe I my suffisaunce.
>
> [V, 763]

Love was too strong to allow her to remember, but her
glimpses of the truth and Pandar's hints at it were enough to
make Chaucer's more serious readers understand why, after
his complete surrender to love, Troilus was inevitably to go
from weal to woe.

But they would hardly have been satisfied with the conduct of the story and the fate assigned to Troilus if in his
world he had never had the opportunity to choose the way to
felicity. If Destiny had had complete control over him, then,

according to the *Troilus,* "yonge, fresshe folkes" would have little choice as to where they would place their hearts; and Chaucer's appeal, however pious and sincere, would have been vain. The control of Destiny is not complete, however, in the life of either Criseyde or Troilus. We cannot deny its importance in their lives: because of the "lawe of kynde" Troilus must love [I, 237-8]; Troy is destined to fall [I, 68; V, 1541-7]; Criseyde must leave and Troilus live thenceforth in pain because of fatal destiny [V, 1-7] and it is Fortune's decree that prevents Troilus and Diomede from killing one another [V, 1763-4]. Forces and events completely beyond the lovers' control affect their lives greatly.

But the story does not depend on destined events alone, nor is the final unhappiness of either owing only to fate. They are free to choose what they wish, and as they choose they determine their lot. (Chaucer's philosophical reconciliation of these elements we do not know; the *Troilus* is not, as are the *Divine Comedy* and *Paradise Lost,* a philosophical poem; but it is controlled by Chaucer's philosophy as *Tom Jones,* for example, is controlled by Fielding's conception of the natural goodness of man.) When Pandar is preparing to reveal Troilus's love for Criseyde, he tells her that every one has a chance to have good fortune and that she should take hers before it slacks [II, 281-91]. And when he tells her of Troilus's plight, and asks for her pity at least, she says that since one ought to *choose* the lesser of two evils, she will give Troilus some encouragement rather than endanger her uncle's life [II, 470-2]. Destiny has no hand here, but the interplay mentioned above is seen when we seek the reason for her loving Troilus. "Who yaf me drynke?" [II, 651] she asks as she sees him ride by; but that she will love him is not determined then; there follows her clear and deliberate meditation as to whether or not she will give him her love. From her words to Troilus when he first enters her closet at Pandar's, we know that such thought did influence her. As well as the excellence of love, which none may or should attempt to resist, the sight of his loyalty and service also led her to have pity on him [III, 988-94]. Moreover, as Troilus takes her in his arms, at last able to see the pleasant side of life, he says to her:

> Now be ye kaught, now is ther but we tweyne!
> Now yeldeth yow, for other bote is non!
> [III, 1207-8]

But Criseyde snatches the last word to impress upon him that she is there only because she is willing [III, 1210-11].

Finally, when Criseyde is untrue to Troilus, although sorrowful, she acts deliberately. In order to heighten the dramatic effect of the betrayal through suspense, Chaucer tells us, at the beginning of Book V, that Destiny sends Criseyde from Troy and decrees that Troilus must thenceforth live in pain [V, 1-7]. But Destiny does not make Criseyde faithlessly turn to Diomede. She deliberately gives up her intention of returning to Troy because she enjoys Diomede's clever talk, respects his great estate, fears the perils of Troy, and needs help [V, 1023-9]. Later

> the bet from sorwe hym to releve,
> She made hym were a pencel of hire sleve.
> . . . .
> And for to helen hym of his sorwes smerte,
> Men seyn—I not—that she yaf hym hire herte.
> [V, 1042-3; 1049-50]

In both instances she acted for a definite purpose, in itself a good one but not when related to all other ends. No one knew better than she that the fault was hers, and the pitifulness of her last lament lies in her clear-sightedness accompanied by an equal blindness:

> Al be I not the first that dide amys,
> What helpeth that to don my blame awey?
> But syn I se ther is no bettre way,
> And that to late is now for me to rewe,
> To Diomede algate I wol be trewe.
> [V, 1067-71]

Earlier, as she left Troy, she accused the constellation of her birth for her forced departure from the city [IV, 743-6], but here she recognizes that the fault is her own. And Chaucer, in spite of his pity which will not allow him to chide her further, could not excuse her guilt [V, 1093-9], which he mentions again at the end of the story [V, 1775].

When we turn to Troilus, we find that if we took his own word, we should look no further. When Criseyde's departure is almost certain, although he desires above all things to prevent it, Troilus is unable to do so. Forces beyond his control make his will of no avail; so great is his despair that he prepares to die, for he is lost since, as he sees life at the time, "al that comth, comth by necessitee" [IV, 953-9]. To prove his statement he reviews the arguments of the "clerkes" on the subject of divine providence and free-will; he decides that those who deny the existence of free-will must be right [IV, 960-1078]. Dramatically the soliloquy is perfect, but it reaches the wrong conclusion to fit the facts of the world Troilus lives in. He decides the question as he does because his will is thwarted; his philosophizing started from its conclusion.

His trouble was not that he lacked free-will but that he had used it unwisely. Once again we see the interplay of necessity and free-will in his world, and we see that his unhappiness depended on his own choice. To love was inevitable, and Troilus loved by "lawe of kynde"; yet the individual could control the love born of nature. Pandar set forth the doctrine when he told Troilus that Criseyde was suited to love a worthy knight and that he would hold it for a vice in her unless she did [I, 987]. She was free to and did choose Troilus. And we know from his own words that Troilus once had the power to control his own love for Criseyde. When he returned from the temple where he first saw her, he not only "took purpos loves craft to suwe" [I, 379] and "gan fully assente Criseyde for to love" [I, 391-2]. He also sang of his love and acknowledged that he had no right to complain of its burning, for only if he consented could it be as strong as it was in him [I, 407-15]. After his song, he acknowledged the god of Love's mastery of his spirit, thanked him for his favor, and vowed to live and die in the service of Criseyde [I, 421-7].

Thus his "sorwes" began, and serving as the background against which this action took place for the reader was the fact that no human pleasure, however good, could be sufficient for the individual's complete happiness. Professor Gilson has pointed out that on this fact rested the whole Christian conception of love.[7] Later than Chaucer, Thomas à Kempis wrote:

> How small soever anything be, if it be inordinately loved and regarded, it keepeth thee back from the highest good, and defileth the soul.[8]

And Dante had learned in Purgatory:

> Nor Creator nor creature, my son, was ever without love, either natural or rational; and this thou knowest.
>
> The natural is always without error; but the other may err through an evil object, or through too little or too much vigour.

While it is directed to the primal goods, and in the secondary moderates itself, it cannot be the cause of sinful delight.

. . . .

innate with you is the virtue which giveth counsel, and ought to guard the threshold of assent.

. . . .

Wherefor suppose that every love which is kindled within you arise of necessity, the power to arrest it is within you.[9]

It was with this in mind, it was according to this scale of values that Chaucer retold the tale of Troilus's unhappy love. Boccaccio's treatment of the problem was not satisfactory. He showed how Troilus, who led his life according to the dictates of the tradition of courtly love, ultimately found only sorrow because Criseyde, like most young women, was vain and fickle:

O youths, in whom amorous desire gradually riseth with age, I pray you for the love of the gods that ye check the ready steps to that evil passion and that ye mirror yourselves in the love of Troilus, which my verses set forth above, for if ye will read them aright, and will take them to heart, not lightly will ye trust in all women.

A young woman is fickle and is desirous of many lovers, and her beauty she esteemeth more than it is in her mirror . . . she hath no feeling for virtue or reason, inconstant ever as leaf in the wind.[10]

But as this description will not do for Chaucer's Criseyde, so Boccaccio's solution will not do. Even as Chaucer told of Criseyde's guilt, he had only pity for her:

And if I myghte excuse hire any wise,
For she so sory was for hire untrouthe,
Iwis, I wolde excuse hire yet for routhe.

[v, 1097-9]

At no time do we feel that Criseyde is unworthy of love; she was gracious and kind, neither desirous of many lovers nor unmoved by virtue; we cannot feel that Troilus was well rid of her. We can only accept the fact that, gentle and lovely as she was, Criseyde could not stand fast in "trouthe." Because she did not and because he had placed all his hopes of happiness on her, Troilus suffered. Although he did nothing ungentle or ignoble, although "he loved chivalrye, trouthe and honour, freedom and curteisye" and was faithful to all that he thought best, yet his portion in life was pain.

Swich is this world, whoso it kan byholde;
In ech estat is litel hertes reste.
God leve us for to take it for the beste!
                                                    [v, 1748-50]

Chaucer's comment is not that women are fickle and men
foolish to love them, but rather: *Sunt lacrimae rerum, et
mentem mortalia tangunt* [The universe bids forth our tears,
and mortal things do move the mind]; for he saw men seeking lasting peace and happiness in things unstable by nature
and moved by forces beyond their control. But Troilus could
not be blamed or scorned for caring; Pandar's Horatian
acceptance and warning of inevitable change was no sufficient substitute for the joy which Troilus thought to have.
And it covered only half the problem as Chaucer saw it and
as a modern poet has stated it:

Teach us to care and not to care.

Pandar could not, with all his kindly and worldly wisdom,
keep Troilus from sorrow. But the solution was clear since
the tale was told in reference to the beliefs and ideas of the
Christian tradition. St. Augustine, in his *Confessions,* wrote
of his seeking for peace:

Be not foolish, O my soul, nor become deaf in the ear of thine
heart with the tumult of thy folly. Hearken thou too. The Word
itself calleth thee to return: and there is the place of rest imper-
turbable, where love is not forsaken, if itself forsaketh not. Behold,
these things pass away, that others may replace them, and so this
lower universe be completed by all his parts. But do I depart any
whither? saith the Word of God.[11]

It was in contrast with this conception that Troilus's woe was
seen. Chaucer's conclusion was but the direct statement of
the ideas and beliefs which gave full meaning to Troilus's
situation and sorrows. And it is, I think, aesthetically essential
as well as intellectually consistent, for by these lines only is
the final emotional resolution achieved. Not only is the appeal
to "yonge, fresshe folkes" consistent with the implications of
the tale; it also completes and fulfills them. Chaucer was not
finished until he had written the epilogue, for the *Troilus* was
not a completely objective representation left to speak entirely for itself, but a tale with comment as was Boccaccio's.

Chaucer found in Boccaccio an artistic guide, but in his story and comment no adequate treatment and explanation of the experience set forth. The case of Troilus was but part of a whole in which, as Theseus said in the *Knight's Tale*:

> speces of thynges and progressiouns
> Shullen enduren by successiouns,
> And not eterne, withouten any lye.   (I[A] 3013-15)

And one part of wisdom was, he added:

> To maken vertu of necessitee,
> And take it weel that we may not eschue,
> And namely that to us alle is due.   (I[A] 3042-4)

The whole of wisdom Chaucer set forth in his *Balade de Bon Conseyl*

> That thee is sent, receyve in buxumnesse,
> The wrastling for this world axeth a fal.
> Her is non hoom, her nis but wildernesse:
> Forth, pilgrim, forth! Forth, beste, out of thy stal!
> Know thy contree, look up, thank God of al;
> Hold the heye wey, and lat thy gost thee lede;
> And trouthe thee shall delivere, it is no drede.

This is the summary of the attitude of the man who wrote the *Troilus* and the *Canterbury Tales*. The epilogue of the *Troilus* is not, as some have seen it, an inconsistent repudiation of life by one who seems to have enjoyed and accepted it. It is rather, like the *Balade de Bon Conseyl*, the expression of the belief and feeling on which Chaucer's acceptance of life was based. The "trouthe" that will deliver one is the "trouthe" placed in Him who, as the poet said in the epilogue, "nyl falsen no wight, . . . That wol his herte al holly on him leye." It was because he did believe "trouthe" would avail in the end that Chaucer, in spite of sorrow which he saw and felt, could accept life as he did in the Canterbury Tales and would have Troilus say for him as did another earthly lover in Dante's Paradise—

> Non però qui si pente, ma si ride.
> [Yet here we repent not, but smile. Par., ix, 103.]

Notes

[1] W. C. Curry, "Destiny in Troilus and Criseyde" [reproduced above, pp. 34-70; see pp. 66 ff.].

2 J. P. Tatlock, "The Epilog of Chaucer's *Troilus*," *MP*, XV (1920-21), 146.

3 G. L. Kittredge, *Chaucer and his Poetry* (Cambridge, Mass.: Harvard University Press, 1915), p. 143.

4 See R. K. Root, ed., *The Book of Troilus and Criseyde* (Princeton: Princeton University Press, 1945), Introduction, p. 1.

5 F. N. Robinson, ed. *The Complete Works of Geoffrey Chaucer* (Boston: Houghton Mifflin Co., 1957), pp. 388-9.

6 Dante, *Paradiso*, III, 70-2, 79-87; trans. P. W. Wicksteed (London: J. M. Dent & Sons, *The Temple Classics*, 1930).

7 Etienne Gilson, *The Spirit of Mediaeval Philosophy*, trans. A. H. C. Downes (New York, 1936), p. 271.

8 *Of the Imitation of Christ*, III, 42.

9 Dante, *Purgatorio*, XVII, 91-9; XVIII, 62-3, 70-2; trans. Thomas Okey (London: J. M. Dent & Sons, *The Temple Classics*, 1930).

10 N. E. Griffin and A. B. Myrick, trans. *The* Filostrato *of Giovanni Boccaccio* (Philadelphia: University of Pennsylvania Press, 1929), VIII, 29-30.

11 Augustine, *Confessiones*, IV, 11; trans. E. B. Pusey (London: J. M. Dent & Sons, *Everyman's Library*, 1932).

8

The Two Moralities of Chaucer's *Troilus and Criseyde*

ALEXANDER J. DENOMY, C.S.B.

In the *Troilus and Criseyde* Chaucer's avowed purpose is to recount the double sorrows of the Trojan prince in loving the daughter of the traitor priest Calchas. In the first three books he tells of the suffering that Troilus underwent before his love was brought to a successful issue; in the last two, of his pangs and torments when separated from Criseyde, his futile expectation of her, and her infidelity. In his little tragedy it is quite evident that two moralities are involved: that which informs the romance itself and according to which the characters act and live; and that of Chaucer and the world in which he lived and wrote. Chaucer the Christian lived according to Christian morality based on the commandments of God, the teaching of Christ and of His Church; so did the world of the late fourteenth century. As regards the relationship of the sexes, it taught the sinfulness of extra-marital relations and sexual self-indulgence, the ideal of self-mastery and self-discipline. From the point of view, then, of Chaucer

Reprinted, by permission of the Congregation of St. Basil and of the Royal Society of Canada, from *Transactions of the Royal Society of Canada*, Vol. XLIV, Ser. III, sec. 2 (June, 1950), pp. 35-46. For a critical review of Father Denomy's views on courtly love, see Theodore Silverstein, "Andreas, Plato, and the Arabs: Remarks on Some Recent Accounts of Courtly Love," *MP*, XLVII (1949-50), 117-26. For an interpretation of Andreas Capellanus which differs from Father Denomy's see D. W. Robertson, "The Subject of the *De amore* of Andreas Capellanus," *MP*, L (1952-53), 145-61.

and of his audience and readers, the story of Troilus and Criseyde was immoral and their love sinful and damnable.

If that were all, one might dismiss the romance as unchristian and Troilus and Criseyde as devoid of Christian principles. But there is something more. Troilus and Criseyde are not immoral Christians, though their speech, dress, and social customs are those of fourteenth-century England. Nor are they self-indulgent pagans, though the scene of their activity is laid in pagan Troy. The fact is that they are courtly lovers living according to a code of morality wholly divorced from Christianity and paganism, a code of morality that is not only unchristian but heretical and which had been condemned as such some hundred years before Chaucer wrote his story. According to the code of Courtly Love, their love and behaviour are necessary and praiseworthy, their love a source of ennoblement and growth in excellence.

The existence of the elements of Courtly Love in the *Troilus and Criseyde* has often been noted and studied—by Dodd, Kirby, Young, by almost all who have had occasion to write on the romance. This paper is confined to the morality of Courtly Love which informs the story, its basis, and how Chaucer met the challenge of its antinomy to Christian morality.

If we would know the basis of the morality of Courtly Love, then it is only fair to go back to the troubadours of the twelfth century of the south of France who introduced it into literature. For them, the basic, essential characteristic of Courtly Love is the irresistibility of love on the one hand and the ennobling force of love on the other. No one is exempt from the service of the god of love who rules this world, while extra-marital sexual love, sinful in Christian eyes, is the ennobling force in this world. Mark that it is not merely *an* ennobling force; it is the *sole* source of worldly worth and excellence. These are the two characteristics that make Courtly Love be Courtly Love. The other characteristics, conceits, and affectations are but trappings of these essential principles, assimilated to them as they might be assimilated to any other conception of human love. The personification of love as a god, the conception of this world as his kingdom, the feudalistic relationship of lover and beloved, his humility and timidity, her haughtiness and disdain, the physical manifestations of unrequited love, the moaning and groaning, wailing and whining, tears and sighs, the need of secrecy and stealth, the fear of gossip and scandalmongers are not peculiar to Courtly Love but are universally human and belong to the general body of love literature. It is, however, these very trappings—so ludicrous when exaggerated—that have obscured the essential factors of Courtly Love, have caused it to be confounded with romantic love, and have brought it so into disrepute among critics and historians of literature that its very existence in literature has been challenged.

From these essentials of Courtly Love, its irresistibility and the conception of it as the sole source and font of human worth and excellence, follows the moral code that governs the actions of lovers. Since love is irresistible, then nothing done under the compulsion of love can be immoral; since man is worthless unless he acts under the compulsion of love, the necessity of practising love is incumbent on every man. Therefore, Courtly Love not only approves and encourages whatever fans and provokes sensual desire, it not only condones fornication, adultery, and sacrilege, but it represents them as necessary sources of what it calls virtue.[1]

Furthermore, love must be in accord with the nature of man, not with the nature that he has in common with the animals but with his *rational* nature. Love is a union of heart and mind as well as of bodies. What is contrary to Courtly Love is sensuality for its own sake, the enjoyment of fleshly delights of and for themselves. This is not love but lust, the counterfeit of true love. Such love is practised by the wanton and the promiscuous. Hence, in the courtly code the importance of fidelity as one of its greatest virtues and infidelity as one of its greatest vices.

In the *Troilus and Criseyde*, Chaucer expounds the might and goodness of love in the Proem to Book III, and in the song of Troilus in praise of love late in the same book [1744-71], a song which picks up again the thought and theme of the Proem. In these passages, he teaches the doctrine taken from Boethius [*De cons.* II. m.8], and ultimately from Plato [*Symposium* 186A-B, *Timaeus* 32C] that it is universal love which rules the world, celestial and earthly, which unites all varied beings in harmony, and directs and disposes all things to goodness. It is in love that all beings have their existence and from which they derive their worth:

> God loveth, and to love wol nought werne;
> And in this world no lyves creature
> Withouten love is worth, or may endure.   (III, 12-14)

> Algates hem that ye wol sette a-fyre,
> They dreden shame, and vices they resygne;
> Ye do hem corteys be, fresshe and benigne.   (III, 24-6)

Love dominates all things, binds them together and to itself, so that all creatures desire to unite themselves to love as to their final end; human love is a phase of that universal law that brooks no opposition:

> So wolde God, that auctour is of kynde,
> That with his bond Love of his vertu liste
> To cerclen hertes alle, and faste bynde,
> That from his bond no wight the wey out wiste.
>   (III, 1765-8)

> Ye folk a lawe han set in universe;
> And this knowe I by hem that lovers be,
> That whoso stryveth with yow hath the werse.
>   (III, 36-8)

Chaucer sets forth these same characteristics expressly in two other passages: the "Cantus Antigone" and the poet's digression on the nature of love following Troilus' scorn of lovers and mockery of love. In the former, Antigone sings in praise of love a song that is designed to calm Criseyde's fear and anxieties at the dominance of love over her. It was composed, as Antigone says, by

>   the goodlieste mayde
>   Of gret estat in al the town of Troye,
>   And let hire lif in moste honour and joye.   (II, 880-2)

In the "Cantus" Chaucer establishes in positive fashion the ennobling effects of love:

> And thanked be ye, lord, for that I love!
> This is the righte lif that I am inne,
> To flemen alle manere vice and synne:
> This dooth me so to vertu for t'entende,
> That day by day I in my wille amende.   (II, 850-4)

Then in negative fashion he points out that love is not a vice or a servitude:

> And whoso seith that for to love is vice,
> Or thraldom, though he feele in it destresse,
> He outher is envyous, or right nyce,
> Or is unmyghty, for his shrewednesse,
> To loven; for swich manere folk, I gesse,
> Defamen Love, as nothing of him knowe.   (II, 855-60)

In his aside on the nature of love, the poet makes two points. First, it is in accord with man's nature that he should love. Just as the cavorting Bayard is made to realize by the lash that he is a horse subject to the laws that govern horses, so Troilus is made to realize by a look from Criseyde that he is a man subject to love by his very nature:

> For evere it was, and evere it shal byfalle,
> That Love is he that alle thing may bynde,
> For may no man fordon the lawe of kynde.   (I, 236-8)

Secondly, it is fitting that this should be so because of the effects of love:

> And trewelich it sit wel to be so.
> For alderwisest han therwith ben plesed;
> And they that han ben aldermost in wo,
> With love han ben comforted moost and esed;
> And ofte it hath the cruel herte aspesed,
> And worthi folk maad worthier of name,
> And causeth moost to dreden vice and shame.
>   (I, 246-52)

Therefore, since love is so virtuous by its very nature and cannot be gainsaid, one may not refuse to be subject to love:

> Now sith it may nat goodly ben withstonde,
> And is a thing so vertuous in kynde ,
> Refuseth nat to Love for to ben bonde,
> Syn, as hymselven liste, he may yow bynde.   (I, 253-6)

In these passages, the poet sets forth the theory of the irresistibility of love and of its ennobling power; the theory is put into practice in the action of the romance. Both essentials are apparent throughout. Once caught by love dwelling in the subtle streams of the eyes of Criseyde, Troilus feels its irresistible force. He has no choice but to surrender completely to it:

> O Lord, now youres is
> My spirit, which that oughte youres be.
> Yow thanke I, lord, that han me brought to this.
>   (I, 422-4)

In his complaint to Pandarus before he reveals the name of
his beloved, he apostrophizes love:

> Love, ayeins the which whoso defendeth
> Hymselven most, hym alderlest avaylleth. . . .
>
> (I, 603-4)

And Criseyde, in defending herself to Troilus against the
charge of arousing his jealousy, explains to him the force
that drives her to love him:

> Lo, herte myn, as wolde the excellence
> Of love, ayeins the which that no man may
> Ne oughte ek goodly make resistence. . . .   (III, 988-90)

In fact, the role of Fortune seems to be to help by external
necessity bring to consummation the love that drives Troilus
by inner necessity. Chaucer seems to have linked these two
forces as the *deus ex machina* of his romance: joining the
inner necessity of love to the exterior necessity of Fortune.

Never do the lovers exhibit the least concern or remorse
for what in Christian eyes is illicit and sinful love. There is no
moral barrier to forbid Criseyde practising love. After all, as
she says, she is no celibate bound by vow. Her concern is for
the secrecy that must protect her honour and her good name.
In the Greek camp she is remorseful at her infidelity but never
at her love. When, near the beginning of the poem, she
weighs the pros and cons of granting Pandarus' pleas that she
accept Troilus as her servant in love, she says:

> Shal I nat love, in cas if that me leste?
> What, par dieux! I am naught religious.
> And though that I myn herte sette at reste
> Upon this knyght, that is the worthieste,
> And kepe alwey myn honour and my name,
> By alle right, it may do me no shame.   (II, 757-63)

And much later, after she becomes the beloved of Troilus,
when he tries to persuade her to fly with him before the exchange is made, it is her good repute that is uppermost in
her mind:

> And also thynketh on myn honeste,
> That floureth yet, how foule I sholde it shende.
>
> (IV, 1576-7)

The effect of love in Troilus is apparent once Pandarus
gives him hope of its successful issue:

> For he bicom the frendlieste wighte,
> The gentilest, and ek the mooste fre,
> The thriftiest and oon the beste knyght,
> That in his tyme was or myghte be.
> Dede were his japes and his cruelte,
> His heighe port and his manere estraunge,
> And ecch of tho gan for a vertu chaunge.   (I, 1079-85)

After the union of the lovers, Troilus tells Pandarus of the "newe qualitee" he feels (III, 1654). Following his second meeting with Criseyde, Chaucer describes the effect that love has had on Troilus:

> And this encrees of hardynesse and myght
> Com hym of love, his ladies thank to wynne,
> That altered his spirit so withinne.   (III, 1776-8)

Not only did love effect an increase of worth, but it drove out every vice contrary to courtliness:

> Thus wolde Love, yheried be his grace,
> That Pride, Envye, and Ire, and Avarice
> He gan to fle, and everich other vice.   (III, 1804-6)

The irresistibility of love, love as the sole source of human worth, the moral code of Courtly Love based on these two principles, were formally condemned on March 7, 1277, by Archbishop Stephen Tempier at Paris as manifest and execrable errors. Among the 219 propositions then condemned as contrary to orthodoxy and good morals, the following expressly related to Courtly Love: (1) Simple fornication is not a sin.[2] (2) Chastity, i.e. abstinence by vow from illicit things, is not a greater good than perfect abstinence, i.e., abstinence from licit things; in other words, the clergy are no more bound to continence than are lay folk; the married are no more bound than the unmarried.[3] (3) Continence, the virtue by which one abstains from venereal pleasures, is not essentially a virtue, i.e. a principle of good works.[4] (4) It is impossible that sin be committed in the superior powers of the soul, i.e., in the mind and will; thus sin is a result of brute passion and not of love.[5] (5) Finally, a body of propositions aimed at the destruction of the role of reason and its liberty of judgment in the exercise of the will. The will acts under the constraint, necessarily, of the desired object. The appetible object is the sole cause of the motion of the will.[6]

How did poets and writers who were Christian and how

did a world that was Christian accept a conception of love so
at variance with Christian morality and orthodoxy. The *De
amore* of Andreas Capellanus "the egregious," written 1184-6,
makes this very clear—by the device of the double truth. It
explains the antinomy between Courtly Love and Christianity
not in terms of reconciliation and compromise—they are
basically irreconcilable—but as they might exist side by side,
each within its own sphere: the mundane alongside the
spiritual, the natural alongside the supernatural, the temporal
alongside the eternal, the philosophical alongside the theological.

Andreas' main purpose in the *De amore* was to provide a
pseudo-philosophical and logical basis for the ideas and ideals
of the troubadours. By reason and by arguments based on the
nature of love and of man, he showed that love is the greatest
good in this world, that it constitutes earthly felicity and
beatitude, and that it is the font and origin of all good here
on earth. Andreas sought to show as a necessary conclusion
of reason that, if man is viewed solely as a rational and
natural creature, subject only to the laws of nature and reason, then reason and nature demand that he enrol in the
army of the god of love, that he seek the pleasures of the
flesh so that he may be ennobled and grow in virtue and in
worth.

As a scholar and as a cleric, Andreas was quite aware not
only of the immoral but also of the heretical implications involved in the *De amore*. So he wrote the *De reprobatione
amoris,* the rejection and condemnation of Courtly Love.
There he replaced the natural and rational conception of man
of the *De amore* with the Christian conception of man as a
supernatural creature, a child of God by grace, with an end
wholly different from the natural beatitude he had proposed
in the *De amore*. In presenting the case of Christian morality
against Courtly Love, Andreas appealed to Scripture and to
divine authority to show as true that man must set aside all
human love and seek the love of God alone, that human love
is loathsome and sordid, evil and the source of evil, that
women by their very nature are weak and vicious, infected
with every vice and frailty.[7]

In the *De amore* we are exclusively on the level of reason
and nature; in the *De reprobatione* on that of faith and grace.
Thus there is built up an opposition between the *De amore*

and the *De reprobatione*, between the rational and natural teaching of the former and the theological teaching of the latter. In them is seen erected an opposition between nature and grace, between reason and faith, between philosophy and theology. What Andreas taught to be necessary according to nature and reason, he teaches to be false according to grace and Revelation. Thus emerges in his work the doctrine of the so-called "double truth."

Included *nominatim* in the condemnation of 1277, therefore, was the *De amore* grouped with Latin Averroists' dogmas and the teachings of those "who say that things may be true according to philosophy but not according to Faith just as if there were two contradictory truths."[8]

It is not unreasonable to suppose that Chaucer knew of the condemnation of 1277, one of the great events in the history of medieval philosophy. With his interest in, and knowledge of, philosophical problems and with the opportunity he had of acquiring knowledge of them at home, in France and Italy, he could very easily have been acquainted with the condemned propositions and the so-called double truth with which Courtly Love is so intimately connected. Chaucer must have been aware of the dangers involved in writing a romance of Courtly Love—the risk of an accusation of teaching or, at least, of upholding immorality and the accusation of heresy. Andreas Capellanus had been condemned on both counts.

Chaucer, I think, consciously set out to meet these dangers by three devices. Unlike Andreas, he was not teaching Courtly Love *ex professo*. He was concerned not with giving Courtly Love a logical or philosophical basis but with using it as a background for a story he had to tell. In the case of Andreas, heresy is actually and expressly taught and defended. With Chaucer an immoral and heretical teaching is utilized as a vehicle.

Both made retractions, Andreas in his *De reprobatione amoris*, Chaucer in his Palinode at the end of the poem and in a more general way at the end of his *Canterbury Tales*. There is, furthermore, this difference between them. Andreas, as a Christian, rejects, disapproves of, and condemns Courtly Love but he does not repudiate it; [for him] as a philosopher, it remains the necessary conclusion of reason and nature. His method was to establish a truth of the philosophical order but contrary to faith and then to posit along with that philo-

sophical truth the doctrine of faith. These two, the doctrine
of faith and the truth of the rational order, remain side by
side as if in separate compartments. Chaucer not only rejects,
disapproves of, and condemns, he repudiates Courtly Love as
vain, ephemeral, and fallacious, the blind effect of passion,
and that not only in the Palinode but within the very fabric
of the story itself. Courtly Love is repudiated both from the
pagan and from the Christian standpoint.[9] In a passage closely
imitated from the *Teseide* (XI, 1-3), where Boccaccio is describing the death of Arcite, Chaucer relates that after Troilus
is killed, his spirit ascends to the eighth sphere and from that
vantage point looks down on the world in which he had lived.
He sees then the vanity of his love in comparison with the
"pleyn felicite" of the heathen heaven; he condemns and repudiates man's blind pursuit of pleasure and the slavery of
the passions:

> And dampned al oure werk that foloweth so
> The blynde lust, the which that may nat laste. . .
> (v, 1823-4)

It is such love that has brought to naught his great worthiness,
his high character, and his royal estate. It is only then that
Chaucer exhorts the repudiation of all human love, licit and
illicit, as worldly vanity and a transitory thing, in favour of
the love of Christ who through love redeemed us all:

> And syn he best to love is, and most meke,
> What nedeth feynede loves for to seke?   (v, 1847-8)

Andreas, as he himself tells us, wrote his *De amore* from
experience and from personal knowledge. His manifest purpose was to teach his young friend Walter the theory and
practice of the art of love. Rightly does he call his teaching
"haec doctrina nostra" ["this, our teaching"]. His is the
moral responsibility for the doctrine contained therein. Chaucer states again and again that he is not writing on love from
personal knowledge gained from experience or from his own
feelings on the subject.[10] In *The House of Fame,* he had told
us that he knew nothing of love: "I kan not of that faculte"
(I, 248) and in *The Parliament of Fowls* he states that all he
knew of love came from books:

> For al be that I knowe nat Love in dede,
> Ne wot how that he quiteth folk here hyre,

> Yit happeth me ful ofte in bokes reede
> Of his myrakles and his crewel yre.
> There rede I wel he wol be lord and syre. . . .
>   (8-12)

So in the *Troilus and Criseyde* it is to definite sources, to authorities that he appeals: "Lollius," "myn auctour," "bokes olde." His purpose is to tell a story. He is careful to disavow any claim to originality:

> Forwhi to every lovere I me excuse,
> That of no sentement I this endite,
> But out of Latyn in my tonge it write.
> Wherfore I nyl have neither thank ne blame
> Of al this werk, but prey yow mekely,
> Disblameth me, if any word be lame,
> For as myn auctour seyde, so sey I.   (II, 12-18)

He refuses to be blamed should anyone be displeased at the actions of Troilus and the manner in which he won his beloved. It is his contention that different countries and times have their own laws and customs in matters of love. So, too, individuals differ in their approach to it. The love of Troilus and Criseyde belongs to antiquity, and to his modern English world what was valid a thousand years ago seems now foolish and strange. His stand is that whether his readers or audience like it or not, this is the story as he found it. If perchance he had added anything of his own, then it is for them to do as they wish with it. As for those who are adepts in the art of Courtly Love, what he has said they may use at their own discretion.

Chaucer's presumptive status is that of a non-participant in love—a rank outsider. As far as love and lovers are concerned, his role is that of its clerk, their servant and instrument to gladden them and advance them in their individual cause. He is not a participant because, as he puts it, "for myn unliklynesse" (I, 16)—his unsuitableness. Here and in *The House of Fame* where the eagle tells us that the poet has served Cupid and fair Venus "withoute guerdon" (II, 619), that he has never had part in the art of love (II, 628), the poet is thought to allude to his physical build and to his un-romantic personality (as he does again in the Prologue to *The Tale of Sir Thopas* (698 ff.) and in the *Lenvoy a Scogan* (25-8). His purpose in so doing was not merely to ward off chaff while reading aloud among his social superiors. I think there was the fear of incurring blame and displeasure, perhaps official, for what he knew to be not only immoral but also heretical. Chaucer did strive for orthodoxy. In the words of the good Parson:

> . . . this meditacioun
> I putte it ay under correccioun
> Of clerkes, for I am nat textueel;
> I take but the sentence, trusteth weel.
> Therfore I make a protestacioun
> That I wol stonde to correccioun.
>
> (Pars. T., prol., 55-60)

If it were not in fear, could it not be to salve a conscience thoroughly Christian, a conscience revolted at the utter incompatibility of Courtly Love with the tenets of Christian morality and faith? The direction of the *Troilus and Criseyde* to the moral Gower and to the philosophical Strode would assume something more than merely conventional form. Indeed, there were moral and philosophical doctrines that cried aloud for correction: the irresistibility of love, the ennobling power of love, and the doctrine of the double truth on which the necessity of the first two rested. Apart from the trappings of Courtly Love found in the *Tales* —for example, in the "deerne love" of *The Miller's Tale,* in the complaint of the peregrine falcon on the faithless tercelet in *The Squire's Tale,* the love of Aurelius for the faithful Dorigen in *The Franklin's Tale*—it is significant, I think, that Chaucer never after the *Troilus and Criseyde* ventured to write a full-fledged romance of Courtly Love. If you will recall, Chrétien de Troyes never ventured into that field after his *Lancelot.*

At the very end of *The Canterbury Tales,* the *Troilus and Criseyde* is included in Chaucer's more general retraction along with his other works that betray worldly vanity, that are consonant with or tend towards sin, that are lecherous. These have been his guilt, these have been his sin:

> Wherfore I biseke yow mekely, for the mercy of God, that ye preye for me that Crist have mercy on me and foryeve me my giltes; and namely of my translacions and enditynges of worldly vanitees, the whiche I revoke in my retracciouns: as is the book of Troilus; the book also of Fame; the book of the xxv Ladies; the book of the Duchesse; the book of Seint Valentynes day of the Parlement of

Briddes; the tales of Caunterbury, thilke that sownen into synne; the book of the Leoun; and many another book, if they were in my remembrance, and many a song and many a leccherous lay; that Crist for his grete mercy foryeve me the synne.

Notes

1 Cf. A. J. Denomy, *"Fin' Amors:* The Pure Love of the Troubadours, Its Amorality, and Possible Source," *Mediaeval Studies,* VII (1945), 142-3, 175-9.

2 "Quod simplex fornicatio, utpote soluti cum soluta, non est peccatum" ["That simple fornication, as between a single man and single woman, is not a sin"]. *Chartularium Universitatis Parisiensis,* ed. Denifle and Chatelain, I (Paris, 1889), no. 183, p. 553. Cf. Pierre Mandonnet, *Siger de Brabant et l'Averroisme latin au XIIIe siècle* (Louvain, 1908; 2nd ed.), II, no. 205, p. 190.

3 "Quod castitas non est maius bonum quam perfecta abstinentia" ["That chastity is not a greater good than perfect abstinence"]. *Chartularium,* no. 181, p. 553; Mandonnet, no. 209, p. 190.

4 "Quod continentia non est essentialiter virtus" ["That continence is not in essence a virtue"]. *Chartularium,* no. 168, p. 553; Mandonnet, no. 208, p. 190.

5 "Quod non est possibile esse peccatum in potentiis animi superioribus. Et ita peccatum fit passione non voluntate" ["That it is impossible for sin to exist in the superior powers of the soul. Thus, sin arises from passion not from will"]. *Chartularium,* no. 165, p. 552; Mandonnet, no. 167, p. 189.

6 Cf. A. J. Denomy, "The *De amore* of Andreas Capellanus and the Condemnation of 1277," *Mediaeval Studies,* VIII (1946), 118-25.

7 *Ibid.,* 125-48.

8 "Dicunt enim ea esse vera secundum philosophiam, sed non secundum fidem catholicam, quasi sint due contrarie veritates" ["For they say that those things are true from the standpoint of philosophy, but not from the standpoint of the catholic faith, as if there were two opposed truths"]. *Chartularium,* p. 543; Mandonnet, p. 175.

9 Cf. Karl Young, "Chaucer's Renunciation of Love in *Troilus and Cressida,"* MLN, XL (1925), 270ff.

10 Cf. Marshall W. Stearns, "A Note on Chaucer's Attitude towards Love," *Speculum,* XVII (1942), 570-4.

9

The Significance of Chaucer's Revisions of *Troilus and Criseyde*

CHARLES A. OWEN, JR.

The substantial revisions that Chaucer made in *Troilus and Criseyde*, occurring as they do in a poem so carefully constructed, should give us important insights into Chaucer's own conception of his work. What aspects of it did he feel to be inadequate? What elements was he trying to strengthen, to bring out more clearly?

The revisions apparently started even as he was writing the work. Professor Root found evidence in the manuscripts that the proems to Books II, III, and IV were detachable from Chaucer's fair copy.[1] If these passages were added, as seems likely, they were added before the poem was finished and probably before Chaucer had written very far into the fourth book. For the proem to that book invokes the aid of the Furies and Mars in words that make it clear that this was originally to be the final book of the poem:[2]

> This ilke ferthe book me helpeth fyne
> So that the losse of lyf and love yfeere
> Of Troilus be fully shewed here   [IV, 28].

The evidence here adduced points to two significant conclusions. Chaucer was intent on even more clearly defining the structure of his poem, on stressing the distinct tone of

Reprinted, by permission of author and publisher, from *Modern Philology*, LV (1957-8), 1-5. Copyright, 1957, by the University of Chicago.

each of his books. At the same time, he was exploring his subject matter for the structure most appropriate to it. What at one time he felt confident of bringing to a close in four books resisted the pattern he was seeking to impose, a pattern foreshadowed in the opening lines of the *Parlement of Foules* and in keeping with medieval notions of tragedy. In the *Parlement of Foules* he had written of love:

> The lyf so short, the craft so long to lerne,
> Th' assay so hard, so sharp the conquerynge,
> The dredful joye, alwey that slit so yerne.

Here we find the same emphasis on the development of love that a *Troilus and Criseyde* in four books would have presented. But, as Chaucer worked on the end of his poem, he discovered more in the slipping away of "dredful joye" than a stereotype of medieval tragedy, than the sudden fall from high estate, the quick turn of fortune's wheel. He found matter as revealing of his characters, as significant thematically, and demanding a treatment as extensive as what he had earlier covered in his first two books.

The symmetry that resulted [from the story's extension into a fifth book] helped to set off the contrasting parallels that had always been an important part of Chaucer's design. The prayers at beginning and end, Troilus' two sorrows, his manner of wooing Criseyde and Diomede's, the impending union and the impending separation of the lovers, the intrusion of love into society and the intrusion of society into love, balanced one another across the keystone of the third book and at the same time helped to define one another by contrast.

This structure of contrasting parallels explicit in Pandarus' "Of two contraries is o lore" (I, 645) was accentuated by the next major step in revision.[3] The addition of Troilus' hymn to love at the end of Book III [1744-71] and of his ascent to the eighth sphere at the end of Book v [1807-27] reinforced both the symmetry of structure and the definition by contrast in the poem.

Troilus' ascent to the eighth sphere, from which he looks back on the earth and laughs inwardly at the passions and vanity of worldly life, balances and contrasts with his earlier laughter, his mocking of lovers in the first book. Thus the consummation of love in the third book is framed by the two

contrasting sorrows; those, in turn, by the two contrasting
laughters; and those, in turn, by the two contrasting prayers.
The two prayers point up the opposition between courtly love
and the love of God, the "two contraries" that form "o lore"
both in the exaltation of the third book and in the betrayal
of the fifth. The first laughter is one of ignorance and pride.
But, even so, it helps to give the first sorrow its comic overtones, especially when recalled by Pandarus after Troilus'
confession. For the second sorrow, however, for the human
weakness that makes betrayal inevitable, only a cosmic vision
can create a comic perspective. By permitting us to follow
Troilus to this cosmic vision, Chaucer provides a transition to
the deeply religious tone of the ending as well as a contrast to
the earlier laughter. The stanzas are evidence that Chaucer
recognized the artistic problem inherent in the Christian
ending of his poem and that he was aware in his efforts to
solve it of the symmetry of design as an important structural
element.

The symmetry of the poem as a whole is mirrored by the
symmetry of the third book, especially after Chaucer added
Troilus' hymn to love at the end of the book. These stanzas
translated from Boethius match the stanzas in the proem
translated from Boccaccio, both passages emphasizing the
power of love. Between these two exaltations of love the
action of the book takes place, the meeting of the lovers in
Deiphebus' house and their second meeting in Pandarus'
house inclosing the great central consummation scene. Why
did the discovered symmetry of his subject matter so appeal
to Chaucer? Why did he seek to strengthen it in these two
added passages? One of the possible reasons—the strengthening of the contrasting parallels through which he had already
sought to sharpen and define his subject matter—has already
been given. Another reason is connected with the series of
nature images through which the fulfilment of love is in part
envisaged. These images which cluster around the consummation— the lark in the grasp of the hawk, the trembling
aspen leaf, the woodbine entwining the tree, the nightingale
singing securely—suggest the world of nature in which the
cycle of growth, maturity, and decay is inevitable. The symmetry of the poem thus brings love into relation with the fate
of living things in nature and suggests both the inevitability
of the end and the infinite variety of forms within the basic

pattern. Love in this world follows a course in which the nature of the lovers expresses itself and yet confirms fate. It is both free and predestined.

The relationship of this point to Troilus' soliloquy in the temple [IV, 953-1085] is apparent, but, before taking up the effect of this third added passage, something more needs to be said about the song to love and the ascent of Troilus to the eighth sphere. We have already seen how Troilus' cosmic vision after death served as transition to the religious view of the action at the close. By linking this view more effectively with the poem, the passage enhances the impact of the religious ending. At practically the same time, Chaucer was writing for Troilus his hymn to love in which worldly love is given its most exalted expression. Love is here the cosmic principle that holds in concord the elements, the peoples, the spheres:

> "And if that Love aught lete his bridel go,
> Al that now loveth asonder sholde lepe,
> And lost were al that Love halt now to-hepe."
>   [III, 1762-4]

The two "contraries" seem irreconcilable. On the one hand, the love of Troilus for Criseyde ennobles the lovers and brings them in contact with the power that rules the universe. On the other hand, the choice of any but Christ as an object for devotion leads to inevitable betrayal:

> "And loveth hym, which that right for love
> Upon a crois, oure soules for to beye,
> First starf, and roos, and sit in hevene above;
> For he nyl falsen no wight, dar I seye."
>   [v, 1843-5]

That Chaucer should be strengthening both these irreconcilables in his revision of the poem shows, I think, his own conviction that, though irreconcilable, both were valid. Love between man and woman was capable at its best of generating a blessed state and a cosmic vision. The surrounding betrayals, while they validate the religious vision at the end, do not invalidate the love. The two ideals are held in a sort of tension by the poem, and only by the aid of both can we see either the full meaning of love or the full meaning of betrayal, meanings which it is the aim of the poem to define.

By far the longest and apparently the final addition to the poem is the 19-stanza soliloquy by Troilus on God's fore-knowledge and man's free will [IV, 953-1085]—like the hymn to love, a translation from Boethius. In this soliloquy, which comes just before the critical meeting between Troilus and Criseyde at the end of the fourth book, Troilus echoes Boethius in the *De consolatione,* finding in God's foreknowl-edge a clinching argument against freedom and responsibility for man and ignoring the later argument of Philosophy in which she convinces Boethius of his error. He ends his think-ing on the subject still in uncertainty and still in despair:

> "Almyghty Jove in trone,
> That woost of al this thyng the sothfastnesse,
> Rewe on my sorwe, and do me deyen sone,
> Or bryng Criseyde and me fro this destresse."
>
> [IV, 1079-82]

Perhaps the most interesting problem connected with this long passage is how Chaucer could have allowed his hero to pon-der his problem at such length and give so little thought to Criseyde. The answer would seem to be either extreme in-eptitude on Chaucer's part or a motivated avoidance by Troilus. The second solution becomes more plausible when we recognize in the final lines (the ones that were earliest written),[4] not just a conclusion to the argument, but a decision by Troilus— a decision to leave his fate in the hands of al-mighty Jove rather than follow Pandarus' suggestion and carry off Criseyde. The long soliloquy on fate and free will, in which Troilus carefully avoids facing the specific altern-atives, represents his internal struggle: Can he take effective action to retain Criseyde? Or is action futile in a predestined world? The general terms in which he argues his problem re-sult from the idealism of his nature in part, but they also represent his instinctive recognition that no thought is possible if he allows the impending loss of Criseyde to engross his mind. His decision to leave everything in the hands of God releases him from his effort to think things through, permits him once more to bring Criseyde and the overwhelming hope-lessness of their position consciously to mind. It also accounts for his lack of initiative in the meeting with Criseyde. Finally, however, he is so appalled by the flimsiness of Criseyde's plans for return that he is forced to fall back on Pandarus' suggestion. Even then he yields to Criseyde after only a feeble effort to persuade her. And on the morrow he helps to deliver her into the hands of the "sodeyn Diomede."

Chaucer added the soliloquy then because he wanted to focus attention at this point on Troilus and show Criseyde's departure as more clearly dependent on Troilus' decision. That we are to see this deference for Criseyde as admirable and at the same time misguided is clear from a number of passages. Both Troilus and Criseyde later regret their not having followed Pandarus' advice. Diomede needs no friend's aid to win Criseyde from what she recognizes, even in yielding, as a nobler love. And much earlier Criseyde's dream of the eagle had shown her instinctive need of a decisive lover. The soliloquy further performs the function of internalizing the action at this crucial point in the fourth book, so that we shall be aware of the characters as sentient human beings struggling against their own ignorance and a hostile world to think their way through their problems. In this respect it matches Criseyde's efforts in the second book to think out her proper response to Troilus' love. The irony of Troilus' coming to a decision through a train of thought that rejects freedom of the will was perhaps no small part of the passage's appeal to Chaucer.

Finally, the passage calls attention to the problem of freedom of the will. Does it represent Chaucer's own position in the matter? Certainly the role of destiny is a big one in the poem. Though Pandarus and later Diomede make effective conscious decisions, the efforts of men to shape their ends are for the most part weak and futile. So long as we think of freedom in terms of conscious choice, the poem gives little scope for it, especially for the lovers. On the other hand, the action in the poem is determined in large measure by the character of the actors. Troilus may be struck suddenly by love, but his response to the situation is an expression of his character. Throughout the poem we watch men and women moving and thinking and feeling. Frequently they are victims of their own self-deception. But their actions emerge; they are not imposed. Chaucer was presenting, I think, the paradox of Boethius in his poem. To the intelligence of the Maker all is known and determined in an eternity that is ever present. The Maker is God in the world, the Poet in his poem. But within the world of time and to the limited awareness of man some things are determined, other things are free. As Boethius put it, the sunrise is determined, but the man walking is free. We can see this paradox in the poem working in the fate of the lovers, which we know from the start, which yet we watch them work out and choose and deserve. We can see it also in the fate of the city which casts such an influence over the fate of the lovers. Troy is doomed from the start, and the first action in the poem is Calchas' desertion of what he knows to be a lost cause. But at the very moment when the fate of the city is casting its most fateful influence over the lovers, we watch the Trojans, in parliament assembled, choose Antenor, the city's betrayer, despite Hector's arguments to the contrary, despite the clear immorality of the procedure.

In *Troilus and Criseyde* Chaucer was working out his subject in the same experimental way that led to such a large proportion of fragments in his complete works. Though his revisions started, as later in the *Canterbury Tales,* before the poem was finished, they were not nearly so extensive. For the only time in his career Chaucer's inspiration carried him through, not just to a conclusion, but to a subsequent revision of the completed poem. The changes he made had both formal and thematic significance. Not only did they strengthen the contrasting parallels and the symmetry of the poem's structure, but they made more explicit the thematic oppositions which the poem holds in tension, the opposition between fate and free will, the opposition between love and "charity."

Notes

1 Root, R. K. ed. *The Book of Troilus and Criseyde* (Princeton, 1945), pp. xii f.; see also Root, *The Textual Tradition of Chaucer's Troilus* ("Chaucer Society, First Series," Vol. XCIX [London, 1916]), pp. 23 ff.

2 See Root's edition of the poem, n. 6 of the introduction, the last paragraph on p. xiv; and Kemp Malone, *Chapters on Chaucer* (Baltimore, 1951), p. 120.

3 For Root's discussion of the following three passages added by Chaucer in revision [Troilus's hymn to love, III, 1744-71; his ascent to the eighth sphere, V, 1807-27; his soliloquy on fate vs. free will, IV, 953-1085] see his *Textual Tradition,* pp. 155-57, 216-21, 245-48, and 249 f.

4 See Root, *Textual Tradition,* pp. 218 f.

10

The Aube in Chaucer's *Troilus*

R. E. KASKE

In the medieval poetry of the Continent, one of the most distinctive lyric types is the aube, or dawn-poem. At its center is a simple dramatic situation, obviously related to the conventions of Courtly Love: A lover has spent the night secretly with his lady; shortly before morning they are awakened, usually by the warning of a watchman who has seen the first light of dawn; one or both voice their grief at the necessity of parting, and the lover sadly takes his leave. The lyric and dramatic possibilities of this situation are developed primarily through the manipulation of conventional motifs—for example, the lady's dispute with the watchman about the actual closeness of dawn; her arraignment of day for returning too soon; the lovers' mutual pledge of faithfulness and commitment of one another to God's protection; the danger of discovery by their enemies, particularly the lady's husband; and very often, their last-minute relapse into love-making despite such dangers. In the present paper, I will attempt to analyze the first and longer of the two "aube-passages" in *Troilus* (III, 1415-1533, 1695-1712) as a purposeful adaptation of this traditional poetic form.

However the aube may have reached Chaucer, it must have held a somehow significant place in his cultural reper-

Unpublished paper delivered before the Chaucer Group at the meeting of the Modern Language Association, Chicago, 1959. Printed with the author's permission. All translations are by the author.

tory. His echoes of the form in *Troilus* have long been recognized; and in a recent article[1] I have shown the existence of a parodic aube in the *Reeve's Tale*, centered in the farewell speeches of Aleyn and Malyne (4236-47). Aleyn's speech is a little thesaurus of aube-clichés, duplicated many times over in Continental examples of the form:

> "Fare weel, Malyne, sweete wight!"
> The day is come, I may no lenger byde;
> But everemo, wher so I go or ryde,
> I is thyn awen clerk, swa have I seel!"   (4236-9)

Parodic incongruities are created by the surrounding situation itself; by the inelegant name "Malyne"; by Aleyn's anticlimactic burst of Northernisms in the final line; and by his substitution of "clerk" for the more conventional probability, "knyght." In such company, the lines with which Chaucer introduces Aleyn's speech—

> Aleyn wax wery in the dawenynge,
> For he had swonken al the longe nyght   (4234-5)

—clearly burlesque a contrasting situation in the aube, where the lover's limitations are apt to be less neatly synchronized with the arrival of dawn. In Malyne's reply, the opening and closing lines are a pair of commonplaces frequently juxtaposed in the aube—the granting of leave or *congié,* and the hope of God's protection for the lover:

> "Now, deere lemman," quod she, "go, far weel! . . .
> And, goode lemman, God thee save and kepe!"   ,
>   (4240, 4247)

Here, however, they sandwich incongruously Malyne's businesslike confession about the stolen meal (4241-6). And finally, Chaucer's modest description of her grief seems obviously designed to contrast with the more impressive lachrymal achievements of aube-ladies at such moments:

> And with that word almoost she gan to wepe.
>   (4248)

The argument for this parody in the *Reeve's Tale* is of course strongly supported by the existence of our acknowledged aube-passages in *Troilus.* The parody once admitted, however, demonstrates in turn that Chaucer was familiar enough with the aube not only to imitate it straightforwardly, but also to use the poetic form itself as a vehicle for comic allusion. One wonders inevitably whether he has made similarly oblique uses of the aube in *Troilus*.

The question is complicated at the outset by the fact that nearly all our surviving examples of the medieval aube—including those most pertinent to our problem—are in languages that Chaucer presumably did not know. Briefly, the significant parallels to Chaucer's imitations of the form are all found in either French, Provençal, or German. On the one hand, the French *aubade* survives only in from four to six widely differing examples; while on the other, the Provençal *alba* is represented by eleven examples and the German *tagelied* by well over one hundred through the fifteenth century, including the most fully developed and dramatic ones.[2] This untidy distribution creates no real weakness in our argument for the parody in the *Reeve's Tale*, most of whose comparatively simple motifs are common to the *aubade*, the *alba*, and the *tagelied*. The long exchange of speeches in *Troilus*, however, represents a much more complex development of the form, hardly paralleled except in the German *tagelieder*. In interpreting the aube of *Troilus*, then, how far can we rely on this sizeable body of German poems—clearly belonging to a generally similar type, but so far as we know unlikely to have influenced Chaucer directly?

It seems to me that if the aube in *Troilus* does somehow reflect a traditional poetic form, the major components of that form can be recognized also in the *tagelieder*. A fundamental correspondence is the development of the basic situation by an exchange of speeches between the lovers—a development found in most *tagelieder*, but in only one highly uncharacteristic Romanic aube.[3] Again, the sequence of aube-motifs in *Troilus* follows an order generally familiar in the *tagelieder*: the discovery of dawn by the lady; the complaint about the shortness of night and the arrival of day; the expression of the pains of parting; the question concerning faithfulness and the answering pledge; and the final appeal for God's protection.[4] Both of these patterns in *Troilus* result to a great extent, of course, from Chaucer's direct dependence on Boccaccio's *Filostrato* (III, 43-53) and the prose *Roman de Troyle;* for the moment, my point is simply that within the aube-tradition as we know it, they are matched only in the *tagelieder*. A more specific correspondence—not paralleled in the *Filostrato*—is provided by the astronomical description of dawn that introduces the aube of *Troilus*, including references to Lucifer the morning-star (1417-18) and the heaven of the fixed stars (1419-20). Such passages are unknown in Romanic aube; in the *tagelieder* they form a progressively consistent and elaborate motif, marked by especially frequent references to both the *morgenstern* and the *firmament*.[5] Finally, there are the extended addresses to night and day in *Troilus* (1427-70), practically all of which are Chaucer's addition; within the aube, as we shall see, direct addresses of this kind are found nowhere but in the *tagelieder*. Though individually any of these correspondences might be explained as coincidence, I would find it difficult to believe that this combination of them did not point to a conventionalized and fairly distinct poetic form, which must be assumed as somehow underlying both the *tagelieder* and the aube of *Troilus*. Later evidence can be found in the famous "aube-passage" of *Romeo and Juliet* (III, v, 1-64), whose basic pattern is also closely paralleled in the *tagelieder* but not in Romanic aube. This whole argument for the relevance of the *tagelied*, in turn, speaks indirectly also for the relevance of the less fully developed Provençal *alba*, since every motif in the *alba* that is in any way pertinent to our present problem is duplicated in either the French *aubade*, or the *tagelied*, or both. My governing assumption in the remainder of this paper, then, is that all our extant specimens of the aube in French, Provençal, and German—together with Chaucer's own parody of the form in the *Reeve's Tale* —have at least potential relevance for a cautious interpretation of the aube in *Troilus*.

A second complicating factor is Chaucer's dependence on the *Filostrato* for well over half of what I consider to be the first aube-passage. My proposed explanation is that Chaucer saw in this part of the *Filostrato* a latent aube-pattern inadvertently created by the narrative and Boccaccio's treatment of it, and that through various changes and additions he elaborated this hint into a recognizable aube. His result, however, is an aube whose broadly conventional design embraces a number of striking individual departures from what our surviving evidence seems to present as "typical"—some of them introduced by Chaucer, others adapted or simply carried over from the *Filostrato*. In particular, Chaucer seems

to have bestowed on Troilus several speeches usually assigned to the lady in an aube, and on Criseyde certain speeches
usually assigned to the lover, thus enriching a theme sometimes detected in other parts of the poem: the reversal of the
roles of man and woman as they are popularly or romantic-
ally conceived. Apart from some incidental burlesque of the
aube-form itself, the total effect of these distortions is to
give the human shortcomings of Troilus and Criseyde added
dimensions—both comic and pathetic—by projecting them
against the idealized unreality of the lovers in a more conventional aube.

At the beginning of our scene in the *Filostrato,* Criseida
hears the cocks crow for morning and exclaims,

> "Now it is time to rise,
> If well we wish to conceal our desire."   (III, 43, 3-4)

On the lips of Chaucer's Criseyde, the exhortation becomes,

> "For tyme it is to ryse and hennes go,
> Or ellis I am lost for evere mo!"   (1425-6)

No doubt the change is dictated partly by Chaucer's changes
in the situation itself, with Criseyde's waiting-women now
lodged in the adjoining room; but it would be difficult not to
recognize it also as a small signpost in his characterization of
Criseyde. Speeches on the necessity of parting and the pre-
servation of the lady's honor are commonplaces in the
medieval aube—most of whose ladies, in the courtly tradition
at any rate, have small patience with such irrelevancies. A
particularly strong example is the lady in an *alba* by Raimon
de la Sala, who replies to her watchman's report that he has
seen her husband already dressed and armed:

> "You alarm us not at all;
> Nor think, because of weapons,
> That I forego the play of my lover,
> Who lies happy in my arms. . . ."[6]

When the parting *is* urged by the lady, her emphasis is practically always on either the virtues of secrecy or the safety
of her lover. In the courtly *tagelieder,* a familiar pattern
makes her defy the first warnings of dawn but weaken when
she realizes the lover's actual danger. The lady's honor,
predictably enough, is a standard concern of both lover and
watchman, and in the late popular *tagelieder* the lady's con-

cern for her own honor increases almost to the point of
respectability; in only one of them, however, is there a real
parallel to Criseyde's explicit self-concern.[7] Chaucer's omis-
sion of the rest of our stanza in the *Filostrato* (43, 5-8)—in
which Criseida's desire for renewed lovemaking actually
suggests a common aube-motif—seems clearly to contribute
to this same characterization.

Chaucer's largest single addition to the aube-passage is the
arraignment of night spoken by Criseyde (1427-42) and the
arraignment of day spoken by Troilus (1450-70—the latter
represented by three lines in the *Filostrato* (III, 46, 4-6), and
both apparently modelled to some extent on a passage in the
Filocolo (I, 173). In the aube as we know it, Troilus' rhetorical address to day is paralleled only among the *tagelieder*,
in which such protests are a fairly frequent major motif and
with a few late exceptions are voiced by the lady. The
extreme is found in an apparently comic *tagelied* from a
fourteenth- or fifteenth-century manuscript, where the lady
personifies day as a somewhat unimaginative intruder:

> "Sir Lady-Robber, what do you want here?
> I, and many a noble woman, have small wish for you,
> And would gladly do without all your sun's brightness.
> Alas! that you don't stop and think—
> No woman has there been so lovely,
> So rich in charms,
> That you have not been anxious to reclothe her by such a
> deed."[8]

Criseyde's wish for longer night (1427-8) is a commonplace,
freely assigned to either of the lovers in an aube. Other
references to night are found chiefly in the later *tagelieder*,
and are much less frequent, elaborate, and uniform than the
addresses to day; where they do occur, they seem more characteristically assigned to the lover than to the lady.[9] On the
basis of this admittedly imperfect pattern, I would suggest
that within the context of his aube Chaucer has reversed the
conventional assignment of these two speeches—a suggestion
that will be supported indirectly by other details as we proceed.

The next seven stanzas (1471-1519) follow the *Filostrato*
fairly closely. In the process, however, they sharpen certain
contrasts between the two lovers, which in this new environment appear as inversions of familiar aube-motifs. For

example, Troilus' expression of his unwillingness to part
(1472-4), of his grief at parting (1475-80), and of his
burning desire to return (1481-4), are all decidedly more
elaborate and intense than any corresponding feelings voiced
by Criseyde; and the clear contrast between the fervor with
which Criseida in the *Filostrato* invites Troilo's return (III,
50), and Criseyde's almost noncommittal expression of the
same idea (1515-17), seems to leave no doubt about the
deliberateness of Chaucer's emphasis. Now it would be
obvious folly to overlook the general appropriateness of
such contrasts in the light of Courtly Love convention—not
to speak of womanly reserve. Yet in the aube, with a few
notable exceptions, it is the lover who is more nearly re-
signed to the necessity of parting, while the lady emotionally
opposes or laments his departure and begs for his quick return.[10] Chaucer's familiarity with such a pattern is strongly
implied by the parody in the *Reeve's Tale*, where Malyne's
almost weeping evidently burlesques this very convention of
extravagant grief.

Troilus' hesitant request for assurance (1485-91) and
Criseyde's long answering promise of faithfulness (1492-
1518) coincide with a motif that is particularly prominent in
the aube. Though there are strong exceptions, its prevailing
pattern seems to be that in which the lady introduces the
question of faithfulness, and the lover replies with an elaborate pledge in what might be described as the superlative
mood—illustrated, for example, in a *tagelied* by the Minnesinger Rubîn:

> She said: "Show me a lover's loyalty,
> And give me in the center of thy heart a place,
> That there I may be ruling lady."
> Then spoke the gallant knight:
> "Thy love has over my body so great a power,
> No greater might it be.
> Thou dwellest in my heart, woman most pure,
> So that never can a dearer thing befall me
> Than if I may see thee again, all wondrous.
> My heart will I pledge thee for thine own."[11]

The best evidence for a reversal of these speeches in *Troilus*,
however, is again the parody in the *Reeve's Tale*—whose
comic point seems clearly *not* to lie in a reversal of speakers,
and whose brief but highly conventional pledge of loyalty is
put into the mouth of Aleyn.

Criseyde's pledge is followed by Troilus' final brief reply (1525-6), corresponding to that of Troilo in the *Filostrato*,

> "I commend thee to God,
> And leave with thee my soul." (III, 51, 7-8)

This commitment of the loved one to God's care is a frequent motif in the aube, where it is freely assigned to either the lover or the lady. In addition, a sprinkling of miscellaneous appeals to God—though evident enough in most medieval romantic poetry, including *Troilus itself*—seems particularly characteristic of the aube, where the situation lends itself rather colorfully to such sentiments. In the *Filostrato,* the one reference to God in our entire scene is Troilo's appeal just quoted; in the aube of *Troilus* there are eleven such appeals (1430, 1437, 1456, 1470, 1481, 1501, 1503, 1509, 1512, 1518, 1526), most of them uncommonly gratuitous—Chaucer's playful bow, I take it, to this marked rhetorical feature. In particular, Criseyde's speech of reassurance builds up a kind of desperate concentration of them, apparently with the added implication that the lady is protesting too much—

> "As wisly verray God my soule save. . . ." (1501)
> "And, for the love of God that us hath wrought. . . ."
> "And, if I wiste sothly that to fynde, (1503)
> God myghte nat a poynt my joies eche. . . ." (1508-9)
>
> "For I am thyn, by God and by my trouthe! . . ."
> (1512)
> "As wisly God myn herte brynge at reste. . . ." (1518)

It is Troilus, however, who climaxes the series with a comparatively meaningful appeal to God, which by contrast strikes a note of painful sincerity:

> "Farewel, dere herte swete,
> Ther God us graunte sownde and soone to mete!"
> (1525-6)

This appeal to God for a speedy reunion—substituted by Chaucer for Troilo's commitment of his lady to God during his absence—corresponds to another though obviously related aube-motif. Concerning its possible conventional assignment within the aube, our evidence is, I think, too ambiguous and too limited in quantity to be very compelling; the most one can say is that the appeal itself seems a little more natural to

the lady's stationary and comparatively passive situation, and
that our surviving examples do seem, if anything, to point a
little more in her direction:

> "Alas for this, how will he return?
> May the protection of the Most High lead him once more
> into my arms."[12]

A stronger piece of evidence, however, is Chaucer's own
assignment of Malyne's two dispersed aube-lines in the
Reeve's Tale (4240, 4247)—which, though they under-
standably do not mention the lover's return, parallel the
speech of Troilus rather closely in their expression of farewell and of the hope for God's protection.

A final dramatic detail, setting off Chaucer's aube-passage
rather than falling within it, is the return of Troilus to his
own palace. The action itself appears also in the *Filostrato*:

> When Troilo had returned to the royal palace,
> Silently he went off to bed,
> To sleep at ease a little, if he could.   (III, 1-3)

Chaucer's version, however, produces what has always struck
me as a rather curious change of tone:

> Retorned to his real paleys soone,
> He softe into his bed gan for to slynke,
> To slepe longe, as he was wont to doone. . . .
>   (1534-6)

The last line seems brought about partly by Chaucer's own
understanding of the Italian,[13] and the passage that follows
(1537-47) turns the picture to other uses; still, it is hard to
see how Chaucer could have remained unaware of the touch
of farce created by his lines 1535-6.[14] In courtly aube, the
curtain falls discreetly on the lover's departure, preserving
around it an air of ardor undiminished and heroism som-
brely undaunted in the face of the undescribed separation and
hardships ahead. At the close of the aube in *Troilus* it is as
though the curtain had momentarily stuck, affording a small
anticlimactic glimpse of a world in which flesh and spirit have,
alas, their limitations. The joke is revived, as we have seen—
though with some decline in delicacy—to introduce the aube
of the *Reeve's Tale*.

A paper of this kind takes manifest advantage of its
audience, inflicting on them a body of documentation con-

tinually alluded to but seldom produced. Let me emphasize, therefore, that for none of these individual motifs is the evidence of the medieval aube quite so conclusive as one would wish. In every instance there are exceptions to the patterns I have been invoking as "conventional"; and in a few instances the number of examples available is suspiciously slight. What my collected data does show, however, is that within this recognizable frame Chaucer's handling of each of these motifs is nearly unparalleled so far as our examples go, or is the less usual of two distinct alternatives, or is in some other way peculiar. I suppose that even this pattern may not be altogether convincing—especially when one takes into account Chaucer's direct use of the *Filostrato,* and our own necessary reliance on the evidence of the *tagelieder* for several motifs. To it, however, we must add first the significant contrasts with Chaucer's own aube-parody in the *Reeve's Tale;* secondly, the several details in my analysis that are supported by the evidence not only of the medieval aube, but also of Chaucer's own alterations of the *Filostrato;* and third, the instances in which our combined evidence from the aube and the *Filostrato* agrees with, or heightens, touches of irony or burlesque for which the first hint is provided by the text itself—as for example Criseyde's "I am lost for evere mo," her string of appeals to God, and Troilus' homecoming. My proposed reversal of speakers seems to gain in plausibility from a somewhat similar reversal near the end of Book IV, where a substantial part of Criseyde's long speech (1667-82) is spoken in the *Filostrato* by Troilo (IV, 164-6).

If this interpretation is generally acceptable, the aube of *Troilus* takes form as a highly original thematic device, adding not only to the comedy in the psychological relations between Troilus and Criseyde, but also, less directly, to some of the motivations at work in their pathetic final outcome. Like all such interpretations, it points to further difficult questions. Does Pandarus—the sole confidant, sympathizer, and general accessory—assume temporarily the role of the watchman, who in the aube frequently plays a similar part? More important, to what extent does this unconventional "aube" remain at the level of sophisticated psychological comedy alone; and to what extent may it contribute also to an equally sophisticated philosophical or moral theme, such as have now and again been proposed for *Troilus?* I am not certain. Let me close, however, with a final provocative detail from the complaint of Troilus to day:

> "What profrestow thi light here for to selle?
> Go selle it hem that smale selys grave;
> We wol the nought, us nedeth no day have."
>
> (1461-3)

Besides apparently anticipating Criseyde's use of the "graving" image (1499), this unusual concept surely echoes Ecclesiasticus 38:28,

> So every craftsman and designer
> Who spends the night as well as the day,
> Who engraves small graven seals,
> And his diligence varies the image. . . .[15]

These diligent gravers of small seals form part of a catalogue of craftsmen (Ecclus. 38:26-39) whose skills are necessary to a city, but who nevertheless fall short of the highest wisdom. Against this context Troilus' exclamation sounds very much like a piece of unconscious irony, implying that while light may be useful enough in such secondary occupations, the works of profounder wisdom—like his own—are best matured in the dark.

Notes

[1] "An Aube in the *Reeve's Tale*," *ELH*, XXVI (1959), 295-310, which may serve also as an introduction and bibliographical supplement to the present paper. For a pair of slighter echoes in the *Merchant's Tale*, see "January's 'Aube'," *MLN*, LXXV (1960), 1-4.

[2] For the pertinent bibliography, see "Aube in the *Reeve's Tale*," p. 297, n. 8.

[3] The "Un petit devant le jor," ed. Karl Bartsch and Leo Wiese, *Chrestomathie de l'ancien francais* (12th ed.; Leipzig, 1920), pp. 218-20 (*CAF*).

[4] Among the courtly *tagelieder*, see especially Walther von der Vogelweide, "Friuntlichen lac," ed. Carl von Kraus (11th ed.; Berlin, 1950), pp. 123-6; and among the late popular *tagelieder*, "Woluff, woluff," ll. 55 ff., *Liederbuch der Clara Hätzlerin*, #23, ed. Carl Haltaus (Quedlinburg, 1840), pp. 27-8. Many other examples contain the same basic sequence with one or two omissions.

[5] For references, see Friedrich Nicklas, *Untersuchung über Stil und Geschichte des deutschen Tageliedes* (Germanische Studien, 72; Berlin, 1929), pp. 42-5, 109-10.

6 "Dieus, aidatz," ed. Karl Bartsch, *Provenzalisches Lesebuch* (Elberfeld, 1855), p. 101, ll. 56-62. See also the "En un vergier," st. 3, ed. Carl Appel, *Provenzalische Chrestomathie* (6th ed.; Leipzig, 1930), p. 90; Cadenet's "S'anc fui belha," st. V, ed. Appel, *Der Trobador Cadenet* (Halle, 1920), p. 81; the "Gaite de la tor," st. 3-5, *CAF* p. 168; Walther, especially 89:25-30, p. 125; and for further references in the *tagelieder*, Walter De Gruyter, *Das deutsche Tagelied* (Diss., Leipzig, 1887), pp. 34-7, 62-4, and Nicklas, *Untersuchung*, pp. 50 ff.

7 "Von hocher art," ll. 331-6, *Hätzlerin* #27, ed. Haltaus p. 36. For references to the subject generally, see De Gruyter, pp. 32, 37, 61, 65-6; and Nicklas, pp. 139-40.

8 "Ich singe, ich sage," st. 2, ed. Friedrich Heinrich von der Hagen, *Minnesinger* (Leipzig, 1838), III, 427. Other notable examples are Walther, 88:16-20, p. 123; Von Wissenlô, "Swer hînte," 3:4-7, and "Der wahter," st. 2, ed. Karl von Kraus, *Deutsche Liederdichter des 13. Jahrhunderts (Tübingen, 1952)*, I, 593-4 (*DL*); Heinrich Teschler, "Ein wahter sanc," ll. 13-8, ed. Bartsch, *Die schweizer Minnesänger* (Frauenfeld, 1886), p. 97 (*SM*); and Konrad von Würzburg, "Ich sihe den morgensternen,' ll. 31-8, ed. Ernst Scheunemann and Friedrich Ranke, *Texte zur Geschichte des deutschen Tageliedes* (Altdeutsche Übungstexte, 6; Bern, 1947), p. 27 (*TGT*). See also De Gruyter, pp. 34-5, 63; and Nicklas, pp. 51-2, 127-8. In Romanic aube, hatred of day is expressed by the lady, though not as a direct address, in the refrain of the "Cant voi l'aube," *CAF* p. 190. Troilus' rebuke specifically to the sun (1464-70)—itself adapted largely from Ovid's *Amores* i. 13, where the speaker is the poet or a male persona—finds a parallel within the aube in a spirited protest by the lady of Oswald von Wolkenstein's "Ich spür ain luft," ll. 43-7, *TGT* p. 33. Addresses to day and the sun are assigned to male speakers in some Renaissance approximations of the aube—as for example in the last two tercets of Ariosto's *Capitolo VIII*, and in Donne's "The Sunne Rising."

9 See especially the anonymous "In der naht wise," st. 2 and 5, ed. Von der Hagen, III, 428; and further, Nicklas pp. 107-8.

10 See generally De Gruyter, pp. 34-9, 62-7; and Nicklas, pp. 53-9, 69-71, 116-31. Note, however, the strong similarity between the speech of the lover in the *alba* "Us cavaliers," ll. 41-5, ed. Appel, *Prov. Chrest.*, p. 91; and that of Troilus in ll. 1481-3.

11 "Wie kunde leider," 1:7-9, 2:1-9, *DL* p. 355. Note also, for example, Ulrich von Lichtenstein, "Got willekomen," st. 7, *DL* p. 469; Ulrich von Winterstetten, "Tougenlîchen lac," 3:5-8, *DL* p. 526; and Ulrich von Singenberg, "Swer minneclîche," ll. 33-44, *TGT* pp. 12-3. And see generally De Gruyter, pp. 37-8, 66-7; and Nicklas, pp. 132-3.

12 Wolfram von Eschenbach, "Ez ist nu tac," ed. Karl Lachmann, rev. Eduard Hartl (Berlin, 1952), I, 8, ll. 7-8. For other examples, see perhaps Von Wissenlô, "Der wahter," 3:4-7, *DL* p. 594; perhaps Jakob von Warte, "Guto rîter," ll. 28-30, *SM* p. 255; *Hätzlerin* #12, ll. 51-4, ed. Haltaus p. 14; perhaps #19, ll. 49-50, *ibid.* p. 23; #23, ll. 91-108, 113-4, *ibid.* p. 28; and #115, ll. 27-8, *ibid.* p. 86.

13 The corresponding line in the *Filostrato* (53, 3) is "per dormir s'el potesse alquanto ad agio"; Chaucer apparently renders *ad agio* by

"as he was wont to doone," renders the idea of *alquanto* by "longe," and omits *s'el potesse*. The *Roman de Troyle,* ed. L. Moland and C. d'Héricault, *Nouvelles françoises en prose du XIVe siècle* (Paris, 1858), p. 187, paraphrases the line, ". . . et mist à son aise, au mieulx qu'il peut, pour essayer à dormir s'il pourroit."

14 The observation they invite is apparently a favorite with him; see "January's 'Aube'," pp. 3-4.

15 Though the Vulgate *signacula* here would normally be rendered by "seals" rather than "small seals," it seems plausible enough as the inspiration for Chaucer's "smale selys" in view of the general diminutive force of the ending *-culum.*

11

The Dual Time-Scheme in Chaucer's *Troilus*

HENRY W. SAMS

The general impression and effect of *Troilus and Criseyde* is one of continuous action over one season between spring and winter, and Chaucer conceived it so. There are in the poem two concentric and contradictory time-schemes; one of them is based upon the formal dating of the books, the other upon a porportionately spaced series of seasonal images. The second of these time-schemes is the one with which this paper is concerned. A skeletal series of seasonal images is used to produce an artistic illusion of unity without disturbing the actual history of event. Of course, not all of the images in the poem contribute to this sequence, but none of them disturbs it; those which are not part of the structure are irrelevant. I shall trace the sequence of these structural images, maintaining at the same time its relationship to the formal time-scheme of the poem and to the *Filostrato*.

The time consumed in the story of Troilus and Criseyde is about three years (v, 8-14),[1] but within this limit the action falls into two sequences of short duration. The first sequence is that which begins with Troilus' first sight of Criseyde in the temple and ends with the consummation of their love. Roughly, this sequence occupies two months. The first book begins in April (I, 158-61), and the second begins in May

Reprinted, by permission of author and editor, from *MLN*, LVI (1941), 94-100.

(II, 50-56). The main part of the action in the third book—that is, the third book up to and including the meeting in Pandarus' house—continues in May, as the conjunction of Saturn and Jove in Cancer, which occurred in May, proves.[2]

By a passage to which I have already referred (V, 8-14) we know that about three years elapse between the meeting at Pandarus' house and the beginning of the fourth book. There is no way, however, to tell exactly how long the action of the last books is, for Chaucer refuses to say. The nature and sequence of events indicate that it was a matter of a few months. Actually the poem occupies two months at the first and about six months at the last of its total time of duration, which is at least three years; there is a gap of about three years in the middle of the poem.

Boccaccio does no more than to tell us at the beginning of his poem that it is spring, and at the end, that it is again spring. Chaucer's formal dating does not come from his immediate sources. Wherever Chaucer got his formal time-scheme, it is apparent that he regards it as essential. The dating of the fifth book (V, 8 ff.), with its introduction of a three year break in the middle of the poem, is the most important of his innovations. Perhaps it may be accounted for as an attempt to ameliorate Criseyde's crime. It is more likely that Chaucer had some unaccountable impression that in adapting this stanza (cf. *Teseide* II, 1; and *Thebaid* IV, 1-2) he was more nearly retaining the truth of the Troy story. Perhaps Mr. Root's suggestion[3] that by this device of formal dating Chaucer "contributes to this sense of the actual," which is the most remarkable characteristic of the poem, is the correct one. Wherever Chaucer got his formal time-scheme, and for whatever reason he included it, he seems to have regarded it as a thing more or less beyond his direct control; and to preserve in his poem the unity of a single action, a unity which Boccaccio left undisturbed by formal datings, Chaucer devised a second, concentric time-scheme based upon a sequence of images.

It is important to bear in mind that the two time-schemes do not start from the same point. The first book is dated in April (I, 155-61) by a stanza corresponding in position with Boccacio's general statement that his story begins in spring time (*Fil.* I, 18). The dating is in strict accord with convention, and the "swote smellen floures" are standard properties.

The second book is dated in the same fashion (II, 50-56), but there is no corresponding dating in Boccaccio. The formal time-scheme begins, then, "with newe grene, of lusty Veer the pryme." On the other hand, the second scheme begins earlier in the season, lags behind the formal dating, and keeps pace with the emotional climate of the story. In the consideration of the artistic time-scheme we may identify the images which concern us as those which are applied in simile to the characters.

The first image of importance to our structure is spoken by Troilus when in the privacy of his room he complains that love afflicts him.

> But also cold in love towardes the
> Thi lady is, as frost in wynter moone,
> And thow fordon, as snow in fire is soone.   (I, 523-25)

This figure is taken from a corresponding place in the *Filostrato* (I, 53), but Chaucer's taking it is less significant than his not taking another figure which Boccaccio used only three stanzas later. Boccaccio's figure is this: "If thou, lady doest this, I shall revive as a flower in the fresh meadow in spring time" (*Fil.* I, 56). Chaucer's general tendency is to temper the concettism of Boccaccio's characters, but in this instance he had an explicit reason for rejecting Boccaccio's figure. Obviously, it is a spring-time figure, and the characters, despite their April setting, are not yet in harmony with it.

This divergence of seasons, ever narrowing, is maintained into the second book, undisturbed by the conventional dating on "Mayes day the Thrydde." The background is constantly that of flowers, meads, and the season of love, but the climate of the story itself is not so. Gradually the imagery of the story converges toward that of the setting; the limit can only be, of course, at the climax of the plot. When Criseyde is first shaken by Pandarus' shrewd arguments for love, this is the simile applied to her:

> But right as when the sonne shyneth brighte
> In March, that chaungeth ofte tyme his face,
> And that a cloude is put with wynd to flighte,
> Which oversprat the sonne as for a space,
> A cloudy thought gan thorugh hire soule pace,
>
> (II, 764-68)[4]

The events which follow are toward a happy consummation of the love affair, and when Pandare returns to Troilus with good news, Chaucer uses a simile which shows clearly the progress of this second, subliminal spring. It is translated from a corresponding passage in Boccaccio's version (*Fil.* II, 80).

> But right as floures, thorugh the cold of nyght
> Iclosed, stoupen on hire stalke lowe,
> Redressen hem ayein the sonne bright,
> And spreden on hire kynde cours by rowe,
> Right so gan tho his eighen up to throwe
> This Troilus . . .   (II, 967-72)

Book three is comparatively barren of developed images, but the one notable image which occurs is emphasized by the weakening at this point of the formal time-scheme. This image is taken with some changes from Boccaccio (*Fil.* III, 12), but it is expanded with the evident desire to make it the "pryme" of the illusory year.

> But right so as thise holtes and thise hayis,
> That han in wynter dede ben and dreye,
> Revesten hem in grene, when that May is,
> Whan every lusty liketh best to pleye;
> Right in that selve wise, soth to seye,
> Wax sodeynliche his herte ful of joie,
> That gladder was ther nevere man in Troie.
>   (III, 351-57)

The sequence of imagery from the beginning of the poem through the third book is in effect the story of the coming of a spring; that it is deliberately so we may judge from the facts that it accords with the development of the plot, and that images in the Italian source are apparently adopted or rejected with this structure in mind.

The beginning of the fourth book is, of course, the beginning of the tragic conclusion of the story; it is also the point of reversal in the year of images. This point is indicated by what is perhaps one of the most striking departures from the source in the entire poem; there is no question but that some definite critical idea led Chaucer to it. Boccaccio describes Troilus at the moment when Troilus hears that Cressida is to be exchanged for Antenor:

Ev'n as the lily, after it hath been turned up in the fields by the plough, droopeth and withereth from too much sun and its bright color changeth and groweth pale, so at the message brought to the Greeks . . . did Troilus . . . (*Fil.* IV. 18)

If Chaucer had adopted this image, it would have seemed a logical development from an earlier one in his poem (II, 967-72), but he did not adopt it. He wanted an image which conveyed not only the pathetic aspect of Troilus' misfortune, but also the idea of autumn. The images portray the coming and passing of a summer. The simile which Chaucer used to replace Boccaccio's is this:

> And as in wynter leves ben biraft,
>   Ech after other, til the tree be bare,
> So that ther nys but bark and braunche ilaft,
>   Lith Troilus . . .   (IV, 225-28)

This image, like the one in the third book, carries the weight of the story; we are not told until book five that three years have elapsed since Troilus first saw Criseyde. Thus the imaginary time-scheme is reinforced at the very point where the formal time-scheme collapses; and a hiatus of three years does not disturb the unity of the poem.

The fifth book continues the poetic year by more subtle devices than those that have preceded, for the general effect has been established. In the second stanza we learn that Phebus has melted the snows three times since the story began. Single lines now achieve the end to which five-line similes were devoted earlier. When Troilus makes his pathetic visit to Criseyde's empty house, "As frost, hym thoughte, his herte gan to colde." (V, 535) This line does not come from Boccaccio. Not only does Chaucer invent this line for the purpose, but also he omits, with the passage in which Deiphoebus discovers Troilus' love for Cressida, a simile of coming spring and greening meadows (*Fil.* V, 78).

The song of Troilus to the horned moon is part of a special phase which the imagery of the waning year takes in the last book; Chaucer makes use of darkness to obtain the effect he desires. In the long scene of Troilus' waiting at the gate for Criseyde's return, Boccaccio employs a brief description of the closing of the city for the night (*Fil.* VII, 11). Chaucer adopts it:

> The warden of the yates gan to calle
> The folk which that withoute the yates were,
> And bad hem dryven in hire bestes alle,
> Or al the nyght they moste bleven there.
>
> (v, 1177-80)

The sombre coloring of the last book is in contrast to the bright season of the middle of the poem.

There are, then, two complete and concentric time-schemes in *Troilus and Criseyde*: the one is the actual, basic time-scheme of three years; the other is the practical, artistic scheme of one year, or the coming and departure of one summer. The advantage of such a plan is obvious; it combines truth to conventional sequence with artistic unity. The fact that it is self-contradictory bothers no one. The thing to be desired is a general effect of artistic unity, and that this poem has that effect is beyond question.

Notes

1 R. K. Root, ed. *The Book of Troilus and Criseyde* (Princeton, 1926), pp. xxxiii-xxxiv.

2 An objection may be raised to this hypothesis on the ground of Pandarus's speech (II, 1298), but in this passage "yeres two" is no more than a good round number to give point to a generalization (T. A. Kirby, "A Note on *Troilus*," *MLR*, XXXIX [1934], 67-8). It is also worth noting that Troilus refers (III, 360-2) to "Aperil the laste," for this places the third book within the first year of the story (Root, p. xxxiii).

3 Root, p. xxxiii.

4 This image has no parallel in Boccaccio, though the passage of which it is a part is an almost literal translation of *Fil.*, III, 69, 75-7. The image itself is taken from Boethius *De cons.* i. m.3. 7-10.

12

Elements of Epic Grandeur in the *Troilus*

DANIEL C. BOUGHNER

The reader with both the *Filostrato* and the *Troilus* before him is struck at the outset by Chaucer's reversal of the situation of Boccaccio. In the "Proemio" of the former a young poet represents himself as passionately in love with the lady Fiammetta (Maria d'Aquino), whose absence he laments by a story which will enable him to sing in his "Florentine idiom and in a very appealing style" his own sorrows and plead his own case.[1] But Chaucer poses as an outsider in matters of love, and tells the story with a detachment that signalizes the changes he has introduced. These have increased the length of the story from 5704 to 8239 lines. Many are in accord with the doctrine of the medieval rhetoricians as it was expounded by Mattieu de Vendôme and Gaufred de Vinsauf.[2] That doc-

Reprinted, by permission of author and editor, from *ELH*, VI (1939), 200-10. Cf. Robert D. Mayo, "The Trojan Background of the *Troilus*," *ELH*, IX (1942), 245-56; Mayo argues that Chaucer failed to exploit the Trojan background of his story and thus qualifies Kittredge's contention (approved by Boughner) that Chaucer "Trojanized" the poem. For a quite different stylistic approach to the *Troilus*, see Charles Muscatine, *Chaucer and the French Tradition* (Berkeley: University of California Press, 1957), pp. 124-65; Muscatine finds in the *Troilus* not, as Boughner does, a "high style" traceable to medieval rhetorical theory and practice but a double style "alternatingly conventional and naturalistic" and reflecting "two equally admirable, equally incomplete attitudes to life" deriving from the French romance and fabliau traditions.

trine was based chiefly on the *De Inventione* of Cicero, the
Epistola ad Pisones of Horace, and the *De Rhetorica ad
Herennium* . . ., [and] it applied to poems in Latin. Of its
three divisions [disposition, amplification and abbreviation,
and stylistic ornamentation], disposition received relatively
little attention from the theorists, being concerned chiefly with
the problems of beginning and ending a poem.... The theorists
conceived of amplification, [which belongs to the] second
division, as the principal function of the writer. Chaucer uses
many of the devices of amplification. One of these is description, which was sometimes considered the supreme object of
poetry. Since its essential function was to award praise or
blame, it had two parts, the physical, comprising a treatment
of each feature including the brows and the interval that
separates them, and the moral. Chaucer follows this prescrip-
tion, as in the lines that interrupt the narrative in Book Five
[v, 799-840], to pen little portraits of Criseyde, Troilus, and
Diomede. He writes of Criseyde:

> And, save hire browes joyneden yfere,
> There nas no lak.   [v, 813-14]

And seizing on the fundamental qualities of her character, he
says:

> Ne nevere mo ne lakked hire pite;
> Tendre-herted, slydynge of corage.   [v, 824-25]

A second device is the digression, chiefly in the form of *sententiae* or proverbs, with which the *Troilus* is salted. A third is
the apostrophe, used to reinforce an expression of feeling. This
might take the form of an *exclamatio,* a passionate outcry addressed to persons dead or absent or to personified abstractions. The invocations in the poem exemplify this. One of the
most memorable apostrophes is the exhortation to young folk
at the end of the poem [v, 1835-48]. . . . A fourth of these
devices is the *prosopopeia*, or words lent to persons dead or
absent or to inanimate objects. Chaucer uses this artificial
device rather sparingly . . . but its narrower form, personification, occurs often. One of the most moving [occurrences]
comes when Troilus, his love consummated, begs Night to
tarry [iii, 1429-42]. Another device is the periphrasis, the
amplification of a statement to the end of raising it to a
higher stylistic level. . . .

> The dayes honour, and the hevenes ẏe,
> The nyghtes foo,—al this clepe I the sonne.   [II, 904-6]

And still another is the *expolitio* [elaboration] (closely related to the preceding), as in Chaucer's invocation of Venus:

> O blisful light, . . .
> O sonnes lief, O Joves doughter deere,
> Pleasance of love, O goodly debonaire.   [III, 1-4]

The authors of the medieval *artes poeticae* distinguished three levels of style, the simple, the middle or mixed, and the high or sublime, a distinction that had been one of the foundations of Ciceronian doctrine and that remained in force in the Middle Ages. The models were Virgil's *Eclogues* for the simple, his *Georgics* for the middle, and the *Aeneid* for the high style. To achieve the high style, a writer used two kinds of ornament, *modus gravis* [the laborious manner] and *ornatus facilis* [easy embellishment]. The first was characterized by the use of tropes, in which human emotion and aesthetic feeling find utterance. Chaucer used these extensively, but not to the point of being mannered. A particularly interesting metaphor is "dulcarnon," used by Criseyde for her dilemma which Pandarus tries to argue away, with its rich associations of science running back through Arabic to Euclid.[3] The second consisted chiefly in the employment of the "colors of rhetoric," word-schemes and figures of thought from which resulted ingenious patterns of sound and sense familiar to students of the later prose in euphuism. Chaucer, of course, uses some of them—alliteration, for example, without ceasing—but he subordinates them in the *Troilus* to graver matters of style. Sometimes he secures a powerful effect at once emotional and spiritual in an elaborate anaphora:

> Swich fyn hath, lo, this Troilus for love!
> Swich fyn hath al his grete worthynesse!
> Swich fyn hath his estat real above!
> Swich fyn his lust, swich fyn hath his noblesse!
> Swich fyn hath false worldes brotelnesse!   [V, 1828-32]

A similarly heightened use of this rhetorical device occurs a few lines later:

> Lo here, of payens corsed olde rites!
> Lo here, what alle hire goddes may availle;

Lo here, thise wrecched worldes appetites;
Lo here, the fyn and guerdoun for travaille
Of Jove, Appollo, of Mars, of swich rascaille!
[v, 1849-53]

. . . Though the theorists wrote for the instruction of poets using Latin, Chaucer availed himself of their precepts to raise his English poem above the level of any but the best vernacular literature. We can in all probability thus explain the ornateness he has added to his original.

But what of the more fundamental and pervasive change, the alteration of the whole tone of the poem? It is not surprising that the theories and example of Dante provide us with a possible explanation. In the *De vulgari eloquentia* he defends the speech of the people as "nobler" than the learned and artificial Latin, and he finds in it qualities of excellence and courtliness that make it a fit vehicle for poetry when used for the best thoughts of men of the highest excellence.[4] The subjects worthy of this illustrious vernacular must be useful, or deal with safety and the public good; must be pleasurable, or deal with love; and must be right, or deal with virtue. [In particular, these subjects, respectively], as Virgil indicated, are prowess in arms, the fire of love, and the direction of the will. For tragedy, when "the stateliness of the lines as well as the loftiness of the construction, and the excellence of the words" agree with the greatness of the subject, Dante would have his poet use "the higher style." If, he says, "our subject appears fit to be sung in the tragic style, we must then assume the illustrious vernacular language." Those things "which we have distinguished as being worthy of the highest song are to be sung in that style alone"—namely, arms, love, and virtue. When a poet purposes to sing of these, "let him drink first of Helicon," and submit himself to "the habit of the sciences." Those who, "innocent of art, and science," trust to genius alone, merely display their folly. Only after "strenuous efforts of genius" and "constant practice in the art" should the poet adjust the strings of his lyre and "boldly take up his plectrum and begin to ply it." Dante's models are the classic poets, for, he says, "the more closely we copy the great poets, the more correct is the poetry we write"; and from them we may learn how to write in a style having "flavor and grace and also elevation."

Dante was, of course, the greatest exemplar of his theories. And by the third quarter of the fourteenth century, the Florentines were sufficiently proud of his name to appoint Boccaccio in 1373 to expound the *Divine Comedy*. Thus began the first *cathedra dantesca* [chair of Dante studies] and the first formal exposition of a poem in the vulgar tongue. Boccaccio told his fellow citizens that he honored Dante for having revealed the glory of the Florentine idiom, which was sweeter and lovelier than Latin; his works, he asserted, "have concealed within them the sweetest fruits of historical or philosophical truth."[5] Though Chaucer could not have heard reports of the epochal lectures on his first Italian journey, which ended in May, 1373, he might have learned of them later. Certainly he followed the example of Dante with respect to his native idiom.

In his *De genealogia deorum*, Boccaccio had already set forth and defended the attributes of poetry written in the high style.[6] Such poetry, he insists, is to be sharply distinguished from that which is merely ornate (and the most faithful devotion to the rhetorical doctrines of the medieval theorists would have issued only in ornateness), because it aims to teach as well as to delight. It "veils truth in a fair and fitting garment of fiction," which does not impair the truth but much enhances its power over men. Poets of this rank, Boccaccio declares with Dante in mind, "raise flights of symbolic steps to heaven." To them, a thorough schooling in the Liberal Arts, in science moral and natural, in history, literature, archaeology, and geography—in the full cycle of medieval knowledge—is necessary. The *De Genealogia* made available some of the learning that its author regarded as indispensable. Now the highest poetry, Boccaccio thought, was ancient poetry, and "the essential matter of ancient poetry was myth," which was a source of "spiritual energy" that it was his task to revive. He conceived of the old mythology, Professor Osgood points out, "not as mere make-believe, but as describing, however dimly, the operations of the Celestial Hierarchy"; and so he identified the gods of mythology with planetary influences and pointed "the alliance between the old paganism and the astrology" that was accepted by Dante and the fourteenth century. Finally, Boccaccio says that the poet belongs to the number of philosophers since he "tries with all his powers to set forth in noble verse the effects, either of Nature herself, or of her eternal and unalterable operation." In Virgil, in Dante, and in Petrarch, "the sap of philosophy runs pure"; and in them "all that is clear and holy in the bosom of moral philosophy is presented in so majestic a style, that nothing could be uttered for the instruction of mankind more replete, more beautiful, more mature, nay, more holy." From Italy, it would seem, from the principles and practice of Dante and Boccaccio, came the inspiration to tell the story of Troilus in the mother tongue with the dignity and elevation of the high style.[7]

Many of Chaucer's additions to the *Filostrato* are in accord with these principles and may properly be called elements of epic grandeur. First are the "proems." That of Book One shows that Chaucer had taken to heart Dante's advice to emulate the great ancients. It announces the theme, after the manner of classical epic, the love-tragedy of Troilus; it sets the tone of the whole poem and prepares the reader for the irony of the author's treatment. The "Proem" of Book Two is a metaphorical statement of the change for the better in the fortunes of the young lover, and resembles Dante's leaving the *Inferno* for the *Purgatorio*,[8] but there is a note of underlying tragedy and inescapable destiny. The ecstasy of the lovers is prefigured in the "Proem" of Book Three by the invocation of Venus, whose role is sometimes that of the pagan deity, sometimes that of the planet with astrological influence, the power of love and the unifying principle of the universe. Perhaps no passage in the *Troilus* better illustrates the use of mythology in the manner urged by Boccaccio. It also indicates the heightened emotional content and the deepened philosophical import of the poem. And again, the "Proem" of Book Four sets the tone and announces the matter of that division, how Fortune cast Troilus "out of his lady grace" and her faithlessness.

Chaucer enhances this epic dignity by means of the invocations, another device of classical epic. In Book One, Tisiphone, "cruel furie," becomes a symbol of sorrow and pain, a conception owing much to Dante.[9] The appeal to Clio, Muse of history, serves notice that the material related in Book Two is a matter of sober record. The prayer for aid to Calliope, Muse of epic poetry, suggests that the poet was rising to a higher level of composition in Book Three. And at the end of this book, Chaucer again addresses Venus and the Muses to thank them for the inspiration he had received [III, 1807-14]. The invocation to the Furies and to "cruel Mars" foreshadows the more sorrowful matter of Book Four. And in Book Five, Chaucer's divine aids are the Fates, the ministers who will carry out Jove's decree of infelicity and death for Troilus [V, 3-7].

To infuse the *Troilus* with "flavor and grace and also elevation" superior to the *Filostrato,* Chaucer has, as Dante prescribed, copied the ancients also in the large number of mythological allusions he has introduced. Many come from Ovid, such as Niobe weeping for her children [I, 699-700], or the agony of Tityus torn by the vultures in hell [I, 786-8], or the Calydonian boar hunt [V, 1464-79].

But Chaucer has also scattered through his poem, in contrast to Boccaccio, such a multitude of other classical touches as to constitute what Professor Kittredge calls a "Trojanization" of the situation.[10] It is necessary to offer as examples only a few of these in order to show how thoroughly they have been harmonised with and how much they contribute to the atmosphere of high romance that predominates throughout the poem. Thus among Calchas' divinations that presage the fall of Troy are the oracle of Apollo, the lots cast like the ancient *sortes,* and augury [IV, 114-17]. Again, Troilus adjures Venus by her love of Adonis, Jove by his love of Europa, Mars by his love of Venus, Phoebus by his love of Daphne, Mercury by his love of Herse, Diana, and the Fates to grant him success [III, 712-35], and he wishes that his night with Criseyde might be as long as Jupiter's with Alcmena [III, 1427-8]. He vows that he will love her after he is dead and dwelling in torment with Proserpine, but she hopes to live with him in the Elysian Fields, like Orpheus and Eurydice [IV, 470-6, 785-91]. She swears by the celestial gods, by every nymph and infernal deity, by the satyrs and fauns, and calls on Atropos to break her thread of life if ever she is false; and she asserts that Simois, the river that runs through Troy, shall turn back its current before she will be unfaithful [IV, 1541-53]. In all, there are about 100 such touches. Their effect is not only, as Professor Kittredge says, "to intensify an atmosphere of high antiquity," but also to ornament and to exalt the poem.

Chaucer has shown here as in all his poems a perfect control of the learning in which Dante and Boccaccio would have the serious poet steep himself and use at will to raise the tenor of his subject. For example, the reference to "Orcades and Inde" is good medieval geography [v, 969-71]. Pandarus' discussion of the significance of dreams is likewise in accord with the science of the day [v, 360-85]. A good understanding of physiology is equally clear [i, 306-7; iii, 1088-9]. But just as accurate and especially characteristic of his work is the elaborate use of astronomy and astrology. He utilizes myth and astronomy for definitions of time, and tells the hour by the sun's progress through the heavens. Accordingly, the passage of the Moon from Aries to the end of Leo serves to measure the period of Criseyde's absence from Troilus, or ten days [iv, 1590-6]. As the Moon nears the end of Leo, a complicated astronomical statement of time shows that the ten days are almost over [v, 1016-20]. Astronomy woven with myth marks, with references to Phoebus and Zephirus, the passage of three years [v, 8-13].

The movements of the stars in their courses affect the doom of Troy and the conduct of the persons. Chaucer depicts these astrological influences as subject to the will of God, as Dante and Boccaccio had explained. Thus Pandarus discovers whether the Moon is propitious for his visit to Criseyde [ii, 74-5]. Later Venus in the seventh house is favorably placed for the success of Troilus' love [ii, 680-6]. As if to heed Boccaccio's advice, Chaucer often blends myth and astrology. Thus Troilus thanks Venus both as a deity and as a "wel-willy" planet [iii, 1255-7]. Again, he prays to her as the goddess of love and as an astrological influence to intercede with Jupiter and turn aside evil planetary influence, and he appeals to the gods who are identified with the several planets [iii, 715-32]. Criseyde is forced to stay with Pandarus by the remarkable conjunction of Jupiter, Saturn, and the crescent Moon in the sign Cancer, which causes a heavy downpour of rain [iii, 617-26]. These allusions are used in the manner of Boccaccio in the ornate *Teseide* and after Dante's fashion in the *Divine Comedy*; and like them Chaucer touches the imagination and sheds an astral lustre on his poem.

But the most profound change made by Chaucer, the philosophizing of the story, has deepened its meaning. He belongs to that illustrious company of excellent poets visioned by

Dante, who body forth grave subjects in a style not merely
ornate, but sublime; for he undertakes to write, as Boccaccio
had said, of moral philosophy in so majestic a form that nothing could be uttered for the instruction of mankind more
powerful. After the manner of Dante, he incorporates into
his poem the philosophy of Boethius, and from Dante he
borrows the elevated conception of Fortune as the agency of
divine providence and the address to the Blessed Trinity which
brings the *Troilus* to a close [v, 1541-5, 1863-5]. Among these
Boethian elements, which increase the tone of artistic and
spiritual elevation of the poem, especially significant are the
discussion of Fortune in which Troilus blames and Pandarus
defends the fickle goddess [I, 837-54], Criseyde's complaint
against false felicity [III, 813-36], Troilus' hymn to love as the
bond of all things [III, 1744-71], and his soliloquy on the conflict between God's foreknowledge and man's free will [IV,
953-1085]. The last two passages, significantly enough, were
introduced by Chaucer in revising the poem after publication.
A third similar insertion consists of the stanzas which follow
the soul of Troilus on its flight through the heavens. These
new passages, all in the grand manner, strengthen and give
climactic emphasis to the philosophical interpretation of the
story. Their cumulative effect is to exalt the *Troilus* to the
level of those supreme poems in which tragedy is interpreted
in the light of moral values that give human beings an anchor
of hope in a world of bitterness and insecurity.

Dante would have his poet write of arms, love, and virtue
in tragedy. Chaucer has treated these subjects in a tragedy in
the medieval sense of the term. He has disposed the nine of
Boccaccio's tale into five books suggesting the five acts of
tragic drama, with a tragic insistence on an overruling destiny.[11] From his position of ironic detachment, moreover, the
poet acts as a kind of tragic chorus. Many of his moralizing
comments are of this sort, interpreting the conduct and emotions of his actors and pointing his lesson. Thus he studiously
corrects the impression that Criseyde's was "a sodeyn love"
[II, 666-79]; or he summarizes the status of the action [*e.g.,*
III, 491-511], or turns, profoundly moved at the end, in lines
adapted from the *Paradiso* to a sublime invocation to the
Blessed Trinity.[12] These tragic elements put the reader in the
position of the gods on Olympus observing the struggles of

pitiable humans against ineluctable fate; they enforce the lesson of eternal Christ and true felicity. There is nothing like this in the *Filostrato*. A narrative that had been a young man's vehicle of intense but personal appeal has become in Chaucer's handling a high romance of universal appeal, ennobled by certain epic features, which depicts and interprets one of the central human experiences.

Notes

1 See Nathaniel E. Griffin and Arthur B. Myrick, *The Filostrato of Giovanni Boccaccio* (Philadelphia: University of Pennsylvania Press, 1929), pp. 114-31.

2 See Edmond Faral, *Les Arts poétiques du XIIe et du XIII siècle* (Paris: Edouard Champion, 1924) for both texts and studies of these medieval rhetoricians. See esp. pp. 61-2 and 85 on amplification as the poet's principal function; pp. 75-84 on description; p. 74 on digression; pp. 70-2 on apostrophe, or exclamation; pp. 72-3 on prosopopoeia, or personification; p. 68 on periphrasis; pp. 86-9 on the three levels of style; and pp. 89-90 on tropes suitable for the *modus gravis*. See also J. M. Manly, "Chaucer and the Rhetoricians," *The Proceedings of the British Academy*, XII (1926), 95-113 [reprinted in R. J. Schoeck and J. Taylor, eds. *Chaucer Criticism: The Canterbury Tales* (Notre Dame, Indiana: University of Notre Dame Press, 1960), pp. 268-90], and Traugott Naunin, *Der Einfluss der mittelalterlichen Rhetorik auf Chaucers Dichtung* (Bonn, 1930).

3 III, 930-36. [For explanation of the metaphor, see R. K. Root, ed. *The Book of Troilus and Criseyde by Geoffrey Chaucer* (Princeton: Princeton University Press, 1945), pp. 481-2. Briefer explanation in notes to the Robinson edition of Chaucer's works.]

4 In A. G. Ferrers Howell, tr. *The Latin Works of Dante* (London, 1904), pp. 4 and 54-67; see also pp. 69-71, 78-80, 86-8, and 94.

5 E. Hutton, *Boccaccio* (London, 1910), pp. 256-72; see also pp. 249-52.

6 See Charles G. Osgood, *Boccaccio on Poetry* (Princeton: Princton University Press, 1930; reprinted, New York: The Liberal Arts Press, 1956); for the ideas of the following paragraph, consult pp. xiv, xvi-xxi, xxxv, xxxviii-xl, 21, 39-42, 52-4, 76-9.

7 Root, *The Book of Troilus*, p. xlv.

8 *Ibid.*, p. 435.

9 J. L. Lowes, "Chaucer and Dante," *MP*, XIV (1917), 719.

10 G. L. Kittredge, "Chaucer's Lollius," *Harvard Studies in Classical Philology* (Cambridge, Mass., 1917), pp. 50-4.

11 Root, *The Book of Troilus*, p. xlix. [See also Curry's elaboration of the point, pp. 34-70 above.]

12 *Ibid.*, pp. 564-5.

13

Distance and Predestination in *Troilus and Criseyde*

MORTON W. BLOOMFIELD

For we are but of yesterday.—Job viii.9

IN *Troilus and Criseyde* Chaucer as commentator occupies an unusual role. It is indeed common for authors to enter their own works in many ways. Writers as diverse as Homer, Virgil, Dante, Cervantes, Fielding, Thackeray, and George Eliot all do so. Sometimes, as with Fielding, the author may keep a distance between himself and his story; sometimes, as with Dante, he may penetrate into his story as a major or the major character; and sometimes, as with Homer, he may both enter and withdraw at will. When Homer directly addresses one of his characters, he is deliberately breaking down, for artistic reasons, the aloofness to which he generally holds.

Chaucer also frequently appears in his own works, usually as one of his dramatis personae, and participates in the action.[1] Although he is not always an important or major character, his actions or dreams within the work frequently provide the occasion for, or give a supposed rationale to, his literary creations. Chaucer the character's decision to go on a pilgrimage to Canterbury provides the ostensible justification for the *Canterbury Tales*. His dreams as a character, following a great medieval literary convention, give rise to the *Parlement of Foules* and the *Hous of Fame*.

Reprinted, by permission of author and editor, from *PMLA*, LXXII (1957), 14-26.

In *Troilus and Criseyde* Chaucer plays his artistic role with a striking difference. Here he conceives of himself as the narrator of a history, of a true event as the Middle Ages conceived it, which happened in the past; and as historian he meticulously maintains a distance between himself and the events in the story. His aloofness is similar to and yet different from Fielding's in *Tom Jones* or Thackeray's in *Vanity Fair*. In these works the authors look upon their puppets from their omniscient, ironical, humorous, and at times melancholy point of view and make comments on them or their predicaments, using them as excuses for brief essays or paragraphs on different subjects. In *Troilus* Chaucer does not look upon his characters as his creations. His assumed role is primarily descriptive and expository. Though we are continually reminded of the presence of Chaucer the historian, narrator, and commentator, at the same time we are never allowed to forget that he is separate from the events he is recording.

Troilus is not a dream vision nor is it a contemporary event. It is the past made extremely vivid by the extensive use of dialogue, but still the past. Chaucer cannot change the elements of his story. As God cannot violate His own rationality, Chaucer cannot violate his data. Bound by his self-imposed task of historian, he both implies and says directly that he cannot do other than report his tale.

If we assume that Chaucer is a painstaking artist—and it is impossible not to—it is clear that the nature of the role he assumes has an extremely important meaning in the economy and plan of the poem. Why, we must ask, does Chaucer as character-narrator continually remind us of his aloofness from and impotence in the face of the events he is narrating? An historian takes for granted what Chaucer does not take for granted. A Gibbon does not tell us constantly that the events of the decline and fall of the Roman Empire are beyond his control. That is an assumption that anyone reading a true history makes at the outset. Chaucer introduces just this assumption into the body of his work, continually reminding us of what seems, in the context of a supposed history, most obvious. What is normally outside the historical work, a presupposition of it, is in the history of Troilus and Criseyde brought into the poem and made much of. This unusual creative act calls for examination.

We must also wonder at the quantitative bulk of Chaucer's

comments on the story. Frequently, even in the midst of the action of the inner story, we are reminded of the presence of the narrator—sometimes, it is true, by only a word or two. We cannot dismiss these numerous comments merely as remarks necessary to establish rapport with the audience under conditions of oral delivery. The few remarks of this nature are easy to pick out. If we compare the simple comments made by the narrator in, say, *Havelock the Dane* or any other medieval romance with those made by the *Troilus* narrator, I think the difference is plain.

Although many stanzas belong completely to the commentator *in propria persona* and others pertain to the events of the tale, so many are partly one or the other, or merely suggest the presence of a narrator, that a mathematical table which could reveal the actual percentage of commentator stanzas or lines would be misleading and inaccurate. Anyone who has read the poem must be aware of the presence of the commentator most of the time; one is rarely allowed to forget it for long. And even more impressive than the number of comments are the times and nature of the author's intervention. At all the great moments he is there directing us, speaking in his own person close to us and far from the events of the tragedy which he is presenting to us within the bounds of historical fact.

This sense of distance between Chaucer as character and his story is conveyed to us in what may be designated as temporal, spatial, aesthetic, and religious ways, each reinforcing the other and overlapping. For the sake of clarity, however, we may examine each in turn as a separate kind of aloofness.

The aspect of temporal distance is the one most constantly emphasized throughout the poem. Chaucer again and again tells us that the events he is recording are historical and past. He lets us know that customs have changed since the time when Pandarus, Troilus, and Criseyde lived. The characters are pagans who go to temples to worship strange gods and are caught up in one of the great cataclysms of history. Their ways of living are different from ours. Their love-making varies from the modern style. They lived a long time ago, and Chaucer, to tell their story, is forced to rely on the historians. In order to understand their actions, we must make an effort in comprehension. Yet, says Chaucer, diversity of custom is natural. At times, it is true, Chaucer is very anachronistic, but he still succeeds in giving his readers (or listeners) a feeling for the pastness of his characters and their sad story and for what we today call cultural relativity.[2]

Throughout, Chaucer tries to give us a sense of the great sweep of time which moves down to the present and into the future and back beyond Troy, deepening our sense of the temporal dimension. He tells us that speech and customs change within a thousand years (II, 22 ff.) and that this work he is writing is also subject to linguistic variability (v, 1793 ff.). Kingdoms and power pass away too; the *translatio regni* [transference of royal power] (or *imperii* [imperial rule]) is inexorable—"regnes shal be flitted/Fro folk in folk" (v, 1544-45). The characters themselves reach even farther backward in time. Criseyde and her ladies read of another siege, the fall of Thebes, which took place long before the siege of Troy (II, 81 ff.). Cassandra, in her interpretation of Troilus' dream (v, 1450-1519), goes into ancient history to explain Diomede's lineage. We are all part of time's kingdom, and we are never allowed to forget it.

Yet, as I have already mentioned, Chaucer vividly reconstructs, especially in his use of dialogue, the day-by-day living of his chief characters. This precision of detail and liveliness of conversation only serve to weight the contrast between himself in the present and his story in the past, to make the present even more evanescent in the sweep of inexorable change. It is the other side of the coin. These inner events are in the past and in a sense dead, but when they occurred they were just as vivid as the events that are happening now. The strong reality and, in a sense, nearness of the past make meaningful its disappearance and emphasize paradoxically its distance. If there are no strong unique facts, there is nothing to lament. We cannot escape into the web of myth and cycle; the uniqueness of the past is the guarantee of its own transience. This is the true historical view and this is Chaucer's view. For him, however, even unique events have meaning, but only in the framework of a world view which can put history into its proper place.

Not frequently used, yet most important when it is, is the sense of spatial distance which Chaucer arouses in his readers. The events of the poem take place in faraway Asia Minor. Chaucer creates a sense of spatial distance by giving us a

shifting sense of nearness and farness. At times we seem to be
seeing the Trojan events as if from a great distance and at
others we seem to be set down among the characters. This
sense of varying distance is most subtly illustrated in the fifth
book when Chaucer, after creating a most vivid sense of
intimacy and closeness in describing the wooing of Criseyde
by Diomede, suddenly moves to objectivity and distance in
introducing the portraits of the two lovers and his heroine
(799 ff.)—a device taken from Dares. With the approach of
the hour of betrayal, as we become emotionally wrought up
and closely involved, Chaucer the narrator brings us sharply
back to his all-seeing eye and to a distance. The same technique may also be seen elsewhere in the poem. This continual
inversion of the telescope increases our sense of space and
gives us a kind of literary equivalent to the perspective of
depth in painting.

Chaucer, in his insistence on cultural relativity, not only
emphasizes chronological but also geographic variability. "Ek
for to wynnen love in sondry ages,/ In sondry londes, sondry
been usages" (ii, 27-28). Above all we get this sense of
spatial distance in the final ascent of Troilus to the ogdoad,
the eighth sphere,[3] where in a sense he joins Chaucer in looking down on this "litel spot of erthe" and can even contem-
plate his own death with equanimity.

The sense of aesthetic distance[4] is evoked by the continual
distinction Chaucer makes between the story and the commentator, between the framework and the inner events. Although his basic "facts" are given, Chaucer never lets the
reader doubt for long that he is the narrator and interpreter
of the story. Once, at least, he adopts a humorous attitude
towards his dilemma. He insists that he is giving his readers
Troilus' song of love (i, 400 ff.), "Naught only the sentence"
as reported by Lollius but "save oure tonges difference"
"every word right thus." This attitude is, however, rare. But
it is not unusual for Chaucer to insist upon his bondage to
the facts. Yet he strains against the snare of true events in
which he is caught. Indeed Chaucer tries again and again,
especially where the betrayal of Criseyde is involved, to fight
against the truth of the events he is "recording." He never
hides his partiality for that "hevennysh perfit creature" (i,
104), and in this attitude as in others he notifies us of the
narrow latitude which is allowed him. As he approaches the

actual betrayal, he slows down; and with evident reluctance, as his reiterated, "the storie telleth us" (v, 1037), "I fynde ek in the stories elleswhere" (v, 1044), "men seyn—I not" (v, 1050) show, he struggles against the predestined climax. The piling up of these phrases here emphasizes the struggle of the artist-narrator against the brutality of the facts to which he cannot give a good turn. As a faithful historian, he cannot evade the rigidity of decisive events—the given. Criseyde's reception of Diomede cannot be glossed over.[5] All this makes us more aware of Chaucer the narrator than ordinarily and increases our sense of aesthetic distance between the reporter and what is reported, between the frame and what is framed.

Finally we may call certain aspects of Chaucerian distance religious. Troilus, Pandarus, and Criseyde are pagans who lived "while men loved the lawe of kinde" (*Book of the Duchess*, 1.56)—under natural law. The great barrier of God's revelation at Sinai and in Christ separates Chaucer and us from them. Chaucer portrays them consciously as pagans, for he never puts Christian sentiments into their mouths.[6] He may violate our historic sense by making lovers act according to the medieval courtly love code, but not by making them worship Christ. They are reasonable pagans who can attain to the truths of natural law—to the concept of a God, a creator, and to the rational moral law but never to the truths of revealed Christian religion. Chaucer is very clear on this point and in the great peroration to the poem he expressly says

> Lo here, of payens corsed olde rites,
> Lo here, what alle hire goddes may availle;
> Lo here, thise wrecched worldes appetites;
> Lo here, the fyn and guerdoun for travaille
> Of Jove, Appollo, of Mars, of swich rascaille!
>
> (v, 1849-53)

In general, until the end of the poem, Chaucer, as we shall see, plays down his own Christianity for good reason. He even, at times and in consonance with the epic tradition which came down to him, calls upon the pagan Muses and Furies, but he does not avoid the Christian point of view when he feels it necessary to be expressed. Although the religious barrier is not emphasized until the conclusion, we are left in no doubt throughout as to its separating Chaucer from his characters. This sense of religious distance becomes at the end a vital part of the author's interpretation of his story.

A close study of Chaucer's proems written as prefaces to the first four books bears out the analysis offered here. In these Chaucer speaks out, and from his emphases and invocations we may gain some clues as to his intentions. At the beginning of the first proem, we are told of the subject of the work and of its unhappy fatal end. Chaucer does not allow us to remain in suspense at all. He exercises his role as historical commentator immediately at the outset. Tesiphone, one of the Furies, is invoked as an aid. She is a sorrowing Fury, as Dante had taught Chaucer to view her. She is responsible for the torment of humans, but she weeps for her actions. She is also in a sense the invoker himself who puts himself in his poem in a similar role. Chaucer is also a sorrowing tormenter who is retelling a true tale, the predestined end of which he cannot alter. Though ultimately he is to conquer it through religion, Chaucer the commentator is throughout most of the poem a victim of the historical determinism of his own poem. Although it is set down in the introduction to the poem, we may not understand the full meaning of Chaucer's entanglement and the escape provided by Christianity until we reach its end. There the Christian solution to the dilemma of the first proem is again presented but deepened by our knowledge of Troilus' fate and by a greater emphasis. Then, we shall have followed through the sad story under Chaucer the commentator's guidance and the answer is plain. In the proem, on the first reading, however, the problem and the solution cannot be clear in spite of Chaucer's open words. We too must discover the answer.

On the other hand, in the first prologue, he does tell us, so that we may understand, that he the conductor and recorder of his story is like Troilus after the betrayal, unhappy in love. In the *Book of the Duchess*, the dreamer's unhappiness in love is assuaged within the dream and inner story by the grief of the man in black, whose loss of his beloved foreshadows what would have happened to the dreamer's love in one form or another, for all earthly love is transitory. Death is worse than unhappiness in love. Chaucer the *Troilus* narrator who dares not pray to love "for myn unliklynesse" is also going to learn in his tale that the love of the Eternal is the only true love. Actually Chaucer, because he conceives of himself as historian, has already learned before he begins.

Hence, it is not quite accurate to say as above that he is going to learn, for he already knows. The reader, however, unless he is extraordinarly acute, remains in ignorance until he
finishes the whole work. He discovers in the course of the
experience of the history what Chaucer already knows and
has really told him in the beginning, for Chaucer concludes
his first proem by calling on all lovers both successful and
unsuccessful to join him in prayer for Troilus. It is, he says,
only in heaven, in the *patria* of medieval theology, that we
can find lasting happiness. Troilus will find a pagan equivalent
for this in his pagan heaven at the end. One cannot, however,
quite believe Chaucer here until one reads the poem and
finds that he is deadly serious when he prays that God
"graunte" unhappy lovers "soone owt of this world to pace"
(I, 41). It is the love of God which is the answer to the
love of woman and of all earthly things.

In other words, Chaucer in his introduction to the poem
indicates his bondage to historical fact, his own grief at this
position, the problem of the unhappiness in this world he,
like Troilus and all unhappy lovers, must face, and the only
true solution for all the lovers of this world.

The second proem appeals to Clio, the Muse of history,
and alludes to the diversity of human custom and language.
The sense of history and cultural relativity manifested here
emphasizes the distance in time which temporal barriers impose. "For every wight which that to Rome went/Halt not o
path, or alwey o manere" (II, 36-37).

The opening of Book III calls upon Venus, goddess of love,
and, although it makes other points as well, underlines again
the pagan quality of the history. Venus in her symbolic,
astrological, and divine role conquers the whole world and
binds its dissonances and discords together. It is she who
understands the mysteries of love and who explains the apparent irrationality of love. The proem closes with a brief
reference to Calliope, Muse of epic poetry, as Chaucer wishes
to be worthy, as an artist, of his great theme of love.

Finally, in the last proem, we have an appeal to Fortune
the great presiding deity of the sublunar world. Here as always she suggests instability and transience. Chaucer then
alludes to the binding power of his sources. He closes his
prologue with an invocation to all the Furies and to Mars
with overtones suggesting his unhappy role as commentator

and the paganness of the story he is unfolding.

These proems cannot be completely explained in terms of my interpretation, for they are also, especially the third and fourth, appropriate artistically to the theme of the books they serve to introduce and the various stages of the narrative. In general they emphasize the tragic end of the tale, the unwilling Fury-like role Chaucer has to play, the historical bonds which shackle him, the pity of it all, the aloofness and distance between the Chaucer of the poem and the history itself he is telling, and the one possible solution to the unhappiness of the world. Nor are these sentiments confined to the prefaces. They occur again and again throughout the body of the poem. Chaucer takes pains to create himself as a character in his poem and also to dissociate this character continually from his story.

The attitude of Chaucer the character throughout makes it possible for us to understand the crucial importance of the concept of predestination in the poem. In the past there has been much debate in Chaucerian criticism over the question of predestination in *Troilus*. We know that Chaucer was profoundly interested in this question and that it was a preoccupation of his age. It seems to me that, if we regard the framework of the poem—the role that Chaucer sets himself as commentator—as a meaningful part of the poem and if we consider the various references to fate and destiny in the text, we can only come to the conclusion that the Chaucerian sense of distance and aloofness is the artistic correlative to the concept of predestination. *Troilus and Criseyde* is a medieval tragedy of predestination because the reader is continually forced by the commentator to look upon the story from the point of view of its end and from a distance. The crux of the problem of predestination is knowledge. So long as the future is not known to the participants in action, they can act as if they were free. But once a position of distance from the action is taken, then all can be seen as inevitable. And it is just this position which Chaucer the commentator takes and forces upon us from the very beginning. As John of Salisbury writes, "however, when you have entered a place, it is impossible that you have not entered it; when a thing has been done it is impossible that it be classed with things not done; and there is no recalling to non-existence a thing of the past."[7] All this presupposes knowledge which is impossible *in media re*. It is just this knowledge that Chaucer the commentator-historian gives us as he reconstructs the past. Hence we are forced into an awareness of the inevitability of the tragedy and get our future and our present at the same time, as it were.

Bound by the distance of time and space, of art and religion, Chaucer sits above his creation and foresees, even as God foresees, the doom of his own creatures: God, the *Deus artifex* who is in medieval philosophy the supreme artist and whose masterpiece is the created world. But Chaucer is like God only insofar as he can know the outcome, not as creator. Analogically, because he is dealing with history, and, we must remember, to the medieval Englishman his own history, he can parallel somewhat his Maker. He is not the creator of the events and personages he is presenting to us; hence he cannot change the results. On the other hand God is the creator of His creatures; but He is bound by His own rationality and His foreknowledge. The sense of distance that Chaucer enforces on us accentuates the parallel with God and His providential predestination. We cannot leap the barriers which life imposes on us, but in the companionship of an historian we can imitate God *in parvo*. As God with His complete knowledge of future contingents sees the world laid out before Him all in the twinkling of an eye, so, in the case of history, with a guide, we share in small measure a similar experience. The guide is with us all the way, pointing to the end and to the pity of it. We must take our history from his point of view.

It is, of course, as hazardous to attribute opinions to Chaucer as it is to Shakespeare. Yet I suspect both were predestinarians—insofar as Christianity allows one to be. It is curious that all the great speeches on freedom of the will in Shakespeare's plays are put into the mouths of his villains—Edmund in *Lear*, Iago in *Othello*, and Cassius in *Julius Caesar*. This is not the place to discuss the relation of Chaucer to fourteenth-century thinking or to predestination, but I think he stands with Bishop Bradwardine who, when Chaucer was still very young, thundered against the libertarians and voluntarists because they depreciated God at the expense of His creatures and elevated man almost to the level of his Creator. Even the title of his masterpiece *De causa Dei* reveals clearly his bias. God's ways are not our ways and His grace must not be denied. His power (i.e., manifest in predestination) must be defended. Chaucer is probably with him and others on this issue and in the quarrel over future contingents which became the chief issue[8]—a reduction of the problem to logic and epistemology as befitted a century fascinated by logic and its problems. Regardless of Chaucer's personal opinion, however, I think I have shown that one of the main sources of the inner tensions of *Troilus* is this sense of necessity of an historian who knows the outcome in conflict with his sympathies as an artist and man, a conflict which gives rise to a futile struggle until the final leap which elevates the issue into a new and satisfactory context. This conflict causes the pity, the grief, the tears—and in a sense the ridiculousness and even the humor of it all.

Yet, throughout, the maturity of Chaucer's attitude is especially noteworthy. Predestination which envelops natural man implicates us all. Only from a Christian point of view can we be superior to Troilus and Criseyde and that is not due to any merit of our own, but to grace. As natural men and women we too are subject to our destiny whatever it may be. Chaucer links himself (and us) with his far-off characters, thereby strengthening the human bond over the centuries and increasing the obectivity and irony of his vision. We are made to feel that this is reality, that we are looking at it as it is and even from our distance participate in it.

There is no escape from the past if one chooses to reconstruct artistically, as Chaucer does, the past from the vantage ground of the present. Chaucer's creation of himself in *Troilus* as historian-narrator and his emphasis on the distance between him and his characters repeat, in the wider frame of the present and in the panorama of complete knowledge, the helplessness and turmoil of the lovers in the inner story. The fact that Chaucer regards his story as true history does not, of course, make his point of view predestinarian; in that case all historians would be committed to a philosophy of predestination. The point is that the author creates a character —himself—to guide us through his historical narrative, to emphasize the pitiful end throughout, to keep a deliberate distance suggested and stated in various ways between him and us and the characters of the inner story. He makes his chief character awake to the fact of predestination towards the end of the story and at the conclusion has this character join, as it were, us and Chaucer the character—in space instead of time

—in seeing his own story through the perspective of distance. It is all this which gives us the clue. The outer frame is not merely a perspective of omniscience but also of importance and is in fact another level of the story. It serves as the realm of Mount Ida in the *Iliad*—a wider cadre which enables us to put the humans involved into their proper place.

Every age has its polarities and dichotomies, some more basic than others. To believing medieval man, the fundamental division is between the created and the uncreated. God as the the uncreated Creator is the unchanging norm against which all His creatures must be set and the norm which gives the created world its true objectivity. The true Christian was bound to keep the universe in perspective: it was only one of the poles of this fundamental polarity. The city of God gives meaning to the city of the world.

The impasse of the characters can only be solved on this other level and in this wider cadre. Actually for Troilus and Criseyde there is no final but merely a temporary solution— the consolation of philosophy—from which only the betrayed lover can benefit. Troilus begins to approach his narrator's viewpoint as he struggles against his fate beginning in the fourth book. The political events have taken a turn against him, and he tries to extricate himself and his beloved. But he is trapped and, what is even worse, long before Criseyde leaves he becomes aware of his mistake in consenting to let her go. In spite of her optimistic chatter, he predicts almost exactly what will happen when she joins her father. And he tells her so (IV, 1450 ff.). Yet like one fascinated by his own doom he lets her go. He struggles but, in spite of his premonitions, seems unable to do anything about it.

It has long been recognized that Troilus' speech in favor of predestination (IV, 958 ff.) is an important element in the poem. It certainly indicates that Troilus believes in predestination, and I think in the light of what we have been saying here represents a stage in Troilus' approach to Chaucer. When, in the pagan temple, he finally becomes aware of destiny,[9] he is making an attempt to look at his own fate as Chaucer the commentator all along has been looking at it. The outer and inner stories are beginning to join each other. This movement of narrator and character towards each other in the last two books culminates in the ascent through the spheres at the end where Troilus gets as close to Chaucer

(and us) as is possible in observing events in their proper
perspective—*sub specie aeternitatis*. As Boethius writes in
the *Consolation of Philosophy*

> Huc [Nunc] omnes pariter uenite capti
> Quos fallax ligat improbis catenis
> Terrenas habitans libido mentes
> Haec erit uobis requies laborum,
> Hic portus placida manens quiete,
> Hoc patens unum miseris asylum. (III, m.10)

Or as Chaucer himself translates these lines

> Cometh alle to gidre now, ye that ben
> ykaught and ybounde with wikkide cheynes
> by the desceyvable delyt of erthly
> thynges enhabitynge in your thought! Her
> schal ben the reste of your labours, her is
> the havene stable in pesible quiete; this
> allone is the open refut to wreches.

From this vantage point all falls into its place and proper proportion. Troilus now has Chaucer's sense of distance and
joins with his author in finding what peace can be found in
a pagan heaven.

Just before this soul journey, Chaucer has even consigned
his very poem to time and put it in its place along with all
terrestrial things (v, 1793 ff.) in the kingdom of mutability
and change. As Chaucer can slough off his earthly attachments
and prides, even the very poem in which he is aware of their
transitory nature, Troilus his hero can also do so.

Thus towards the end, in the last two books, we see the
hero beginning to imitate his narrator and the narrator, his
hero, and the distance set up between the two begins to lessen
and almost disappear. A dialectic of distance and closeness
which has been from the beginning more than implicit in the
poem between God, Chaucer the commentator-narrator, and
the characters—notably Troilus—of the inner story, becomes
sharply poised, with the triangle shrinking as the three approach each other.[10] A final shift of depth and distance, however, takes place at the end. The poem does not come to a
close with Troilus joining Chaucer. A further last leap is to
establish again, even as at the beginning, a new distance.
Beyond the consolation of philosophy, the only consolation
open to Troilus is the consolation of Christianity. In the last
stanzas, Chaucer the narrator escapes from Troilus to where

the pagan cannot follow him; he escapes into the contemplation of the mysteries of the Passion and of the Trinity, the supreme paradox of all truth, which is the only possible way for a believing Christian to face the facts of his story. The artist and the historian who have been struggling in the breast of Chaucer can finally be reconciled. Here free will and predestination, human dignity and human pettiness, joy and sorrow, in short all human and terrestrial contradictions, are reconciled in the pattern of all reconciliation: the God who becomes man and whose trinity is unity and whose unity is trinity. Here the author-historian can finally find his peace at another distance and leave behind forever the unhappy and importunate Troilus, the unbearable grief of Criseyde's betrayal, the perplexities of time and space, and the tyranny of history and predestination.

Notes

1 On this point in connection with the *Canterbury Tales,* see Professor E. Talbot Donaldson's stimulating "Chaucer the Pilgrim," *PMLA,* LXIX (1954), 928-36 [reprinted in R. J. Schoeck and J. Taylor, eds. *Chaucer Criticism: The Canterbury Tales* (Notre Dame, Indiana, 1960), pp. 1-13]. I am indebted to Professor Donaldson for several suggestions made orally to me and which I have woven into this article—notably the root idea of n.10 below.

2 See Morton W. Bloomfield, "Chaucer's Sense of History," *JEGP,* LI (1952), 301-13.

3 Although irrelevant to the point I am making about the sense of distance in the journey to or though the spheres, there is some question as to the reading and meaning here (v, 1809). I follow Robinson and Root who take the reading "eighth" rather than "seventh" as in most manuscripts. Boccaccio uses "eighth," and there is a long tradition extending back to classical antiquity which makes the ogdoad the resting place of souls (see Morton W. Bloomfield, *The Seven Deadly Sins* East Lansing, 1952, pp. 16-17 ff.). Cf., however, Jackson I. Cope, "Chaucer, Venus and the 'Seventhe Spere'," *MLN,* LXVII (1952), 245-246. (Cope is unaware of the ogdoad tradition and also assumes that Troilus is a Christian.) There is also the problem of the order in which the spheres are numbered. If the highest is the first then the eighth sphere is that of the moon, the one nearest the earth. Root believes Chaucer is following this arrangement. However, as Cope points out, Chaucer in the opening stanza of Bk. III names "Venus as the informing power of the third sphere" and therefore must be using the opposite numbering system. Troilus then goes to the highest sphere, that of the fixed stars. E. J. Dobson ("Some Notes on Middle English Texts," *Eng. and Ger. Stud.,* Univ. of Birmingham, I [1947-48], 61-62) points out that Dante, *Paradiso* XXII, 100-154, which is Boccaccio's (and hence Chaucer's) source of this passage in the *Teseide,* makes clear that the emendation to "eighth" is justified.

4 Needless to say I am not using this phrase in the sense given it by Edward Bullough in his " 'Psychical Distance' as a Factor in Art and an Aesthetic Principle," *Brit. Jour. of Psychol.*, v (1913), reprinted in *A Modern Book of Esthetics, An Anthology*, ed. Melvin Rader, rev. ed. (New York, 1952), pp. 401-428. He refers to "distress" between the art object on the one hand and the artist or audience on the other. The distance here referred to is within the poem, between the character-narrator Chaucer and the events.

5 Chaucer sets himself the problem of interpreting Criseyde's action here by his sympathetic portrayal of her character and by his unblinking acceptance of the "facts" of his history. Boccaccio evades it by his pre-eminent interest in Troilus. Henryson gives Troilus an "unhistorical" revenge. Shakespeare has blackened Cressida's character throughout. Christopher Hassall, in his libretto for William Walton's recent opera on the subject, makes Criseyde a victim of a mechanical circumstance and completely blameless. Only Chaucer, by a strict allegiance to the "historical" point of view, poses the almost unbearable dilemma of the betrayal of Troilus by a charming and essentially sympathetic Criseyde.

6 The only exception is to be found in the Robinson text where at III, 1165 we find the reading in a speech by Criseyde "by that God that bought us both two." I am convinced that the Root reading "wrought": for "bought" is correct. It would be perfectly possible for pagans to use "wrought" but not "bought." If we admit "bought" it would be the only Christian allusion put into the mouths of the Trojan characters and would conflict with the expressedly pagan attitude of these figures. I now take a stronger position on the matter than I allowed myself to express in "Chaucer's Sense of History," *JEGP*, LI (1952), 308, n. 17. Various references to grace, the devil (I, 805), a bishop (II, 104), saints' lives (II, 118) and celestial love (I, 979) need not, from Chaucer's point of view of antiquity, be taken as Christian.

7 *Policraticus*, II, 22, ed. C. C. I. Webb (Oxford, 1909), I, 126; trans. Joseph B. Pike, *Frivolities of Courtiers* (Minneapolis, 1938), p. 111. Incidentally it should be noted that Calchas' foreknowledge through divination is on a basic level the cause of the tragedy.

8 On this dispute in the 14th century, see L. Baudry, *La querelle des futurs contingents* (Paris, 1950), and Paul Vignaux, *Justification et predestination au XIVe siècle* (Paris, 1934).

9 The location of this speech is not, I think, without significance. The end of pagan or purely natural religion is blind necessity, and in its "church" this truth can best be seen.

10 Another triangle has its apex in Pandarus who is, of course, the artist of the inner story as Chaucer is of the outer one and as God is of the created world. Pandarus works on his material—Troilus and especially Criseyde—as his "opposition numbers" do with their materials. All are to some extent limited—Pandarus by the characters of his friend and niece and by political events; Chaucer by his knowledge and by history; God by His rationality. All this is another story, however; my interest here is primarily in the triangle with Troilus as apex.

14

Chaucer's Point of View as Narrator in the Love Poems

DOROTHY BETHURUM

Chaucer writes about more varieties of amatory experience than any other English poet except Shakespeare. Whether in this abundance we have God's plenty or the devil's I will leave to Dryden and Father Denomy and try to comment only on his point of view as he relates the love visions and *Troilus and Criseyde*.

The convention exemplified in the love visions of Machaut, Froissart, and other of Chaucer's near contemporaries is that the narrator of the events—or sentiments—is himself implicated in them and writes from experience. That is the tradition handed on not merely from the Troubadours, but from Ovid as well, who boasts himself in the *Ars Amatoria magister* (II, 744), *doctus* (III, 18) in the art. What he has to say is not the opinion of a mere mortal, but an oracular pronouncement. This is a part of Ovid's sophisticated, complex point of view; it allows him all sorts of sallies and retreats, and is reinforced by his pretended susceptibility to every feminine charm. In the *Remedia* he is more in love than ever and unable to take his own remedies. The troubadour William IX likewise calls himself undoubted master, so learned that he could give advice to anyone.[1] And, indeed, the essential thing to remember is that the tradition passed on from the trouba-

Reprinted, by permission of author and editor, from *PMLA*, LXXIV (1959), 511-20.

dours all the way to the fashionable French poets of Chaucer's generation was a lyric tradition, with the poet expressing his own feelings. There is great difference, to be sure, between the lyric impersonality of the troubadours—we know only that they love—and the personal detail we can piece out about Machaut's late involvement with *la jeune Peronelle* or Froissart's with his "Marguerite," but both assume an implicated poet. It would at this late date be supererogatory to stress the social and literary conventions that in the late Middle Ages clustered around the figure of the troubadour, more often well born than not, addressing amatory verses to his sovereign lady. It became, this very image, the model of courtly behavior, what the well-bred man *must* do, poet or squire.

In the *Roman de la Rose* also the narrator is of course the Lover himself, and he tells his story with the simplicity of youth and with the correctness of Love's servant. He knows that Reason's wise and unexciting advice is not now for him. His despair at times, tempered, to be sure, within the range of good behavior, is genuine, his bursts of hope equally so. Boccaccio, from whom Chaucer borrowed most, is presumably moved to write by no other aim than to set forth his love for Fiammetta. And at the other extreme of love poems Dante also is deeply involved, perhaps most deeply of all. It is not necessary to assume the historical or autobiographical fidelity of the positions taken by these poets, for that is not the question. The point is that they all adopted a position that demanded identification with the idealistic courtly view of love current from the twelfth to the fourteenth centuries.

The courtly view of love to which Chaucer is committed in the poems I am discussing, essentially a justification and ordering of the drives of life, an attempt to make them serve man's highest ends as well as that of preserving the race, had received for thoughtful people stimulus and sanction from the Neoplationists of Chartres in their magnificent elevation of Nature and, by implication, of Eros. In Bernardus Sylvestris' *De mundi universitate* [*On the Created Universe*] and in the two works of Alanus that most influenced mediaeval literature, the *Anticlaudianus* and *De planctu naturae* [*On the Complaint of Nature*],[2] Nature is the principal character. She is appointed by God the *universalis vicaria procreatrix* [universal procreative agent], Chaucer's "Vicaire of the almighty Lord," to whom is delegated the ordering of the world. She is Plato's World Soul, familiar to intellectuals throughout the early Middle Ages, but made accessible to poets and thence to courtly society through the compelling form given the goddess and her work by Bernardus and Alanus, particularly the latter.

The fable of Bernard's work and of Alain's *Anticlaudianus* is the same: Nature on behalf of uncreated matter approaches Nous (God's providence) to beg that form be given to un-formed matter; in other words, to recognize the principle of Plenitude. Bernard's work turns out to be a catalogue of the glories of the created world, very detailed, very learned, and finds its climax, of course, in the creation of man. Alain's *Anticlaudianus* is concerned wholly with the shaping of the perfect man. It is much longer than Bernard's and did much more to make the natural man respectable, even divine. But when the perfect man emerges, his virtues, his prowess are purely secular. That is, there is no appeal to grace or to the redemptive powers of Christ.[3] Man stands complete in the equipment of a gentleman. . . .

The interesting thing about it is that Alain's essential hedonism looks like something else. So serious is his tone, so elevated his speech, so poetically fresh and vigorous his teaching that he makes the noble fulfillment of man's earthly duties seem his highest end. Alain's humanism has religious fervor and gives the stamp of sanctity to his teaching. I do not mean to imply that he is anti-Christian, but simply that the Platonic notion of man's perfectibility if he follow his best *natural* guides so impressed him that he gave perhaps specious religious sanction to the *service d'amour*. Nature is divine and Eros a sacred power.

The great release and joy that came from such a belief has nothing in common with libertinism. It is simply the enormous satisfaction, even delight, of finding the created universe good and man a proper part of it. His internal order corresponds to the external order. The high moral tone of Alain's idea of love in the second part of *De Planctu* is grounded on his idea that Nature is herself responsible for man's moral nature, as well as for the stability and continuity of the created universe; in other words, that reason is *natural* to man, and that the demands of one part of his nature do not conflict with those of another. As de Lage has well pointed out, in Alain's sys-tem the old notion of natural morality (evolved from Cicero,

Seneca, perhaps St. Paul, and the early Fathers) is here
brilliantly reinforced by Nature's control over both physical
and moral life. Kant and Wordsworth and Coleridge found
in this idea when they recovered it the same ecstatic joy that
informs the *Anticlaudianus* and the last part of the *Roman de
la Rose*, though none of them applied it to love as did the
Middle Ages. I think it was not Jean de Meun who first made
this idea acceptable, but Alain de Lille.

A second strain in Alain's thought which influenced Chaucer is the Neoplatonic idea of the ladder of love. Love of man
leads to love of God, and this belief also gave stimulus and
approbation to the great interest in sexual love displayed in
the Middle Ages.

It is this Neoplatonism that Chaucer knew most about and
that seems to have fixed the temper of his thought. Aside from
his familiarity with Alain he was open to the same essential
currents of thought through Macrobius' treatment of Scipio's
dream and through Boethius, perhaps the strongest influence
on him, and through the *Roman de la Rose*. Whether it was
that he was widely read in all of this or whether the appeal of
the Neoplatonic Eros was naturally congenial to him it created
the atmosphere in which the love visions and *Troilus* were
conceived. His trust in a beneficent Nature, autonomous and
intelligible because she is the "Vicaire of the almighty Lord,"
forms the basis of his all-embracing sympathy.[4] This sympathy expresses itself in different forms in the *Book of the
Duchess* and in the *Miller's Tale*, but it is always there. But
when he began to write the *Book of the Duchess* and the
House of Fame these ideas were unformed, to be sure, and
philosophical speculation was far from his intent.

II

What of the traditional form did Chaucer use in the beginning? First, his love visions are indeed dreams, and the
implication of that is, I think, rather simple in the beginning.
Chaucer is not quite romantic enough or idealistic enough to
see the dream as the reality, as did perhaps his troubadour
predecessors, though he became familiar with Alain's use of
the dream to represent the realization of the ideal in form.[5]
The dream serves mainly for aesthetic distancing. It is a
vision within the poem, two degrees from reality, and allows

an even further idealization than we ordinarily expect in a
poem. Later its meaning is ambivalent, for even the pre-
Freudian mediaevalists suspected that there might be psychological revelation in dreams. In the *Book of the Duchess*
the dream offers a relief from reality in that in it the Dreamer
escapes his own sufferings, the knowledge of which he nevertheless carries along. It offers also a charming idealization of
love and a genuine expression of grief. What cuts across the
dream is a suggestion of the comic view of life in the
Dreamer's simplicity and fecklessness, qualities that are present in the *House of Fame*, the *Parlement*, the Prologue to
the *Legend of Good Women*. They are even imitated or
parodied by Pandarus after Chaucer had given up the vision
for straight narration.

When we turn to the lyricism that was so persistent a feature of the love visions, there we find a sharper break. Chaucer is a narrator, and though he twice boasts of having written
the conventional lyrics, the examples of this style that he has
left us are not impressive. In the genuine love visions he meets
the demand for the first person but fails to exhibit his bleed-
ing heart. In two of the visions, however, the *Book of the
Duchess* and the Prologue to the *Legend*, he accepts the convention of the narrator as himself Love's servant.

The *Book of the Duchess* is closest of all to the conventions, being so closely dependent upon Machaut's and Froissart's poems. Features not found in their works, such as the
"screen of ladies" when the knight first sees his beloved, show
that Chaucer was fairly widely read in courtly literature. It
is natural, then, that in this first poem the narrator should be
the sorrowing lover. As Mr. Bronson has so well said, his
involvement here is the ideal complement to the Knight's
own sorrow; "the Knight becomes the dreamer's surrogate."[6]
His state is given as the cause of his sleeplessness and reiterated
from time to time. When he has read the story of Ceyx and
Alcyone he says, as a joke, although he is not at all in the
mood for joking (l. 239), that he also would make Morpheus
an offer. He reminds us of his suffering. And in the course of
the Knight's long recital of the virtues of his lady the Dreamer
applauds his choice thus:

> "By oure Lord," quod I, "y trowe yow wel!'
> Hardely, your love was wel beset;
> I not how yo myghte have do bet."
> "Bet? ne no wyght so wel," quod he.

"Y trowe hyt, sir," quod I, "parde!"
"Nay, leve hyt wel!" "Sire, so do I; . . .
Yow thoghte that she was the beste."   (1042-59)

Notice that the Dreamer never says she was the best, for that superlative is reserved for his own cruel charmer; he merely says "yow thoghte."

Yet the Dreamer is certainly not the conventional rejected lover. Chaucer's is far from Machaut's pose or Froissart's, for it is not his sufferings that are the subject of the poem. The Dreamer is like Conrad's Marlow, the screen through which the real emotion is filtered. And his qualities are far from those of the conventional poet. His obtuseness, his failure as a lover, his ignorance of the classical gods that all polite society tossed about, his direct and humorous speech set him off at a great distance from the knightly subject of his poem, the perfect lover. The effect is comic, of course, yet it provides the ideally tactful form in which a bourgeois poet may record the grief of his patron, the chief knight of the realm, for the death of his wife. As has been often pointed out, irony plays over the whole poem, but the crowning irony is that at the end neither Knight nor Dreamer has his lady. "Golden lads and girls all must/As chimney sweepers come to dust." Death overtakes even the successful lover. Chaucer has promised this in the prologue when Ceyx says to Alcyone at the end of her dream, "To litel whil our blisse lasteth." This line is not in Ovid, and, as Kittredge noted, this awareness of mortality Chaucer had even when young. It constitutes his principal, though not the only, realistic criticism of the dream of love he has described. It is made possible by the position he has taken as narrator.

What is also made possible by his role is some sort of acceptance of death. It is never made explicit, and indeed the proffer of pious advice about being superior to Fortune is satirized by the very naivete of the Dreamer, and the reality of the Knight's grief emphasized by its being beyond the reach of this fatuous talk. Nevertheless, the presence of the simple-minded Dreamer and his ready, if uneloquent, sympathy when he finally does learn the truth binds together the May garden and the reality of love with its ultimate loss in a mutable world, and the reader is presented with the other side of the Garden of Love, which, though it may be painfully difficult to accept, is also in Nature's plan.

Before we consider the other poem in which Chaucer is in

a way a devotee of love, the Prologue to the *Legend*, we ought to see what sort of role he had built up for himself before he wrote it. The *House of Fame* is a love vision, and here the narrator, Geoffrey Chaucer, is the principal character. He is the one who has the adventures. But the poem is not about love, for he is not the man to have amatory experiences. As he wrote to Scogan, Cupid did not bother even to notice people as "rounde of shap" as they both were. The *House of Fame* abounds in conventional features of the vision, though the dream occurs in December and even within it there is no garden in May, without ever really touching love. But the summary of Dido's story, the ground of Jove's interest in Chaucer, even the variety of the amatory experience treated in the Eagle's list of what the poet will hear about love (ll. 677-698)—all promise the usual treatment. The poem turns out to be a parody of the love vision—that is why the dream is in December—principally because of the character of the narrator.

It is a highly personal poem, full of chit-chat about Chaucer's affairs, with a dig at his wife, all of which must have been vastly amusing to its audience. There is nothing original in giving it this turn. Machaut and Froissart were not reluctant to speak of their affairs in their poems. But neither made of himself a comic figure as Chaucer does. He is a dimwitted, insensitive grind, so occupied with his business and his books that he does not even know the current gossip. He has, how-ever, in his feckless way served Love faithfully as Venus' clerk, always writing in his honor and always without reward. He makes quite a point of it for 27 lines (614-640). Jove's pity is inevitable. The implication is, I think, that the tidings of love he is to hear will furnish more material for his poems, for certainly mere tidings of how other people fare would not be the reward a lover looked for.

Here begins the opposition that goes all the way through the poems under discussion—books versus life, authority versus experience. For good or for bad, Chaucer's pose is that of the devotee of books. All he knows about love he reads in books, and he trusts them. So far does this preference go that when the Eagle offers to identify the constellations he has read about, he shows no interest and says he believes the stories all right without seeing the Raven, Bear, etc. Besides, the light hurts his eyes. It always does. The narrator of all these poems trembles at the thought of experience. It is his way of casting the shadow of dubiety upon the glittering idealizations of love that were the current fashion at the court.

He is the perfect sounding-board for the Eagle's professorial loquacity, as indifferent to his pedagogical zeal as our students are to ours. It all increases the element of parody in the poem. For what sort of celestial journey is this? The journey of Nature to heaven in Bernard's *De Mundi*, of Wisdom's in the *Anticlaudianus*, Scipio's or Dante's—all these were deeply serious in intent. This one is comic to a high degree, with a middle-aged fat civil servant journeying through the celestial spheres in the claws of an eagle to hear a little gossip.

In the end the poem turns out to be about fame, and Geoffrey is as indifferent to fame as he was inexperienced in love. Both love and fame to nothingness do sink. As Professor Baum has said, experience itself in this poem is disillusioning, Fame's good will not worth struggling for.[7] And, though we lack the ending, that of the *Parlement of Foules* would be suitable enough: he returns to his books.

Why it is that the poem pulls in two ways, promising a love vision and then shifting the subject, we can only surmise. It may be that Chaucer intended in the beginning to write about love (in his way) but that his apparently recent reading of the *Somnium Scipionis*[8] with its quite different slant led him to echo what Africanus taught the younger Scipio about the unreliability of Fame. The ambivalence of the term *Fama* allows the shift from tidings (rumor) to Fame.

This withdrawal of the narrator from love constitutes not merely the only possible position for a bourgeois poet writing for a courtly and largely feminine audience, but it allows him increasingly his own ironic and realistic comment on the fashionable subject. This becomes explicit in the *Parlement of Foules,* and now that he is at home in his role, he can write about love freely, from many points of view. This poem seems to me by far the best of the love visions. It is both rich and brilliant, with all the gusto of the *House of Fame* and with variety so great that its critics are as disputatious about its meaning as the avian parliament in its debate. In the introduction the opposition between books and experience is sharpened, and Chaucer announces a sort of credo in the fourth stanza:

> For out of olde feldes, as men seyth,
> Cometh al this newe corn from yer to yere,
> And out of olde bokes, in good feyth,
> Cometh al this newe science that men lere.

He is again rewarded for reading a book, this time the *Dream of Scipio*. Africanus is so moved by his devotion to the vision that he takes him into the Garden of Love. But what good does it do a poor dull fellow who has lost his taste for love as a sick man loses his appetite? As he stands outside the gate with its two inscriptions he acts like Criseyde, not knowing whether to risk it or not, until Africanus has to remind him that he will be a mere observer, not participator, and that he will get material for his poems:

> Yit that thou canst not do, yit mayst thow se
> . . . .
> And if thow haddest connying for t'endite,
> I shal the shewe mater of to wryte.

What he shows him is Paradise, and Chaucer writes of it freely, delightedly. But the very fact that he is substituting description for participation emphasizes the unreality of the Garden. It is the dream of love that all men with imagination have at some time and that none ever completely realizes. The description is done *con amore*, the details carefully enumerated to fill out all aspects of the sensual experience, and if it remains on an earthly level, it is only being true to the tone of the *Roman de la Rose*, with something of the untroubled joy that Alain's interpretation had made possible in this context. It is, indeed, Alain's own Natura who rules the garden, she who redresses the losses caused by death by means of her powerful drive. She is the "creative passion of God at work on the earth." Her aide is Love—Venus or Eros—whose manifestations are all good from the universal point of view that regards variety as the great end of creation,[9] and who constitutes the bond of union in all existence, that universal cohesive force that keeps the world going. (Chaucer celebrates this aspect best in *Troilus*.)

In the beginning of the poem the narrator states that though he has not experienced love "in dede" and does not know its "dredful joye," he has studied it long in authoritative books and hopes some time to understand it. There is con-

scious ambiguity in the "certeyn thing to lerne" that he sought
in the Dream of Scipio, but it can hardly be doubted that it is
knowledge about love that he seeks.[10] His position of the
ignorant but eagerly receptive seeker for knowledge makes
description his only function, for he can not judge what he
does not know.

The picture of the Garden of Love is little touched by
irony. It is full-blooded voluptuousness common enough in
Italian literature but difficult to find in English. Irony is all-
pervasive, however, in the latter part of the poem. It allows
Chaucer to set forth the courtly ideal and all the middle-class
criticism of it with equal delight. The acceptance of selfish
cuckoo, sentimental turtle dove, conventional ardent courtly
lovers alike rests upon Chaucer's acceptance of Nature's
beneficent fullness where all serve some purpose, and also
upon the fact that all are somewhat ridiculous. For none has
his eye on the "comune profyt," and the undifferentiating
narrator in his detachment takes the universal point of view.
But perhaps to God the "comune profyt" is served by earthly
folly as well as by earthly wisdom, and perhaps the difference
between them is not great.

In any case, Africanus' promise is made good; Chaucer has
"mater of to wryte," and he takes his poetic duties seriously.
The ardor of his invocation to Venus anticipates that in
Troilus:

> Cytherea! thow blysful lady swete,
> That with thy fyrbrond dauntest whom the lest,
> And madest me this sweven for to mete,
> Be thow myn help in this, for thow mayst best;
> . . . .
> So gif me mygth to ryme and ek t'endyte.   (113-9)

This stanza combines his dedication to writing about love and
his desire to understand it and to write well. At the end of
the poem his knowledge is apparently still incomplete—

> I hope, ywis, to rede so som day
> That I shal mete som thyng for to fare
> The bet, and thus to rede I nyl nat spare—

but it is not experience from which he hopes to profit better,
but from further study of his books.

The Prologue to the *Legend of Good Women* has the look
of making unusual concessions to the conventions. It is a

palinode answering the palinode of *Troilus and Criseyde,* and though there are many literary models for it, it may actually have been demanded by the ladies, as it says. Chaucer's retraction, when he gets into the legends themselves, is too perfunctory to be entirely genuine, but he does his best in the beginning. He reverses his position, apparently, and professes himself a devotee. So hotly does he love the daisy that he leaves his beloved books when May comes to go out and assume an attitude of abject devotion, leaning on his elbow to gaze at the flower. The daisy is, of course, some woman; not even Wordsworth could find in that miserable little English daisy "the clernesse and the verray lyght/That in this derke world me wynt and ledeth." Even in the F version this devotion seems to have gone against the grain with Chaucer, for he excuses himself, saying it is the French poets who can really praise the marguerite, as indeed they did, and he is only coming after them picking up the scraps. This is *vers de société,* glancing over the courtly fashions of the moment—the cult of the marguerite, the parties of the flower and the leaf, the light and never serious treatment of love. What has *Troilus* to do in that company![11]

Though he begins the poem with this profession of devotion it turns out that his adoration is for some disembodied she whose identity he does not even know until the God of Love tells him at the end of the Prologue that it is Alcestis (or Queen Anne) he has been worshipping all this time. And before the Prologue has progressed far Chaucer has reverted to his usual position when Alcestis pleads for him that he is really too stupid to understand what he has translated and will use any material that comes to hand, just so he can write something. Nor does he really understand Love's service. Here there is an amusing slight change. Alcestis does not say that Chaucer is unsuccessful in love, but "thogh he lyke nat a lovere bee" (F 490), and in the G version,

> While he was yong, he kepte youre estat;
> I not wher he be now a renegat.   (400-401)

Perhaps it is the slightest gesture of defiance. A court poet had to pay *some* compliment to ladies, but he had never been willing to pay the usual ones. The Prologue is, in fact, an elaborate and graceful compliment to Queen Anne, in which any real participation in love would be grossly out of place.

As much space is given to her queenly pity as to his defection, and her defense of him amounts in a way to his justification.

In the G version the explicit reference to the Queen is deleted, and the devotion is considerably cooler. It takes place within the dream, for one thing, and even there it is less extreme. The G version adds also a detail that must be ironic in citing those arch anti-feminists Jerome and Walter Map as defenders of faithful women, especially when the brides of Christ are expressly excluded:

> And this thing was not kept for holynesse,
> But al for verray vertu and clennesse.

It looks as if books and art had come out second best on this occasion, but I do not think they have. The beginning of the Prologue is notorious for its roundabout way of getting into the story, and what the delay amounts to is a thumping defense of authority, of what can be read in books. When the poet leaves them to go and peer at a daisy it is a little funny. This reliance on the "olde bokes" clears the poet of all responsibility. If they led him astray once in the case of *Troilus* and the *Roman* (and he never admits that they did), he nevertheless returns to them at the end of the Prologue to prove the opposite case of woman's faithfulness and man's perfidy. What else can he do who has "noon other preve?" This time, when it comes to rewards for reading and writing, there is an appeal for a more useful patron than Jupiter or Africanus. Alcestis says she will pray the God of Love that he charge his servants to help the poet along and reward his labor well. I trust they did.

The mask of the Fool—that is what Chaucer hit upon as the ideal reflector of life's extravagances, and he could have found no better. He is the ancestor of Swift in presenting these idealizations through a dullard who can not understand or respond. Through his pose he keeps the true comic spirit, maintaining the *ewige kleine*. It does not condemn the ideal, but marks it as pretty far from normal human experience.

III

In *Troilus and Criseyde* Chaucer's position changes somewhat. Though he emphasizes his detachment and ignorance—

he does not "dar to love, for myn unliklynesse"—and insists throughout the poem that he is completely dependent on "myn auctour," he is of course more deeply involved than in any other of his stories. For this is no longer a dream, an allegory of love in which the writer describes his vision. It is a romance, straight narration, and to be able to realize the values of love in the brilliant concretion the story gives us, its narrator must be also the sympathetic participator. His reiteration that he is only an outsider and the power and truth of his picture are completely contradictory and produce the ambivalence that is so strikingly characteristic of the poem.[12] Indeed, it makes high comedy of his pose, and must have been one of the great sources of delight to its first audience.

There has always been a conflict between Chaucer's pose of detachment and his identification with his subjects. A really detached writer tells his story as Chrétien told his, and the result is coldness. The nearest Chaucer came to detachment was in the third book of the *House of Fame,* and it was there possible because Fame did not move him very deeply. Love does, and in *Troilus* his identification with his characters is so complete that he cries out in pain as the story moves to its sad end.

There is another facet also to his attitude towards his story. The love of Troilus and Criseyde is not unique; it is presented as an illustration of Love's wonderful works.

> For evere it was, and evere it shal byfalle,
> That Love is he that alle thing may bynde;
> For may no man fordo the lawe of kynde.
>
> (I, 236-238)

When the author intervenes in the story, as he so frequently does, it is often to speak in his own person of Love's power, as in I, 211-259. The Proem of the third book is a great Neoplatonic invocation to the love that sustains the universe, as is Troilus' hymn in the third book to "thou holy bond of thynges." The lovers do not boast that they surpass all others in their feeling, nor does their creator so present them. They illustrate that "every wyght, I gesse,/That loveth wel meneth but gentilesse." At the height of their joy Chaucer says:

> I kan namore, but thus thise ilke tweye,
> That nyght, betwixen drede and sikernesse,
> Felten in love the grete worthynesse.
>
> (III, 1314-16)

And he appeals to his audience to recognize their emotions:
"This, trowe I, knoweth al this compaignye." The poem is in
fact a sort of exemplum, and this fits Chaucer's pose as narrator. Since he can not pay Venus the usual service of love,
he will write in her honor. As far as the narrator himself is
involved in the whole religion of love which is so prominent
a feature of the poem, that is his position, from his parody of
the pope's title in I, 15—"For I that god of loves servauntes
serve"—until the end, where he pays tribute to another God.
This universality conditions the philosophical tone of the
poem.

As the story sweeps him on, another contradiction emerges.
Chaucer's consciousness of himself as artist is more emphasized here than in the love visions, and makes explicit his
necessary involvement. From the Proem of Book I, where he
bids lovers pray for him, not that he succeed in love, but that
he write well, to the ending, where he prays God that no one
copy his book wrong or mis-meter it, he has his art always
before him. At the climax of his story he appeals in agony of
need to Venus to help him do justice to the *joie d'amour*.
(She heard his prayer.) At the same time he emphasizes his
complete dependence on the books. In the love visions the
fact that the poet is relating a dream relieves him of responsibility; one can not order his dreams. In *Troilus* Chaucer gets the same effect by reiterating his passive role. He
can not direct the story; he merely translates what is before
him. "Of no sentement I this endite." It isn't his feeling, but
his author's.

His own imprisonment in the story builds up toward the
end; in Book V he grieves that he can not exonerate Criseyde
and "falsen my matere," and, projecting the story far back
in time, he refers often to the "olde bokes." But the compulsion is not that of the "olde bokes," nor yet, I think, of
any faith in the historicity of his characters. It is the compulsion of the artist face to face with the naked fact of human frailty, and torn by pity that a creature so charming as
Criseyde could be capable of infidelity. Chaucer has exactly
the freedom of any artist, and he makes the same choices.

Shakespeare chose to write about the improbable, almost incredible, circumstance under which a man not given to jealousy could murder his wife in a jealous rage. Chaucer chose to write about conditions under which a woman made for love and deeply capable of its best service could betray her lover. We do not know what *Othello* cost Shakespeare, but Chaucer describes his sorrow.

The effect of Chaucer's insistence on his lack of freedom is that he maneuvers himself into exactly the position of the reader, and his intense involvement is that of the fascinated reader or hearer, knowing how the story must end and dreading to see Troilus sign his soul out to the Grecian tents where Criseyde lay that night. It is a masterful position, not quite that of the Fool who related the love visions, but it leaves him equally helpless before the story. For, like Dante, he can now have it both ways. Dante's poem in its magnificent architecture, the journey, sets out the justice of God; but Dante as a figure moving through the system can express man's pity. Throughout the *Inferno* his tears flow for the condemned. Otherwise we could not bear the poem. Chaucer also has it both ways. He presents Eros in all its glory and nobility. Where is the great chain of Love that binds all creation together expressed with more passion, even religious fervor, than in the Proem to Book III? And where is the *service d'amour* and the *joie d'amour* nobler or truer? What is there more to say? Only what Chaucer does implicitly say: Love is wonderful, the most wonderful thing in the world. I don't have it, but the books say it is, and successful lovers say it is. Troilus and Criseyde both said it often, but at the end of the poem neither has it. The truth is, nobody has it in its perfection— or has it very long. That is what Chaucer always knew. "To litel whil our blisse lasteth." And by putting himself exactly in our position, he has presented the ideal vision and his sober realistic comment on it.

For the reader brings to the poem his own knowledge of the instability of all human relations. If Troilus and Criseyde are illustrations of love's powers, their short happiness is also an illustration of the mutability that marks all earthly life. Not for nothing did Chaucer give them their universal role. Hence the ending of the poem.[13] Chaucer's pity and irony join in his wish to spare the "yonge fresshe folk" love's sorrow, but he knows nevertheless that "may no man fordo the lawe of kynde." If one could love God solely he would never know Troilus' sorrow, but for most youth on this earth that is not a possibility. Nor is it desirable, if the human race is to continue.

What Troilus ultimately sees is the absurdity of earthly life, but that vision in its entirety is not possible save from some celestial height. What is sometimes possible is the tragic vision of life which presents its ineluctable contradictions as a mystery. That vision Troilus did not get, because his view came from the realm where causes are known. Criseyde comes nearer expressing it, but she is not of stature heroic enough to achieve it. Nor is it possible to Chaucer, for he found the answer to the dilemma of man's idealism and his frailty in Christian dogma. Yet the poem marks the point where the mediaeval idea of tragedy almost becomes that of the seventeenth century.

IV

Let us attempt to define Chaucer's attitude to love. I do not think it possible for any modern to do this satisfactorily, for we lack knowledge intimate enough to reveal it. Certainly it was not a static one, and within the poems we have been discussing there is clear development up to the complex and subtle presentation in *Troilus,* while the *Canterbury Tales* offer another chapter. Even within one work there is action and reaction, as in *Troilus.* But within these limitations perhaps something can be said.

For one thing the reaction at the end of *Troilus* can not be taken to mean that Chaucer was urging all youth to renounce earthly love and enter a convent. And if not, and if one lives in the world, one must obey the law of kind and love, for love, as Chaucer so eloquently says, is the great teacher of virtue. It cured Troilus of his pride and Criseyde of her self-centeredness, and each "tho (their vices) gan for a vertu chaunge." "Thus wolde Love, yheried be his grace!"

It is not sufficiently recognized by some modern critics, it seems to me, that mediaeval counsels of perfection took account of two spheres, a secular and religious, two states of life, an active and a contemplative.[14] Some of the recent criticism[15] seems to proceed on the assumption that the conduct enjoined upon the religious is demanded of everybody, that celibacy is a universal ideal. We do not need the Wyf of Bath to answer that attitude; St. Thomas himself has done it. But I do not know on what other grounds Professor Robertson could find the garden of the *Roman de la Rose* the scene of idolatry and evil and the God of Love "Satan decked out in fine 'humanistic' trappings" (p. 43). It could not be on the ground that the love celebrated in the *Roman* does not produce offspring, for that is the point of Nature's eloquent (and long-winded) defense of Love in the second part. Only Alain exceeded Jean de Meun in his celebration of fertility. And Genius not only expressly excommunicates all who fail to use Nature's powers as they were intended but says further in good Neoplatonic terms that the entrance to Paradise is through the earthly Garden of Love.[16] To be sure, it is not expressly stated that the Lover and his Rose produced sixteen children after their union, but to claim that the love celebrated is sterile and the *Roman* a denunciation of earthly love in favor of heavenly is to ignore almost everything Nature says and the whole movement of the poem. It is to impose upon it a scheme of thought to which there is little evidence that Guillaume or Jean de Meun adhered.

In view of the sheer bulk of secular literature produced in the twelfth, thirteenth, and fourteenth centuries, and in view of the mediaeval preoccupation with sexual love, it seems to me impossible to deny that secular active life, admittedly ruled by different canons from those imposed upon clerics, was then as now the principal interest of most people. Alain de Lille's performance is a good example of how possible it was for even a cleric to shift from one sphere to another. He was a theologian of wide repute and wrote ten works on theology and morality, but he produced also two secular works from which theology is entirely absent.

Nor am I convinced that in the secular world there was the agonizing opposition between sexual love and *caritas* that we are led to believe. In Chaucer's poems anyway the Neoplatonic conviction that love of man leads to love of God, and its corollary, the chain of love that keeps the universe in being, are too enthusiastically described to allow us to believe that Chaucer himself found them unacceptable. Nor does the somewhat uneasy searching of the *Parlement* necessarily mean that *caritas* and *eros* were at war in Chaucer's mind,[17] but rather that to him as to us the nature of love is the most important thing one can know and the most difficult in its moral and spiritual implications.

But the criticism of Father Denomy and Professor Robertson is leveled against all of courtly love because it does not lead to marriage. Here it is not necessary to enter that controversy. What is necessary is to note that we can not expect, even in Chaucer's time, that the idealism of courtly love had been successfully transferred to marriage, for, although two hundred years separate Chrétien and Chaucer, social conditions had not changed to the point where the aristocracy could marry for love, much less the nobility. Hence it would have been irrelevant to talk about marriage in this connection. If love came after marriage, that was all to the good, but it would have disrupted the whole social and economic organization to make it a prerequisite for marriage. If poets are going to write about love they must write about love, not about a religious sacrament or a social institution. Hence the ambiguity in some of Chaucer's poems. The *Book of the Duchess* is written in the terms of courtly love, but Blanche *was* John of Gaunt's wife. In the *Parlement* there is no mention of marriage, but birds do not have priests.

The open acceptance of Katherine Swynford at the court in the long twenty years that she was John of Gaunt's mistress[18] would indicate that the society that formed Chaucer's audience could tolerate an extramarital liaison; and when Boniface IX made the Beauforts legitimate and Richard II elevated one of them, a mere boy, to a bishopric, it was clear that neither the church nor the king took Gaunt's defection very seriously. We do not know enough about this affair to say whether it was, like Chad Newsome's and Mme. de Vionnet's, a "virtuous attachment," or whether it fulfilled the stringent demands of courtly love, but the facts that it lasted so long and that Gaunt finally married Katherine forbid the assumption that it was mere philandering. It *may* have seemed to the court exactly what the older poets were talking about.

Courtly love was probably the purest form of sexual love the western world has known, being unmixed with social ambition, pride, desire of wealth, or even the laudable interests of family. That was its trouble. Like Mr. Warren's "pure poetry,"[19] it was too pure, and in a complex social world it would not do. Troilus' ruin came from his intense preoccupation with Criseyde, to the exclusion of everything else, but his sin was not to Chaucer a mortal one, for Troilus goes to the only heaven a pagan can know.

It seems to be assumed sometimes that the love poets of the Middle Ages thought they were writing about perfect and stable felicity and then described something that fell short of it. But they were not; they were writing about human love. The troubadours and the Italian poets knew no satisfied love; they knew desire, *courtoisie,* the elevation that comes from loving the *donna angelicata.* But peace and security they do not talk about at all. They know it is not to be had. And at the end of the *Roman,* when Genius compares the earthly garden with the heavenly, he is not repudiating the earthly; he is only saying what everybody knows, that human happiness is unattainable, that lasting felicity is not an earthly commodity. But the greatest happiness that *is* possible in the sublunar realm comes from love. And to that I think Chaucer would subscribe.

Chaucer's balance is a delicate one. The Neoplatonic terms in which his favorite authors saw the universe—the Immutable has expressed himself in change, but the mutable is his work and lovable—is in agreement with his own delight in the visible world. But that is not the whole story. After the first ardor of youth he begins to find in learning the stability the world of human relations lacks. His interest in science, in philosophy, his critical sceptical mind, his absorbed delight in a fine book—when he read the *Somnium Scipionis* "al that day me thoughte but a lyte"—define the kind of man to whom learning is an absolute necessity. The heart of Chaucer's position as narrator is to set off the contrast between books and experience, between the stable world of learning and the fragile world of love. He knows another kind of stability also, a belief in an immutable God who "nyl falsen no wight," and this becomes most valuable to him when love brings most pain. But his trust in the stable did not lead him to undervalue what he seems to have considered mortal man's best experience on this earth. From his appreciation of *both* worlds comes his incomparable poise.

Notes

1 See *Les Chansons de Guillaume* IX, ed. Alfred Jeanroy (Paris, 1913) IX, 13-16.

2 The best edition of the *Anticlaudianus* is that of R. Bossaut, Paris, 1955. *De planctu* has not been recently edited but is in Migne, *Patrologia Latina*, Vol. ccx, and in Th. Wright's *Satirical Poets of the Twelfth Century*, Vol. II. *De planctu* was translated by Douglas Moffat, Yale Studies in English, Vol. xxxvi (1908), and *Anticlaudianus* by Wm. H. Cornog, Philadelphia, 1935. For recent studies of Alanus, see J. Huizinga, *Über die Verknüpfung des Poetischen mit dem Theologischen bei Alanus de Insulis* (Mededeelingen den Koninklijke Akademie van Westenschappen, Afdeeling Letterkunde, Deel 72, Serie B, No. 6, Amsterdam, 1932); Raynaud de Lage, *Alain de Lille*, Montreal and Paris, 1951; and R. H. Green, *Speculum*, xxxi (1956), 649-674.

3 Huizinga makes this point in the article cited above.

4 The achievements of the early scholastics, especially the Chartrists, in establishing the autonomy and reality of the natural world are described in the work of de Lage cited above and in G. Paré, *Le Roman de la Rose et la Scolastique Courtoise*, Paris and Ottawa, 1941. See also, on the School of Chartres, B. Geyer, *Überwegs Grundriss der Geschichte der Philosophie*, Teil 2 (*Die Patristische und Scholastische Philosophie*), Berlin, 1928.

5 Alain's use of the dream to embody the *form* which is closer to God's idea than the waking experience appears in both his poems. . . .

6 B. H. Bronson, "The *Book of the Duchess* Reopened," *PMLA*, LXVII (1952), 863-81.

7 Paull F. Baum, "Chaucer's *The House of Fame*," *ELH*, VIII (1941), 248-256.

8 I do not consider irrefutable Miss Shackford's evidence that he did not know the *Somnium* at first hand when he wrote the *House of Fame*. See "The Date of Chaucer's *House of Fame*," *MLN*, xxxi (1916), 507-508.

9 Thomas Aquinas accepted the principle that a universe in which there were no evil would be less good than the one we have because less varied. *Summa contra Gentiles*, III, 71, argues the perfection of the universe from its variety. "Its beauty results from the ordered unity of good and evil things," tr. English Dominican Fathers (London, 1928), III, i, 177.

10 On this point see J. A. W. Bennett's *The Parlement of Foules*, Oxford, 1957, chs. I and II.

11 It looks a little as if the Prologue were a reaction from the pain of *Troilus*, something similar to Shakespeare's reaction from *Romeo and Juliet* in *A Midsummernight's Dream*.

12 Professor Donaldson, in his criticism of the poem in *Chaucer's Poetry*, New York, 1958, pp. 965-980, has written sensitively of Chaucer's role as narrator and the ambiguity it creates. See also Morton Bloomfield, "Distance and Predestination in *Troilus and Criseyde*," *PMLA*, LXXII (1957), 14-26 [reproduced above, pp. 196-210].

13 I agree with Professor Donaldson that the ending is not an afterthought nor inconsistent with the story, though it flows from Chaucer's strong reaction to the unhappy outcome.

14 See Thomas Aquinas' moderate discussion of the two in *Summa Theologica*, II, CLXXIX-CLXXXII, with his pronouncement that personal temperament should dictate one's choice in this matter.

15 For example, Father Denomy's *The Heresy of Courtly Love*, New

York, 1947; and D. W. Robertson, "The Doctrine of Charity in Mediaeval Literary Gardens: A Topical Approach through Symbolism and Allegory," *Speculum*, XXVI (1951), pp. 36 ff.

16 *Roman de la Rose*, ed. E. Langlois (Paris, 1924), ll. 19505-32. See the whole of Genius' speech of excommunication.

17 Cf. R. M. Lumiansky, *RES*, XXIV (1948), 81-89.

18 See Armitage-Smith, *John of Gaunt* (London, 1904), ch. XVI and Appendix VI, iii.

19 R. P. Warren, *Selected Essays* (New York, 1958), pp. 3 ff.

15

The Pattern of Consolation in *The Book of the Duchess*

JOHN LAWLOR

The Book of the Duchess will always hold a special attraction for students of Chaucer, since it is the first extended work to come from his hand. If criticism is in general no longer in danger of seeing "the great mass of Chaucer's work [as] simply a background to the *Canterbury Tales*,"[1] there is still every reason for concerning ourselves with the emergence of Chaucer's characteristic powers, especially his power of setting an "unmistakable, individual stamp"[2] on all he uses from common mediaeval stock. *The Book of the Duchess* offers features of peculiar interest in this respect, and we are indebted to many scholars for their comparison of French poetry with Chaucer's appropriation from it. More generally, the poem has not lacked critical attention, and after the work of Kittredge[3]—surely the best single treatment of the poem to date—there might seem little to be said concerning the general lines of interpretation. Asserting the delicacy of the central design—a dullness of the Dreamer which draws the Bereaved Knight to describe with growing ardor his love suit and its happy fulfilment—Kittredge is led to conclude his examination on the highest plane. He finds Matthew Arnold "speaking with limited sympathy and imperfect comprehension" when he "would exclude [Chaucer]

Reprinted, by permission of author and editor, from *Speculum*, XXXI (1956), 626-48.

from the fellowship of his peers on the strength of a formula, because he lacked 'high seriousness.' "[4] This is indeed a marked change from earlier charges of incompetence,[5] and later studies have in general followed Kittredge in his approach to the dullness of the Dreamer and his appraisal of the effective ends to which the matter of courtly love has been directed. In one of the best of more recent treatments, Professor Patch[6] reminds us that in such an undertaking as this, the attempted consolation of one of the most powerful men of Chaucer's day, "there could be no false step," and he goes on to observe that the background of French courtly love poetry is used to remind us "of the fundamental equilibrium in nature."[7] The "high frivolity of Courtly Love" makes for an essential difference in tone from *"Lycidas, Adonais,* or *Thyrsis,* where we are invited merely to weep or at least to recollect our emotion in tranquillity." But the poet's purpose is "to afford comfort": and in this he has "counted on a sensitive understanding in his reader, and on a friendliness that reached across barriers."[8]

It would seem, however, that not all students of Chaucer are thus readily persuaded. Manly declared that "the poem bears all the marks of immaturity":[9] Professor H. S. Bennett, in a more recent publication, appearing in an authoritative series, speaks of "the absence of any profound emotion or piercing thought."[10] A more specific objection has been made by Professor C. S. Lewis. He warmly praises the description of the Duchess, and finds the poem "a true elegy," the poet's choice of the dream form having rendered possible "a more intimate picture of his patron's loss than would have been seemly on any other terms."[11] But Professor Lewis finds Chaucer attempting "to do better than he is yet able"; the dialogue between Knight and Dreamer is to bring out "dramatically"

> the impatient self-absorption of grief on the part of the lover, and his demands on the dreamer's close attention. But [Chaucer] does this so clumsily that he sometimes makes the one seem a bore, and the other a fool, thus producing comic effects which are disastrous, and which were certainly not intended.[12]

More recently, Professor Kemp Malone has expressed certain forthright views on the artistry of this work. Kittredge's explanation of the Dreamer's dullness is "ingenious but not wholly convincing"; both the Dreamer's lovesickness and his dullness are to be understood more simply. "Chaucer was not the man to miss a humorous effect"; "wherever Chaucer speaks one is justified in looking for humor and one usually finds it": and the fact that the Dreamer has overheard the plain statement of bereavement and yet in the dialogue ignores it is to be understood as an attempt to gain "the greater virtue of dramatic irony" by deliberately sacrificing "the virtue of consistency." The irony thus aimed at lies behind the "fool's part" Chaucer must play and "Chaucer has to pay for what he gets." Yet the comic element thus introduced "into the very heart of his elegy" does not spoil Chaucer's elegiac effect—"a piece of technical virtuosity beyond praise." Professor Malone does not enlarge upon this aspect of Chaucer's achievement; his treatment concludes with praise of the realism of the dialogue in this poem; an illustration that Chaucer "from the beginning of his literary career . . . set his own stamp on everything he took."[13]

It is clear that the humor of this poem offers possible misunderstanding where it does not provoke outright censure. This is inseparably linked with the whole pattern of consolation that the poet offers in the "high frivolity" of courtly love. If we establish that pattern, it may be easier to assess the nature and effectiveness of the humor it involves. Further, as a wealth of literary convention is involved in this first extended poem of Chaucer's, we may have fresh grounds for judging the development of Chaucer's skill in placing "his own stamp on everything he took."

I

The natural starting-point of inquiry is with courtly love. The origin and progress of the sorrowful Knight's love affair are clearly conceived in those traditional terms that have their ultimate source in *The Romance of the Rose.* The relation of this to the pattern of consolation offered will be discussed later. But at the outset it must be observed that the use of these conventions does not immediately involve departure from a prosaic world of married love to a sophisticated fiction of adultery. Readers of Professor C. S. Lewis's *The Allegory of Love* might be forgiven for supposing that love is only "courtly" when it is adulterous.[14] Lewis indeed has allowed that the loves of Troilus and Criseyde "are so nobly conceived that they are divided only by the thinnest partition from the lawful loves of Dorigen and her husband." But for him the fact of adultery remains the decisive test: so Chaucer, he holds, has in *Troilus and Criseyde* "brought the old romance of adultery to the very frontiers of the . . . romance of marriage." But "he does not himself cross the frontier" though "his successors will soon inevitably do so."[15] To this we can only reply that Chaucer's Dorigen and Arveragus are wedded courtly lovers. Like the love portrayed in The Knight's Tale, their love finds its issue in marriage; and their courtly relationship is maintained within the marriage bond. Arveragus is "Servant in love and lord in mariage"—and this is true "lordshipe":

> Sith he hath bothe his lady and his love;
> His lady, certes, and his wyf also,
> The which that lawe of love acordeth to.
>
> *(CT,* V [F], 796-8)

Again, as one writer has observed, a union of "romantic love and marriage is assumed in the majority of the knightly romances that took their present form in late fourteenth century England."[16] Even if we turn to *Troilus and Criseyde,* we find Pandarus, the high-priest of all who love *paramours,* equating a man's "love" and his "wife" for the purpose of his lesson to Troilus on the acceptance of separation:

> Syn day by day thow maist thiselven se
> That from his love, *or ellis from his wif,*
> A man mot twynnen of necessite,
> *Ye, though he love hire as his owene lif.*
>
> (v, 337-40)

Father Mathew draws attention to the significance of a fourteenth-century Anglo-Norman allegory where the courtly conventions are linked with marriage: the lovers, being married "remain *amys et amye* and such good loving rightly used can please and serve God and bring them to a joy without end."[17] Yet it is not necessary in this matter to go far afield. In *The Owl and the Nightingale,* as Atkins pointed out, the Nightingale, while forwarding the merits of love poetry, has reservations to make against the tradition of *amour courtois,* where "marriage was represented as a hateful form of slavery, and the husband as an odious tyrant *(le vilain, le gelos).*"[18] . . .

The Owl, in her sharp fashion taking the Nightingale to task for her preoccupation with maidens, agrees in the praise of married love. Many a merchant and many a knight loves and cherishes his wife ("Luueþ an hald his wif ariht").

The point would hardly be worth making, were it not apparent that it is sometimes overlooked, and this may lead to deeper misunderstanding. Towards the end of his treatment of *The Book of The Duchess*, Kemp Malone makes this observation:

> Throughout the dialogue the man in black presents his love affair in strictly courtly terms. Marriage is nowhere mentioned, and the following passage makes it clear that the affair was not physically consummated:
>
> > My lady yaf me al hooly
> > The noble yifte of hir mercy,
> > Savynge hir worship, by al weyes,—
> > Dredles, I mene noon other weyes.
> >
> > (1269-72)
>
> In other words, John of Gaunt's happy marriage with Blanche could not be represented as such but had to be turned into an extra-marital love affair for the sake of conformity to the conventions of courtly love. And as it would never do to have the Duchess give herself to a lover, the affair had to be presented as a love in which the desires of the flesh could not be satisfied and must be sublimated.[19]

This is indeed a curious comment. Certainly if there were warrant for restricting the term "courtly love" to "extra-marital" love affairs, it would be necessary to conceive the poem as sophisticated fiction. But even if this were so, it would still be difficult to see the logic of Professor Malone's contention that the love portrayed can have no physical fulfilment. What the dialogue presents is the experience of the lover from the first sight of his Lady up to his final acceptance by her. "The noble yifte of hir mercy" is not *le don de merci amoureux* in the old tradition, the yielding of the Lady's person, but her acceptance of the lover, and the plighting of troth with him. All other suitors drop out of sight: he becomes her man, and is taken "in her governaunce." The story of fulfilled love has reached its climax. The sorrow and hardship of love's service, the first failure and redoubled grief, all are now at an end. From this point forward

> Our joy was ever ylyche newe;
> Oure hertes wern so evene a payre
> That never nas that oon contrayre
> To that other, for no woo. (1288-91)

Precisely because the present sorrow is to be matched against past happiness the story of this love reaches its climax in the region of fulfilment; the suitor is accepted. Marriage, and the physical fulfilment of love, as such have no immediate place in this design: they are neither suppressed nor made explicit. What is relevant to the pattern of consolation the poet offers is the perfect fulfilment of the lover's service. The "conventions of courtly love" as poets and writers of romance can use them in the fourteenth century are not restricted to "extra-marital" associations. The truth appears to be that the color and warmth of *amour courtois,* the stylized attitudes and tender protestations, the cries for mercy and the proofs of constancy, have found their own effective sphere within the framework of a romantic love that finds its issue in marriage. . . .

The point need not be labored, though it is of fundamental significance in the history of English sentiment. The color and tenderness of *amour courtois* do not, in the English tradition, have any final quarrel with the romantic love that aspires to fulfilment in marriage. In this respect, of course, our tradition differs from that of Continental literature, where the serious treatment of the passion of love is to be looked for in the adulterous liaison; and critics who come to our literature with the continuing French tradition in mind may well be inclined to register disapproval of English handlings of traditional love themes. One recalls Professor Vinaver's original disappointment at Malory's treatment of Tristan and Iseult ("comédie larmoyante"), and his repudiation of Malory's "well-intentioned" attempts to inculcate "stability," "the virtue of the common man," as also Malory's making Lancelot himself warn a lady against those who use "peramours": they "shall be unhappy, and all thynge unhappy that is aboute them."[20] Approached from the French tradition, Malory's attitude may well seem disastrously wrongheaded, even "unbecoming."[21] But if we bear in mind the quiet appropriation of the leading sentiments and attitudes of *amour courtois* by poets celebrating a "virtuous" love, our judgment of Malory may be sensibly different. Such appropriation of *amour courtois,* it should be noted, will lay increased emphasis on the notion of constancy, the "stability" that has always been a leading characteristic of the Courtly Lover. In the general consideration of what is and what is not "courtly" love, too

much can be made of the arranged marriage as the enemy of
"free" and therefore courtly passion. "Matches of interest,"
says Professor Lewis, were "the drab background against
which [courtly] love stood out in all the contrast of its new
tenderness and delicacy."[22] These are sound words, no doubt,
for courtly love in its newness. But if we turn to the later
Middle Ages in England, and not to imaginative literature
but to actuality, we shall find that the very letters which contain prosaic details of the financial terms of a projected marriage offer us also the language of romantic passion, caught
from the older tradition and in no way altered to placate any
imagined hostility between romantic adultery and a church
wedding. John Paston III writes to Margery Brews offering,
as the phrase still runs, both his heart and his hand. The very
letter is a form of contract—"thys bylle wretyn with my lewd
hand and sealyd with my sygnet to remayn with yow for a
wyttnesse ayenste me, and to my shame and dyshonour if I
contrary it." But this does not preclude the suitor from beginning by offering "syche por servyse as I now in my mynd owe
yow, purposyng, ye not dyspleasyd, duryng my lyff to contenu
the same"; and from ending with a prayer for mercy on his
sufferings:"And, mastress, I beseche yow, in easyng of the
poore hert that somtyme was at my rewle, whyche now is at
yours, that in as short tyme as can be that I may have knowl-
age of your entent and hough ye wyll have me demeanyd in
thys mater. . . ."[23]

So, too, though the negotiations dragged on into February
of the following year, Margery Brews could write to her lover
in terms that perfectly match her role of romantic lover and
obedient wife-to-be. He is both "Ryght reverent and wurschypfull, and my ryght welebeloved Voluntyne"; and, again,
she begins a letter "Ryght wurschypfull and welebeloved
Volentyne, in my moste umble wyse, I recommande me un to
yowe."[24] If ever the arranged marriage were to be an obstacle
to any romantic feelings, it should have been so in Margery's
case: and palpably it was not. It would appear that "love
will find a way," even through protracted negotiations for a
financial settlement—a way to make articulate the dignity and
aspiration, as well as the bitter-sweetness, of passion. The
sentiments and stylized attitudes of *amour courtois* can be
appropriated by those who have no thought of loving *paramours* but seek to be united in marriage.

II

If then it may be allowed that Chaucer is making no forced transition from the world of married lovers to a region appropriate only to adulterous passion, we may ask what is the significance of his whole mode of presentation? It is clearly, as the critical tradition has long perceived, to portray attainment of the highest earthly good. The love so long and so faithfully pursued reaches in this case perfect fulfilment—perfect, because now forever inviolate: the Lady is dead. There is no mention of religion in this poem, notes one critic, but the love-religion has its own consolation to offer. The pattern of this consolation, and the means of its communication, now concern us.

The first thing to notice is that so far from softening the impact of courtly love, Chaucer displays it in all its brightest colors. May morning, birdsong, the friendly animal that leads him away from the hunt through the darker thickets to meet the Knight—all are used in their first freshness. What has been said above concerning *amour courtois* and marriage is offered as evidence that no final incongruity or sense of mere artifice need be felt by Chaucer's audience as the tale of love unfolds in the traditional French setting. But what is of the highest importance to the effect Chaucer is contriving is that there is no blurring of the original images sacrosanct to the code of *amour courtois*. He desires to invoke the full power of the Enchanted Garden, all the ardors and ecstasies of Love's servants, sharply and traditionally defined, to convey the full glory of a love that comes to its appointed fulfilment. It is, one feels, a most apposite image that Professor Coghill[24a] employs when he blazons the "heraldry" of this poem. All the weight of an honored tradition, the most glowing colors known to the poet and his audience for the depiction of human felicity, are displayed in their pristine freshness. Precisely because no doubts or uncertainties attach to this story, "the colours and shapes," as Professor Coghill observes, "are determined in advance and meticulously placed." It is, to be sure, a funeral hatchment: but the colors and the detail of the quarterings shine out above the tomb. For once, the story of fulfilled love is true. There remains one decisive touch to add, at the climax of fulfilment. *Le don de merci amoureux* [the gift of love's mercy] will be understood by the audience as the Lady's acceptance of the suitor. But so potent has been the evocation of the world of *amour courtois* that emphasis is required, at this moment of intensity, to guard all who listen against one flicker of misunderstanding. Yet even at this point, the emphasis upon the Lady's "worship" is adroitly handled within the dramatic setting of the poem. The Dreamer is a man of humble estate, one who uses the best courtesy he can towards his superior, and is treated by him with the utmost consideration. The Knight, in the old and honorable sense, "condescends" to his inquirer; looking back, the Dreamer realizes "He made hyt nouther towgh ne queynte." The more important, then, that what is involved in the Lady's yielding should be put beyond any possibility of doubt for this humble listener:

> "My lady yaf me al hooly
> The noble yifte of hir mercy,
> Savynge hir worship, by al weyes —
> Dredles, I mene noon other weyes."   (1269-72)

For a moment some of the Knight's earlier intensity comes back, as he recalls the figure, momentarily silent, before him— a listener sworn to attend with the best understanding he can command:

> "I telle the upon a condicioun
> That thou shalt hooly, with al thy wyt,
> Doo thyn entent to herkene hit."   (750-2)

The device of a listener who is the Knight's inferior has enabled Chaucer to present the full and exemplary story of a love-suit. Now, as that story comes to its climax in the acceptance of the suitor, the device serves once more to preserve the matchless decorum of this love.

The consolation thus brought about carries the implicit appeal, What shall be put in the balance against perfection? The consolation offered to the husband who has suffered the loss of his wife is explicit—though with a world of difference in tone—in the words of Pandarus to Troilus who suffers the absence of Criseyde, his lover:

> "— I pray the, tel me now
> If that thou trowe, er this, that any wight
> Hath loved paramours as wel as thow?"   (v, 330-2)

(It is appropriate, we may observe in passing, that Pandarus must go on to state that "Necessite" cannot be fought against.) This theme of consolation, the happiness of requited love, is used, as Professor Patch has remarked, to remind us of "the fundamental equilibrium in nature." But it brings into play another theme, closely and subtly allied to it, which is of great importance to the pattern of consolation the poet offers. *Amour courtois* knows the pangs of lovesickness, of enforced separation, and even of deprivation by death; but it considers no pain equal to that caused by infidelity. As the highest conceivable good in this system is reciprocated passion, so its deepest misery is inconstancy—or, to give it the plainest name, treachery. Not even loss by death can equal loss by disaffection. This theme of consolation is skilfully prepared at the outset of the poem; the Dreamer is himself one who knows what it is to suffer in love's service. It is here that we first encounter humor, and it will be as well to proceed warily, until we have established the kind of humor that is being offered us.

In the first twenty-nine lines, we are told that the poet is sleepless, and in this extremity ("Purely for defaute of slep") is indifferent to all things:

> For sorwful ymagynacioun
> Ys alway hooly in my mynde.   (14-15)

This, all men will agree, is "agaynes kynde":

> For nature wolde not suffyse
> To noon erthly creature
> Not longe tyme to endure
> Withoute slep and be in sorwe   (18-21)

Yet there is no remedy, and death appears the only ending to this course; for

> Defaute of slep and hevynesse
> Hath sleyn my spirit of quyknesse
> That I have lost al lustyhede.   (25-7)

What is here feigned of the poet's wretchedness is the plain truth of the patron's situation. Chaucer is thus enabled to make his Dreamer a substitute-figure,[25] through whom he can make an appeal for a cessation of grief without the indelicacy of more direct approach. It would be extremely unwise to take these lines in a spirit of mock ruefulness: but

equally it would be alien to Chaucer's purpose to take them
au grand sérieux. Chaucer's delicate humor enables him to
do two things—to plead for an end of uncontrolled grief (and
thus to prepare a receptive mood for this poem); and at the
same time to sound, with the major theme of consolation (the
perfection of the Knight's love), a note of consolation peculiarly audible within the world of courtly love. The lines in
which the poet's unhappiness is stated are, it is well known,
modelled closely on French poetry, lines 1-15 being a direct
imitation of the opening of Froissart's *Paradys d'Amours*.
But there is a transition from the woes of the lovesick to a
deeper note of unhappiness: lines 23-29 (the expectation of
death as a release from meaningless life) are modelled upon
a passage which occurs early in Machaut's *Jugement dou Roy
de Navarre*. In this poem, it will be recalled, Machaut had
begun by dwelling on the wretched state of the world:

> Les merveilles et les fortunes
> Qui au jour d'ui sont si communes
> Qu'on n'oit de nulle part nouvelle
> Qui soit aggreable ne belle . . .
> [The prodigies and misfortunes
> So common today
> That on no side does one hear news
> Agreeable or pleasant . . .]

The occasion of Machaut's poem is peculiarly appropriate to
Chaucer's undertaking. Writing at the beginning of the winter of 1349, the French poet had begun by grimly recalling
the honors of the Black Death as the worst instances of human misery yet recorded. In the 430 lines he devoted to the
dark events of the preceding year—

> des orribles merveilles,
> Seur toutes autres despareilles,
> Dont homme puet avoir memoire
> [horrible prodigies
> Beyond all others
> Which man can recall]

—there is no obvious preparation for what is to follow.
Machaut's is in every sense a Winter poem: and yet its subject, when at last unfolded, has the traditional setting of
Spring—for it is a continuation of a love-theme previously set
forth in the *Jugement dou Roy de Behaingne*. In fact, as it is
entitled in some manuscripts, this poem is *Le Jugement dou*

Roy de Navarre contre le Jugement dou Roy de Behaingne.
In these two poems, as Lowes notes, lies "the suggestion for
[Chaucer's] central situation,"[26] for the *débat* which begins
in the *Behaingne* opens with a woodland meeting between
two persons who have suffered loss in love. What is, however, of the highest importance for Chaucer's theme is that
Màchaut's *débat* is upon which is the greater loss—that of a
Knight whose lady has played him false, or that of a lady
whose lover has died? At the outset of his poem, Chaucer,
writing, like Machaut, a "Winter" poem, with the terrors of
Plague all too fresh in men's minds, has no need to dwell
upon "melancolye." But he has taken the first step in the design of his poem by conveying the poignancy of love-sorrow,
and, for those who have ears to hear, establishing a connection between the sorrow of unfulfilled love and the sorrow of
fulfilled love abrupted by death. Chaucer's poem, too, is to
turn back to Spring. Perhaps we may say of his design, at this
point, what Machaut's editor says of the poem Chaucer is
recalling: "sur ce fond sombre et tragique, la gracieuse aventure allait se détacher en couleurs d'autant plus vives" [against
this dark and tragic background, the gracious adventure
would stand out in colors all the brighter for it].[27]

The device of the poet as sorrowful lover is significant and
far-reaching. It at once allows the telling of a dream upon
the love-sorrow occasioned by death (Ceix and Alcyon):
and in that dream the desire of every bereaved lover to see
again the lost one is deftly communicated. But, further, it
determines the reactions of the Dreamer in the course of his
inquiry. Since the Dreamer is himself an unhappy lover, he
can sympathize with love's distresses, and make bold to pur-
sue his questioning. But since his predicament is that of the
nearly hopeless lover, who has served eight years without ad-
mission to his lady's favors, there is the more subtle reason
for his embodying, by a pretended incomprehension, the
witness of a world that conceived as the highest good of all
the fulfilment of love. The Dreamer is indeed not without
experience of a kind: but he is lamentably dependent upon
doctrine for all except the experience of unrequited love. This,
as I understand it, is the real authority, within the world of the
poem, for his pretended misconception of the Knight's loss.
Nothing, it may be said in passing, could so perfectly preserve the balance between poet and patron. The doctrines

held in innocence will allow the Dreamer to probe with
apparent artlessness: and it is a gentle and all-pervading irony
that in fact it is the Dreamer who must be instructed in
heartfelt experience. If we attend to the Dreamer's reactions
his role as love's doctrinaire will become clearer.

When he comes upon the rueful Knight and hears his
lament, we are reminded at once of the Dreamer's own
melancholy that brings him near to death; in both cases,

> Hit was gret wonder that Nature
> Myght suffre any creature
> To have such sorwe, and be not ded.   (467-9)

There is no question for the Dreamer that the Lady is dead.
But what is unknown to him is whether the Lady had in
fact accepted the Knight's service. This is the primary distinction to be made by the doctrinaire servant of love before the
true weight of loss can be assessed. Can the Knight's sorrow
be at worst the double misery of an unrequited love now
placed forever beyond the reach of hope? This lies behind
the Dreamer's reflection, before he enters upon conversation
proper with the Knight:

> Anoon ryght I gan fynde a tale
> To hym, to loke wher I myght ought
> Have more knowynge of his thought.   (536-8)

The Dreamer is perhaps not quite the fool that criticism
often supposes. We have been very ready to allow that in the
attempt to draw out the Knight, Chaucer has portrayed the
Dreamer as merely dull, and thus actually or feignedly for-
getful of what he has heard. It is however worth asking
whether this "dullness" does in fact exist as a mere expedient
towards the Knight's unlocking his heart; and whether the
forgetfulness is equally arbitrary. Kittredge takes the lines
quoted above as direct evidence ("the plainest language")
that the Dreamer, knowing the Lady is dead, wishes "to
afford the Knight the only help in his power—the comfort
of pouring his sad story into compassionate ears."[28] I would
suggest that we take these lines even more "plainly"; the
Dreamer seeks to know more, namely the precise nature of
the Knight's grief. Chaucer has brought us to the situation
from which the *débat* of Machaut's two poems springs. There,
too, there were two servants of love; and there, too, a greet-
ing was given by one and ignored by the other in the distrac-

tion of bereavement. Now it remains for Chaucer's Dreamer
to ask the nature of his mourner's grief; for, in Machaut's
poem, the Knight who addresses the bereaved Lady can offer
consolation of a kind:

> Mais vraiement
> On trouveroit plus tost al\
> igement
> En vostre mal qu'en mien.
> [But in truth
> One would find solace sooner
> From your sorrow than from mine.]

Such consolation as this is certainly not for Chaucer to
offer· in his own person. Where Machaut had been an onlooker, and a *débat* could be conducted, with the verdict lying for
the Knight, Chaucer presents himself as the humblest of
love's followers. The more reason that, instead of rival claims
to the title of greater loss, to be referred, at the poet's suggestion, to a judge, Chaucer should contrive for us a situation in
which the Dreamer, knowing love only as unfulfilled desire,
should in effect be a judge of what to him can only be a
matter of authority, not experience. Hence the shift in this
poem away from its analogue's *débat* to a simpler process of
question and answer. The Dreamer seeks to know more: is it
grief at love forever unfulfilled, or grief at Death's interrup-
tion of love in its fulfilment? On this turns the whole pattern
of consolation that the poet offers. Those of his audience who
catch the allusion, in similarity of situation, to the *débat* of
the two *Jugement* poems, can perceive what the poet in sheer
delicacy of feeling will not make explicit. On his side, the
Knight has no conception of any grief like to his own. The
Dreamer can therefore invite him to speak of his sorrow, and
this will reveal ultimately the fact of fulfilled love. But in the
telling the Knight and his interlocutor do not remain unchanged. Not only does the Knight gain in strength and ardor;
his would-be comforter also begins to change his role, though
equally unwittingly. When the "case" is finally established,
judgment, and the consolation it implies, may not be so easy
a matter as the Dreamer at the outset had every reason to
expect. For the moment, we are concerned with the Dreamer
holding the initiative, establishing the nature of the case before proceeding to judgment.

III

We start with two servants of love. He who has never been

admitted to the service of a lady comes face to face with a
lover whom

> deth hath mad al naked
> Of al the blysse that ever was maked.   (577-8)

The invitation to the Knight to speak of his sorrow is an invitation, though the Knight knows it not, to bring his case
for trial. Further, the telling itself may "amende" the sorrow
—though not, ultimately, by any such means as either the
Knight or his interlocutor conceives:

> With that he loked on me asyde,
> As who sayth, "Nay, that wol not be."   (558-9)

So, in face of this apparent incomprehension, the Knight
begins by railing against Fortune, and the loss of his "queen"
in Fortune's game of chess with him; only to meet with the
common counsel to despise what Fortune can do. The poet's
device is to offer in the world of the poem, as the threshold
of consolation, what would in reality sound all too heartless.
The contempt of Fortune is a note that can be sounded in
the world of courtly love: and its presence at this point in the
poem allows the transition by which the Knight, protesting
that this loss is above all others, can be besought by love's
neophyte to tell *all*:

> "Good sir, telle me al hooly
> In what wyse, how, why, and wherfore
> That ye have thus youre blysse lore."   (746-8)

The notion of Fortune is a delicate reminder of the whole
code by which the Knight has lived and prospered. We have
seen Pandarus consoling Troilus—no man can escape "necessite." In the same system, and for the same reason, no lover
can plead merit to win his lady's yielding: all lies in hope.
This is a realm in which the god of love is omnipotent. The
lesson known to all lovers is, as Kittredge observes, submission
to the god—"in his grace and favor was their only hope:
for no man's heart was in his own control."[29] This the Knight
perceives in his own outcry against Fortune; the recall of his
"fruitless wish" to have managed his game better, as Professor C. S. Lewis observes,[30] anticipates *Lycidas*. It is a cry
that is instantly revoked—

> "For Fortune kan so many a wyle,
> Ther be but fewe kan hir begile—"   (673-4)

and the Knight perceives that he cannot blame Fortune for
her greed:

> "Myself I wolde have do the same,
> Before God, hadde I ben as she."   (676-7)

If this is the beginning of recognition that the loss of the
best reflects back upon the heaven of the past as well as forward to the hell of the present, it is instantly submerged:

> "And whan al this falleth in my thoght,
> Allas! than am I overcome!"   (706-7)

There has been no doubt in the Dreamer's mind that the
Lady is dead: now, when the contempt of Fortune fails as
initial consolation, it remains to bear witness to the lover's
final credo—no loss is to be compared with infidelity. Gently,
yet eagerly, the disciple of love asks to be told the whole
story of this love, feigning ignorance that the Lady is dead.
Gently, for

> "whoso wiste al, by my trouthe,
> My sorwe, but he hadde rowthe
> And pitee of my sorwes smerte,
> That man hath a fendly herte—"   (591-4)

but eagerly, for this love if fulfilled will surely prove the
final truth that fulfilment of love is not to be weighed against
any loss, even that of death. As this love of the Knight's is to
be tested by the highest standards, the Dreamer is slow to
allow that it is an outstanding instance, and this enables the
poet to raise the account to a level of hyperbole, deftly sus-
tained by humor. We move back from the winter of present
discontent to the spring of first enchantment, and there is a
lightening of tension. Now the roles are delicately altered;
love's doctrinaire has his own condescension to make. The
Dreamer is willing to concede that this is indeed an admirable
love-suit: he can well believe that the Knight thought his lady
the best,

> "And to beholde the alderfayreste,
> Whoso had loked hir with your eyen."   (1050-1)

But this will not serve for the Knight:

> "With myn? nay, alle that hir seyen
> Seyde and sworen hyt was soo."   (1052-3)

In the establishment of the Knight's "case" there is, besides the overt humor of the situation, an inward humor
appropriate to the relation of poet and patron. The conception of the Dreamer is shaped in terms of a bookish servant
of love, whose unshaken doctrinaire position issues in kindly
self-possession. So the Knight himself becomes precise upon
the use of terms of doctrine. He would, he says, have loved
this Lady had he every attribute of greatness, strength, and
wisdom:

> "I wolde ever, withoute drede,
> Have loved hir, for I moste nede—"   (1073-4)

and at once he interrupts himself—

> " 'Nede!' nay, trewly, I gabbe now;
> Noght "nede," and I wol tellen how . . . "   (1075-6)

The same effect is gained at the next interjection by the
Dreamer, who observes:

> "Me thynketh ye have such a chaunce
> As shryfte wythoute repentaunce."   (1113-14)

Skeat glosses these lines, "You are like one who confesses,
but does not repent." This is hardly satisfactory: *shryfte* must
mean not "confession" but absolution, and *repentaunce*, con-
trition. I take it that the Dreamer is humorously admonishing the Knight for the sadness of his resolve not to leave his
Lady. The implication, charged with some complacency, is
that there is, after all, such a thing as the reward of faithful
service. The Dreamer well knows that the Lady is dead; but
he does not know whether love has been fulfilled. So, consistently with his catechism throughout, he pretends to treat
the love-suit as still in progress, in order to lead to the question
of fulfilment. The Knight's constancy is assured: very well,
then, can he have failed to declare his love to the Lady? Let
the Knight answer this, and then we can proceed to the matter of his "loss." To the Knight this seems the final proof of
the Dreamer's obtuseness: he retorts in despair,

> "thow nost what thow menest;
> I have lost more than thou wenest." (1137-8)

The Dreamer at once replies, pressing the questions that will
reveal all, and thus allow "loss" to be placed in its true perspective. He is, as men say, cruel in order to be kind:

> "What los is that?" quod I thoo;
> "Nyl she not love yow? ys hyt soo?
> Or have ye oght doon amys,
> That she hath left yow? ys hyt this?
> For Goddes love, telle me al." (1139-43)

We have come to the crucial question, and from this point
forward all element of doubt upon the fulfilment of this
love affair is to be removed. The story of the love-suit follows
perfectly the pattern of the highest and best, even to the
first failure and the continued service, until at last fulfilment
is won and long enjoyed:

> "Al was us oon, withoute were.
> And thus we lyved ful many a yere
> So wel, I kan nat telle how. (1295-7)

Not merely has the suitor been admitted to his Lady's favor;
their continuing relationship as lovers is perfection itself.

For the first time in the poem the Dreamer has a question
to ask which he had not foreseen. The telling of the story
of perfected love has submerged all other considerations but
one. His reservations concerning the nature of the Dreamer's
love have gone; and with them have gone both the doctrine
on which they were based, and the very memory that the
Lady is no more to be found. In the Dreamer's unfeigned forgetfulness at this last stage the poet pays his final tribute to a
loss which leaves the world poorer. The issue is not the fore-
gone conclusion that the allusions to Machaut's two poems
would suggest. The "case" when brought eventually to trial
turns out to be not the superiority of fulfilled love to all considerations of loss, but the naked force of loss when love has
reached a perfect fulfilment. This is the final and surprising
assertion for which the poet's audience is not prepared. And
yet, we recall, in the world of courtly fiction, the judgment
given in the first of Machaut's poems had to be reversed in
the second. The mere oscillation between "verdicts" is the
measure of the tradition's final limitations. At the end of

Chaucer's poem pity is born of the Dreamer's innocence—
pity, "a naked, new-born babe." The pattern of consolation
reaches final strength and sincerity from the unswerving recognition of a sorrow that will not be lessened by any doctrine
of the greater or less in human loss. The loss is absolute: and
the last consolation the poet offers is that of perfect understanding. For now the Dreamer has had his wish, "For Goddes love, telle me al"; and what the Knight had sadly told him
at the outset is the only truth that remains:

> "whoso wiste all, by my trouthe,
> Mý sorwe, but he hadde rowthe
> And pitee of my sorwes smerte,
> That man hath a fendly herte."   (591-4)

The work of consolation has been done. Beginning with
the appeal to cease from lamentation, which is against
"kynde," the poet has continued by recalling the glory of perfect fulfilment in love, with its subtle reminders of the final
code of all lovers—that Fortune is not to be railed against,
since the heaven of requited love is to be granted not for the
lover's deserving but of the Lady's grace; and that the loss
of this heaven by death is not so great a disaster as its loss by
infidelity. These are the consolations of the religion of love.
They come with peculiar force in that here the world of
fulfilled desire is placed forever beyond the reach of change.
But the last "consolation" the poet offers is that of perfect
understanding. The pretended misunderstanding of the
Knight's loss had stood for a deeper misunderstanding—the
superiority of authoritative doctrine over heartfelt experience.
As the pretended misunderstanding is dropped, so with it goes
the attempted consolation, though not before it has done its
work. We turn in a moment from the golden past to the black
present. Chaucer's last offering is naked sympathy:

> "Is that youre los? Be God, hyt ys routhe!"   (1310)

IV

It may be thought no accident that the best-loved line in
Chaucer ["For pitee renneth soone in gentil herte"] speaks of
pity and the *cuor gentil:* and the unrivalled pathos displayed
in the close of the *tragedye* of Troilus is justification enough,
if justification were needed, for Lowes's placing that poem in

the region of "The Mastered Art." If we seek for a specifically Chaucerian characteristic it is to be found above all in the rare combination of objectivity and pity—fidelity to the fact without either rancor or sentimentality. If this is the hall-mark of Chaucer's treatment, the "unmistakable, individual stamp" which warrants the work as his, however many and diverse the sources on which it draws, this early poem on the death of Blanche the Duchess may deserve to stand higher in our estimation, for it offers an entry upon this central mystery of Chaucer's art.

We have seen how all proceeds from the conception of the Dreamer as the bookish servant of love, his unshaken doctrinaire position, and its final inadequacy to experience where the experience is of perfection itself. The plight of the hapless lover is one that comes naturally and humorously to the poet of a courtly and erotic tradition. For the poet by his very craft is dependent upon the "auctoritees"; his place in the great tradition of his calling is the least because it is the last. So, with Love, he can be only the god's doctrinaire servant; and it is a jest which affords many possibilities. He can, for example, be the one whose service is recognized with the promise of an appropriate reward in *The House of Fame*. As the Eagle, sent from on high, tells the poet, it is meritorious service of its kind, and it is to receive its adequate recompense. You have served Love, he says benignly,

> "Withoute guerdon ever yit . . .
> And peynest the to preyse hys art,
> Although thou haddest never part."   (*HF*, 619, 627-8)

The poet will therefore be given more material for his book-ish service. Indeed, so devoted is he to his books that he is not even an observer of the reality around him:

> "But of thy verray neyghebores,
> That duellen almost at thy dores,
> Thou herist neyther that ne this."   (*HF*, 649-51)

What is treated as pure comedy in *The House of Fame* is the same situation that is deftly employed in *The Book of the Duchess*. Here, too, Chaucer represents himself as, for the most part, hearing "neyther that ne this." But because it is the same situation, we are not to suppose that it is invested with the same kind of humor.

A further kind of humorous effect is to be found when
bookish devotion leads not to approval from on high, but to
outright condemnation. For the poet may choose the wrong
"auctoritees"; and it will be for the God of Love himself to
appear and impose penance. Let the bookish servant of Love
take heed to his books:

> "Was there no good matere in thy mynde,
> Ne in alle thy bokes ne coudest thow not fynde
> Som story of wemen that were goode and trewe?"
>
> (*LGW*, [G], 270-2)

Again, in both the Pandarus of Chaucer's love-tragedy, and
in the author himself as he turns with increasing frequency
to his books when Criseyde begins her fatal descent, we catch
another note of humor. But how delicate a humor this is!
The recognition of the two worlds of "experience" and
"auctoritee" allows the poet his greatest reaches into tenderness and pathos. The note of the real can be touched without
stridency or false emphasis when we move in a world of
gentle scepticism for the absolute wisdom of the "auctoritees."
Pandarus can begin by offering the standard consolation to
Troilus, now separated from his love:

> "But, Troilus, I prey the, tel me now
> If thow trowe, er this, that any wight
> Hath loved paramours as wel as thow?"
>
> (*TC*, v, 330-2)

But Pandarus must continue with the recognition from common experience that "necessite" keeps no covenant: and,
banishing the world of learned conjecture upon the significance
of dreams, he plainly tells Troilus that if he continues to
languish he will seem cowardly in the eyes of a world that
knows nothing of his love, So, in a manner analogous to that
of *The Book of the Duchess,* it is Pandarus who must attend
to the reality of suffering. Now it is Troilus who hopes and
Pandarus who begins to have no doubt of the sad outcome,
while he none the less

> bisily did al his fulle myght
> Hym to conforte, and make his herte light,
> Yevyng hym hope alwey, the tenthe morwe
> That she shal come, and stynten al his sorwe.
>
> (v, 683-6)

As the story runs to its appointed end, it is the sufferer who
revives in ardor, and the consoler, Pandarus, who comes to
the realization of the truth:

> And to hymself ful sobreliche he seyde,
> "From haselwode, there joly Robyn pleyde,
> Shal come al that that thow abidest heere.
> Ye, fare wel al the snow of ferne yere!"
>
> (v, 1173-6)

So, in the end,

> "What sholde I seyen? I hate, ywys, Cryseyde;
> And, God woot, I wol hate hire evermore!"
>
> (v, 1732-3)

But Chaucer himself cannot come to this pass. It is for
him to follow his authorities; and if they are not to be relied
upon unreservedly, by the same token there is room for
neither outright affirmation nor simple denial. As Criseyde
moves downwards he will remind us that it is "the storie
telleth us" of her beginning to yield. On the other hand, he
finds "ek in the stories elleswhere" that she wept for Diomede's hurt at the hands of Troilus. And when it comes to
full surrender, we have it only upon report: "Men seyn—I
not—that she yaf hym hire herte." Certainly, "the storie telleth
us," her grief was bitter. Let no one assume she yielded soon
to the "sodeyn" Greek:

> There is non auctour telleth it, I wene.
> Take every man now to his bokes heede;
> He shal no terme fynden, out of drede.   (v, 1088-90)

In a world where "experience" and "auctoritee" are the two
courts of appeal, particular truth is not simple. What is
smilingly conveyed at the outset of *The Legend of Good
Women* is an unwillingness to believe upon authority what
can be tested by experience. What is revealed in *Troilus and
Criseyde* is the foundation of pity in a complementary
scepticism. The "books" tell us of Criseyde's guilt; Pandarus
will "hate" Criseyde: but their creator does not find it so
easy a matter to pronounce judgment:

> Ne me ne list this sely womman chyde
> Forther than the storye wol devyse.
> Hire name, allas! is punysshed so wide,

> That for hire gilt it oughte ynough suffise.
> And if I myghte excuse hire any wise,
> For she so sory was for hire untrouthe,
> I wis, I wolde excuse hire yet for routhe.   (v, 1093-9)

Humor, then, especially the humor of the doctrinaire servant of love's mysteries, can be the necessary foundation of pathos. The world of "auctoritee" can be used not to override the realm of "experience," nor yet to rival it, but to place it in a perspective where neither condemnation nor correction has final warrant, but only pity is the adequate response. In the "mastered art" of *Troilus and Criseyde* Chaucer comes to the threshold of what later is to be called "realism." Criseyde is not to be upbraided: one more step and we should be in the region of creative art where she is not to be blamed — *tout comprendre, c'est tout pardonner*. But that is not a step which Chaucer takes; for it, too, represents a kind of overbalance. To suspend judgment is not to abolish it. So, in the early work of *The Book of the Duchess,* there is no final shelter behind the world of doctrine. Pity has the last word; but consolation is not laid aside before it has served an end. Towards this final effect, in both poems, humor and even outright comedy can play a part. The Pandarus who fetches a cushion for the kneeling Troilus is intended as no final criticism of the values of the *tragedie.* So, in the earlier work, a point even of comic absurdity can be reached not in order to destroy, by gaining a monstrously gratuitous effect, but in order to reaffirm the values asserted. Perhaps the most striking instance occurs when the account of the Lady passes from physical description to the enumeration of her virtues. It is essential to the main pattern of consolation that the love between the Knight and his Lady shall be the unique example of all that is best in the courtly tradition. So "goode faire White" must have all the highest attributes of the ladies of romance. The description of her physical presence, so often praised by critics, is, as has frequently been noted, greatly indebted to the courtly tradition. Kittredge points out that the very description of her eyes—

> But ever, me thoght, hir eyen seyde,
> "By God, my wrathe is al foryive!"   (876-7)

—is taken from Machaut, and he continues by noting Chaucer's device for establishing the truth of this description. "In *his* lady, the Knight protests, this was not an affectation.

> Hyt was her owne pure loking,
> That the goddesse, dame Nature,
> Had mad hem opene by mesure,
> And close. . ."[31]

This is characteristic of Chaucer's method of conveying the present truth of all that poets have feigned. Blanche is to be a Lady unparalleled; like "the soleyn fenix of Arabye,"

> "ther livyth never but oon,
> Ne swich as she ne knowe I noon."   (983-4)

But precisely in as far as this Lady is the exemplar of all courtly attributes, there is the danger of mere hyperbole—the risk that what is conveyed in terms of the courtly conventions may be received as merely conventional.

To forestall this, Chaucer deftly introduces comedy. The Lady's proud beauty is not to be identified with the sophisticated cruelty of those who "holde" a "wyght in balaunce" and send them questing over the known world to prove their devotion. Here Chaucer, taking the catalogue of lovers' exploits from *Le Dit dou Lyon* and adding (as Lowes notes)[32] his own vivid topographical touch,[33] deliberately involves comic absurdity:

> "She ne used no such knakkes smale."   (1033)

His audience laughs; the false hyperbole of mere over-elaboration is destroyed—and the rest passes unscathed. The portrait of "goode faire White" is the portrait of a great Lady of romance. There is no invasion of the world of private recollection. The picture is conceived and constructed in the terms of traditional praise; and this Chaucer can draw upon freely, for the cynic has been disarmed. The "argument" can proceed unhindered, for what has been handed over to mockery, though it is no less a part of the developed courtly tradition, has no place in the praise of Blanche. The humor, then, of this poem is a delicate balance, proceeding initially from the rueful plight of a pair of lovers, one the doctrinaire student, the other the embodiment of perfect service. As in his *tragedie,* Chaucer here shows us a reversal of roles: the well-grounded servant of love must learn eventually the local and unique force of suffering through the experience of another.

By the means employed in *The Book of the Duchess,* a sense of proportion in grief is not counselled, but conveyed. Not before the work of healing has begun does the poet add the final touch of unswerving sympathy. Since the whole balance of effect—the *decorum* of the poem—turns upon delicate idealization, what can be gently ridiculed is mere exaggeration. In both *tragedie* and elegy, pity is the ultimate offering. The health of Chaucer's imagining appears to be no late growth. It was not lightly that Dryden called him "a *perpetual* fountain of good sense."

V

It is thus that the central tradition of the Enchanted Garden is preserved intact in Chaucer's elegy: until in the close it is seen as safe forever. The immemorial enemies of the Garden can have no entry here. The peculiar difficulty of elegy as an art form is that it must contend with two extremes of mere nature, each, it is not to be doubted, present in all experience of bereavement. One is the impulse to seek for consolation in the idealization of past happiness: the other the rejection of all consolation in the overmastering sense of loss. Consolation of itself has a hollow ring: and the rejection of it is a suffering in silence where it is not the difficult art of lament. Moreover, when the loss is not the poet's own, elegy is indeed a precarious undertaking; for consolation may sound heartlessly doctrinaire, and any attempt to share the sense of absolute loss a perilous intrusion. In Chaucer's poem something unique is done: we have both consolation and a rejection of it—but not before it has done its work. Neither invalidates the other; consolation does not cancel pity, nor pity render consolation void. By introducing the mourner himself, Chaucer has succeeded in this most difficult of modes. The pattern of consolation works by implication—the Knight is brought to celebrate again the heaven of requited love. That, for the poet's audience, involves its own theme of comparison in loss. Death, it seems for the moment, is robbed of the greater glory. The Dreamer who comes to offer consolation is made to listen and eventually to learn what manner of love this is that has come to its fulfilment. He who knows of love only from the outside begs to be told all. So the Dreamer must learn of love not by "auctoritee" but by the "experience" of a lover. As the Dreamer becomes a disciple, so there recedes into the background the world of comfortable values he has brought with him. When the story of fulfilled love is told, then the Dreamer knows what loss is. Doctrine capitulates: only pity remains. As elegy, this poem offers the best of two worlds of "consolation"—they are caught up in one pattern by the skillful deployment of the personality of the Dreamer. In the end, the poet learns from his patron: and the gate to the garden of the Rose is closed forever.

In this, we may in some respects be reminded of *Lycidas*. For Milton, too, the past is golden, the lines that recall it mellifluous and traditional; for the past is seen as unalterably past. And in Milton's poem, too, there is tension between what may be thought to be true and the overmastering sense of loss:

> For so to interpose a little ease,
> Let our frail thoughts dally with false surmise.
> Ay me! Whilst thee the shores, and sounding Seas
> Wash far away . . .

But the garden of youthful endeavor and conventional ceremony can give no final consolation to the poet of *Lycidas*. His thoughts and energies are bent upon present and future. The enemy has made headway, and tasks too long postponed press upon him, the survivor. So, in Milton's poem, elegy turns away from eulogy to the poetry of battle. The recollection of beliefs and ideals held in common with the dead draws the poem away from fruitless lament into purposeful statement, while at once lessening the sting of grief and allowing due ceremony for "the Laureate Herse where Lycid lies." There can be "leisure for fiction" when farewell is said to a world that can never be recalled. So Milton turns a key upon the world of pastoral innocence. Equally, with whatever great differences of effect, Chaucer's poem marks his leave-taking of an Enchanted Garden. We are never to have from him the *comedye* promised at the end of *Troilus and Criseyde*. "Succesful panegyric," observes Professor Lewis, "is the rarest of all literary achievements and Chaucer has compassed it."[34] But not, one thinks, so much in his presentation of "goode faire White," as in the whole world of innocence and fulfilled desire of which she is the center. The *genre* of French courtly love poetry has found its perfect setting in this English garden. If it is, in a later jargon, a poetry of "escape,"[35] it has found its justification in a world that is secure from alteration, from the shadows of events to come, from the insidious victories of age and ugliness, the play of circumstance and the lingering sickness of life. The Enchanted Garden of French courtly poetry has been, in the profoundest sense "translated." Deschamps perhaps wrought better than he knew in his praise of Chaucer: but certainly he has chosen the right terms of address to the English poet—

> qui as
> Seme les fleurs et plante le rosier . . .
> Grant translateur, noble Geffroy Chaucier.

Notes

1 C. S. Lewis, *The Allegory of Love* (Oxford, 1936), p. 161.

2 J. L. Lowes, *Geoffrey Chaucer* (Oxford, 1934), p. 95.

3 G. L. Kittredge, *Chaucer and his Poetry* (Cambridge, Massachusetts, 1915), pp. 37-72.

4 *Ibid.*, p. 72.

5 *Cf.*, among others, R. K. Root, *The Poetry of Chaucer* (Boston and New York: Houghton Mifflin, 1906), pp. 60-63. *The Book of the Duchess* "deserves attention" as "a mark from which one may measure his subsequent literary development." "Intrinsically its value is but slight . . . taken as a whole, it furnishes but weary reading." (*Ibid.*, pp. 60-61.)

6 H. R. Patch, *On Rereading Chaucer* (Cambridge, Massachusetts, 1939), pp. 25-36 ("The Court of Love").

7 *Ibid.*, p. 33.

8 *Ibid.*, pp. 35-36.

9 J. M. Manly, *Some New Light on Chaucer* (London, 1926), p. 66.

10 *Chaucer and the Fifteenth Century*, The Oxford History of English Literature, II, 1 (Oxford, 1947), p. 36.

11 *Op. cit.*, pp. 168-169.

12 *Ibid.*, p. 170. We may notice in passing that Mr. Lewis has begun by saying "*If the poem has any faults*, apart from its occasional lapses in style and metre . . ." (italics mine). The transition from this to "disastrous" effects is somewhat startling, especially in view of the high praise accorded to the imagery of "satisfied love," which has "a symbolic fitness that is beyond the contract of conscious allegory." We are left with the puzzling conception of a highly successful achievement which yet displays "disastrous" faults.

13 Kemp Malone, *Chapters on Chaucer* (Baltimore, Maryland, 1951), pp. 38, 24, 39, 38, 39, 41. (The last observation echoes Lowes, *op. cit.*, p. 95.)

14 *Cf. op. cit.* p. 2, where the "characteristics" of Courtly Love (referred to in the Index as "its four marks") are given as "Humility, Courtesy, Adultery, and the Religion of Love."

15 *Ibid.*, p. 197.

16 Gervase Mathew, "Marriage and *Amour Courtois* in late four-teenth-century England," in *Essays presented to Charles Williams* (Oxford, 1947), p. 132. Father Mathew notes the significance of The Knight's Tale and The Franklin's Tale in this connection. *Cf.* also George Kane, *Middle English Literature* (London, 1951). In his chapter on "The Middle English Metrical Romances," Professor Kane notes the differences from conventional *amour courtois* in *Partonope of Blois*, the fragmentary *Sir Firumbras* (which hardly observes courtly convention at all), *William of Palerne*, and *Sir Degrevant*. Professor Kane's comment on *William of Palerne* is especially relevant: here was an author who elected "to use as gracious ornaments some of the outward rituals of the courtly love convention while rejecting its fundamental principles of service and adultery" (p. 51).

17 *Op. cit.* p. 132. The allegory is in Arundel MS. XIV (College of Arms): Father Mathew expresses indebtedness to C. West's analysis (*Courtoisie in Anglo-Norman Literature*, pp. 144-150). Dr. West's concluding observations (pp. 167-169) are of special interest. The "doctrine, with its various implications, of marriage as the fulfillment of love is regularly exemplified in the romances." "The point of view of the author [of the allegory referred to above], and his attitude to *amour courtois*, may fairly be taken as typical of the outlook of Anglo-Norman writers in general."

18 *The Owl and the Nightingale*, ed. J. W. H. Atkins (Cambridge, England, 1922), Introduction, p. lix.

19 *Chapters on Chaucer*, pp. 39-40.

20 *Malory* (Oxford, 1929), pp. 54, 48, 46-47.

21 *Ibid.*, p. 48. In his edition of the Winchester MS (*The Works of Sir Thomas Malory*, Oxford, 1947) Professor Vinaver acknowledges Malory's sense of purpose in remodelling his material. Malory's alterations to his source in the *Book of Sir Tristram* at the outset reestablish "the normal sequence of incidents," and in general "do much to relieve" the "tedium" of the uninspired matter of this book: and there is appreciation of Malory's changes in the status and appeal of Lancelot as the embodiment of earthly chivalry. On Malory's "New Arthuriad," Professor Vinaver modifies his earlier view that "mere condensation of narrative" could account for "the essential quality of his rendering." (Introduction, p. lxxii; pp. lxxv-lxxviii; p. lxxxi, n. 3.) But in his commentary, dealing with Lancelot's rebuke to the notion of loving "peramours," Professor Vinaver's view remains substantially unchanged. Malory "simply had no knowledge of the refined courtly philosophy which lay behind his story." (Vol. III, pp. 1402-04.) As Professor Vinaver is the first to allow, his own "natural tendency has been to place Malory, not against his native background, but against that of mediaeval French fiction" (Preface, p. viii). It remains for subsequent inquiry to assess Malory's background of English romantic sentiment. There can, of course, be little question that Malory's *primary* interests lay elsewhere.

22 *Op. cit.*, p. 13.

23 *The Paston Letters*, ed. James Gairdner (London, 1900), Vol. III (Edward IV-Henry VII), No. 774 (pp. 158-160). Gairdner conjectures the date of this letter as c. 1476.

[24] *Op. cit.,* Nos. 783 and 784 (pp. 170, 171).

[24a] Nevill Coghill, *The Poet Chaucer,* Home University Library (Oxford University Press, 1949), p. 23.

[25] On the psychology of 'substitution', see Bertrand H. Bronson, '*The Book of the Duchess* Re-opened', *PMLA,* LXVII (1952), 863-81, esp. 870-2.

[26] Lowes, *op. cit.,* p. 101.

[27] E. Hoepffner, *Oeuvres de Guillaume de Machaut,* Société des Anciens Textes Français (Paris, 1908), I, lxvii.

[28] Kittredge, *op. cit.,* p. 52.

[29] *Op. cit.,* p. 63: cf. Patch, *op. cit.,* p. 31: "the deity who controls a world where things like Blanche's death can happen must indeed be capricious, ruthless, guided by no rational plan."

[30] *Op. cit.,* p. 169.

[31] Kittredge, *op. cit.,* pp. 65-66.

[32] Lowes, *op. cit.,* p. 101.

[33] The "Drye se" and the "Carrenar," or Black Lake, seem perfectly appropriate not only to the idea of remote and arduous journeying, but also to the fruitlessness of the errand when heartless beauty is to be served.

[34] Lewis, *op. cit.,* p. 169.

[35] *Cf.* J. S. P. Tatlock, *The Mind and Art of Chaucer* (Syracuse, New York, 1950), p. 31.

16

The Unity of Chaucer's *House of Fame*

PAUL G. RUGGIERS

In many ways the most tantalizing of Chaucer's vision poems, the *House of Fame* continues to present a serious problem of interpretation to students of medieval poetry. The views of many writers who have dealt with the poem have tended to leave its meaning unresolved, and the steady accumulation of theories, while not obscuring the intention of the work, has unfortunately not clarified into a unified whole a poem in which Chaucer's rapidly developing powers are revealed at every turn.[1] The often repeated charge against the *House of Fame* that it lacks a clear plan, and Coghill's remark that it seems the least successful of Chaucer's longer poems sum up, in spite of more appreciative words, the general attitude of perplexed dissatisfaction with it.[2] A close reading of the work should convince the most reluctant reader that Chaucer was here, if not in complete possession of his artistic powers, nearing the goal of facility and force such as are to be seen in the structural strength and psychological validity underlying his major poetry. A comparison of the *House of Fame* with the *Book of the Duchess* and the *Parliament of Fowls* offers a clue to the problem of its unity, and in spite of the stumbling blocks in the way of a totally satisfactory analysis of the poem as an organic whole, I should

Reprinted, by permission of author and editor, from *SP*, L (1953), 16-29.

like to present what I consider its binding principle in terms of the progressively universalizing impulse which determines its form.

I shall attempt to show that the first book of the *House of Fame* presents us with a love story in which Fame, much like Fortune, plays an important role in the lives of two lovers; that the second book, while maintaining both the motive power of a love-vision and the force of a quest, gives us a view of an orderly universe, of which Fame is a part, in which all things seek and find their proper resting place; that the third, satisfying the demands of the quest and the love-vision, reveals the actual distribution or withholding of renown in such a universe. Book II, while transitional, is of great importance because it establishes the philosophical formula for the poem; with Book III it provides a kind of commentary on the exemplum of Book I.[3] Whatever was to have been announced in the grand climax by the man of great authority may have been intended to provide an answer to the common consideration of the Middle Ages, the relationship of men to the mutable world through the agency of Fame.

I

The first of the enigmas of the poem seems always to have been the first book, with its emphasis upon the story of Dido and Aeneas. Does Chaucer devote this book almost entirely to the story of the *Aeneid* and in particular to the ill fortune of Dido simply because the poem is a love-vision? Why then call the poem the *House of Fame*? What is the connection between this book and the books that follow? What, for that matter, is the relation between the activities of Venus and those of her sister Fortune?

Two writers, W. O. Sypherd and Howard Rollin Patch, have amply demonstrated these connections for us. Sypherd's argument, stated briefly, is that Chaucer's conception of the Goddess Fame was greatly influenced by the current notions of the goddesses of Love and Fortune, and that the idea of Fame or Rumor was enlarged by adding to her simple functions of hearing tidings and spreading them abroad, the more powerful attribute of sitting as a divinity to decide on the worldly fame of mankind. Chaucer would find some authority for such an equation of the three deities in love-visions and in his own reading and translation of Boethius. Even the companies of suppliants at the court of Fame, Sypherd writes, are ultimately dependent upon the general notion of the court of the god and goddess of Love.[4] To these identifications Patch gives his further support: "Fortune is never quite free from the charges of those who are discontented with their fame. As her gifts include glory, so we find her pretty much responsible for our reputation, good or bad." And again: "Fortune actually does or undoes the work of the God of Love. We may remember that in many ways her traits . . . resemble those of the love deity. . . . These divinities, Fortune and Love, become sufficiently identified for Venus to take over the characteristics of her sister goddess, and by the time of *Les Eches Amoureux* we find Venus turning a wheel and exalting and debasing mankind."[5]

What I am suggesting is simply that the functions of the three goddesses are so similar as to result in a conflation of their activities and the effects of their power over men. There is sufficient practical identification of these important deities in the House of Fame ("Geffrey" himself is going to the House of Fame, sister of Fortune, for love tidings) to warrant the recounting of a fateful love story in a poem which is to be concerned chiefly with the meting out of fame. Further, by structural analogy with the *Book of the Duchess* and the *Parliament of Fowls* where Chaucer's method is to juxtapose a preliminary reading from a book with the ensuing vision for purposes of profounder implication and meaning,[6] the *House of Fame* provides us with a specific account of Dido caught in the contrivances of Venus, or the fortunes of love, and of Fame, as an introduction to what "Geffrey" is to behold in the third book, the goddess Fame doling out her favor and disfavor with random caprice to mankind, in matters of love as well as in the countless other pursuits of men. It is important to notice that when Dido cries out against her fate, her complaint is specifically lodged against wicked Fame, the lament being a neat blend of the two phases of Fame's functions, rumor and reputation (I, 349-60). . . . The evil fortune of love, the slander, the loss of reputation, all of which Dido laments in the first book, point towards the third book where Fame is seen in action. There is in Chaucer's epitome of the *Aeneid,* with its emphasis upon the story

of Dido and Aeneas a sufficient foreshadowing of his theme
to warrant the long so-called digression of the third book
where Chaucer relates the method by which Fame distributes
her dubious favors. For his purposes the unhappy catastrophe
of love is the work of a divinity whose name might easily be
Fortune, or Fame, or Venus; their roles are interdependent;
they operate in similar circumstances. We need not complain
that Chaucer has not told us that this is an exemplum; we
need not look for the explicit moral drawn in the manner of
Gower or Machaut or Jean de Meun. In none of the early
love-visions does Chaucer state the purpose of the preliminary
reading, for as Bronson, Clemen, and most recently, Malone
have shown, all that follows the reading from a book is in a
sense a commentary on what has gone before.

The presence of the eagle at the end of Book I and his
subsequent role in the poem raise the old question of Dantean
influences upon Chaucer, a question that has a certain importance in an interpretation of the work.[7] The eagle which
appears at the end of Book I is generally acknowledged to be
derived in part from the eagle which carries Dante aloft in
Purgatorio IX. If this is so, we cannot very easily dismiss
the possibility that Chaucer was fully aware of the significance
of this episode for the *Divine Comedy* as a whole. It will be
remembered that in the valley of negligent princes Dante is
assailed by thoughts of the corruption and decay of Empire.
A golden eagle, aptly the symbol of empire, law and justice,
Jove's bird, snatches the dreaming Dante into the fiery sphere;
the dream is a prophetic one, or as it has been called, a pre-
fatory one, and whatever specifically was revealed to Dante in
it, Dante falls away from the purging vision with a sense of
the disparity between the ideal of the empyrean and the
defective milieu of this earth. The eagle itself is but a fore-
cast of another eagle which Dante is to see, the lecturing,
rebuking eagle of Paradise, the bird of God formed by the
just rulers who collectively represent Divine Justice. In this
circle of heaven Dante is confronted with the great mystery
of God's justice with special regard to whether or not the
righteous heathen were saved. The question is answered after
the manner of St. Paul; that is, it is declared unanswerable.
Divine Justice must always remain a mystery beyond the
reach of human knowledge; Dante must be content to see
that some of the righteous heathen are saved, and that the

will of God, embracing and exceeding ours, is its own standard in the choice of the elect. Both the eagle of Jove in
Purgatory and the eagle of God in Paradise seem implicit in
Chaucer's talking bird. He appears to have adopted the device of the flight from the *Purgatorio* and the meaning of
that flight from the *Paradiso*. Chaucer's eagle, the agent of
high comedy, not of serious moral drama, and the messenger
of Jove, enables him to approach an understanding of the
activities of Fame, her casual bestowal or withholding of
favor; her caprice, or in short, her injustice is apparently her
only standard. The implication for Chaucer, as it was an open
rebuke for Dante, is the same: Who is Chaucer that he should
attempt to judge this mystery and to fathom its operations?
The eagle comes, in the conclusion to Book I, at a calculated
moment. Just as Dante needed to be presented with his reassuring vision, so Chaucer now needs his reassuring answer
to what he has just recently seen. He prays,

> "O Crist!" thoughte I, "that art in blysse,
> Fro fantome and illusion
> Me save!" (I, 492-94)

Is he perhaps asking how this cruel love which he has just
witnessed can be the magnificent love of which Boethius and
Dante both speak, ordering the stars in their courses and
binding men and women in a sacred tie? The eagle comes
miraculously to lead him to an answer.

Such seems to me to be the relationship between Book I
and the remainder of the poem. And if we can perceive that
relationship, then we will also discover that from the very
beginning of the poem Chaucer's genius has taken hold of
its direction; it comes more and more to life in bursts out of
the very core of his subject, which is a facet of the problem
of evil, the role of capricious circumstance in men's lives,
whether in the realm of the passions or elsewhere. And as we
shall see, he yields himself up to his scheme with an enthusiasm that is always sufficiently held in check to make the
poem conform to the requirements of his guiding principle. It
seems presumptuous to assume that Chaucer did not learn
from Geoffrey de Vinsauf and Boethius, if not from his own
hard application to the art of poetry, that the creative artist
refrains from plunging carelessly into his task, but first
"aperceyveth in his thought the forme of the thing that he

wol make" before he shapes his idea and clothes it with words
(Boethius *De cons.* iv. pr. 6, 90-5; cf. *TC*, I, 1065-9).

II.

There can be little disagreement over the purpose and
function of Book II of the *House of Fame*. Its clear statement by the eagle that "Geffrey" is to be carried away from
the uninspiring daily rounds of his life to the House of Fame
where he may hear tidings of love, indicates the motive of the
dream. The chief difficulty of interpretation has arisen, of
course, from our inability to adjust what is promised in the
long list of love's circumstances cited by the eagle (II, 672-
99) to what Chaucer actually sees in Book III when he is in
the House of Fame. Our general tendency is to feel that the
author has lost the main thread of his narrative and has
abandoned, if only in part, his original direction. As I have
stated above, it is my belief that Chaucer has not relinquished
his theme, the reward of love tidings for the weary poet; in
the universalizing process, in the conflation of the three goddesses, the love motive has been absorbed into the larger
scheme of the mystery of adverse circumstance, and in
particular into the accident of fame. All that evolves after
the promise of the eagle does so naturally and smoothly:
Chaucer protests that he cannot understand how so many
items of news could reach the goddess Fame, whereupon the
bird launches into his long explanation of the basic order of
the universe, and with it, the analogy between the widening
circles resulting from throwing a stone in water and the
widening circles of sound (which is merely broken air) seeking their natural resting place in Fame's palace.

The function of the book is of course to serve as a statement of purpose, the quest for tidings, and to provide in
Boethian terms the basic scientific and theological formula
of the orderly universe. Its narrative thread is spatial, and
thus the book is structurally, as well as geographically, transitional.

The generally accepted notion has been that at the time of
the writing of the love-visions Chaucer had as yet only imperfectly assimilated the substance of his reading, abundant as
it was, in continental sources. And yet, one of the satisfying
aspects of Chaucer's art has always been his ability to co-

ordinate into an interesting and artistic whole the most heterogeneous materials. This creative synthesis is perhaps best seen in the *Nun's Priest's Tale* where we find the humors, dream psychology, Bradwardine on God's foreknowledge and man's free will, and a parody of Vinsauf's elegy—all cleverly subordinated to his main scheme. One may wonder on occasion whether Chaucer's audience must not have been impressed and bewildered by the confusing array of Chaucer's gifts alongside those of other writers, and whether those who were well-read would not find that they were forced to adjust their recollection of the meaning of a reference in its original context to its new use; but Chaucer's borrowings from Boethius, for example, are extraordinarily successful in the *House of Fame.* The explanation in Boethian terms that "every thing . . . hath his propre mansyon, / to which hit seketh to repaire, / ther-as hit shulde not appaire" (753-56), is beautifully absorbed into the scheme of the passing of report to the House of Fame where it finds its natural resting place. And when, following his exultant little prayer at God's mighty creation, Chaucer resorts to a direct quotation from the *Consolatio* (iv. m. 1), the reference is peculiarly apt and corroborates the tone of subtle irony throughout. The lines read:

> And thoo thoughte y upon Boece,
> That writ, "A thought may flee so hye,
> Wyth fetheres of Philosophye,
> To passen everych element;
> And whan he hath so fer ywent,
> Than may be seen, behynde hys bak,
> Cloude," and al that y of spak.   (972-78)

The poem he is referring to occurs at a point in the *Consolatio* where Boethius is about to learn from the lady Philosophy her views on the existence of evil in the world. Through her tutelage he has been gradually freed from the taint of earth and is now to be made "parfit of the worschipful lyght of God" in a sphere to which one day his soul will return as to its natural home. Chaucer must have liked the passage for its power as well as for its adaptability to his narrative: he too is, in his dream, surmounting the earth; he too has beheld the order and beauty of God's creation; he too will receive an answer, in the form of a demonstration in the House of Fame, to one phase of the problem of evil in God's world.

Indeed the whole flight through the upper air is so closely
supported by the Boethian references that one catches a hint
of the sublime usually denied to Chaucer, the sublime of
high comedy. The eagle's amusing disquisition on order in
the universe set side by side with the passage of report to the
House of Fame, the retreating of the earth beneath them as
they mount higher and higher, the precarious relationship of
poor Geoffrey to the eagle form the substance of Book II
in a lively sweep of narrative related with great deftness and
comic awareness, an extraordinary sample of the literature
of the journey. Chaucer seems here really to have enjoyed
his work, for in its lines he had lavished most of his energy
in creating the learned bird and the simpleton foil. The
general interest is high because the book serves as a transition
from earth to heaven and because the journey, with its
scientific apparatus, becomes Chaucer's primary object.

III.

The "lytel laste bok" is the source of most of our difficulties
in interpreting the *House of Fame* as a unified whole because
it contains the second of the so-called artistic blemishes (the
Dido-Aeneas story is the first) in the poem, and because in it
Chaucer seems to have lost the original direction of the narrative and shifted his emphasis from love tidings to the
vicissitudes of fame. This emphasis upon the granting or
withholding of fame constitutes no real difficulty if we consider that Dido and Aeneas are part of the human comedy
and that their relationship is conditioned by the intermingled
activities of Love and the two sister goddesses, Fame and
Fortune. One cannot shake off the conviction that in this
book Chaucer has his mind set squarely on his goal. The
extravagant invention, the embellishment of glorious names,
the energy and the enthusiasm with which the poet pushes
towards a conclusion would seem collectively to indicate his
singleness of purpose; the fact that the poem does not in its
present state fulfill its earlier promise of tidings of love is no
warrant that such tidings were not to be forthcoming. The
long account of the nine companies of petitioners in the court
of Fame, suing for their desired reputation or oblivion, it is
entirely possible, is not a digression at all but an organic part
of the action, the logical demonstration of Chaucer's ideas

about Fame and her influence upon the lives of men. The relationship to Dante which I have indicated earlier suggests that the mysterious and capricious injustice of the Lady Fame is to Chaucer's poem what the impenetrable mystery of God's justice is to the *Divine Comedy;* both poets are led to the threshold of an answer by an eagle who is the messenger of the Almighty. In his own poem, he deals with the problem not so much of God's justice working itself out in the world (although he may have meant that to be a part of the final resolution), but with a collateral consideration that may have had its genesis in his reading of Boethius, the subjection of men to the capricious circumstance of Fame. It is my persuasion that the third book says what Chaucer intends it to say, that Fame and her influence, like that of her sister Fortune, is ever present as a conditioning factor in men's lives, and that men should fasten their hopes on something more stable, over and above this capricious power. Chaucer knew well from Boethius and Dante that there is a tremendous gap between the fame that the world offers and the personal satisfaction in abiding by the laws of his art and eschewing the lures of the inconstant Lady Fame. His own humorous and dispassionate attitude towards the influence of Venus in his life is too well known to mention here; humorous though it be, Chaucer's position with regard to Fame is stated in his answer to the passerby who asks him if he has come in search of fame for himself:

> Sufficeth me, as I were ded,
> That no wight have my name in honde.
> I wot myself best how y stonde;
> For what I drye, or what I thynke,
> I wil myselven al hyt drynke,
> Certeyn, for the more part,
> As fer forth as I kan myn art. (III, 1876-82)

This is Boethius' own lesson well learned, that inner peace cannot be bought on the world's terms. To it Chaucer adds a faith in oneself, which in his words suggests a faith in God-given talents. He refuses to be overwhelmed by the accidents of fortune or fame.

Chaucer has not forgotten his original purpose, the eagle's promise of love tidings as his reward. He falls away easily from the larger theme of Fame's injustice. I have always known, says he, that men desired fame, praise, reputation, but until now, I knew nothing of her house, her appearance, her method of passing judgments. These are not the tidings I mean. And he is led to the nearly whirling house of tidings with its many openings to let out sounds and its open doors to let in all kinds of news. The catalogue of the kinds of tidings which are to be found in the whirling house deserves to be compared with the earlier rehearsal of tidings cited by the eagle in BOOK II, 672-99, for in the list of BOOK III, it should be noted, Chaucer has passed from his emphasis upon love and its phases to life itself, in which love and its various circumstances form only one small part of the picture:

> And over alle the houses angles
> Ys ful of rounynges and of jangles
> Of werres, of pes, of mariages,
> Of reste, of labour, of viages,
> Of abood, of deeth, of lyf,
> Of love, of hate, acord, of stryf,
> Of loos, of lore, and of wynnynges,
> Of hele, of seknesse, of bildynges,
> Of faire wyndes, and of tempestes,
> Of qwalm of folk, and eke of bestes;
> Of dyvers transmutacions
> Of estats, and eke of regions;
> Of trust, of drede, of jelousye,
> Of wit, of wynnynge, of folye;
> Of plente, and of gret famyne,
> Of chepe, of derthe, and of ruyne;
> Of good or mys governement,
> Of fyr, and of dyvers accident.   (1959-76)

And it will be remembered too that of the nine companies of petitioners, only two of them, the sixth and seventh, are made up of those who desire fame "as wel of love as other thyng," a sign that the love element has been absorbed into a larger framework. This departure from the motive of love tidings exclusively seems to my mind to be the inevitable result of the universalizing impulse behind the broader concept of Fortune in any of her cults. The steadily expanding compass of the successive books of the *House of Fame* demonstrates in small Chaucer's whole development as an artist as he masters a literary type, absorbs a new and liberating philosophy from Boethius, and creates a new form. BOOK III is an attempt to stay within the tradition of the love-vision while at the same time widening its scope to include more direct observation, more invention and detail. None of Chaucer's early poetry seems so clearly to discover to our eyes the poet utilizing convention but putting it aside for larger and profounder patterns of thought.

The remainder of the poem, its description of the House of Rumor, the final scrambling in a corner of the House where men are talking of love tidings, is a fulfillment of the eagle's promise (never quite lost from view) that Chaucer was to have as his reward a journey to the House of Fame where he would hear such tidings. More than that, it is Chaucer's method of disassociating his enlarged and more grandiose conception of Fame or reputation from the meaner view of her as mere rumor or report, as she had been in classical literature. By supplying the poem with a House of Rumor where reports are received and intermingled before Lady Fame decides what will be done with them, he preserves the grander picture of Fame by subordinating rumor to a mere device in her hands, no longer equating her with it.

As for the name of the man of great authority who was presumably to present the tidings, the guess of triumph which Bronson looks forward to is yet to be made. The identification of the man of authority with an actual historical personage, with Richard II or John of Gaunt for example, has been so unsatisfactory as to lead Robinson to write that the "identity of the person and the nature of the connection seem now beyond the range of conjecture" (p. 887 [2nd ed., p. 779]). A recent and interesting suggestion, offered in the form of a question by R. C. Goffin, is that Boccaccio may be the man of authority,[8] but the suggestion of a literary figure raises the ghosts of other writers from whom Chaucer borrowed or who turned from the matter of books to the matter of life for their subjects. There is, however, another figure whose influence is manifest not only in this poem but in all of Chaucer's major work and whose philosophy might have supplied a resolution for the demand for tidings. I mean, of course, Boethius himself.

Coghill has written that Chaucer's liberation from the influence of the love-vision was the result of his reading and translation of Boethius in whom he had found his new formula, the turn of Fortune's wheel.[9] My own impression is that Chaucer had already discovered the formula and was in the *House of Fame* prefiguring the many subsequent uses to which it could be put. Perhaps had we the completed poem

the precise use of the formula would have been revealed by
the man of great authority in a sane and dispassionate pronouncement incorporating the theme of the untrustworthy
fortunes of love into the larger picture of the instability of
fame in general, a pronouncement voicing the conviction that
only disillusion must result from an abuse of the passions and
the folly of trusting the inconstant goddesses.[10] That Boethius
could supply Chaucer with an answer to suit the needs of the
House of Fame may be seen from the long concluding speech
by Theseus in the *Knight's Tale* where Chaucer has borrowed
from the *Consolatio* a part of the Boethian love song to bring
his tale to an end. Boethius himself could certainly have
supplied a statement on the falseness of the glory that the
world offers; and there is a sufficient broadening of the meaning of "love" in his philosophy to warrant the assimilation of
the earthly passion of Dido and Aeneas into the "fayre
cheyne of love" established by the "Firste Moevere" in whose
plan for the world good and evil fame, like good and evil
fortune, are a part.

Would Chaucer's high comedy support such a conclusion?
My feeling is that it would, for though Chaucer knew that
men desired fame and praise, and then came to know where
Fame dwelt and how she dealt out her favors, he did not
know that like her sister Fortune, Fame is part of a system
by which the "purveiaunce" of God is carried out, and in
which even the personal tragedy of Dido has meaning. And
this the man of great authority might have told him. Our task
is to recover something of the vision implicit in Caxton's
words: In the *House of Fame* Chaucer "towchyth . . . ryght
grete wysedom & substyll understondying. . . . For he wrytteth
no voyde words / but all hys mater is ful of hye and quycke
sentence."

Notes

1 For a summary of the various theories which have accrued to the
House of Fame the reader is directed to F. N. Robinson's edition, *The
Complete Works of Geoffrey Chaucer* (Boston, 1933), pp. 886-87 [(2nd
ed.; Boston, 1957), pp. 778-9], and to Bertrand H. Bronson, "Chaucer's
Hous of Fame: Another Hypothesis," *University of California Publications in English* III (1932-1944), 171 ff. All quotations from Chaucer
are from Robinson's text.

2 Nevill Coghill, *The Poet Chaucer* (Oxford University Press, 1949),
p. 49. Coghill is far from alone in this attitude. For Emile Legouis,

Geoffrey Chaucer, trans. L. Lailavoix (London, 1913), pp. 87-88 and for W. C. Curry, *Chaucer and the Mediaeval Sciences* (New York, 1926), p. 233, the poem lacks careful selection of materials or demonstrates an incomplete assimilation of Boethius and Dante. Percy Van Dyke Shelly, *The Living Chaucer* (The University of Penn. Press, 1940), p. 84, feels that Chaucer had more matter than he could digest, and Marchette Chute, *Geoffrey Chaucer of England* (New York, 1946), p. 110, surmises that possibly Chaucer had no clear plan in mind and merely intended to ramble along in the "easygoing medieval way on the general subject of 'fame' until he was through." The most recent expression of this view is that of J. S. P. Tatlock, *The Mind and Art of Chaucer* (Syracuse University Press, 1950), p. 59, who writes that the first part of the poem is undefined and motiveless, and that only in the latter parts of the work is there any concentrated aim.

3 Critics have come more and more to accept the introductory reading from a book in the early love-visions as having the full force of an exemplum. Perhaps the fullest treatment of this rhetorical device in the vision poems is that of Wolfgang Clemen, *Der Junge Chaucer, Kölner Anglistische Arbeiten* (Bochum-Langendreer, 1938), pp. 39-42, 96-99, and 168-70. Clemen's views have been anticipated in part by Bronson, "In Appreciation of Chaucer's *Parlement of Foules*," *University of California Publications in English* III (1932-1944), 199-201, and have been followed for the most part by Kemp Malone, *Chapters on Chaucer* (The Johns Hopkins Press, 1951), pp. 28-29, 51. Needless to say, I am in debt to all of these.

4 W. O. Sypherd, *Studies in Chaucer's 'Hous of Fame,'* (Chaucer Society, 1907), pp. 16-17, 71, 114 ff.

5 Howard Rollin Patch, *The Goddess Fortuna in Mediaeval Literature* (Cambridge, Mass., 1927), pp. 112 and 96. That Chaucer was well aware of this practical identification of Love and Fortune may be seen from *A Complaint to his Lady*, ll. 33-36; *Fortune*, l. 50; *Troilus and Criseyde*, IV, 323 ff.

6 The arguments of those who disagree on the relationship of the preliminary reading to the rest of the poem are impressive. Cf. John Edwin Wells, *A Manual of the Writings in Middle English 1050-1400* (New Haven, 1916), p. 634: "Scholars have pointed out that [the *Book of the Duchess*] . . . lacks unity and proportion in its proem (most of which is a complete story practically independent of the rest of the poem). . . ." And p. 646: "[The *Parlement*] exhibits the tendency to disproportion of treatment and lack of unity, that appears in much of Chaucer's work, especially that of his earlier years. There is the same difficulty in getting to his story." With respect to the *House of Fame* perhaps the most recent statement of this school of thought is that of Tatlock, p. 58: ". . . the highlighting of the Dido-Aeneas love story . . . is like the long beginnings of the *Book of the Duchess* and the *Parliament of Fowls* in having little appropriateness and much decorative force and a great deal of intrinsic value in that it introduced ill-read auditors to the distinguished *Aeneid,* to Ovid's *Metamorphoses* and Cicero's *Somnium Scipionis*. The lighter literature of the Middle Ages did not highly value unity. . . ."

7 Coghill, p. 48, has summarized the matter of Dante's influence

upon Chaucer succinctly. Chaucer, he writes, was "struggling to look forward to a newer and a more controlled way of writing. He had now read Dante, and was beginning dimly to show in his own verses the first fruits of his reading. Not only are there individual lines taken from *The Divine Comedy*, but there is the palpable effort to organize his material something after the manner of Dante. . . . Upon the general unwieldiness of his subject-matter (no poetical sin by the standards of Jean de Meun) Chaucer was trying to impose something of the logical shaping power of Italian poetry."

8 "Quiting by Tidings in *The House of Fame*," *Medium Aevum*, XII (1943), 44. [A possible occasion for the poem as part of the entertainments in the Inns of Court has been suggested by R. J. Schoeck in "A Legal Reading of Chaucer's *Hous of Fame*," *University of Toronto Quarterly*, XXIII (1954), 185-92; the man of authority might then have been one of the officers of the revels.]

9 *The Poet Chaucer*, p. 64.

10 Cf., the similar conclusion drawn by Paull F. Baum, "Chaucer's *The House of Fame*," *ELH*, VIII (1941), 255-56. "The ultimate tidings of love from the man of authority would have inevitably been a . . . disappointment and disillusion."

17

An Interpretation of Chaucer's *Parlement of Foules*

CHARLES O. MC DONALD

The main lines which any investigation of the *Parlement of Foules* must follow have been firmly traced out,[1] and disagreement is limited to the interpretation and weight assigned to specific details. However, such disagreement concerning details may effect considerable alterations in our judgment of the unity and value of the poem.

To describe briefly the unity of the *Parlement of Foules* before beginning a detailed analysis, I would say that the poem has as its subject matter love, but love considered from a very special point of view — that of an entire spectrum of varying types of love experience which the poet is trying to define and analyze. Through the use of contrasted pairs—the golden *versus* the black side of the garden gate, the lush natural beauty of garden *versus* the sterility of the abstract personifications, Priapus *versus* Venus, and the birds of low degree *versus* the "foules of ravyne" — this spectrum of love experience is set up. Through the idea of "commune profyt," and particularly through the figure of Nature, a norm is established by which these types of love can be viewed in their proper perspective and the extreme ends of the spectrum may be treated with a delicate humor and irony. This is the essence of the poem in which Nature plays the role of a

Reprinted, by permission of author and editor, from *Speculum*, XXX (1955), 444-57.

tolerant mediator between apparently contradictory points of view, and in which the usual roles of the naive and sophisticated are delightfully reversed. These statements are the barest summary of what follows.

The poem opens with an aphorism, *Ars longa, Vita brevis*, usually applied to writing in general and poetry in particular, but which here applies as well to the art of love:

> Al this mene I by Love, that my felynge
> Astonyeth with his wonderful werkynge
> So sore, iwis, that whan I on hym thynke,
> Nat wot I wel wher that I flete or synke.   (4-7)

When the poet thinks of the complex emotion he has set out to analyze, consternation arises within him at being so innocent of knowledge of it. The poet's perplexity in the presence of Love is underlined by the following stanza in which he reads both "Of his myrakles and his crewel yre" (l. 11). All that the poet can say at the present time is that if Love *will* be Lord, then, "God save the King," and with this wryly humorous dismissal of the problem he turns to other things. However the keynote of all the subsequent action is hit in this initial presentation of love's "myrakles and his crewel yre." Love immediately suggests a double-standard to the poet, or at any rate two extremes which may result from cultivating his acquaintance. We shall see both these aspects presented at some length before the poem concludes.

The poet tells us of his habit of reading which has led him to read this day an old book for the purpose of ascertaining "a certeyn thing" (l. 20). What this thing is he does not tell us, and we must not be too hasty in identifying it. The thing he seeks must have some relationship to that "newe science" (l. 25), which he, as well as others, seeks from books and which, probably, has connections with the art of love which he has already characterized as so puzzling to him.

His reading has been "Tullyus of the Drem of Scipioun" (l. 31) which in seven chapters gave him a complete conspectus of heaven, hell and all the intermediate stations of the universe, so that, theoretically at least, he is in good case to find what he is looking for. He summarizes the dream so as to emphasize the function of the narrative as a way toward salvation for the desiring soul, which, according to Africanus, can make its way to heaven immediately upon death only by working for the "commune profyt," a phrase he uses twice (ll. 47 and 75). The souls which belonged to transgressors of the law or "likerous folk" (l. 79) shall be whirled about the universe in torment, until finally forgiven, they too, come into heaven. Although we cannot yet, with any certainty, say what the "certeyn thing" is, we may agree with R. C. Goffin [*op. cit.*, p. 499] in saying that the *Dream* does establish a partial concern with salvation as one of the *motifs* of the poem, and a salvation to be attained most easily through working for the common good. We need not say that this regimen of conduct necessarily excludes all lovers. It rejects only those, as Macrobius says, "qui se corporis voluptatibus dediderunt" [who have given themselves over to carnal pleasures], but it certainly puts limitations on the conduct of all others in a variety of ways as we shall see.

All of this moral reading-matter is very well, but the poor poet prepared for bed when darkness fell,

> Fulfyld of thought and busy hevynesse;
> For bothe I hadde thyng which that I nolde,
> And ek I nadde that thyng that I wolde.   (89-91)

Macrobius had let him down; a way of salvation he had seen, but evidently that was not what he sought. Of what use is a mode of salvation to a poet of love in full pursuit of his trade? The answer comes back quickly enough when Africanus appears and tells the poet that for so diligently perusing his old book, "sumdel of thy labor wolde I quyte" (l. 112). There may, after all, be a really direct connection between love and salvation.

Before we begin to follow Africanus we come to the stanza which more than any other has puzzled the commentators:

> Cytherea! thow blysful lady swete,
> That with thy fyrbrond dauntest whom the lest,
> And madest me this sweven for to mete,
> Be thow myn helpe in this, for thow mayst best!
> As wisly as I sey the north-north-west,
> When I began my sweven for to write:
> So yif me myght to ryme and ek t' endyte!   (113-119)

To list the interpretations made for this stanza would take more space than it would be worth, but it seems most likely to me that Manly's interpretation [*op. cit.*, p. 288] of the words "north-north-west" as meaning "in an unpropitious

position" (cf. Hamlet's "I am mad but north-north-west"),
or, as Bronson suggests, "hardly at all" [*op. cit.*, p. 203] thus
giving the stanza an ironic cast in which the poet is slighting
Venus rather than asking her for inspiration, is the correct
way in which to read it in view of the treatment accorded
Venus later in the poem.

At any rate, we quickly return to Africanus, and as the
Roman takes the poet by the hand, we begin to get echoes
of Dante's excursion under the guidance of Virgil, gently
ironic in tone. The garden-gate definitely recalls the gate of
Hell in Dante's *Inferno,* but here the verses inscribed over
the door are tantalizingly ambiguous; one side, in gold, boding
good to the wayfarer, the other, in black, boding ill.

The gate however is more important than this simple explanation would suggest; it is one of the key elements in the
poem. The phrasing of the mottoes is important. The golden
one:

> "Thorgh me men gon into that blysful place
> Of hertes hele and dedly woundes cure;
> Thorgh me men gon unto the welle of grace,
> There grene and lusty May shal evere endure.
> This is the wey to al good aventure.
> Be glad, thow redere, and thy sorwe of-caste;
> Al open am I — passe in, and sped thee faste!"
>
> (127-133)

The black one:

> "Thorgh me men gon," than spak that other side,
> "Unto the mortal strokes of the spere
> Of which Disdayn and Daunger is the gyde,
> Ther nevere tre shal fruyt ne leves here.
> This strem yow ledeth to the sorweful were
> There as the fish in prysoun is al drye;
> Th' eschewing is only the remedye!"   (134-140)

This gate seems to symbolize two distinct kinds of love to
be found in the garden: love according to Nature, which
promises ever-green joy, and love of a more courtly kind
which leads to barren sorrow and despair. A further dimension is thus added to the poet's concern with Love's "myrakles
and his crewel yre" which began the poem. The golden inscription uses no words reminiscent of the French courtly
romances, and the "welle of grace" clearly suggests a kind of

love which is holy, is approved of by God. The joyful side of love could have been pictured in much more specifically "romance" or "courtly" terms if the poet had so wished by the expedient of introducing the opposite numbers of Daunger and Disdayn—for example, Bialacoil and Pleasaunce—but they do not appear; instead "grene and lusty May shal evere endure," an entirely different order of description than that lavished on the sorrow-causing allegorical abstractions, because of whom "never tre shal fruyt ne leves bere." The elements of natural beauty, used also by the French courtly poets, are here given a new and vital function as symbols serving in themselves as a vivid contrast to the allegorical personifications of the courtly tradition rather than as mere ornamental surroundings for them. "Grene and lusty May" defines a kind of love differing not only in results but in essence from that defined by Daunger and Disdayn.

The poet is inspired to enter by the first inscription but deterred by the second. This is a critical moment for one who has read, as the poet has, so many tales of Love's "myrakles and his crewel yre," and Chaucer capitalizes on the inherent drama of the situation in a humorously ironic fashion. Africanus claps the poet on the shoulder and whisks him through the gate not at all in the manner of Dante's Virgil, commenting that the inscriptions do not apply to the poet, "For thow of love hast lost thy tast, I gesse, / As sek man hath of swete and bytternesse" (ll. 160-161). This is only half-true as the poet has already shown us by saying, as he viewed the inscriptions. "That oon me hette, that other dide me colde" (l. 145). The concept of love, fostered by Nature, has definite appeal for the poet, while the concept of love beset by Daunger and Disdayn has not.

The moment the poet steps inside, the feeling of apprehension leaves him, and he exults in the natural beauty around him:

> But, Lord, so I was glad and wel begoon!
> For overal where that I myne eyen caste
> Were treës clad with leves that ay shal laste,
> Ech in his kynde, of colour fresh and greene
> As emeraude, that joye was to seene.   (171-175)

Obviously this is a garden in which "lusty May" predominates and where Daunger and Disdayn have little inhibiting power upon the fecundity and growth of the vegetable inhabitants of

the region at least. Again the contrast in the use of natural
and allegorical imagery is quite different from that of the
French poems in which natural objects were just so much
more allegorical furniture, undifferentiated in purpose from
the personifications themselves.

Then begins the description of the garden, drawn from
Boccaccio's *Teseida,* but not without certain changes which
entirely alter the effect of the original.[2] One may note after
Emerson[3] that lines 188-189 and 199-210 are original with
Chaucer. Each of these passages is a picturesque addition to
the natural detail of the garden which enhances its character
as an "ideal state of nature," and Chaucer elaborates Boccaccio's list of trees with characteristic delight while altering
and subduing the allegorical figures of the *Teseida.* One may
note also that Chaucer has transposed the stanzas in Boccaccio's poem dealing with Venus (63-66) to a position
directly after that which describes Priapus (60), and has
placed the two intervening stanzes (61 and 62), which describe the bows of Diana's maidens that decorate the temple
and the paintings of the famous lovers upon the walls, at
the very end of his account. If we were to agree entirely with
R. A. Pratt[4] that Chaucer was translating from his source in
a hurry and without much care, such alterations in the place-
ment of whole stanzas would be completely inexplicable, but
if we credit Chaucer with some sense of design in his own
poem then the reason may become apparent. Chaucer has
increased the natural detail of the garden considerably, and
we may attribute this solicitude on his part to that preference
for a joyous love in accord with nature which we have noticed
in the preceding passages. Let us begin to take note of the
changes in the personnel of the garden and the way in which
they are described in Boccaccio:

> E poi vide in quel passo Leggiadria
> Con Adornezza ed Affabilitate,
> E la ismarrita in tuto Cortesia,
> E vide l'Arti ch'hanno potestate
> De fare altrui a forza far follia,
> Nel loro aspetto molto isfigurate:
> Della immagine nostra il van Diletto
> Con Gentilezza vide star soletto.
>
> (VII, 55)

> [And she saw, in her passing, Grace
> With Adornment and Affabilty

> And Courtesy completely confused,
> And she saw the Arts which have power
> To make others by force to commit folly,
> In their appearance greatly disfigured:
> Vain Delight in our image,
> With Gentleness, she saw standing alone.]

And Chaucer:

> Tho was I war of Pleasaunce anon-ryght,
> And of Aray, and Lust, and Curteysie,
> And of the Craft that can and hath the myght
> To don by force a wyght to don folye—
> Disfigurat was she, I nyl nat lye;
> And by hymself, under an ok, I gesse,
> Saw I Delyt, that stod with Gentilesse. (218-224)

Note how *Leggiadria* (Grace) becomes in Chaucer the Romance "Pleasaunce," and *Affabilitate* (Affability) becomes "Lust," although *Arti* is given a relatively literal rendering, "Craft." However, when Chaucer comes to Diletto ("Delyt") he inserts the natural detail of the "ok," consistent with his other uses of natural objects in referring to the joyous aspects of love. In the next stanza of Boccaccio, after literally rendering *Bellezza* as "Beaute" and *Giovenezza* as "Youthe," but omitting *Piacevolezza* (Attractiveness), he translates Boccaccio's *Ardire* (Audacity) by "Foolhardynesse," then renders literally *Lusinghe* as "Flaterye," and finally Ruffiani (Pimps) is completely deserted in favor of "Desyre," while two more figures corresponding to nothing in the original, "Messagerye" (the sending of messages) and "Meede" (Merit, Desert), both commonly associated with courtly love concepts are introduced into the company. We note the use of or substitution of as many romance words in these personifications as possible. The poet is telling us that all the elements of courtly love allegory are present in this garden, but he makes them generally as unattractive as possible by allowing them few qualifying adjectives with which he was so lavish in listing the trees which grew in the garden or which he will use again to such charming effect in the list of birds. By contrast the picture here is bleak and cold, but we must not think that it is cold, as C. S. Lewis contends [*op. cit.*, p. 174], because this is Renaissance, not medieval allegory, for we have seen Chaucer go out of his way to give the common courtly names to his figures. The result of the changes is plain. Only "Delyt" rates the natural detail of the "ok."

Indeed, these personifications are "barren"—with the bar-
renness of Daunger and Disdayn, who inhibit all fertility and
growth.

However, when Chaucer turns to Priapus—a figure who,
incidentally, had, since Roman times, in statuary adorned
Italian gardens as their tutelary deity[5]—he alters Boccaccio
to a more favorable and humorous light. In place of the
Italian, which reads to the effect that the observer in the
temple went on, seeing as she progressed many flowers adorn-
ing the place, he gives the lines (257-259),

> Ful besyly men gonne asaye and fonde
> Upon his hed to sette, of sondry hewe,
> Garlondes ful of freshe floures newe.

Priapus has a place in the temple of courtly love even in
Boccaccio, but it took Chaucer to grasp the full potentialities
of the situation. Certainly Priapus represents love and fertility
at its most natural, and his description is in humorous harmony with what we have noticed before.

Then comes the major change in the passage; the trans-
position of the three stanzas of the Italian devoted to Venus
to their present position where they contrast directly with the
picture of Priapus just presented. It has been noticed by other
commentators that Chaucer here subdues Boccaccio's verse.
Bronson [op. cit., pp. 209-11], gives the best analysis of the
changes, which I shall summarize here:

1. Boccaccio dwells on Venus' beauty; Chaucer does not mention
   it;
2. Boccaccio discovers her virtually naked in bed; Chaucer focuses
   on the bed;
3. Boccaccio gives her loose golden hair; Chaucer binds it with a
   band;
4. Chaucer does not dwell on the beauty of her face as does
   Boccaccio;
5. nor does he mention the beauty of her arms, her bosom, or the
   apples of her breasts as does the Italian;
6. in Chaucer she is satisfactorily covered, while in Boccaccio it is
   as if she had nothing on;
7. Chaucer transfers the fragrance which Boccaccio has assigned to
   her person to the temple itself;
8. Boccaccio dwells on the apple and the victory over Pallas and
   Hera in the valley of Ida which Chaucer omits;
9. Chaucer wholly invents the phrase with which he dismisses her,
   "But thus I let her lye" (279), which Bronson says is proverbially
   applied to dogs.

Even if we discount the ninth "change," which some might challenge, it can be seen from the above that the portrait of Venus, when compared with the original, or even when compared with the brief picture of Priapus, who occupies "sovereyn place" in the temple, is far from the lushness of flattery of Boccaccio. Again the sterility of the courtly conventions is suggested to the reader, and certainly to the writer, who had a description far richer than the one he gave in the very source from which he was translating.

This, then, is a very special garden, as we have suspected ever since we came through the strange gate with its double inscription. It is clearly not the garden of the *Romance of the Rose* nor of any of the conventional "May Morning" poems of courtly love; in fact, in the very real presence of the natural beauty here abounding, the common personifications of the French courtly tradition are put to shame and merely tolerated. The poet is emphasizing what gave him his initial thrill of delight as he entered upon the scene and only fleetingly indicating the presence of those things which threatened pain in the legend in the dark side of the gate. The balance is delicate and subtle, but the position of the heaviest weight is undeniably clear, and produces time and again effects of ironic humor and mild satire at the expense of courtly love.

Again we are in the open, and the poet catches sight of a majestic figure of the "noble goddesse Nature" upon a hill of flowers. As the poet tells us, it was completely fitting that she be here,

> For this was on seynt Valentynes day,
> Whan every foul cometh there to chese his make,
> Of every kynde that men thynke may,
> And that so huge a noyse gan they make
> That erthe, and eyr, and tre, and every lake
> So ful was, that unethe was there space
> For me to stonde, so ful was al the place.   (309-315)

The fowls have come on Saint Valentine's Day, as is their yearly custom, to choose their mates. This again may seem like unnecessary underlining of a relatively simple point, but it is an important one nevertheless, and has definite bearings upon what comes afterwards. Chaucer himself takes pains that no one shall miss it, for he repeats himself in lines 370-371: "Benygnely to chese or for to take, / By hire acord, his formel or his make," and once more when Nature says,

"Ye come for to cheese—and fle youre wey— / Youre makes"
(ll. 388-389). We shall soon see how this develops when the
very first to choose, the royal tercel, paying no heed to Nature's
instructions or to the acknowledged custom, says,

> Unto my *soverayn lady, and not my fere* [i.e., mate],
> I chese, and chese with wil, and herte, and thought,
> The formel on youre hand, so wel iwrought,
> Whos I am al, and evere wil hire serve,
> Do what hire lest, to do me lyve or sterve; . . .
>   (416-420; italics added)

For the moment, however, let us return to the description
of Nature in her glory which contrasts sharply with that of
Venus. Her seat on flowers in the open air is susceptible to
contrast with the dark bed of Venus "in a privie corner,"
and her
>   aray and face,
>   In swich aray men myghte hire there fynde.
>   This noble emperesse, ful of grace, . . .   (317-319)

seems almost like cognizance on Chaucer's part of the details
he had subtracted from Boccaccio's Venus, although he tells
us he was thinking of Alanus' description of Nature in the
"Playnt of Kynde." Next the catalogue of the birds is given,
and anyone who is not yet convinced that the courtly abstractions are barren and frigid in the list which Chaucer
gives of them should read that passage (ll. 218-245), and then
quickly turn to the one now under discussion (ll. 330-363),
of which the latter is six lines longer but infinitely richer.
Again the contrast is meant deliberately, and our feeling for
the natural beauty of the scene increases, while our feeling
for the courtly-love elements within it grows less and less.

We are introduced to the "formel" eagle which perches on
Nature's hand. Our expectancy is aroused; "formel" is not a
generic term for a single species of eagle, but merely means a
female eagle arrived at mating age. When Nature explains the
rules of choosing, her introduction becomes clear, for the
"foules of ravyne," being the ranking members of the assem-
bly, are to have first choice. Immediately, however, a "sour"
note is hit with the speech of the royal tercel already quoted
(ll. 416 ff.). With a swiftness and ironic humor not often
matched in poetry, we are transported by this one line back
into the center of the courtly love tradition which the poet
has been subtly criticizing. The speech of the tercel, perfectly

consonant with his rank, and sympathetically presented, must
have aroused in Chaucer's audience some of the same feelings
in this setting that Madam Pertelotte's learned disquisition to
Lord Chauntecleer elicited in them at a later date. The
formel's "blush" is now clearly apropos, since the protestations
of a courtly lover were subject to the strictest secrecy, and
here they are mentioned in the face of the whole company.
No doubt she as a "formel" had expected the more natural
speech of a petitioner to Nature for her as a mate. No respite
is granted the blushing formel, for a second tercel of "lower
degree" breaks in vigorously as befits his comparative lack of
"gentilesse," and continues with a protestation of his continued faithfulness. Now the merriment must have been
general as the audience realized that here in perfect form
were all the elements of the *demande d'amours* with which
French literature abounded, but used so differently! A third
eagle with an argument all his own joins in the dispute, and
between the three, "from the morwe gan this speche laste /
Tyl dounward drow the sonne wonder faste" (ll. 489-490).
The purpose of the scene is done, and Chaucer does not
attempt to draw it out. Instead he introduces a new but highly
natural development in the course of events: the agitation of
the other birds at this strange turn of affairs:

> The noyse of foules for to ben delyvered
> So loude rong, "Have don, and lat us wende!"
> That wel wende I the wode hadde al toshyvered.
> "Com of!" they criede, "allas, ye wol us shende!
> When shal youre cursede pletynge have an ende?
> How sholde a juge eyther parti leve
> For ye or nay, withouten any preve?" (491-497)

Surely no courtly audience ever reacted this way in the serious
French *demandes!* The birds are not only angered at being
deprived of their natural rights by all the speechifying, but
they are suspicious of speeches themselves as based more on
convention than conviction—an issue which has been in the
back of our minds ever since the inscriptions over the garden
gate. This general uproar is the signal for the richest development of the poem in terms of its irony, the point toward
which it has been working from the beginning.

The three eagles have certainly shown little concern for
the "commune profyt," or for the behests of Nature. For a
moment pandemonium reigns as the goose and cuckoo chip

in with irreverent proposals for ending the dispute—the cuckoo specifically mentioning the "commune spede" (l. 507).
Nature rises to the occasion and, with, for her, an unwonted
sternness, speaks out,

> "Hold youre tonges there!
> And I shal sone, I hope, a conseyl fynde
> Yow to delyvere, and from this noyse unbynde:
> I juge, of every folk men shul oon calle
> To seyn the verdit for yow foules alle." (521-525)

This speech brings into sharp focus the feverish excitement
of the moment and the exasperation of Nature herself as she
searches for a way, "Yow to delyvere, and from this noyse
unbynde"—"noyse" referring as much to the courtly pleas as
to the general commotion. Even patient Dame Nature can
stand only so much from her children, and there is the *motif*
of the common good to be served.

The birds assent to Nature's judgment, and the "foules of
ravyne" elect a tercelet as their spokesman. True to his class,
he mentions first the tested expedient of trial by combat among
the three suitors, and they, in a kind of musical-comedy
chorus, answer with alacrity, "Al redy!" (l. 540). Taking no
notice of their eagerness, which is fitting to their chivalric
characters, he continues to pronounce his judgment that the
formel should chose,

> the worthieste
> Of knighthod, and the lengest had used it.
> Most of estat, of blod the gentilleste, . . . (548-550)

This amusingly naive practicality in the spokesman of the
idealistic aristocracy is ironically contrasted with fully conscious lower-class practicality as the goose steps forward:

> Pes! now tak kep every man,
> And herkeneth which a resoun I shal forth brynge!
> My wit is sharp, I love no taryinge;
> I seye I rede hym, though he were my brother,
> But she wol love hym, lat hym love another! (563-567)

Such eminently practical advice (couched in such eminently
impractical rhetoric) does not set well with the noble sparrow-
hawk who takes the goose sharply to task, "Lo here a parfit
resoun of a goos!" (l. 568).

There is a rather delicate combination of attitudes involved in these developments. We are relieved to hear the

spell of the courtly sentiments broken by plain practical realism, and yet we realize that the conventions are not entirely conventions and that what the birds of prey have been saying has attractions which far outweigh the "resoun of a goos." Chaucer has contrived to enlist our sympathy in part for the noble birds, and when the turtle-dove steps forward, "Nay, God forbede a lovere shulde chaunge!" (l. 582), and blushes, we are in sympathy with her cause as reflecting more clearly the "commune profyt" than what has been said by the goose.[6]

Still the voice of practical considerations will not be denied, and the duck drawls out sarcastically enough to break the mood:

> Daunseth he murye that is myrtheles?
> Who shulde recche of that is recheles?
> "Ye quek!" yit seyde the doke, ful wel and fayre,
> "There been mo sterres, God wot, than a payre!"
> (592-595)

This last has a double significance; "There are more fish in the sea than just two," agreeing with the goose's sentiments, and "There are others waiting here for this to be settled; let's get on with it!" recalling yet another aspect of "commune profyt."

The tercelet feels called upon to defend the proceedings which have thus far occupied all the time, and, in rebuttal to him, the cuckoo puts a point to the second interpretation of the duck's speech which I gave:

> "So I," quod he, "may have my make in pes,
> I reche not how longe that ye stryve.
> Let ech of hem be soleyn al here lyve!"   (605-607)

The cuckoo, it may be remembered, spoke previously of the "commune spede," but his interpretation of it is more warped than any we have met so far. In answer to him the "merlioun" succeeds only in proving by his invective that gentility as well as the cuckoo can be "lewed whil the world may dure," (l. 616).

The argument has passed the amusing stage, and Nature intervenes quickly to restore peace, ordering the formel to make her own choice (ll. 622-623). Nature turns to her "favorite" who is still perched upon her hand:

> "But as for conseyl for to chese a make,
> If I were Resoun, certes, thanne wolde I
> Conseyle yow the royal tercel take,
> As sedye the tercelet ful skylfully,
> As for the gentilleste and most worthi,
> Which I have wrought so wel to my pleasaunce,
> That to yow hit oughte to been a suffisaunce."
>
> (631-637)

The irony of "If I were Resoun," Nature's opposite number
in the allegorical tradition, must not have been lost on Chaucer's audience after all that had gone before, as well as that
of Nature's return to the idea of choosing a mate rather than
a paramour. Quite the best is yet to come, as the formel, still
"sore abasht" by all that has happened, begins to speak
"with dredful voice." After begging a boon, which Nature
kindly grants, she requests a year to think over the whole idea!
The irrelevance of the debate is crowned with a solution more
irrelevant than anything that has yet occurred. The formel's
reply, however, is not entirely devoid of significance in the
general scheme of the poem, for she concludes, "I wol nat
serve Venus ne Cupide, / Forsothe as yit, by no manere
weye" (ll. 652-653). She is specifically rejecting, for the time
being at least, the personages in the garden most commonly
associated with courtly love poetry. The inversion of values
which the poet set out to perform is complete, and the poem
may now progress toward its goal of the common good
achieved through natural married love for the rest of the
birds.

Nature, however, kindly goddess that she is, is unwilling to
see anyone completely unhappy, and so to the eagles goes a
speech of consolation rich in its humor and irony:

> "To yow speke I, ye tercelets," quod Nature,
> "Beth of good herte, and serveth alle thre.
> A yer is nat so longe to endure,
> And ech of yow peyne him in his degre
> For to do wel, for, God wot, quyt is she
> Fro yow this yer; what after so befalle,
> This entremes is dressed for yow alle."   (659-665)

Starting in a tone of consolatory advice, "Be good little eagles
all," the situation begins to get the better of Nature, and the
gentle sigh of relief inherent in the parenthetical "God wot,"
which turns into a broad smile as she continues "for quyt is

she / Fro yow this yer; what after so befalle," is as brilliantly conceived as anything in the poem.

It is but the work of three stanzas to settle the issue for the rest of the birds and send them happily off caroling the praises of "Saynt Valentyn." The irony as well as the thankfulness embodied in the lines of the roundel, "Wel han they cause for to gladen ofte, / Sith ech of hem recovered hath hys make." (ll. 587-588) should not be missed. They certainly do have cause to rejoice after the ordeal they have been put through!

We return to the poet,

> And with the shoutyng, whan the song was do
> That foules maden at here flyght awey,
> I wok, and othere bokes tok me to
> To reede upon, and yet I rede alwey.
> I hope, ywis, to rede so som day
> That I shal mete som thyng for to fare
> The bet, and thus to rede I nyl nat spare.   (693-697)

The dream is at an end. This simple conclusion returns us to the beginning and the "certeyn thing" for which the poet sought in his books, and upon which his dream has, presumably, shed some light, having taken him into one realm of love-experience and shown him its charm. I cannot think that Chaucer here expresses any dissatisfaction with the dream-vision itself such as he felt with his reading upon going to bed. Whether or not he found what he sought he leaves the reader to conjecture, but certainly the concept of "commune profyt" which impressed him so in his reading has provided a perspective through which he has been able to impart his vision to his audience in a unified and effective way.

What those who have attempted to interpret the entire poem as a serious moral problem presented allegorically have missed, I think, is the genial irony—the "good nature"— which infuses the whole. A genuine love of nature and natural conduct is balanced against the artificialities adopted by those who consider love a fit subject for rules and regulations according to an arbitrary, "sophisticated" pattern of courtly conventions. The garden of May and Nature promises joy; that of "Daunger" and "Disdayn," sorrow; the service of Venus and her porter "Richesse" is conducted in a "privie corner" here, while Priapus, in the highest place, is decorated with flowers from the world of Nature by his followers. Nature *in propria persona* reigns, and the birds appear before her to choose their mates, a sharp contrast to the satire embodied in Chauntecleer, who, as "Venus sonne," had his Pertelotte "Moore for delit than world to multiplye." There is no doubt; the common good has been served and through a subtly gentle irony of tone.

Chaucer was to return to this theme and write the tragedy of conventionalized love in *Troilus,* with its austere conclusion in which the artifices of the courtly love tradition are exposed in tragic contrast to the Natural Love of God, and obedience to His commands. In the *Parlement* Chaucer lays his stress upon Love's "myrakles"; in *Troilus* upon Love's "Yre," and the techniques of the two poems differ accordingly, comedy giving way to tragedy, and genially ironic to starkly ironic contrasts between reality and artifice, Nature and convention.

There is, thus, a considerable element of criticism directed against the artificialities of courtly love and the "foules of ravyne" in the *Parlement.* But what of the claims that have been made concerning the ridicule of the lower classes by other critics? It would certainly be a mistake to deny the existence of such an intent on Chaucer's part. The duck, goose, turtle-dove, and cuckoo are richly comic figures, representative, if we may trust the commentators, of various social classes in Chaucer's England.[7] Naturally there is a covert criticism of their characteristic modes of thought inherent in their speeches. The goose is literally a "goose' in matters courtly, but her type of thought would do well in the practical business world of mercantile London or any of the port cities of England to which it is conjectured that the *personae* which she and the duck represent belong. The duck, with his rich vein of sarcasm, betrays an even greater degree of sharp hardheadedness along with a commensurate dulling of feeling on the subject of courtly love. The glutton cuckoo, if by worm-fowl luxury-loving clergy are meant, is in a fair way of being an archetypal figure of the man of the cloth who no longer "eats to live, but lives to eat" and whose notion of the common good is what is good for himself. The turtle-dove who blushes and admits her unworthiness to "give sentence" may represent a kind of country virtue, perplexed in the presence of courtly conventions, but illustrating the gentility and faithfulness which transcends social status as does the fidelity to his congregation of the "Povre Persoun" in the "General Prologue." These are the barest outlines of the possibilities which Chaucer had at hand and which he may have utilized to create a memorably comic cast of characters.

Through admitting that Chaucer has ironically and satirically treated both the "high" and "low" comedy figures of his poem, the central problem of the poem's over-all unity is raised in its sharpest terms. What prevents the poem from splitting into halves? I have tried to suggest that the poem in effect defines a "natural" norm, a perspective from which the author may satirize mere "profyt" on the one hand and mere "romance" on the other. Part of the norm is suggested by the theme of "commune profyt," but that abstract semi-philosophic notion would not suffice to weld the whole together if taken alone.

The figure of Nature herself is the greatest single unifying factor. The combination of "natural" traits given to the goddess is irresistible. She is beauty personified; she has a real sympathy and understanding which all the other characters lack, and she can be exasperated with her children and then laugh herself out of her mood before really chastising them. She can listen with patience to the whole irrelevant *demande* and can seriously consider the possibilities which the lower birds suggest, and she can stop the whole procedure when it threatens the common welfare. She is, in fact, the mediator in the poem spiritually as well as physically. Her position as "the vicaire of the almyghty Lord" (l. 379) refers not only to the Lord Love but also the Lord God and further enhances her stature as an intermediary. It is her depth as a character who would appeal to any audience which made the rest of the poem acceptable to every audience from Chaucer's time to our own. The portrait of her which Chaucer has presented is astonishing in its range; she is capable of embracing "courtly love," "the love between perfect mates" and "sexual love" within her understanding and within the compass of the garden in which she rules. She is the source of all the harmony in the poem, and her character is the essence of the avoidance of any and all pretense. Only against the gentle background which she provides could Chaucer have constructed his double-edged comedy so as to please his listeners. Love, under Nature and within the bounds of sincerity, varying as they may be for the individual, can lead to "commune profyt." Utilizing such a doctrine, Chaucer was able to please his audience by the tolerance of his vision which included not only the individual portraits of the birds but of Nature herself and that for which she stands. Considered in this way, the poem becomes the end-product of a remarkable genius exercising itself in the realms of sympathetic understanding and broad humor.

Notes

1 The critical literature connected with the *Parlement of Foules* is roughly divisible into two parts: (a) proposals of various historical allegories for the situation commemorated in the poem; (b) critical analyses based upon the text itself. A selected bibliography:

(a) Historical allegories; J. Koch, "The Date and Personages of the *Parlement of Foules*," Essays on Chaucer, IV (Chaucer Society, 1877); O. F. Emerson, "The Suitors in Chaucer's *Parlement of Foules*," *MP*, VIII (1910), 45-62; "The Suitors in the *Parlement of Foules* Again," *MLN*, XXVI (1911), 109-111; "What is the *Parlement of Foules?*" *JEGP*, XIII (1914), 566-582; S. A. Moore, "A Further Note on the Suitors in the *Parlement of Foules*," *MLN*, XXVI (1911), 8-12; M. E. Reid, "The Historical Interpretation of the *Parlement of Foules*," *University of Wisconsin Studies in Language and Literature*, XVIII (1929), 60-70; T. W. Douglas, "What is the *Parlement of Foules?*" *MLN*, XLIII (1928), 378-383; E. Rickert, "A New Interpretation of the *Parlement of Foules*," *MP*, XVIII (1920), 1-29; H. Braddy, "Chaucer's *Parlement of Foules* in its Relation to Contemporary Events" (New York University dissertation, 1932).

(b) Critical analyses; J. M. Manly, "What is the *Parlement of Foules?*" *Studien zu Englishe Philologie*, L (1913), 272-290; C. S. Lewis, *The Allegory of Love* (Oxford, 1948), 171 ff.; B. H. Bronson, "In Appreciation of Chaucer's *Parlement of Foules*," *University of California Publications in English*, III, 193-224; R. C. Goffin, "Heaven and Earth in the *Parlement of Foules*," *MLR*, XXXII (1936), 493-499; R. M. Lumiansky, "Chaucer's *Parlement of Foules*; A Philosophical Interpretation," *RES*, XXIV (1948), 81-89; N. Coghill, *The Poet Chaucer* (Oxford, 1949), 57 ff.; Marchette Chute, *Geoffrey Chaucer of England* (New York, 1946), 129-135.

2 The pertinent passages from the *Teseida*, VII, 51-66, are printed in Skeats' *Oxford Chaucer*, I, 68-73, to which the reader may refer for greater detail than space here allows.

3 O. F. Emerson, "Some Notes on Chaucer and Some Conjectures," *PQ*, II (1923), 81-96.

4 R. A. Pratt, "Chaucer's Use of the *Teseida*," *PMLA*, LXII (1947), 605-608.

5 Chaucer was well aware of this tradition as is evidenced by ll. 2034-2037 of "The Merchant's Tale":

> Ne Priapus ne myghte nat suffise,
> Though he be god of gardyns, for to telle

The beautee of the gardyn and the welle,
That stood under a laurer alwey grene.

6 The turtle-dove was traditionally the symbol of faithfulness in love, but especially married love, which casts a rather ironic light on her advice in this connection.

7 See especially Edith Rickert, *op. cit., passim.*